BUSINESS AND ECONOMIC FORECASTING

An Econometric Approach

MILTON H. SPENCER, Ph.D.
Associate Professor of Business Administration
Wayne State University, Detroit

COLIN G. CLARK, M.A. (Oxon.)
Director of the Institute for Research in
Agricultural Economics, University of Oxford
Director of Research, The Econometric Institute, Inc.

PETER W. HOGUET, LL.B.
President, The Econometric Institute, Inc.

1961

RICHARD D. IRWIN, INC.

HOMEWOOD, ILLINOIS

THE IRWIN SERIES IN ECONOMICS

CONSULTING EDITOR

LLOYD G. REYNOLDS

YALE UNIVERSITY

BOOKS IN THE IRWIN SERIES IN ECONOMICS

BUSINESS AND ECONOMIC FORECASTING

An Econometric Approach

. . . The really useful training yields a comprehension of a few general principles with a thorough grounding in the way they apply to a variety of concrete details. In subsequent practice men will have forgotten your particular details; but they will remember by an unconscious common sense how to apply principles to immediate circumstances.

ALFRED NORTH WHITEHEAD

PREFACE

This book is designed to meet the needs of students, consultants, and professional researchers who are interested in the related areas of forecasting and model building. It is also a contribution to the rapidly growing field of business or managerial economics, as that subject has been developing in recent years.[1]

Several books already exist on the subject of business and economic forecasting. The present work is substantially different from these, however, in that it is the only book in the field which:

1. Develops a comprehensive body of forecasting *principles*, and illustrates the application of the principles with numerous models, explained in detail.

2. Uses mainly *graphic* rather than mathematical methods, so that the reader who has had only an elementary course in statistics, and has even forgotten much of it, can still master the principles and techniques involved in constructing the various models. On the other hand, sufficient data are always given so that the models can be developed mathematically if desired.

3. Devotes approximately half of the space to sales models as compared to aggregate economic models, thereby making the work suitable for business as well as economic forecasting.

The book thus emphasizes both the *principles and techniques* of forecasting, by developing and integrating economic and statistical concepts where they are needed. In doing this, several new economic and statistical tools are forged which become part of the forecaster's permanent kit. Thus, the theory and graphic measurement of the celebrated *maximum ownership level*, originated by Roos and Von Szeliski in their classic automobile study of 1938, is fully explained and used effectively in conjunction with a system of life tables or survival functions to develop models of the demand for various consumers' durable goods. Other unique and novel features are also present which professional readers will undoubtedly discover. To this audience in particular, however, we hasten to state that the empirical studies contained in the book are presented for instructional and discussion purposes only and should not necessarily be interpreted as illustrative of the methods currently employed by the authors. Indeed, the various models and techniques developed in the book should be regarded as a *guide* for further research—as a springboard for the development of new and better procedures, and not as a fixed set of rules or methods. If the book merely stimulates others to doubt and to question, and as a result to develop improved theories and models, it will have served its purpose.

---

[1] See, for example, Milton H. Spencer and Louis Siegelman, *Managerial Economics: Decision Making and Forward Planning* (Homewood, Ill.: Richard D. Irwin, Inc., 1959).

The authors are particularly grateful to Mr. Peter Newman of the University College of the West Indies for contributing the section on aggregate econometric models. In addition, Roslyn, Darcy, and Robin Spencer, and Mrs. Harry C. Pernick were generally helpful by their mere presence. Mr. Roberto Hochmann Tauber of Santiago, Chile, assisted considerably in helping to clarify certain portions of the manuscript while working as a graduate student at Wayne State University, as did Mr. Theodore Mattheiss. Messrs. Walter C. Folley, John Cadaret, and James R. Taylor were encouraging at all times, by controlling the senior author's teaching load and making available the necessary calculating equipment and clerical assistance. And Mrs. Judy Johnson co-operated by typing and retyping various portions of the manuscript as it was being hammered into shape. To all of these people we offer our sincere thanks.

MAY, 1961

M. H. S.
C. G. C.
P. W. H.

NOTE TO INSTRUCTORS

The many forecasting models which are presented in Chapters 5 through 9 were purposely terminated in the late 1950's. These models are all presented in rather full detail. Excellent opportunities are provided, therefore, for assigning projects to students. They may be told, for example, to select one or more models, as time permits, and bring them up to date. Or they may develop similar models by collecting their own data, using the text as a guide for conducting the analyses. In any event, the book is reasonably self-contained, and average as well as outstanding students will be challenged in developing models of their choice. The following points, however, should be kept in mind.

1. Students should become familiar with published sources of data, especially the Basic Sources in Chapter 2, to which they will refer frequently.

2. Teachers should encourage students to improvise. For example, the sources of all series are given when they are used in a particular study. It may sometimes happen, however, that the student cannot obtain the identical series. In that case, he should select a substitute or proxy variable, as explained in Chapter 4, which will meet his needs. Thus, in Chapter 7, supernumerary income is used as a purchasing power variable because it is a more refined measure than disposable income when the sale of consumers' durable goods is being analyzed. However, since a series on supernumerary income is not readily available, a disposable income series might be used, and it may or may not be adjusted, depending on the imagination and reasoning ability of the student. Examples and illustrations of similar situations are given in the text when a particular difficulty arises. The student is thus encouraged to seek a way out, or to overcome an obstacle, rather than to let it stop his further progress.

3. Students should be required to write up their complete study in the form of a report, giving the principles, analysis, and illustrations in the same manner as in the text, or as the instructor may designate.

4. Models of various kinds and different degrees of complexity are presented in Part II of the text. The most complicated model is the refrigerator study in Chapter 7, and a project of this type could easily be given as a term assignment or even as a master's thesis, if the student chooses his own product and starts from scratch. And it is also possible that he can find ways to improve upon the technique of the analysis, or to modify it according to his own thinking.

5. In short, the models in this book are designed as a *guide for research*. They should not be viewed as a rigidly fixed set of techniques, but rather as a springboard for the further analysis and development of ideas

based on the reader's imagination and interest. Indeed, students should be *encouraged* to look for improved ways of handling a problem, and to justify their approach in their report. The student who merely "follows the text" in constructing a model is at best meeting only the minimum requirements of the course.

As a teaching suggestion, instructors may find it fruitful to lecture on the first three or four chapters of the text. Then the remainder of the semester can be used for combined discussions and laboratory sessions, during which the students collaborate and work on their models in the classroom under the teacher's guidance. A desk calculator is the only computing equipment necessary for constructing any model in Chapters 5 through 9. Even though the models are developed by graphic methods, instructors can always require the use of mathematical methods if the student has the background and ability. Thus the book is quite flexible and can be taught on various levels.

For teachers who adopt the text, an *Instructor's Manual* is available containing additional material and suggestions.

TABLE OF CONTENTS

PART I. FORECASTING METHODS, MATERIALS, AND TOOLS

PART II. FORECASTING BY SECTORS

PART III. FORECASTING THE TOTAL ECONOMY

INDEX

PART I

Forecasting Methods, Materials, and Tools

The following chapters that comprise Part I are devoted to (1) a survey of the methods of forecasting, (2) a description of the published materials and indexes that serve as helpful guides to professional forecasters, and (3) a sketch of some important quantitative tools that may be employed in business and economic forecasting. The discussion does not do justice to the science of economic measurement, whose history and scope is one of the most interesting and challenging in the field of applied economics, and whose principles constitute the basis of modern forecasting technique. At best, it can only be hoped that the uninitiated reader will gain some insight into the nature of modern forecasting, and that the professional forecaster may learn a few things that will better enable him to establish scientifically sound predictions.

Chapter 1

FORECASTING METHODS

If we could first know where we are and whither we are tending, we could better judge what to do and how to do it.

—ABRAHAM LINCOLN

These words, now a century old, explain as well as any the necessity of forecasting. In a world where the future is not known with certainty, virtually every business and economic decision rests upon a forecast of future conditions. Successful forecasting aims at reducing the areas of uncertainty that surround management decision making with respect to costs, profits, sales, production, pricing, capital investment, and so forth. If the future were known with certainty, forecasting would be unnecessary. Decisions could be made and plans formulated on a once-and-for-all basis, without the need for subsequent revision. But uncertainty does exist, future outcomes are rarely assured, and therefore an *organized* system of forecasting is necessary rather than the establishment of predictions that are based on hunches, intuition, or guesses.

What methods are available to forecasters for predicting future business conditions both for the total economy and for the firm itself? Four common methods will be considered: (1) naïve methods; (2) barometric techniques; (3) opinion polling; and (4) econometrics. In the sections that follow each is discussed from the practical standpoint of their predictive value.

NAÏVE METHODS

Naïve methods of forecasting may be defined as unsophisticated and unscientific projections based on guesses or on mechanical extrapolations of historical data. As a method of prediction, they may include procedures ranging from simple coin tossing to determine an upward or downward movement to the projection of trends, autocorrelations, and other more seemingly complex mathematical techniques. Typically, they are distinguished from other forecasting methods discussed later in that they are essentially mechanical and are not closely integrated with relevant economic theory and statistical data. Nevertheless, they are widely used by professional forecasters, probably because they lend an air of sophistication and precision to mathematically "naïve" executives. Hence, a few of the more common forms used in business should be worth noting.

Factor-Listing Method

One of the earliest forms of forecasting common in the 1920's and '30's and still used by some business firms today may be called the "factor-listing" method. Because it presents an interesting point of departure for the discussion of other forecasting techniques, and because it illustrates how "naïve" some naïve methods can be, it is worth mentioning first.

The factor-listing method is a forecasting procedure whereby the analyst simply enumerates the favorable and unfavorable conditions that will affect business activity as he sees them, and then concludes with little or no evaluation or explanation that business will either be good, bad, or the same next year. The method is well illustrated in Table 1–1, which was prepared at the end of 1953 as part of a forecast of the first quarter of 1954.

Clearly, the list by itself makes no provisions for the quantitative evaluation of each of the factors and their role in influencing business activity; it completely ignores the "weighting" of the true forces that have a bearing on business change. Of course the prediction may turn out to be correct, but correct predictions are sometimes realized merely by chance, and this is what distinguishes a forecasting artist from a forecasting scientist. If 1,000 forecasting artists were to attempt, say, to forecast a rise or fall in production by merely tossing a coin, on condition that those who forecast correctly were to forecast again, here is what would happen if at each round the most probable outcome were realized: On the first toss about 500 out of the original 1,000 would have guessed correctly; on the second toss about 250 out of the 500 would be right; on the third toss, about 125; on the fourth toss, about 62 will have called the correct turn; on the fifth, about 31; on the sixth approximately 16; on the seventh, about 8; on the eighth, about 4; on the ninth 2; and on the tenth, 1. This 1 would then hold the record of having called correctly ten turns out of ten—a most remarkable record for a naïve method! Obviously, one's "record" as a forecasting artist is not a sole criterion of success, for the most elementary principles of probability dictate that eventually the artist must overplay his luck. If forecasting is to be a science, it must be based on the fundamental assumption that small causes of change, since they are too numerous to measure, will cancel each other out and leave the major causes of change to determine the business trend. And when, as often happens, the small causes fail to offset each other, or develop into unexpected major causes, the forecast will be in error. The forecasting scientist, therefore, can at best hope to be right most (more than half) of the time, as determined by the extensiveness and reliability of the data and his own analytical skill.

TABLE 1–1

The major forces affecting the general business outlook for the first quarter of 1954 include:

Favorable	*Unfavorable*
1. *Lower Taxes* On January 1st individual and corporate taxes are to be reduced by $4 billions (annual rate).	1. *Farm Income Off* Farm income is likely to be 10% lower in the first quarter than in the same period this year.
2. *Construction Up* Contracts awarded indicate that construction expenditures in the first quarter are likely to total about $715 billions and set a new record high for that quarter.	2. *Inventory Investment Down* Spending on inventory accumulation is likely to decrease by $2 to $3 billions in the first quarter.
3. *Government Spending High* Total government spending is expected to continue high, with a decrease in federal expenditures to be offset by increased state and local government outlays.	3. *Overtime to Decrease* Manufacturing workers are likely to experience a 2% to 3% decline in the work week.
4. *Big Savings Base* Liquid assets owned by consumers have grown by $10 billions, or 5%, in the past year and now total over $200 billions.	4. *Debt Repayment Absorbing More Purchasing Power* Repayments on installment debt in the first quarter are likely to be $2 to $3 billions greater than in the same period this year.

Conclusion: *The favorable factors appear to be as strong as the unfavorable; consequently, consumer disposable income is expected to continue at its present record high level of $250 billions.*

Source: From a paper by R. J. Eggert, "How to Forecast Your Company's Sales," delivered at American Marketing Association's winter meeting, Washington, D.C., December 29, 1953. Mr. Eggert is Program Planning Manager, Ford Division, Ford Motor Company.

Time Series Analysis

Proceeding from the purely subjective factor-listing method to more objective naïve forecasting procedures, the method of time series analysis may be noted briefly.

A *time series* is a sequence of values corresponding to particular points, or periods, of time. Data such as sales, production, and prices, when arranged chronologically, are thereby ordered in time and hence are referred to as time series. The simple line chart is the most common graphic device for depicting a time series, with the dependent variable such as sales or production or prices scaled on the vertical axis, and the independent variable, "time," expressed in years or months or any other temporal measure, scaled on the horizontal axis. Figure 1–1, which appears in the next section on p. 12, is an illustration of some different kinds of time series frequently encountered in economic and business literature, as are many other series to be discussed throughout this book.

In analyzing time series, which is actually the subject matter of this entire book, the problem is to discover and measure the forces which have caused a series to exhibit its particular fluctuations, in the hope that the causal factors may be projected into the future and the series thereby forecast. Thus the simplest type of naïve projection is a continuity type of model in which the last observed variable serves as a prediction of the future. This occurs, for example, with a forecast which states that next year's sales will be the same as this year's sales (plus or minus, perhaps, a random factor). The underlying assumption, therefore, is that there will be a continuous development of the variable in question. In certain geographical areas where climatic conditions change very slowly, weather predictions can perhaps be made on a short-term basis by the use of this method. Insurance companies might also employ this method in setting premiums based on life tables, on the assumption that death rates, though not constant, change very slowly, and hence the same tables can be used for years at a time. If it produces reliable answers, therefore, the continuity type of model provides an inexpensive method for arriving at predictions. But since few economic series exist which can be predicted in this manner, forecasters have found it necessary to utilize other techniques. It is in this connection that time series analysis arises as a forecasting method which deserves some attention.

Why does a time series exhibit a certain pattern of fluctuations? The answer to this question has typically been that at least four sources of variation are at work in an economic time series: trend, seasonal variation, cyclical variation, and irregular forces. *Trend* represents the long-run growth or decline of the series. *Seasonal* variations due to weather and custom manifest themselves during the same approximate time periods each year (for example, Christmas, Easter, and other seasons of the year during which different types of purchases are made). *Cyclical* variations, covering several years at a time, reflect prosperities and recessions. And finally, *irregular* forces, such as strikes, wars, and boycotts, are erratic in their influence on the particular series, but nevertheless must be recognized.

Of these four forces affecting economic time series, the seasonal is fairly easy to measure and predict. The irregular factor is unpredictable, but can be adjusted by a smoothing out process such as a moving average. Hence the trend, which represents persistent growth or decline, and the cyclical, which is presumably recurrent, are the forces which have occupied the chief attention of forecasters using time series analysis. Some comments as to the implications of trend projections and cyclical analyses are in order, therefore, since these procedures are in wide use by professional forecasters in many firms and industries.

Trend Projections. As a forecasting procedure, the method of trend projection assumes that the recent rate of change of the variable will continue in the future. On this basis expectations are established by projecting past trends, such as least-squares regressions, into the future. This is perhaps the most common method of forecasting used by business firms, not because it is necessarily more accurate than others, but because economic series typically exhibit a persistent and characteristic rate of growth which appears best approximated by a mathematical trend. Accordingly, prediction models of this kind have been used in population forecasting and in stock market forecasting. Companies often project sales several years into the future by this procedure. In basing predictions on trends of past relationships, the trend may be a simple unweighted line, or it may be weighted by attaching greatest importance to the most recent period and successively lesser degrees of importance to periods in the more distant past.

Trend models have been employed both successfully and unsuccessfully in the past. Forecasts based on 1929, 1933, and 1937 were disastrous for companies that employed this method. Yet the method continues in wide use, and for a simple reason. Economic time series do, for the most part, show a persistent tendency to move in the same direction for a period of time because of their inherent cumulative characteristics. Therefore, a forecaster using the method of trend projection will be right as to direction of change more times than he will be wrong, and, in fact, he will be right in *every forecast except* those at the *turning points*. Thus, suppose a series rises for 28 months, waivers or runs about steady for 2 months, and then declines for 20 months—in all, a total of 50 months. A forecaster using the method of trend projection will forecast correctly the month-to-month direction of change at least 48 out of 50 times, which is a score of 96 per cent. And if he tossed a coin for the two uncertain months and guessed one out of two correctly, he could raise his score to 98 per cent—a remarkable record for a naïve method! Yet, counting the percentage of correct forecasts appears to be the standard manner of evaluating a forecaster's performance.[1]

Evidently, it is in the prediction of the turning points rather than in the mere projection of trends that the challenge to forecasting really manifests itself. Only when the turning points can be detected in advance can management proceed to alter its plans with respect to sales effort, production scheduling, credit requirements, and the like. Otherwise, the mere projection of trends implies a forecast of continuance and no essential change in policy, and hence the coordinative (decision-making) function of management reduces to a mere supervisory one.

[1] C. F. Roos, "Survey of Economic Forecasting Techniques," *Econometrica*, October, 1955, p. 364. See also F. Newbury, *Business Forecasting*; W. Wright, *Forecasting for Profit*; and W. Hoadley, Jr., *Determining the Business Outlook*. Some simple criteria for evaluating a forecast are presented in the concluding sections of this and later chapters.

Cyclic Models

When the trend is removed from an annual series of economic data, the residual structure exhibits certain fluctuating characteristics that have been described by economists as *business cycles*. For many years attempts have been made to discover or to prove that a law of oscillation exists in such series, and in some instances the search for periodicity has resulted in outstanding success with respect to prewar series.[2] World War II, however, produced important changes in the structural variables of the economy and altered significantly the phase relationships between time series that had previously exhibited oscillatory characteristics. Nevertheless, the use of cyclic models as a prediction method continues in wide use among forecasters in many business firms.

At the present time, the use of time series analysis in forecasting business cycles commonly employs what is known as the "residual method." The calculation techniques are described in all elementary textbooks on economic and business statistics and need not be illustrated here. What interests us is the nature and assumptions of the method, since the procedure in general plays such a dominant role in the forecasting activities of business firms.[3]

The original data (O) of the series is regarded as being composed of four elements: a secular trend (T), a seasonal variation (S), a cyclical movement (C), and an irregular variation (I). The most common practice is to assume that these elements are bound together in a *multiplicative* structure, so that the relationship is expressed by the formula $O = TSCI$. However, it is also possible to assume that they are *additive*, in which case $O = T + S + C + I$, or that there are both multiplicative and additive relationships such as $O = S + TCI$, or perhaps other combinations. Various theoretical possibilities may exist, but in most practical problems the multiplicative structure is assumed. In any event, the problem for purposes of forecasting is to isolate and measure each of these four factors, by separating out of the total behavior O, the gradual long-term change T, the regular oscillations S occurring with a year, and the regular oscillations C occurring over several years, each measured independently of the others. The problem of assumed relationships between the series, however, is relatively minor when compared to the other measurement problems that arise.

[2] See H. T. Davis, *The Analyses of Economic Time Series*, and C. D. Long, *Building Cycles and the Theory of Investment*. For a simplified presentation, see E. R. Dewey and E. F. Dakin, *Cycles, The Science of Prediction*.

[3] There are other approaches used in measuring business cycles besides the residual method, such as the "fixed regularity" method described in Dewey and Daken, *op. cit.*; the "standard cyclical pattern" method which involves an averaging of link-relative changes in important series, developed in E. Frickey's *Economic Fluctuations*; and the generalizations from specific cycles in individual industries and processes as done by the National Bureau in W. C. Mitchell, *Measuring Business Cycles*. The residual method is the one discussed here.

1. In explaining the cyclical mechanism, whether for the total economy or for a particular firm, there is a controversy over whether the methods of analysis are really valid. Analysts have shown that apparent cycles can result in a series not because a cycle actually exists, but because of the way in which the data are processed. For example, the use of a moving average may induce an oscillation in a resulting series even if a real cycle is nonexistent, or in general, the summing or averaging of successive values of a random series can result in cyclical behavior by the very act itself (known as the "Slutsky-Yule effect"). For these reasons, the conventional method of residual analysis used by most business firms in separating cyclical and random components of time series is by no means a universally accepted procedure and, as a matter of fact, has been strongly questioned by analysts for many years.

2. More recently, the separation of trend and random forces in a time series has also been questioned.[4] The assumption in the residual method is that the long-term and short-term movements are due to separate causal influences, so that appropriate mathematical tools may accordingly be applied. But recent studies of economic series reveal that perhaps the trend in a series is not separable from the short-term movements, and that both may perhaps be generated by a common set of forces. Where series of data are observed at fairly close intervals, the random changes from one term to the next may be large enough to outweigh substantially any systematic (causal) effect which may be present, so that the data appear to behave almost like a "wandering series." In such instances it is difficult to distinguish by statistical methods between a genuine wandering series and one wherein the systematic element is weak. Hence, if the series really is wandering, any movements which appear to be systematic such as trends or cycles would be illusory, and their separation and measurement may be highly hazardous.[5]

Conclusion

It is apparent that the traditional methods of processing time series data—methods that are in extensive use by many business firms[6]—are far from adequate, despite their wide acceptance by many professional business forecasters employed in industry. Evidence already exists, and further research will probably bear out, that the traditional methods of time series

[4] See, for example, M. G. Kendall, "The Analysis of Economic Time Series," *Journal of the Royal Statistical Society*, vol. 66, series A, 1953.

[5] *Ibid.* Kendall points out that an analysis of stock exchange movements revealed little serial correlation (that is, association between successive values) within series and little lag correlation between series. Therefore, as long as individual stocks behave in the same manner as the average for similar stocks, predicting movements on the exchange a week in advance without extraneous information is impossible. (These statistical concepts are treated further both in a later section and in the following chapters.)

[6] Case studies are presented in National Industrial Conference Board, *Forecasting in Industry* (Studies in Business Policy, No. 77).

analysis may provide at best a mere description of a set of data and at worst an enormous waste of time, effort, and expense in arriving at what amounts to nothing more than an illusory explanation of systematic movements.[7] Accordingly, other forecasting procedures must be examined and evaluated if an intelligent choice of methods is to be made.

BAROMETRIC TECHNIQUES

Whereas naïve methods of forecasting, particularly time series analyses, imply that the future is some sort of extension of the past, the use of barometric techniques is based on the idea that the future can be predicted from certain happenings in the present. Specifically, barometric methods involve the use of statistical indicators—selected time series which, when used in conjunction with one another or when combined in certain ways, provide an indication of the direction in which the economy or particular industries are heading. The series chosen thus serve as barometers of economic change. Two particular applications of the barometric approach are commonly employed: leading series and pressure indexes. To some extent they may be overlapping, but they are discussed separately for convenience.

Leading Series

In the history of forecasting, no method has been given more attention than the leading series approach. If a series or index could be discovered that showed leads of, say, six months with substantial regularity, it would indicate successfully the turns in economic activity. Such an indicator would end the quest for a universal "predictor" (and, of course, the need for several thousand professional forecasters). Forecasters have long sought mechanical methods for predicting the future course of business. Andrew Carnegie used to count the number of factory chimneys belching smoke to tell whether business would rise or decline. The Brookmire Economic Service as early as 1911 utilized successive leads in stock, commodity, and money market series to forecast economic change. And the now defunct Harvard Index Chart, constructed by the Harvard Business School in the 1920's, used a similar set of series to forecast changes in business and finance.

In recent decades, the most significant discoveries relating to leading series have come from Geoffrey Moore and his associates at the National Bureau of Economic Research.[8] Moore examined over 800 time series collected by the Bureau covering the period to World War II. He found that twenty-one series had exhibited the greatest consistency either in leading the "reference cycle" (which the National Bureau generalizes from all of

---

[7] Cf. R. C. Sprowls, *Elementary Statistics*. It should be noted, however, that time series analysis does have certain valuable uses. These will be illustrated in Part II where actual forecasting models are constructed.

[8] See his *Statistical Indicators of Cyclical Revivals and Recessions*, Occasional Paper No. 31 (1950).

its series), running coincident with it, or lagging behind it at the turning points (peaks and troughs). The breakdown of the twenty-one indicators, along with their sources, is as follows:

LEADING INDICATORS

1. New incorporations (Dun and Bradstreet)
2. Business failures (Dun and Bradstreet)
3. Residential building contracts awarded (F. W. Dodge Corporation)
4. Commercial and industrial building contracts awarded (F. W. Dodge Corporation)
5. Common stock prices—industrial (Dow Jones)
6. Wholesale commodity price index (Bureau of Labor Statistics)
7. Average hours worked per week in manufacturing (Bureau of Labor Statistics)
8. New orders for manufacturers' durable goods (Department of Commerce)

COINCIDENT INDICATORS

1. Gross national product—quarterly (Department of Commerce)
2. Corporate profits—quarterly (Department of Commerce)
3. Unemployment—inverted (Bureau of Labor Statistics)
4. Nonagricultural employment (Bureau of Labor Statistics)
5. Nonfood wholesale price index (Bureau of Labor Statistics)
6. Industrial production index (Federal Reserve Board)
7. Bank debits outside of New York City (Federal Reserve Board)
8. Freight carloadings index (Association of American Railroads)

LAGGING INDICATORS

1. Personal income (Department of Commerce)
2. Retail sales (Department of Commerce)
3. Manufacturers' inventories (Department of Commerce)
4. Consumer installment debt (Federal Reserve Board)
5. Bank rates on business loans (Federal Reserve Board)

There are thus eight leading indicators, eight that are approximately coincident, and five that are lagging. For forecasting, of course, the leading and the coincident indicators, especially the former, are of primary value, but all three sets are presented here for the sake of completeness. Figure 1–1 presents some recent patterns of both the leading and coincident series as outlined above.

The eight leading series are available monthly, hence it seems that they should provide a useful guide for predicting the future course of the economy. Unfortunately, however, they are not as useful for this purpose as might at first seem, because of their following limitations:

1. They are not always consistent in their tendency to lead. Frequently, some of the series will signal what turns out later on to be a true change, while the remaining series either fail to signal at all or else signal too late to be of much value for prediction purposes.

2. It is not always possible to tell whether the series is signalling an

FIGURE 1–1

MAJOR ECONOMIC INDICATORS

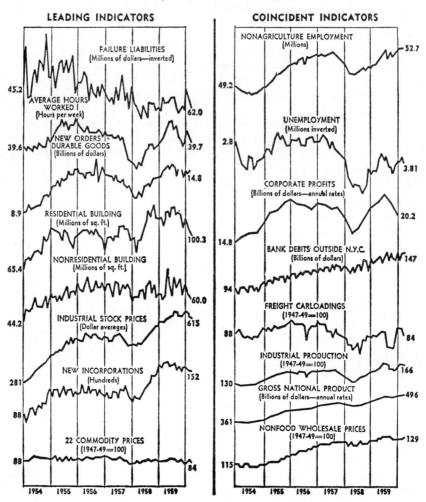

Source: The *New York Times* from Statistical Indicator Associates, April 17, 1960.

actual future turning point of the economy, or whether it is merely exhibiting a wiggle which is of no real significance. In order to be sure whether the variation is actually a true signal of impending change, or merely a false start, it may be necessary to wait a few months for confirmation. But this of course destroys any forecasting advantage which the series may have in the first place, since the eight leading series, whether taken individually or as a composite, can at best be used only for short-term forecasts up to about six months or so.

3. Finally, even if the leading indicators could signal consistently the true turning points of the economy, they would still indicate only the di-

rection of future change, while disclosing little or nothing about the magnitude of the change. Since both are desired, the use of leading series as a forecasting device would seem to be, in the light of this as well as the two previous criticisms, far from the best approach that might be adopted.

Do these criticisms mean that the use of leading indicators for prediction purposes might just as well be abandoned? Not completely. Dissatisfaction with the leading indicators as such resulted in an attempt by Moore to construct so-called "diffusion indexes"—measures in the form of percentages of the eight leading indicators which, each month, are rising or falling. For the period since World War II, the evidence indicates that the diffusion technique has been only moderately successful in predicting the turning points of the total economy, and was not necessarily more successful than certain other forecasting methods that have been used. A chief reason for this, and one which underlies all of the criticisms stated above, is that the leading series are not causally related in a functional sense to the basic factors responsible for them, nor are they weighted according to their intrinsic importance in the economy. Instead, the indicators are selected because of their historical uniformity of performance, and are given equal weights in importance. The most that can be said, therefore, is that leading indicators are at best a supplement to other forecasting devices, and will remain such until more can be learned about their relative significance in the total economy.[9]

Lead-lag techniques are used in various ways by business firms in forecasting their sales. Usually, external correlations are sought between the firm's sales and some outside indicator that is more readily forecast, such as employment. Department store sales, for instance, show an average lag of a few months both at business cycle peaks and troughs. Likewise, the demand for children's and baby clothes can usually be predicted, and sometimes also the modal size by age group, by establishing correlations with past population figures and birth rates. Techniques of this and a similar nature are discussed later in greater detail.

Pressure Indexes

Based largely on the idea that amplitude differences play a significant role in the analysis of business cycles, economists have developed various

[9] A variation of the leading series technique was developed by Ashley Wright in 1949. Wright, an economist with Standard Oil Company (New Jersey), examined about a hundred series and concluded that although their turning points are not simultaneous, they nevertheless tend to cluster around the turning points in general business activity (i.e., the reference cycle) in the manner of a normal distribution, thus providing a basis for forecasting both a turning point and its speed of arrival. Unfortunately, this research has not been followed up in the literature. [*Note:* As this book went to press, publication was announced of a massive new two-volume study, *Business Cycle Indicators* (Princeton University Press, 1961), edited by Moore, in which twelve leading indicators and nine coincident ones are now listed.]

ratio and difference measures called "pressure indexes" as guides to forecasting. Some examples of such indexes used in economic and business forecasting are the following.

1. Durable goods production fluctuates much more widely than nondurable goods production over the course of a business cycle. Hence the ratio of durable to nondurable goods production is sometimes used as an indicator of cyclical change, the ratio tending to increase in prosperity periods and to decline before a business cycle downturn, although there is no clear-cut evidence of the latter.

2. Purchasing agents, in predicting raw materials prices, frequently use a ratio of raw materials inventories to new orders for finished goods. Also, a somewhat rougher indication is given if production of finished goods rather than new orders is used in the denominator.

3. The difference between the rate of family formation and the rate of housing inventory growth is a pressure indicator of the long-term demand for new housing. In the short run, on the other hand, factors such as disposable income and credit conditions are usually more influential in determining the actual rate of construction.

4. Railroads approximate from six months to a year in advance the demand for new orders for railroad cars from the ratio of carloadings (seasonally adjusted) to cars in serviceable condition.

5. The spread between common stock yields and corporate bond yields has sometimes been used as a predictor of stock prices. Classical market theory states that as the spread narrows, the advantage of owning stocks rather than bonds declines, and money flows out of the stock market into the bond market. Figure 1–2, which is self-explanatory, serves as an illustration of the consequent effect on stock prices.

These ratio and difference measures, as well as numerous others that can be devised, may not always be helpful in forecasting the magnitude of change. However, they do serve the useful purpose of providing warning signals of impending developments, and frequently an indication as to the future direction of change. When used in conjunction with other forecasting methods, pressure indexes can accomplish much in the way of establishing quideposts for better prediction.

OPINION POLLING

The opinion polling or sample survey technique of forecasting is a subjective method of prediction, amounting largely to a weighted or unweighted averaging of attitudes and expectations. The underlying assumption is that certain attitudes affecting economic decisions can be defined and measured well enough in advance so that predictions can be made of changing business trends. The results are arrived at by asking people who are directly involved about their expectations as to future economic hap-

FIGURE 1–2

COMMON STOCK YIELDS AND CORPORATE BOND YIELDS

THE GAP IN YIELDS IS NARROW ONCE AGAIN

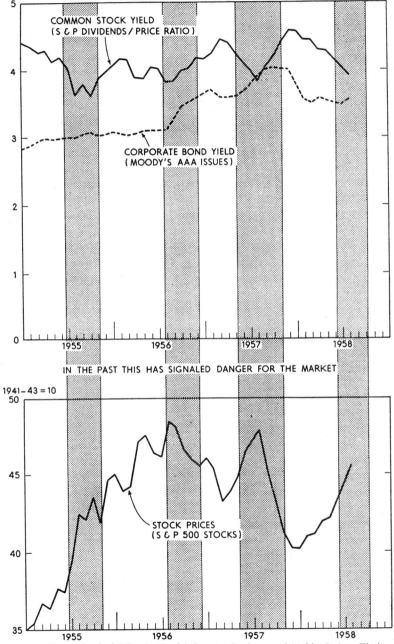

Source: Standard & Poor's; Moody's Investors Service; copyrighted by *Business Week* and reprinted by permission.

penings. Various forms or types of opinion polls are employed both in economic and in sales forecasting, and are discussed below from this standpoint.

Economic Forecasting

Among the best known opinion-polling studies made for forecasting economic activity or some particular phase of it are the following: (1) surveys of businessmen's intentions to spend on plant and equipment, made by the McGraw-Hill Publishing Company, the Department of Commerce, the Securities and Exchange Commission, and most recently by the National Industrial Conference Board; (2) surveys of consumers' finances and buying plans, made primarily by the Survey Research Center of the University of Michigan under the sponsorship of both private business and the Federal Reserve Board, but with the latter's portion of the work taken over by the Census Bureau in 1960; and (3) surveys of businessmen's plans regarding inventory changes, made by the National Association of Purchasing Agents. All of these surveys are made periodically. On the whole, the most successful ones appear to have been the McGraw-Hill survey of expenditure plans for plant and equipment (capital-consuming plans), and the Survey Research Center's surveys of consumers' intentions.

The McGraw-Hill survey covers less than 500 companies, but these account for about 60 per cent of the investment of the important capital-consuming industries. The "record" of these surveys has agreed rather well with actual expenditures, except for a few scattered years where the errors could be accounted for by an unexpected reduction in personal income taxes which stimulated demand (1948) or a failure to anticipate the Korean War (1951). Capital expenditure plans, since they are so dependent on changes in the structural environment of the economy, could not be expected to remain the same under such unusual circumstances. Other than these, however, the McGraw-Hill surveys have provided a basically sound analysis of capital expenditure plans. They cover much the same ground as the government survey mentioned above, but are available earlier (published in *Business Week* magazine) and are widely used for forecasting purposes.

The Survey Research Center of the University of Michigan prepares surveys of consumer finances and buying plans. The surveys, whose sample sizes range from 2,900 to 3,600 cases, are designed to (1) evaluate recent developments among consumers, (2) provide data for testing hypotheses about economic behavior, that is, functional relationships between variables, and (3) determine expectancies for consumer purchases of automobiles, houses, and major appliances. A single survey provides a cross section of data, while consecutive surveys yield time series of such data. The results of these surveys have been both good and bad. On the one hand, the surveys seem to have foretold some of the more important turning points of business since the late 'forties, in particular the recessions of 1948–49, 1953–54, and 1957–58. On the other hand, the surveys have not been useful for predicting the magnitude of change. They have been best suited to predictions covering only a few months at a time, because the average consumer is not a very rational planner and his decisions are affected by a wide array of economic and emotional complexities which he cannot unravel and use as a basis for future buying plans beyond several months. They have been limited to those products that are "planned" for by consumers, such as houses, automobiles, furniture, and major appliances. Of course, the surveys could be conducted more frequently than once a year and could include a broader scope of products. But this would entail expenses that most firms are neither willing nor able to undertake.[10]

Sales Forecasting

Opinion-polling methods are not used just to forecast changes in economic conditions; many business firms employ variations of the method in forecasting sales.

1. *Executive polling*, whereby the views of top management are combined and (subjectively) averaged, is frequently employed. The assumption in the use of this approach is that there is safety in numbers, in that the combined judgment of the group is better than the forecast of any single member. Hence the executives sit as a jury and pass judgment on the sales outlook for the coming year. Generally represented on the jury are those with a divergency of opinions—the sales, production, finance, purchasing, and administrative divisions. In those companies where forecasts of probable events are derived after a sifting and analysis of market reports, sales data, and formal economic forecasts, the executive-polling approach has been fairly successful. Without such careful evaluations, however, the method can easily degenerate to the level of a guessing game yielding nothing more than sloppy and unfounded predictions. Companies employing the executive-polling approach frequently combine it with statistical measures of trends and cycles (that is, naïve methods, discussed above) as a further tool, by raising or lowering the statistical forecast according to their subjective judgment.

2. *Sales force polling* is another variation whereby a composite outlook is constructed on the basis of information derived from those closest to the market. The sales forecast may be built up from salesmen's estimates in co-operation with branch or regional managers, or by going directly to jobbers, distributors, and major customers in order to discover their needs. The advantage claimed for the method is that it utilizes the firsthand, specialized knowledge of those nearest to the market, and thereby gives salesmen greater confidence in their quotas developed from forecasts. On the

---

[10] It has been estimated, for instance, that for $25,000 a year, firms and trade associations could obtain useful small-scale annual studies, and for $100,000 a year they could obtain fairly good surveys more frequently than once a year. See Irving Shweiger, "Forecasting Short-Term Consumer Demand from Consumer Anticipations," *Journal of Business*, April, 1956, p. 100.

other hand, salesmen may be quite unaware of structural changes taking place in their markets, and hence incapable of shaping their forecasts to account for those future changes. Also, sound forecasting requires more time and effort than most salesmen can ordinarily devote, and the result is more likely to be an off-the-cuff guess rather than a prediction based on careful reasoning. Accordingly, firms using this method have usually set up a system of "checks and balances" whereby salesmen's estimates are compiled, checked, adjusted, and revised periodically in the light of past experience and future expectations.

3. *Consumer intentions surveys* are still another version of the opinion-polling method applied to sales forecasting. The Ford Division of the Ford Motor Company, for instance, makes sample surveys of automobile buying intentions which it then projects to a national level of weighting the estimate with the average purchase rate and an index of predicted incomes. Similar techniques are used by other firms in forecasting the sale of appliances, furniture, and other durable goods.

ECONOMETRICS

Forecasting is a science of prediction. Economic forecasting is the science of predicting economic change. It is because change occurs that the need for forecasting arises, for in a stationary economy where the future is merely an extension of the present, forecasting would be unnecessary: what happened yesterday would happen today and would also happen tomorrow. But change does occur, economic activity is not static, and therefore managers must make predictions if forward planning is to be successfully accomplished.

Based on the idea that changes in economic activity can be explained by a set of relationships between economic variables, there has grown up a branch of applied science known as *econometrics*. Breaking the word into its two parts, "econo" and "metrics," it is evident that its subject matter must deal with the science of *economic measurement*. And this is precisely what econometrics does: it explains past economic activity and predicts future economic activity by deriving mathematical equations that will express the most probable interrelationship between a set of economic variables. The economic variables may include disposable income, money stock, inventories, government revenues and expenditures, foreign trade, and so on. By combining the relevant variables, each a separate series covering a past period of time, into what seems to be the best mathematical arrangement, econometricians proceed to predict the future course of one or more of these variables on the basis of the established relationships. The "best mathematical arrangement" is thus a model which takes the form of an equation or system of equations that seems best to describe the past set of relationships according to economic theory and statistical analysis. The model, in other words, is a simplified abstraction of a real situation, expressed in equation form, and employed as a prediction system that will yield numerical results. To the extent that economic theorems and relationships can be verified by subjecting historical data to statistical analysis, then, at least in principle, econometrics as a system of measurement stands as a compromise between pure "ivory tower" economic theory on the one hand, and sheer description of facts and occurrences on the other.

General Aspects

Economic theory deals with the science of choice between alternatives, and its method is to construct simplified models of economic reality on the basis of which certain laws describing regularities in economic behavior are derived. When these models are quantitatively constructed, they are known as econometric models. Such models may be constructed for the total economy for the purpose of predicting future levels of income, employment, and other aggregate economic variables, or they may be constructed for a particular firm or industry in order to predict sales, production, costs, and related economic variables. Both types of models can be useful, of course, in facilitating decision making and planning by government agencies, business executives, labor unions, poltical organizations, and similar groups with a direct interest in economic and business conditions. Hence, both types of models will be discussed and illustrated in later chapters.

An excellent illustration of a relatively simple econometric model of the total economy is presented in Figure 1–3, taken from a famous article on forecasting which appeared in *Business Week* in 1955. This figure is worth a careful reading in order that a proper background be gained for understanding not only the comments which follow, but also the more detailed discussion of econometrics from a statistical standpoint which will be given later.

In practice, econometric models, especially models of the total economy as compared to models of a particular firm or industry, are more complicated than the rather simple one described in the figure. The chief reason for this is that a simple model cannot ordinarily reflect, with forecasting reliability, the major nuances and complex operations of our economy. By identifying and adding new variables to the model, a better explanation of past variations is obtained than is normally the case with a simple model. But further elaborations, although they may improve the accuracy of "fit" of the model up to a point, also increase the cost of the research involved. Hence there is a problem of weighing the increment in research costs against the increment in value of greater accuracy, in order to decide on just how elaborate and complete a model to construct. These concepts will become much more meaningful in the discussion of correlation analysis in Chapters 3 and 4, where some of the techniques of constructing a model are illustrated and explained.

What about the difficulties of employing econometric techniques for

FIGURE 1–3

The Junior Econometrician's Work Kit.

Predict the U.S. Economy for 1956.
Build Your Own Forecasting Model.

DIRECTIONS:

1. Make up a theory. You might theorize, for instance, that (1) next year's consumption will depend on next year's national income; (2) next year's investment will depend on this year's profits; (3) tax receipts will depend on future Gross National Product. (4) GNP is the sum of consumption, investment, and government expenditures. (5) National income equals GNP minus taxes.

2. Use symbols for words. Call consumption, C; national income, Y; investment, I; preceding year's profits, P_{-1}; tax receipts, T; Gross National Product, G; government expenditures, E.

3. Translate your theories into mathematical equations:

(1) $C = aY + b$ (4) $G = C + I + E$
(2) $I = cP_{-1} + d$ (5) $Y = G - T$
(3) $T = eG$

This is your forecasting model. The small letters, a, b, c, d, e, are the constants that make things come out even. For instance, if horses (H) have four legs (L), then $L = aH$; or $L = 4H$. This can be important in the blacksmith business.

4. Calculate the constants. Look up past years' statistics on consumption, income, and so on. From these find values for a, b, c, d, and e that make your equation come out fairly correct.

5. Now you're ready to forecast. Start by forecasting investment from this year's profits. Look up the current rate of corporate profits — it's around $42-billion. The model won't tell what federal, state, and local governments will spend next year — that's politics. But we can estimate it from present budget information — it looks like around $75-billion.

6. Put all available figures into your model. (We've put in the constants for you.)

(1) $C = .7Y + 40$ (4) $G = C + I + 75$
(2) $I = .9 \times 42 + 20$ (5) $Y = G - T$
(3) $T = .2G$

7. Solve the equations. You want values of C, I, T, G, Y. Hints: Do them in this order — (2), (1), (4), (3), (5). In solving (1), remember that I and E are both part of G, $Y = G - T$, and $T = .2G$.

8. Results. (See if yours are the same.) For 1956, consumption will be $260.0-billion; investment, $57.8-billion; GNP, $392.8-billion; tax receipts, $78.6-billion; national income, $314.2-billion. These results are guaranteed — provided that the theories on which they're based are valid.

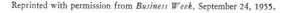

Reprinted with permission from *Business Week*, September 24, 1955.

business and economic forecasting? Can it be assumed that the greater elegance of such models always justifies their use? Perhaps so, but only in the light of two conditions: (1) econometric models, if they are to be useful, require the attention of a full-time research staff, and (2) the models, since they are replicas of dynamic situations, must be revised periodically to allow for the changing weights of the constants or parameters in the equations (that is, step 4 in Figure 1–3). In view of these considerations, the construction of econometric models, whether for a firm or for an economy, has usually been done by professional research or consulting organizations which specialize in this type of activity.

Conclusion

It has sometimes happened that econometric models have failed, under certain conditions, to provide better predictions for the following year than less costly models such as simple trend projections. Does this mean that econometric methods should be abandoned? Where our theoretical understanding and statistical data are good, econometrics can illuminate the darker areas and enhance our ability to predict. For econometrics, to a greater degree than other forecasting methods, is analytical in nature and process-oriented in approach, because its chief concern is to identify and measure changing cause-and-effect relationships through time. In any forecast, certain strong forces always come into play and serve to modify existing relationships. The econometrician is aware of this and constantly watches for the emergence of new forces or for changes in existing ones, so that he can allow for these changes in his operating model. In this manner, a good econometric model automatically incorporates the necessary degree of built-in flexibility, thereby facilitating the model's use for forecasting purposes. Perhaps the most important use of naïve models, therefore, is that they provide a benchmark—a null hypothesis—against which the more sophisticated forecasting methods can be compared. And the econometric method, rather than rivaling the other methods, is probably the only approach which is logically suitable for incorporating or utilizing the best features of them all, as will become more evident in later chapters.

QUESTIONS

1. In your own words, define briefly the various forecasting methods discussed in this chapter. Cite examples of each.
2. What is wrong, if anything, with the "factor listing" approach to economic forecasting?
3. Trend models or projections will usually yield correct forecasts, at least as to direction of change, more often than not. If the distinction between a forecasting artist and a forecasting scientist is that the latter is correct more than half the time, the use of trend models would seem warranted. Yet we have been critical of their use. Why?
4. "After all, in the final analysis, the best forecasting method is obviously the one that yields the highest percentage of correct predictions." Comment.
5. The "residual method" is probably the most common approach employed in industry to forecast cyclical fluctuations. Comment on the use of this method and its significance.

6. (*a*) How may leading series be used to facilitate forecasting? (*b*) What difficulties are involved in employing leading series for forecasting purposes? (*c*) What is a "pressure index"? Cite at least one example and explain its usefulness to management.

7. (*a*) In general, which has been more successful as a forecaster: the McGraw-Hill survey of capital expenditure plans, or the Survey of Consumer Finances? Can you offer a possible economic explanation as to why? (*b*) How many business firms employ opinion-polling methods in sales forecasting? (*c*) Why are opinion-polling methods more often suitable for predicting the sales of new as compared to established products?

8. Of the various forecasting methods discussed in this chapter, what is unique about econometrics?

Chapter 2

FORECASTING MATERIALS

Professional forecasters operate extensively with statistical data, especially time series data which are available in various publications. What are the major sources of published data, and what kinds of statistical series do these sources contain? The answer to this question constitutes the "materials" of forecasting, and will occupy the core of our attention in this chapter. The remaining chapters of the book are then devoted to illustrations and explanations of how particular statistical series are selected and combined in order to produce meaningful relationships for business and economic forecasting.

BASIC SOURCES—GENERAL

The basic sources of statistical data that are used in virtually all types of business and economic research can be grouped under two headings, "general" and "special." Both categories consist of various books, journals, magazines, pamphlets, special reports, and so forth, turned out by commercial publishers, government agencies, research bureaus, foundations, and other public and private organizations. It is obvious, therefore, that a complete listing of statistical sources would be impossible. Fortunately, however, a complete listing is unnecessary, for the great majority of problems that are encountered can be handled by utilizing data obtained from less than a dozen or so of the general sources listed below. If particular needs arise which cannot be satisfied by the general sources, various specialized publications exist which should be consulted. In short, the lesson to be learned from this and the next section is that a great deal more information is available than is readily apparent, and patient searching is often necessary to obtain the desired data. Sometimes, however, the precise data desired are not obtainable, in whch case proxy or substitute statistics must be used, and adjusted if necessary to meet the analyst's requirements. Various examples of proxy data and the statistical adjustments involved will be presented in the illustrative problems and models of subsequent chapters.

General Sources

The following general publications are the main sources of business and economic data. They are readily available in most university and public libraries, and in the research departments and libraries of many companies and government agencies.

1. *The Economic Almanac* (New York: Thomas Y. Crowell Co.) is prepared by the National Industrial Conference Board, a prominent research organization in business economics and management located in New York. The *Almanac* is published annually and is an excellent comprehensive source of business and economic data.

2. *Economic Indicators* (Washington: Government Printing Office) is a monthly publication of important tables and charts, prepared by the Council of Economic Advisors.

3. *Economic Report of the President* (Washington: Government Printing Office) is an annual publication containing some of the most important up-to-date statistics for the national economy and comments about the economy's recent past and future as viewed by the President's Council of Economic Advisors.

4. *Federal Reserve Bulletin* (Washington: Board of Governors of the Federal Reserve System) is a monthly publication providing comprehensive coverage of financial data, both public and private. It includes statistics on such diverse financial matters as international gold movements, debt, savings, banking operations, mortgages, interest rates, and credit, and it contains indexes of business activity such as department store statistics and industrial production.

5. *Federal Reserve Charts on Bank Credit, Money Rates, and Business* (Washington: Board of Governors of the Federal Reserve System) is a useful, comprehensive chart book published monthly that includes an annual historical supplement and hence is a valuable companion to the *Federal Reserve Bulletin*.

6. *Monthly Labor Review* (Washington: U.S. Department of Labor) is a monthly publication containing the great majority of such data as consumer prices, wholesale prices, housing, and wages, developed by the Bureau of Labor Statistics.

7. *Statistical Abstract of the United States* (Washington: Government Printing Office) is published yearly by the Commerce Department and provides in one volume a comprehensive summary, on an annual basis, of government statistics published during the year.

8. *Survey of Current Business* (Washington: Office of Business Economics, U.S. Department of Commerce) is a monthly publication containing the best monthly and quarterly data available on national income, personal income, and various business statistics that are widely used in business and economic research. Subscribers, in addition, receive a weekly leaflet containing current tables and charts. Several supplements to the *Survey* are

also published, of which *Business Statistics*, a biennial, is worth special mention because of its comprehensive monthly coverage of numerous business and economic series back to 1929.

These eight publications constitute the basic statistical sources from which a wide variety of information can be obtained. All of them are available at nominal cost, usually a few dollars each, whether for a year's subscription to a journal or for one of the annual publications. In addition to these, at least two basic sourcebooks are of use: Arthur H. Cole, *Measures of Business Change* (Homewood, Ill.: Richard D. Irwin, Inc., 1952), and Richard M. Snyder, *Measuring Business Changes: A Handbook of Significant Business Indicators* (New York: John Wiley & Sons, Inc., 1955), which together describe the nature of several hundred statistical series and barometers covering virtually all areas of business and economics. A few business magazines, such as *Business Week, Barron's, Forbes, Printer's Ink, Sales Management,* and *Tide,* and newspapers such as *The New York Times* and *The Wall Street Journal,* are also valuable sources of current happenings and statistics in the business world.

SPECIAL SOURCES

The above basic sources also contain a good deal of information, in the form of articles and data, that are of a specialized nature. The following brief listing of special sources, therefore, should be regarded as supplementary to the dozen or so sources given above. Although the listing is by no means complete, it is fairly comprehensive.

Agriculture and Extractive. Mountains of agricultural data are published by the U.S. Department of Agriculture and by the various land grant colleges. Among the chief publications of the former are the monthly *Farm Income Situation*, the annual *Agricultural Outlook Charts*, and the annual comprehensive volume, *Agricultural Statistics*. Concerning the land grant colleges, there is a general index to their publications (most of which are concerned with state and regional problems) in university and public libraries. Statistics on other commodities—copper, lead, zinc, coal, fuel oil, rubber, and many others—are published by the U.S. Department of the Interior, including the Bureau of Mines. One of their major publications is the comprehensive *Minerals Yearbook*. Data on many important commodity series, however, including prices, inventories, and disappearance, can also be found in the *Survey of Current Business* and in various trade magazines, if current information is desired.

Capital Expenditures. In addition to the Commerce Department and SEC survey of capital expenditures published in the *Survey of Current Business*, and the McGraw-Hill survey published in *Business Week*, both of which were mentioned in the previous chapter, there are the MAPI (Machinery and Allied Products Institute) reports on capital outlays published in its *Capital Goods Review*, the BLS (Bureau of Labor Statistics, U.S. Department of Labor) reports on residential building permits and starts, and the F. W. Dodge Corporation reports on contract awards. Many of these statistics, as well as related information and data, can be found in summary form in the *Survey of Current Business* and in the *Federal Reserve Bulletin*, while the monthly government publication, *Construction Review* (obtainable from the Government Printing Office), contains good detailed information on various aspects of construction activity. The most comprehensive measure of capital spending, of course, is the construction and equipment portion of gross national product.

Consumer Instalment Credit. Monthly data on consumer instalment credit are reported in the *Federal Reserve Bulletin*. The statistics published are both by the type and purpose of the credit (for example, automobile, repair and modernization loans) and by the type of lending agency (such as commercial bank or sales finance company). A significant study of consumer credit made by the Board of Governors of the Federal Reserve System in 1957 was entitled *Consumer Installment Credit* and is available in many libraries or from the Government Printing Office.

Government Finance. Various government publications are available from which important financial data pertaining to government activity can be obtained. Among the more important sources are the *Daily Treasury Statement*, the monthly *Treasury Bulletin*, and more comprehensive publications such as *Budgetary Receipts and Expenditures* and *Cash Receipts from and Payments to the Public*, both of which contain receipts, expenditures, and cash flow data. Another useful source is the *Annual Report of the Secretary of the Treasury*. The most comprehensive of all, however, are the annual data in Tables 8 and 9 of *National Income*, published as a supplement to the *Survey of Current Business*.

National Income and Product. Data on gross and net national product, and on national, personal, and disposable income, are available in quarterly form, but two months late, in the *Survey of Current Business*. Estimates only three weeks late are released to the newspapers by the Council of Economic Advisors. Annual data, on the other hand, are available in the general sources listed earlier and in the July issue of the *Survey*. *Business Week*, in the last issue of each month, makes available the data on personal income by states for two months previous, and *Sales Management* magazine publishes its own periodic study of income by counties. Refined measures of purchasing power, called "supernumerary" or "discretionary" income and representing income in excess of basic living costs, are prepared by the Econometric Institute, Inc., and the National Industrial Conference Board.

New Orders. The U.S. Department of Commerce publishes, in its *Survey of Current Business*, general and specific series on new orders for durable and nondurable manufactures; the *Federal Reserve Bulletin* contains a series on new orders for department stores; and various trade associations publish new-orders data compiled from members' reports. New-orders series may be of use in forecasting when, as often happens, particular series can be found which exhibit a leading tendency. Although such series are not too reliable for predicting changes in the total economy (as explained in the previous chapter), they are sometimes found to be of use to business firms for short-term sales forecasting. Frequently, new-orders data, because of their short lead characteristic, are best utilized in combination with other carefully selected series as will be illustrated in subsequent chapters.

Population and the Labor Force. The Bureau of the Census makes available, in its *Current Population Reports*, projections of population, households, and the labor force. These projections are also presented in the *Economic Almanac*, one of the basic sources mentioned earlier. In *Current Population Reports*, the most recent projections for population are available in series P-25, no. 123 (October 20, 1955); for households and families, in series P-20, no. 69 (August 31, 1956); and for the labor force, in series P-50, no. 69 (October, 1956). The January, 1960 issue of the *Economic Report of the President* may also be consulted for several recent population projections.

Prices. In discussing sources of price information, a four-way classification is helpful. (1) "The Consumer Price Index," available in all basic sources, is published by the Bureau of Labor Statistics, which also makes available some further details in its monthly release, *Consumer Price Index*. The Department of Commerce, as an alternative measure, publishes a "Retail Price Index" in the *Survey of Current Business*. (2) Spot prices are made available by the BLS in its "Daily Index of Spot Market Prices," while somewhat similar daily indexes of spot prices are published by Dun and Bradstreet, Dow-Jones and Company, and the *Journal of Commerce*. One or more of these indexes generally appear in leading newspapers as well as in the relevant basic sources. (3) Stock market price averages are available in many daily newspapers, and in the *Survey of Current Business* if monthly data are desired. The best-known averages are those compiled by Dow-Jones and by Standard and Poor's Corporation. (4) "The Wholesale Price Index" is one of the best-known series compiled by the BLS, and is published in all basic sources. Detailed information as to components, breakdowns, and so forth, are also available in various releases issued by the Bureau.

Production. The Index of Industrial Production, prepared by the Federal Reserve Board and available in total as well as in various breakdowns, is published in the *Federal Reserve Bulletin* and in the *Survey of Current Business*. The latter also contains many series on the monthly production of important individual products, while major weekly data can be found in leading newspapers.

Profits, Dividends, Interest Rates and Yields. Corporate profits and dividends, as a division of national income, most closely approximate the true level. However, being based on Bureau of Internal Revenue figures, they are made available three or four years late. Hence, other sources must be sought. The best available are: (1) Federal Reserve estimates of quarterly profits, based on a sample of manufacturing and electric power companies, and virtually all railroad and telephone companies, published in the *Federal Reserve Bulletin*; (2) FTC and SEC joint estimates of quarterly profits based on a large sample of all manufacturing corporations, published in the *Survey of Current Business*; and (3) the *National City Bank Letter*. Dividend data are also reported, based on the first two of the above surveys, in the *Bulletin* and in the *Survey*, as well as by Moody's and by Standard and Poor's Corporation in their own releases and in the *Survey* as well. Both the *Survey* and the *Bulletin* publish, in addition, data on various short-term interest rates, while the Survey also reports Moody's dividend yields on common stocks and Standard and Poor's dividend yield on preferreds, and the *Bulletin* publishes yields on U.S. Government bonds, Moody's series on state and local government bonds by quality ratings, and price-and-earnings ratios on common stocks. A useful publication for more detailed information about bonds, yields, and so on, is *The Bond Buyer*.

Sales. Series on manufacturing, wholesale trade, and retail trade are part of the Commerce Department's monthly "Industry Survey," published in the *Survey of Current Business*. A corporate-sales series also appears in detailed Table 29 of *National Income*, while the *Federal Reserve Bulletin* reports on sales of many individual products and groups, some of which also appear in the *Survey of Current Business*. Many trade associations and trade magazines frequently report useful sales series and related data. Thus, the Automobile Manufacturers Association publishes two annuals, *Automobile Facts and Figures*, and *Motor Truck Facts*, while current information on weekly assemblies is prepared by R. L. Polk and summarized in leading newspapers. The magazine *Electrical Merchandising* often publishes sales series for various kinds of electrical appliances. Similarly, other specialized sources exist for a wide variety of particular products and product classes, to which reference can be made when needed.

Conclusion

The purpose of this and the previous section has been to list and describe the most widely used general and specialized types and sources of statistical data. A complete cyclopedia, of course, would be impossible. However, by touching only on the most essential sources, a sound basis has been laid for further exploration and searching if the need should arise. It is probable, however, that such a need will never arise, for the great majority of business and economic research is based on data obtained from the above-mentioned sources. In fact, for most forecasting work, the basic sources, especially the *Survey of Current Business*, the *Federal Reserve Bulletin*, and perhaps the *Statistical Abstract of the United States* and the *Economic Almanac*, are all that are necessary to maintain a well-organized forecasting operation. This will be further evidenced in later chapters, where numerous forecasting models are constructed utilizing data drawn almost exclusively from these sources.

BUSINESS INDICATORS

Business indicators are statistical series which reflect, in one way or another, economic conditions. Since there are thousands of such indicators—indeed, every statistical series is an indicator of something—we must confine our attention in this section to a discussion of some of the most comprehensive and widely used indicators of business change. In doing so, we familiarize ourselves with the nature of these series, and gain some appreciation of why they are extensively used and frequently quoted by economists, market researchers, financial analysts, and others engaged in business or economic research.

Ideally, an indicator of general economic change, if it is to be used in forecasting work, should fulfill at least four functions. It should: (1) reflect the turning points in economic activity, (2) measure the amplitude of change, (3) measure the rate of economic growth or decline, and (4) have a leading tendency in relation to other series. Unfortunately, no single series evidences all of these characteristics consistently. However, many series exhibit one or more of these characteristics at different times under different conditions. The following comprehensive series, published in the *Survey*, the *Bulletin*, and other sources listed earlier, are important in this connection.

Gross National Product

The most comprehensive measure of aggregate economic activity is gross national product, abbreviated GNP. It is the total amount of final goods and services produced during the year, valued at current market prices; it also represents the expenditure side of the national accounts and includes all governments (federal, state, local), businesses, and individuals. The structure of GNP includes net national product, national income, personal income, and disposable income; their nature, definitions, measurements, and relation to GNP are adequately explained in all elementary textbooks in economics.

The chief advantage of GNP (or other aggregate income and product estimates) for indicating business conditions is its comprehensiveness. This is offset, however, by at least three disadvantages: (1) It is so broad in its coverage that it tends to be somewhat sluggish; (2) all of the component figures cannot readily be estimated on a monthly basis, and even as prepared on a quarterly basis detail must be sacrificed to provide full coverage; and (3) it appears several months late and hence is not sufficiently current for many forecasting problems. In view of these considerations, GNP data are not as widely used in forecasting as might be expected. When they are used, the quarter-to-quarter and year-to-year figures should at best be regarded as indications of the direction of change and, since the figures are rough estimates to begin with, as approximate measures of the amount of change.

Industrial Production

The Federal Reserve monthly index of industrial production is designed to measure monthly changes in the physical volume of output of manufacturing and mining industries, and of electric and gas utilities. Prior to December, 1959, the index measured only manufacturing and mining activity. The inclusion of electric and gas utilities, which accounts for about one third of the difference between the old and the new indexes, provides more complete coverage of power and fuel output, since coal and oil were already included in the old index.

It should be noted that although the index measures directly the output of industries accounting for an important part of total economic activity, it *excludes* certain strategic sectors of the economy such as construction activity, transportation, trade services, and agriculture. The index is not, therefore, a measure of total economic activity, and hence tends to exhibit wider and more frequent fluctuations than a broader series like GNP.

The revision of the index to include electric and gas output now covers the period from January, 1947 on. Some further changes made in the December, 1959 revision are, briefly, as follows: (1) The individual production series, formerly grouped only by "industry" (for example, primary metals and transportation equipment), are now grouped also according to "market"—the three most comprehensive categories being consumer goods, equipment (business and defense), and materials; (2) estimating procedures, seasonal adjustments, and weighting methods have been improved, and some new monthly series have been added; and (3) in order to facilitate analysis of production changes in relation to a more recent period, the detailed breakdowns by industries and market groupings are presented on a 1957 base. However, the total index as well as major groupings continue to be published for an indefinite period on a 1947–49 base, thus keeping in line with the base period used by other federal agencies.

Prices

Changes in prices are reflected by various indexes, three of which are particularly significant: the spot market price index, the wholesale price index, and the consumer price index. All of these are published by the Bureau of Labor Statistics and appear in most of the basic sources mentioned earlier.

1. The daily index of spot market prices is one of the most widely used measures of price fluctuation in the United States. The index measures changes in prices in primary commodity markets of a selected group of twenty-two commodities made up of foods, fibers, metals, and other raw

materials. The commodities are traded on organized exchanges, and the quotations are essentially on a spot basis, that is, for current rather than future delivery. The indexes are published each morning for the previous trading day. Weekly releases are also prepared containing monthly averages, and an annual bulletin of the Bureau of Labor Statistics (BLS), *Wholesale Prices*, contains daily indexes for the entire year. The BLS publishes, in addition to the spot market price index, several group indexes including an all-commodity price index and separate price indexes for foodstuffs, raw materials, livestock and products, metals, textiles and fibers, and fats and oils. In general, the basic commodity price index is more sensitive than the wholesale price index discussed next, because of the latter's broader coverage and inclusion of fabricated and semifabricated goods, the prices of which fluctuate less frequently and less narrowly than the prices of basic commodities. The prompt availability of the spot price index and related group indexes make them useful measures for forecasting, as will be illustrated in Chapter 5.

2. The wholesale price index measures changes in wholesale prices. The term "wholesale prices" refers here to the prices of goods sold in large lots, not to prices paid or received by wholesalers, distributors, or jobbers. Price quotations used in computing the index are those which apply at primary market levels, that is, when the first important commercial transaction for the commodity occurs. The index is designed to reflect price changes for *all* primary market transactions in commodities. It is reported on a monthly basis as the weighted average of a sample of nearly 2,000 commodities, and on a weekly basis as the weighted average of a sample of about 200 commodities. All types of goods from raw materials through finished goods are included. However, there are no quotations for real estate, securities, transportation, or services; nor, for example, is the cost of construction of finished buildings covered, although raw and finished materials used in construction, such as lumber, bricks, and oil burners, are priced. The "all-commodities" index is thus an effective measure of the change in average prices in primary markets, while the various component indexes, arranged in product groups and subgroups (such as, processed foods, metals and metal products, and machinery and motive products) serve as valuable special-purpose indexes for particular types of problems.

3. The consumer price index is defined by the Department of Labor as "a measure of the average change in price of goods and services customarily purchased by families of wage earners and clerical workers living in cities of the United States." The index, computed from a diversified sample of forty-six cities, represents retail price changes of a given-sized "market basket" of goods and services. Eight major categories are represented in the index: food, housing, apparel, transportation, medical care, personal care, reading and recreation, and other goods and services. Separate indexes for each of these groups are published, as well as for their various subgroups. The index attempts to approximate the changes in prices

paid by urban wage-earner and clerical-worker families of two or more persons, and represents about two thirds of all urban families and about 40 per cent of all families in the United States. Despite these constraints, the index is the best and most widely used measure of prices paid by all consumers, and is frequently employed in escalator clauses and wage negotiations. Since it is reported monthly and annually in the basic sources, it (and its components) are often used in various forecasting problems, sometimes in conjunction with certain income variables in order to obtain up-to-date weighted measures of purchasing power, as will be seen in later chapters.

In addition to these indexes, the Department of Commerce publishes implicit price deflators or indexes for expenditure aggregates such as gross national product, personal consumption expenditures, and the like. These deflators provide a useful means of allowing for price changes when dealing with various expenditure aggregates. The implicit price deflators for annual GNP data, covering 1929–59 and expressed on a 1954 base, are provided in Table D–5 of the January, 1960 issue of the *Economic Report of the President*, and the conversion of estimates is explained in *U.S. Income and Output, A Supplement to the Survey of Current Business*, 1958.

Income

A measure of economic activity in general, and of purchasing power in particular, is income. Three distinct but related concepts of income are frequently used by those engaged in business forecasting: personal income, disposable income, and discretionary or supernumerary income. The nature of each may be explained briefly.

1. Personal income is estimated on a monthly and annual basis by the Department of Commerce and is available in the *Survey of Current Business* as well as other basic sources cited earlier. Although frequently used as an indicator of consumer income and purchasing power, personal income, it should be emphasized, does *not* denote money income or spendable income exclusively. To be sure, the largest segment of total personal income, about 70 per cent, is wages, salaries, and other labor income, but the remaining 30 per cent consists of rents, interest, dividends, transfer payments, and income from unincorporated businesses. Personal income data are thus useful for analyzing short-term business changes and long-term economic trends, but not as a measure of spendable income or purchasing power.

2. Disposable personal income, or simply disposable income, is a more accurate measure of actual purchasing power, since it represents personal income less personal tax and nontax payments to governments. Portions of disposable income, however, are income in kind and imputed income, both of which are included in personal income accounts and hence are not actually money incomes at the disposal of persons for spending or saving. Despite these factors, disposable income still serves as a reliable measure of

purchasing power, as will be illustrated in many of the forecasting studies of later chapters. As with personal income, data on disposable income can be obtained from the basic sources mentioned earlier in this chapter.

3. Discretionary or supernumerary income is the most refined measure of consumer buying power available. Conceptually, it represents the flow of money available to consumers over and above their necessary expenditures. Estimates of supernumerary income were first developed and used by Charles F. Roos in his classic study of automobile demand more than twenty years ago (discussed later in Chapter 7), and have since been employed in various other studies, as will be seen subsequently. Recently the National Industrial Conference Board published its description and estimates of discretionary income in W. B. Franklin, *Discretionary Income* (Technical Paper No. 6, 1958). Briefly, the Conference Board estimates discretionary income by subtracting from disposable income the sum of the following three factors: (1) imputed income and income in kind (including employees' lodging, imputed rent on owner-occupied homes, imputed interest, and food and clothing furnished to government employees, the military, and commercial employees); (2) major fixed outlay payments (including mortgage debt repayment, consumer instalment debt repayment, insurance and pension payments, homeowner taxes, and tenant rent); and (3) essential expenditures (including that portion of food outlay necessary to maintain the same average level which prevailed in the years 1947–49, that portion of clothing outlay necessary to maintain per capita physical clothing purchases at their 1951 level, expenses for medical, dental, and health insurance purposes, outlays for household utilities, and purchases of local transportation). The resulting series, called discretionary income, represents "marginal" purchasing power. During the decade of the 'fifties it tended to be a fairly stable proportion of disposable income—about 34 per cent—and has generally been more sensitive to economic conditions because of its marginal or discretionary nature. For forecasting purposes, the use of either variable as a measure of purchasing power is permissible, although disposable income is more frequently employed because of its wider availability. The use of both measures, however, is illustrated in later chapters.

Consumer Instalment Credit

The amount of consumer credit in use has an important influence on consumer purchasing power and hence affects the consumers' goods industries. The use of instalment credit is cyclical in nature, tending to expand in prosperity periods and thereby increase consumer buying power, and fall in recession periods thereby decreasing buying power. Consumers' durable goods industries are the ones most seriously affected by these cyclical swings, since the largest part of the credits are extended either directly or indirectly for the purpose of purchasing such goods as automobiles and major household appliances.

TABLE 2–1

SOURCES OF COMMONLY USED INDEXES*

Name of Index	Prepared by—	Frequency of Publication	Published Regularly in—
A. PRICE INDEXES			
1. Consumer Price Index	U.S. Bureau of Labor Statistics	M	*SCB, FRB, MLR, Business Week, C&FC, S&P, Ec. Ind.*
2. Wholesale Price Index	U.S. Bureau of Labor Statistics	W, M	*SCB, FRB, MLR, Dun's, N.Y. Times, Barron's, C&FC, S&P, Ec. Ind.*
3. Spot Market Prices of 22 Basic Commodities	U.S. Bureau of Labor Statistics	D, W, M	*Barron's*
4. Dow-Jones Commodities Futures	Dow-Jones & Co.	D	*Barron's, Jour. Com.*
5. Construction Cost Indexes	American Appraisal Co.	M	*SCB*
6. Stock Price Averages	Dow-Jones & Co.	H, D, W, M	*SCB, N.Y. Times, Barron's, S&P, Jour. Com.*
7. Stock Price Index, 480 Stocks	Standard and Poor's Corporation	W, M	*SCB, FRB, S&P, Ec. Ind., NICB*
B. QUANTITY INDEXES			
1. Industrial Production	Federal Reserve Board	M	*SCB, FRB, Dun's, N.Y. Times, S&P, Ec. Ind. NICB*
2. Business Activity	*New York Times*	W	*N.Y. Times*
3. Business Index	*Barron's*	W	*Barron's*
4. Manufacturing Production-Worker Employment	U.S. Bureau of Labor Statistics	M	*SCB, FRB, MLR, Dun's, S&P*
5. Steel Production—Per Cent of Capacity	American Iron and Steel Institute	W, M	*SCB, FRB, Business Week, N.Y. Times, Barron's, C&FC, S&P*
C. VALUE INDEXES			
1. National Income	U.S. Department of Commerce	Q	*SCB, FRB, N.Y. Times, S&P, Ec. Ind., NICB*
2. Department Store Sales	Federal Reserve Board	W, M	*SCB, FRB, N.Y. Times, Barron's, C&FC, S&P, NICB*
3. Rural Sales of General Merchandise	U.S. Department of Commerce	M	*SCB*
4. Manufacturing Production-Worker Payrolls	U.S. Bureau of Labor Statistics	M	*SCB, FRB, MLR, Dun's, S&P*
5. Construction Contracts Awarded (Value)	Federal Reserve Board (from F. W. Dodge Corp. data)	M	*SCB, FRB*
6. Regional Trade Barometers	*Dun's*	M	*Dun's*
7. Regional Income Indexes	*Business Week*	M	*Business Week*

* Abbreviations:

H—hourly; D—daily; W—weekly; M—monthly; Q—quarterly.

SCB—*Survey of Current Business* (and weekly supplement)

FRB—*Federal Reserve Bulletin*
MLR—*Monthly Labor Review*
Dun's—*Dun's Statistical Review*

C&FC—*Commercial and Financial Chronicle*
S&P—Standard and Poor's *Trade and Securities Service*
Ec. Ind.—President's Council of Economic Advisers, *Economic Indicators*
NICB—National Industrial Conference Board, *Business Record*
Jour. Com.—*Journal of Commerce*

Source: W. A. Spurr, L. S. Kellogg, and J. H. Smith, *Business and Economic Statistics* (Homewood, Ill.: Richard D. Irwin, Inc., 1954), p. 244.

Data on consumer instalment credit, broken down both by type of credit (for example, automobile, personal loans, repair and modernization loans, and consumers' goods paper) and by type of institution holding the credit (such as, commercial banks, sales finance companies, and department stores) are published regularly in the *Federal Reserve Bulletin*, the *Survey of Current Business*, and various other sources. The use of consumer instalment credit in business forecasting is illustrated in several studies appearing in later chapters.

Conclusion

Numerous indicators in addition to those already mentioned may be cited, but this is unnecessary since the various studies in subsequent chapters will make extensive use of particular indicators as the need arises. It may be mentioned, therefore, that in addition to the indicators already presented, some other useful information that can be obtained includes (1) employment and earnings data provided by the BLS, (2) monetary data provided by the Federal Reserve, and (3) additional activity data such as electric power consumption, railroad-freight carloadings, and sales and inventory data, all of which, along with other useful series, are available in the various basic sources already mentioned. A handy summary of various indexes, along with their sources and frequency of publication, is presented in Table 2–1, and some descriptive charts are shown in Figure 2–1. In a well-organized forecasting operation, up-to-date records and charts of these as well as of particular variables relating to the company and the industry would be maintained, and new relationships continually developed according to management's needs.

QUESTIONS

1. List the general or basic sources of economic and business data, the agencies responsible for the information contained in these sources, and their frequency of publication.

2. (*a*) If you were engaged in research on one or more farm products, and you wanted to obtain data on such factors as yields, prices, production, and consumption, where would you look for current information? For annual information? (*b*) What source would you examine for annual data on copper production, lead prices, and aluminum consumption?

3. Of the various sources listed in this chapter, which two seem to appear most frequently and hence are major sources for the majority of statistical data used in forecasting?

4. (*a*) What is an economic or business indicator? (*b*) If an ideal indicator could be constructed, what characteristics would it have?

5. What are the pros and cons of using gross national product (GNP) as an economic indicator?

6. (*a*) What does the Federal Reserve Index of Industrial Production measure? (*b*) What are some of the things it does *not* measure? (*c*) Does this index fluctuate more widely, or less widely, than GNP? Why?

FIGURE 2-1

Here Are the Instruments for Clocking Busine:

What It Measures

GNP measures the output of all goods and services produced by the economy — or (viewed the other way around) the total income of all producers, including government.

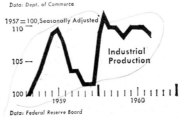

Billions of Dollars, Seasonally Adjusted, Annual Rate

Gross National Product

Data: Dept. of Commerce

FRB Index measures changes in physical output of manufacturing and mining industries, gas and electric utilities.

1957 = 100, Seasonally Adjusted

Industrial Production

Data: Federal Reserve Board

SEC-Commerce Capital Spending survey records business plans for expenditures on new plant and equipment. Later revisions measure actual capital spending.

Billions of Dollars, Seasonally Adjusted, Annual Rate

Capital Spending

Data: SEC-Dept. of Commerce

Manufacturing and Trade Inventories measure end-of-month value of inventories held by manufacturers, wholesalers, retailers.

Billions of Dollars, Seasonally Adjusted

Inventories

Data: Dept. of Commerce

How Good Is It?

Not up to the minute or sensitive an indicator — can take six mon or more to register change in bu ness trend. Quality of data uneve early estimates can be off by se eral billions, though percento error for total usually less than 1 Weakest components: small bu ness income, inventories, savin

Includes 207 series, varying grec in quality — many not based on < tual output but estimated fr man-hours worked and product ity estimates, or from raw materi consumed. The 1959 revision duced reliance on man-hour da

Based on sample of 2,500 comp nies, projected to total by prior y< tax returns. Forecasts for individ< industries often way off, but tot pretty good. Since 1945, quarte forecasts in right direction 3 out 4 times; annual forecasts miss direction only once — in 19 (Korea).

Major errors more likely here th in any other important series. C rent figures, based on small sa ples, subject to big revisions. Fig< for manufacturing is best; retail data weak because based on ports only from chain and depc ment stores. Difficult to adjust ventory figures for price chang

FIGURE 2-1—*Continued*

hat It Measures

using Starts data measure
nber of new housing units
ncluding apartments — on
ich construction is started
h month. Series at right
ers private non-farm hous-
, but data also available
public and farm building.

sus Bureau unemployment
ies tries to measure the
nber of people in the work
ce who are looking for jobs.

nsumer Price Index meas-
·s changes in prices paid
consumer goods and serv-
s by "typical" urban blue-
lar and clerical-worker
nilies.

e Money Supply — defined
demand deposits plus cur-
ncy in circulation — is in-
nded to measure cash im-
ediately available to indi-
duals and businesses.

Thousands of Starts, Seasonally Adjusted, Annual Rate
Housing Starts

Data: Bureau of Labor Statistics

Thousands of Persons 14 Years of Age and Over
Unemployment

Data: Bureau of the Census

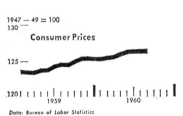

1947 — 49 = 100
Consumer Prices

Data: Bureau of Labor Statistics

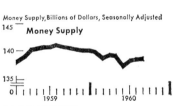

Money Supply, Billions of Dollars, Seasonally Adjusted
Money Supply

Data: Federal Reserve Board

How Good Is It?

New series for which seasonal adjustment is not yet satisfactory.
Some current uncertainty about
housing picture may come from this
series' erratic behavior. Data mainly
from building permits; actual starts
calculated on basis of small sample
—6,000 to 8,500 building permits.

Always a hot number politically.
Definition of "unemployment"
highly debatable. Employment and
unemployment data based on sample of 25,000 — so unemployment
data based on only about 1,000
cases. Depending on number un-
employed, sampling error can be
big as 8%. Seasonal factors difficult to calculate.

Probably overstates amount by
which prices have risen since World
War II by underweighting quality
improvements. Probably under-
states price rises in booms, price
cuts in recessions, because it's hard
to catch all shading of prices. Sampling error virtually impossible to
compute.

Early data subject to revision —
sometimes substantially. Significance of swings may be obscured
by role of "near money" — savings
deposits, S&L shares, some government securities — and changes in
velocity. New York bank deposits
extremely erratic because of big
role of security market transactions.

Reproduced with permission from *Business Week*, October 22, 1960.

7. Define briefly, in your own words, the three most widely used price indexes in the United States. Who publishes these indexes?

8. (*a*) Distinguish between the various measures of income or purchasing power typically used by forecasters. (*b*) Which are recommended as the best measures of consumers' purchasing power? Explain.

9. What class of goods is most seriously affected by fluctuations in consumer instalment credit? Why?

10. In view of your answer to question 9, how should instalment credit and income be treated when forecasting the demand for consumers' durable goods?

Chapter 3   FORECASTING TOOLS

Professional forecasters have only a secondary interest in the past and present behavior of business indicators; their primary interest is in predicting the future course of these indicators, including both their magnitude of change and their turning points. The past and present are thus important, to be sure, but only to the extent that they are useful in shaping scientific estimates of the future.

In Chapter 1, where the subject matter was concerned with methods of forecasting, chief emphasis was placed on the econometric method as representing the type of approach to be followed in this book. In this and the next chapter a nontechnical explanation of certain econometric concepts will be presented. The areas to be covered include a discussion of (1) the statistical basis of econometrics, (2) the method of graphic correlation, and (3) the use of correlation analysis in forecasting. Emphasis will be placed on a literary and graphic (rather than mathematical) presentation so that the reader with little or no background in mathematics can comprehend and even construct for himself the many types of models illustrated in the following chapters. At the end of the next chapter, a supplement on the elements of logarithms will be presented, because many forecasting problems involve the use of logarithms and logarithmic charts, as will soon become apparent. Hence, an elementary explanation of the nature of logarithms may be of use, either as an introduction or as a review, depending on the reader's background in mathematics.

STATISTICAL BASIS OF ECONOMETRICS

Econometrics is a quantitive science about which several books and numerous articles have been written. It should be kept in mind, therefore, that the purpose of this section is to present, within the limits of a few pages, some of the fundamental concepts that underlie econometric research and the interpretation of econometric models. An understanding of the basic concepts discussed here and in the remainder of this chapter will provide the background necessary to comprehend all of the models in this book as well as many others that may be encountered in various publications.[1]

Functional Concept

One of the most important concepts in statistical analysis, as well as in mathematics in general, is the notion of a function. A chief objective of econometrics is to discover functional relations and to measure these relations by statistical means. Since we shall be making estimates of numerous functions in the following chapters, let us see what the concept of a function actually involves.

Definitions. All branches of science are concerned for the most part with the study of relationships among changing quantities. In studying relationships, two technical terms that are usually encountered are *variables* and *constants*. An understanding of these terms is necessary in order to comprehend the concept of a function.

A *variable* is a quantity which may assume any one of a set of values in a particular problem or discussion. The speed of an automobile at different times during a trip, the fluctuations in the price of wheat during the year, and the changes in temperature at different times during the day, are all examples of variables. A *constant*, on the other hand, is a quantity which remains fixed in a particular problem or discussion. Thus the number of days in a week, the number of inches in a foot, and the speed of light in a vacuum are all examples of constants. A constant that never changes in value is sometimes called an *absolute constant*, in order to distinguish it from an *arbitrary constant* or *parameter* which is a constant that may be assigned different values. Most of the constants encountered in business and economic problems are of the latter type, and a main purpose of research, as will be seen shortly, is to discover the probable values of the constants in a particular problem.

In studying variations among changing quantities, it is often found that a change in the value of one variable corresponds to a change in the value of another. When this occurs, a *functional relation* between the variables is said to exist. For example, the quantity purchased of a particular product may depend upon its price. The quantity purchased is then referred to as the *dependent variable* and the price is called the *independent variable*. The dependent variable is thus regarded as a function of the independent variable, the word "function" being used to represent the idea that a relationship exists between the variables.

Functions are conveniently expressed either algebraically in the form of an equation, arithmetically in the form of a table, or graphically in the form of a chart. All three of these methods, particularly the tabular and

---

[1] Some textbooks that may be referred to as supplements to this chapter are G. Tintner, *Econometrics*; L. Klein, *Textbook of Econometrics*; and S. Valavanis, *Econometrics*. Nontechnical discussions of various models appear in M. Spencer and L. Siegelman, *Managerial Economics*.

graphic forms, are employed extensively in the following chapters. A few examples of the algebraic form of expression may be helpful, however, in clarifying the basic ideas.

Conceptually, if Y represents a dependent variable and X represents an independent variable, a statement of functional relationship between the variables may be written $Y = f(X)$. This is read, "Y is a function of X," and means simply that a relationship exists. Other letters, of course, may be used to convey the same idea. Thus, the cost C of sending mail by first class is a function of the weight W; therefore, $C = f(W)$. Similarly, the yield per acre Y on a farm may be a function of the amount of rainfall R; therefore, $Y = f(R)$. Sometimes two or more independent variables, instead of just one, are recognized and included in the parenthesis. Thus the price P of wheat is a function of both the demand D and the supply S, so that the relationship may be expressed conceptually as $P = f(D, S)$. And the sale of television sets T is a function of income I, price P, the number of families F, and other factors, so that the expression may be written $T = f(I, P, F, \ldots)$, where the dots represent the unspecified factors, or simply $T = f(I, P, F)$, since only the specified factors would be included in an actual study.

It should be understood that the expressions above are merely ways of stating conceptually that functional relations exist between certain variables. The actual nature of any particular relationship, however, is not stated, and hence an analysis must be conducted in order to discover if an actual relationship exists. Such an analysis might reveal, for example, that in a particular situation, there exists a linear relation of the form $Y = a + bX$, where a and b are the constants, and Y and X are the dependent and independent variables, respectively. If the values of the constants are found from the analysis to be, say, $a = 3$ and $b = 5$, the nature of the relationship can then be expressed as $Y = 3 + 5X$, and thus a precise rather than mere conceptual statement of dependency can be made.

What value is there in obtaining a precise relationship, as compared to a conceptual one? The answer is that, strictly speaking, the existence of a function implies only that for each value of one variable there is a corresponding value of the other. If, however, the variables chosen can be justified by economic judgment as having a *causal* connection, the precise statement of the relation provides a basis for forecasting the dependent variable on the basis of variations in the independent variable. The development of principles and techniques for accomplishing this objective is a chief goal of econometricians, and will occupy the core of our attention from a forecasting standpoint in this and the following chapters.

Analytical Framework

It is apparent by now that statistical analysis is an indispensable part of econometrics, serving both as a *modus operandi* and as a framework for problem solving. The former function is an operational one and is illustrated in various ways throughout this and later chapters. The latter function, that of providing an analytical framework, is basic to all econometric research, and hence deserves at least brief mention at this point.

Modern statistics, as most readers will recall even from an elementary course in the subject, is based upon the concept of probability. Although there is some disagreement among mathematicians as to the precise meaning of probability, econometricians would generally say that probability deals with the limit that is approached by the relative frequency of an event as the number of trials increases indefinitely. This is an essential concept to keep in mind when reading and evaluating the various econometric studies that will be encountered in later discussions.

Recognizing probability as the most fundamental concept upon which statistical analysis is based, we may outline three aspects of the subject with which the reader is always assumed to be familiar when he interprets the results of econometric investigations.

1. *Statistical Inference.* This is the science of drawing conclusions about a population on the basis of information derived from a sample. All economic relationships, particularly from an econometric standpoint, are regarded as samples from an unknown infinite population of all possible economic relationships, and econometricians employ statistical methods in order to arrive at numerical estimates.

2. *Randomness.* Basic to the entire science of statistical inference is the notion of a randomly determined variable, or as statisticians call it, a stochastic variable. This is a variable that can assume a number of values with given probabilities, as, for instance, when it is stated that with continuous rolls of a perfect die, it can be established with certainty that the probability (that is, limit of the relative frequency) of a given number is $\frac{1}{6}$, or 0.17. The interpretation of randomness may be thought of, therefore, as meaning that any given value of the variable is *independent*: it is not in any way determined by its past values nor does it in any way determine its future values. The importance of this will become more evident in later chapters where, for example, in forecasting a time series of sales, the values may not be entirely independent or, in other words, not randomly distributed in the manner of a stochastic variable, with the result that "autocorrelation" is said to exist.

3. *Point Estimation.* This is a very important part of statistical inference and hence of econometrics. In point estimation, the problem is to derive or predict a single figure as an estimate of the unknown quantity. Two methods commonly used for this purpose are the *method of least squares* and the *method of maximum likelihood*. The method of least squares is more frequently employed by practicing forecasters and is the familiar procedure learned in elementary statistics. It is based on the principle that the sum of the deviations squared when taken from the mean is a minimum (hence the term "least squares") and it chooses the estimate which mini-

mizes the sum of the squared deviations from the chosen value. The method of maximum likelihood, on the other hand, chooses the value which makes the probability of occurrence of the estimate a maximum. Both methods, however, often give the same estimates, and some results of each method will be illustrated in later chapters where empirical studies are discussed.

Thus, with probability as the underlying concept, these three features—statistical inference, randomness, and point estimation—combine to form the analytical framework of modern statistics. Combined with the functional concept, these features comprise the dominant characteristics of econometric analysis, for econometrics is concerned with the numerical evaluation and statistical verification of economic laws or relationships. In a world of uncertainty, econometrics explicitly introduces random variations and leads therefore to probabilistic conclusions. Even though the factual data which serve as the raw material of econometrics are rarely precise, and thereby lead to errors of observation, such errors, quite realistically, are often regarded as random, and methods exist for including them in the general probability scheme of econometric analysis. In short, the objective of econometrics is to predict the most likely course of future economic events, on the basis of relationships revealed in the past, by a sensible method of extrapolation that is not naïve or mechanical.

Correlation and Regression

Modern statistical analysis, as we have just seen, incorporates statistical inference, randomness, and point estimation among its most important features, and these combine to form the skeleton of econometrics. But econometrics with this skeleton alone is like the Pauper without the Prince. The skeleton must be clothed with flesh to make it live, and the tool or *modus operandi* for accomplishing this is the powerful statistical device known as *correlation analysis*. The general concept and technique of correlation will be illustrated by a graphic method in the next section so that it may be comprehended by the nonmathematical reader whose only equipment need be a knowledge of arithmetic and an eye for curves. But on the basis of what should already be familiar from an elementary course in statistics, some simple but essential concepts may be presented at this time, since correlation and its allied activity, regression analysis, are perhaps the most important statistical tools used by econometricians.

The purpose of correlation and regression analysis is to arrive at a mathematical equation, called an *estimating equation, predicting equation,* or *regression equation,* which best discloses the nature of the relationship that exists between a dependent variable and one or more independent variables. Variations in the dependent variable, such as the sale of automobiles, are to be predicted on the basis of variations in one or more independent variables, such as income, number of families, replacement rates, and so on. The independent variables chosen are usually the factors that are believed to be controlling on the basis of economic theory.[2] The ultimate predicting equation that emerges is derived on the basis of statistical or correlation analysis. Where only one independent variable is involved, the statistical analysis is known as *simple correlation*; where two or more independent variables are involved, the analysis is called *multiple correlation*. Conceptually, the relationships may be illustrated by the following example.

If we let Y denote the sales of a product and X its price, then variations in Y will depend upon variations in X, so that the relationship can be written conceptually as $Y = f(X)$. As explained earlier, this is read "Y is a function of X," or "sales are a function of price," and states merely that a dependent or functional relationship exists between the two variables. Of course, any other letters could be used in place of those chosen without affecting the meaning. In this equation, since only one independent variable is involved, the relationship is one of simple correlation. Similarly, if further analysis revealed that not only price, but other factors, such as advertising and income, also had an important influence on sales, the functional relationship could then be written $Y = f(X, W, Z)$ where W and Z now refer to advertising and income, respectively. The equation would now read, "Y is a function of X, of W, and of Z," or "sales are dependent upon price, upon advertising, and upon income." And of course, just as previously, other letters could also be used, if desired, to signify the same fact that a relationship exists. In any event, since more than one independent variable is involved, the relationship is that of multiple correlation.

Now the purpose of correlation and regression analysis, whether simple or multiple, is to derive the actual equation of relationship among the variables rather than the conceptual one stated above. This amounts to saying that the separate independent variables must be weighted in some way, according to their proper importance in their effect upon the dependent variable. In the discussion of correlation in the next section, a graphic method for accomplishing this task will be explained and illustrated. To summarize briefly what was said earlier, however, the desired equation may, for instance, be of the form $Y = a + bX$, which is the equation for a straight line, with Y the dependent variable and X the independent variable. The letters a and b for the particular relationship, however, are not known: they are the weights (the constants or parameters) whose values are to be determined, and it is the purpose of correlation analysis to arrive at their most probable values. When derived, they might, for example, be found to be $a = 8$ and $b = 3$. Then the predicting equation would be $Y = 8 + 3X$, and by forecasting the value of X for any given period in the future, the corresponding value of Y can be predicted by simply substituting for X in the formula. (E.g., at $X = 5$, $Y = 23$; at $X = 10$, $Y = 38$; etc.).

This, very briefly, is a sketch of some of the statistical bases of econo-

---

[2] Economic theory, it may be noted, often provides a useful basis for framing hypotheses, but all models, including econometric models, need not be built exclusively on economic precepts.

metrics. These principles as well as others will be applied and illustrated many times and in various ways as problems are posed and solved in subsequent chapters.

GRAPHIC CORRELATION

Since the chief objective in econometric forecasting is to discover relationships among variables, a method must be found for developing such relationships from empirical data. The method generally employed for this purpose is *correlation analysis* (including regression analysis), the elements of which should be at least vaguely familiar to anyone who has had a course in elementary statistics. In this section, a simple technique for arriving at measures of relationship will be explained, based on the use of nothing more than tabular and graphic methods.

For illustrative purposes, the example to be developed is a price forecasting problem utilizing three series of hypothetical data. These are a price series, a supply series, and a demand series. The study, in other words, will attempt to illustrate how variations in the supply of and demand for a certain product, such as an agricultural commodity, can influence the price of that product, and how a relationship between price, supply, and demand may be derived which may then serve as a guide for forecasting. Thus the example involves a simple supply and demand problem of the type encountered in every elementary economics course. The underlying principles of measurement, however, are probably new to most readers. These principles should be learned at this time, therefore, if their later applications to a great variety of more complex problems are to be understood and appreciated.

Identification of Variables

The first step in the analysis is to define the problem and then to identify the relevant variables that will be involved. This has already been done partially in the preceding paragraphs and hence may be outlined briefly at this time.

The problem is to account for, or explain, the factors that are chiefly responsible for the variations in price of a particular agricultural commodity. Price, therefore, is the dependent variable in this analysis and is designated by the letter Y. And since economic judgment (that is, theory) tells us that prices of agricultural commodities are generally determined by market forces of supply and demand, the letter X_1 may be used to represent supply, and X_2 demand. The problem now crystalizes to that of forecasting the dependent variable, price Y, on the basis of the independent variables, supply X_1 and demand X_2, on the assumption that a functional relationship between the variables exists which may be written in general form for conceptual purposes as $Y = f(X_1, X_2)$. The objective, of course, is to discover the actual nature of this relationship so that it may be expressed precisely rather than conceptually.

After the relevant variables have been decided upon, the time period of the analysis is chosen, and data are secured (usually from the basic sources mentioned in Chapter 2) for each year or observation period. This has been done in the first four columns of Table 3–1. The figures, as already stated, are hypothetical, and are used for illustrative purposes. For convenience, only ten years or observation periods were selected, although something like twenty or more years are typical, for statistical reasons to be mentioned later.

In order to gain some preliminary idea of the relationship among the factors, the three variables are plotted separately on Chart A of Figure 3–1 as ordinary time series. This practice will not always reveal a clear-cut pattern of relationship, but it often gives at least some indication of a connection between the variables, and is desirable in any event for the sake of completeness as will be appreciated subsequently. From an examination of the chart, it appears that price and supply, the latter represented perhaps by production, are inversely related, while price and demand, the latter represented perhaps by consumers' income, are somewhat positively related. Since this is in accord with what is to be expected on the basis of economic reasoning, the analysis may be pursued further in order to develop the specific relationships that are involved. In doing so, the discussion may be pitched at two levels: at an elementary level for the benefit of readers who have little or no knowledge of multiple correlation analysis (such as those who have never gone beyond an elementary course in business statistics), and at a slightly higher level for those who may already have a moderate reading (but not necessarily working) knowledge of the subject. For the latter group some comments labeled "remark" will be interspersed at various points. The beginner with little or no knowledge of correlation analysis can safely skip over these comments in a first reading. However, in rereading and studying the method, these remarks should be included since they form an integral part of the analysis as a whole, and will provide a much stronger foundation for comprehending the results of various econometric analyses in later chapters.

The following discussion is based on the data in Table 3–1, the vertical line between columns (4) and (5) indicating that the information in the columns to the right of the line is to be derived from the given information in the columns to the left.

Arithmetic Means

After the problem is defined and the variables identified and quantified, the totals of the respective series and their arithmetic means may be calculated, as was done near the bottom of columns 2, 3, and 4 of the table. The symbols $\overline{Y}$, $\overline{X}_1$, and $\overline{X}_2$ represent the respective means thus computed. These symbols are read "Y-bar," "X-bar sub-one," and so on, the "bar" being commonly used in statistics to represent a mean.

The computation of the respective means, it may be noted, is optional rather than necessary for performing a graphic correlation, and, in

TABLE 3-1

DATA FOR GRAPHIC CORRELATION

(1) Observation Year	(2) Price Y	(3) Supply X_1	(4) Demand X_2	(5) Regression Estimates Chart B Y_b	(6) Residual No. 1 Chart B (2)−(5)	(7) Regression Estimates Chart C Y_c	(8) Residual No. 2 Chart C (6)−(7)	(9) Calculated Price, P (5)+(7)	(10) Ratio, Actual Price ÷ Calculated (2)÷(9)
1	62	44	60	42	20	20	0	62	1.00
2	22	50	24	37	−15	−20	5	17	1.30
3	52	40	52	45	7	11	−4	56	0.93
4	44	26	28	56	−12	−15	3	41	1.08
5	42	42	42	43	−1	0	−1	43	0.98
6	38	52	46	35	3	5	−2	40	0.95
7	32	44	28	42	−10	−15	5	27	1.19
8	64	32	52	51	13	11	2	62	1.03
9	22	40	26	45	−23	−17	−6	28	0.79
10	54	52	62	35	19	22	−3	57	0.95
Total	432	422	430		1				
Mean	43.2 $\overline{Y}$	42.2 $\overline{X_1}$	43.0 $\overline{X_2}$						
11 Forecast		33	57	51		17	17	68	

FIGURE 3–1. GRAPHIC CORRELATION

CHART A

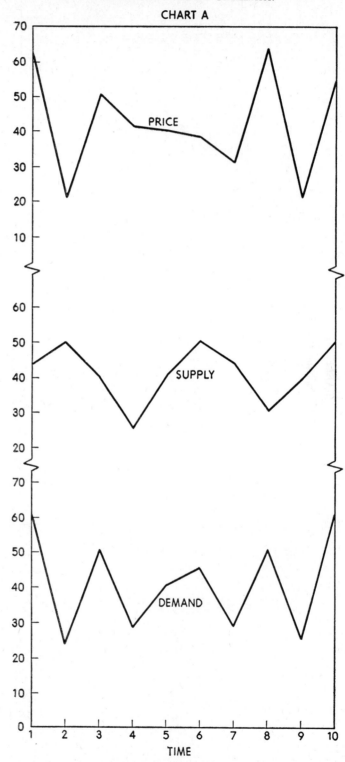

FIGURE 3–1—*Continued*

CHART B

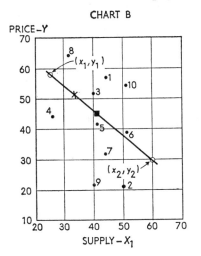

RESIDUAL NO. 1 FROM COLUMN 6   CHART C

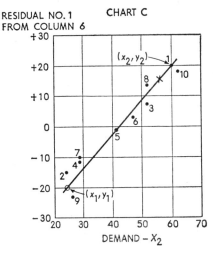

CHART D

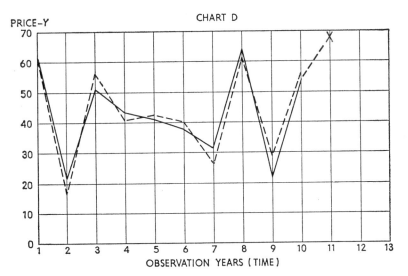

fact, is not done in any of the studies in later chapters. The computations are made here, however, because these mean values will be used as guide-points in fitting freehand regression lines to the data, as will be seen momentarily. With practice in the graphic method, the analyst soon learns to fit good freehand lines without the need of helping devices, and this step can then be eliminated if desired.

Scatter Diagram (Chart B)

The problem is to explain or account for variations in price in terms of changes in the two determining variables, supply and demand. Accordingly, a scatter diagram is plotted of the dependent variable Y against one of the independent variables, such as X_1. These are the dots in Chart B of

Figure 3–1. The order of choice of the independent variables will not affect the analysis, although it is customary to arrange them in decreasing order of importance, such as X_1, X_2, etc., according to their effect on the dependent variable.

Remark. The order of choice can be facilitated by plotting preliminary scatter diagrams between the dependent and each of the independent variables. The independent variable which appeared to have the highest correlation with Y would then be designated as X_1, the next highest as X_2, and so on in that order. Sometimes the relationship can be seen directly from the table so that separate preliminary diagrams are unnecessary to establish the order.

Since the dots must later be identified, they should be labeled by placing next to them the number representing the corresponding observation period from column 1 of the table. The scatter of the dots, as it now stands, represents the simple correlation between Y and X_1. It reveals that there is a tendency for price to be high when supply is low and for price to be low when supply is high. Incidentally, some analysts connect the dots on a scatter diagram in chronological order, so that the time path of the dots can be more readily traced. This has not been done here, but it has been done for almost all of the scatters in later chapters, as can be readily seen by flipping the pages at this time.

Regression Line (Chart B)

The next step is to pass a freehand line through the dots in such a manner that it seems to represent best the pattern of the scatter. The line, in other words, is to be an "average" of all of the dots, and hence may be either curved or straight, depending on what is believed to be the best representation of the pattern. (The implications of this are discussed in the next section.) The meaning of the line will be the same regardless of the type of line, although if a curve is employed there is the further complication of judging the correct type of curvature. In Chart B a straight line was used since there did not appear to be a marked curvilinear relationship. In drawing this line, two guideposts are of some help. (1) If a straight line is used it should be made to pass through the average values of Y and X_1. These were computed earlier as the first step in the analysis, and were recorded near the bottom of columns 2 and 3 of Table 3–1. For Y and X_1, they were 43.2 and 42.2, respectively. These two averages are plotted against each other as a single point and represented on Chart B as a filled-in black square. The line, as can be seen, passes through this point.

Remark. The reason why the line should pass approximately through this point is because of a least-squares principle that all multiple regressions intersect the mean values of the variables. It should be noted, however, that in drawing a *curved* regression line, the best fit is *not* the one which passes through the means of the two series. Only for straight lines does the means rule apply.

(2) Since this is an average line and cannot pass through all of the observations, a second guidepost is that the line should be drawn so that about half the dots are above and half are below the line. Thus, in Chart B, there are five dots above the line and five below. It should be emphasized that, for this second guidepost particularly, it is quite sufficient to approximate the slope or steepness of the line, because any error made can be corrected later on.

Remark. Strictly speaking, this line should be drawn by utilizing what is known as "guidelines" or "drift lines." These are lines based on constant or nearly constant values of X_2, since it is the partial regression (Y on X_1 with X_2 constant) that is wanted. The technique of utilizing drift lines has been explained elsewhere.[3] In the present discussion, attention will be confined to the graphic estimation of the simple regressions (Y on X_1) and the combining of these separate regressions to form a multiple regression, because this approach is simpler and is used extensively in later chapters. Of course, the partial regression will equal the simple regression only when the correlation between the independent variables X_1 and X_2 is zero. Although this extreme condition is not generally expected in a sample, the correlations between the independent variables are often low enough to yield sufficiently good fits. Alternatively, if the correlations are too high, other steps can be taken as will be described in the next section. In any event, the use of drift lines, because of their somewhat more complicated nature, can usually be avoided.

Regression Estimates (Chart B)

As it stands, the regression line in Chart B represents the approximate average or mean relationship between Y and X_1 (price and supply) with X_2 (demand) assumed to remain constant. Accordingly, we can estimate the price that may be *expected* (not necessarily realized) from variations in supply with demand remaining constant. Thus, from Chart B, we observe that for year 1, when supply was 44, the price as would be expected from the regression line was 42, and this figure is then recorded in column 5 of the table for the corresponding year. In like manner, the remainder of column 5 may be filled out for all the remaining observations, by reading from the vertical axis of Chart B the expected price for each observation as determined from the regression line.

At this stage it is possible, though not necessary, to estimate the formula for the regression line in Chart B. In fact, if the formula is estimated, it may be employed to calculate the values to be inserted in column 5, thereby eliminating the necessity of reading the Y values from the chart, and hence reducing the possibility of making visual mistakes.

In elementary statistics, the formula for a straight line is generally given as

$$Y = a + bX$$

[3] *Cf.* Spencer and Siegelman, *op. cit.*, chap. 3.

where *a* represents the Y intercept or the point at which the line crosses the vertical axis, and *b* represents the slope. This formula, called the *slope-intercept* formula because of its constants, is sometimes suitable for estimating from a chart the formula for a straight line. Frequently, however, it poses difficulties for beginning students when, as often happens, the scales of the scatter diagrams do not start at zero. This is especially true when plotting on semilogarithmic or logarathmic paper, since a logarithmic axis can never begin with zero. Another formula must be found, therefore, which can always be used to estimate the equation for a straight line from a chart, regardless of whether the axes begin at zero or not. The recommended equation for this purpose is the *two-point* formula

$$Y = y_1 + \frac{y_2 - y_1}{x_2 - x_1}(X - x_1)$$

where the small letters represent the co-ordinates of any two points on the line. Thus, referring to Chart B, any two points on the line may be selected. The points that have been chosen are those near the ends of the line as shown by the small circles. (Of course, the mean values, represented by the filled-in black square, could also have been used as one of the points, since they are already known. However, since the mean values may not always be calculated for reasons already given, the two values near the ends of the line are chosen instead.) For the point at the left end of the line, the co-ordinate appears to be $x_1 = 25$, $y_1 = 57$. At the right end the value of the point is approximately $x_2 = 60$, $y_2 = 29$. If we let Y_b represent the calculated values of price from the regression line in Chart B, as distinguished from the actual values in column 2, we obtain by substitution in the above equation a formula for price as a function of supply, X_1. Thus

$$Y_b = 57 + \frac{29 - 57}{60 - 25}(X_1 - 25)$$

$$= 57 - \frac{4}{5}(X_1 - 25)$$

$$= 77 - .8X_1. \tag{1}$$

Referring to the table, the regression estimates in column 5 can be estimated by substituting in equation (1) the supply values from column 3, and then computing the corresponding value for Y_b. For example, in year 1 when supply (X_1) was 44, the expected value of price (Y_b) based on the Y-X_1 relationship was

$$Y_b = 77 - .8(44) = 42, \text{approximately,}$$

and this figure is recorded in column 5 for year 1. The remaining figures in column 5 are obtained in the same way, by substituting and solving in the above estimating equation. The equation is thus a substitute for the visual estimation of the points, and is an optional tool which may be employed in the graphic method of correlation. It may be noted that when the data are plotted on logarithmic scales, the formula employed must be modified to account for the difference. This point will be discussed further in the following section.

Residuals (Chart B)

If all the variations in price were due entirely to variations in supply, the dots in Chart B would have fallen along a straight line. As it happened, however, the dots did not fall along a particular line, but instead scattered themselves about the chart in a general downward direction. The regression line was drawn, therefore, to represent the average relationship between price and supply, with the scatter of the dots indicating that factors other than supply may be influencing the price of this commodity. Buying habits, fluctuations in consumers' incomes, and the availability of competing products are just a few of the factors other than supply that may be affecting the price. In order to seek a further explanation, therefore, it is necessary to determine the amount of variation that is unexplained by the association of price and supply. In year 1, for instance, both Chart B and the table show that the expected price as estimated from the regression line was 42 while the actual price realized was 62, a difference between actual and estimated of 20. Similarly, for year 2, the actual price was 22 while the expected price was 37, a difference of −15. These figures are recorded in column 6 of the table. When read from Chart B, they represent the *vertical* deviations or residuals of the dots from the regression line; when derived from the table, which is simpler once column 5 is completed, they are simply column 2 minus column 5.

Remark. The object is to obtain the residual variations between the calculated and actual values. These residuals may be expressed either as a difference or as a ratio, i.e., $Y - Y_b$, or Y/Y_b. The discussion here is in terms of differences; the studies in later chapters are done almost exclusively in terms of ratios. Either one is permissible.

Regression Line (Chart C)

In order to explain further the variations in price unaccounted for by supply, we turn to the next independent variable, demand or X_2. Chart C is now constructed by scaling off on the vertical axis the residuals just recorded in column 6 of the table, while the horizontal axis ticks off the demand series for column 4. Note that a horizontal line, representing the zero value for the deviations, is drawn through the chart (usually near the center) with the plus residuals or deviations above this line and the minus deviations below. (This zero line is the regression line drawn horizontally.) A scatter diagram is again plotted, this time between the column 6 residuals and the demand variable of column 4, and the resulting dots are again labeled with their corresponding observation number. A freehand regression line is fitted to the dots, as before. Note also that the line passes approximately through the filled-in black square which this time represents the mean of X_2 at the zero line.

Remark. Actually, the total of the price deviations in column 6 would have been zero instead of 1 as shown (and hence the mean would have been zero), had the regression line in Chart B been a perfect fit, for it is a mathematical characteristic of the mean that the sum of the deviations about it is zero. Further, it is also a mathematical characteristic of the mean that the sum of the squared deviations from it is a minimum (that is, less than the sum of the squared deviations from any other number in the series). Hence the term "least squares." It is suggested that the latter condition—that the sum of the squared deviations is a minimum from the mean—be used in judging the fit of the separate regression lines. Thus, more weight should be given to a large deviation than to a small one. In Chart C, for instance, observation 9 exercised a relatively greater influence in pulling downward on the left end of the line, as compared to other observations on the chart. With practice, the analyst employing this guide, and perhaps the principle that the sum of the deviations from the mean is zero, can learn to approximate the regressions rather closely. In any event, it should be kept in mind, until discussed further in the next chapter, that there is an underlying assumption here of *no significant intercorrelation* among the independent variables. For when intercorrelation exists, some additional calculations or graph work will be necessary, as explained subsequently.

What does the regression line in Chart C indicate? In economic terms, it represents the average influence of demand on price after allowance has already been made for the influence of supply on price. In other words, it was assumed at the beginning that variations in price were due to several factors, but primarily to supply and demand. In Chart B, the regression line expressed the average relationship between price and the first of these factors, supply. If the variations in price had been due solely to changes in supply, the dots would have fallen along the line and no further analysis would have been necessary. But the dots, instead, scattered about the line, indicating that the deviations or residuals must have resulted from factors other than supply. Accordingly, these deviations, representing price variations caused by nonsupply factors, were plotted against demand in Chart C. The resulting regression line is thus an expression of the average relationship between price and the nonsupply factors which influence it.

The regression line in Chart C may thus be thought of in another manner as well. Since it represents the relationship between price and demand after allowance has already been made for the influence of supply on price, it tells us the amount by which the price will be higher or lower than the price-supply regression line of Chart B according to different levels of demand. To illustrate, in Chart B when supply (X_1) on the horizontal axis is 40, the price (Y) as estimated from the regression line may be expected to be about 45 if demand (X_2) remains at its average value of 43. But in year 9, for example, when supply was actually 40, the level of demand was sufficiently below its average to pull the price down to 22 as compared to what would have been expected on the basis of the partial Y-X_1 relationship. The same idea is shown perhaps more clearly by the table. In year 9, price was 22 (column 2) as compared to the expected 45 (column 5), because demand (column 4) was 26 as compared to its average of 43. In year 3, on the other hand, when supply was also 40, the actual price of 52 was considerably higher than the 45 indicated by the partial Y-X_1 relationship, because the demand level of 52 was sufficiently above its average of 43 to pull the price upward. Hence the second independent variable may be thought of as exerting a "shifting" effect, since the regression line in Chart B will shift up or down according to the actual level of X_2 relative to its average. The same, of course, could be said of any other independent variable once the partial relationships between the dependent and remaining independent variables have been established.

Just as in Chart B where the regression estimates could be obtained either by reading them directly off the chart or by calculating them from a formula, the same can now be done in Chart C. Using the *two-point* formula as before, a point is selected near each end of the line. At the left end, the point is shown by a small circle, the co-ordinates of which appear to be $X_1 = 24$, $Y_1 = -20$. At the right end, the dot representing observation 1 may be used, since it fell directly on the line. The co-ordinates of this point are $X_2 = 60$, $Y_2 = 20$. Letting Y_c represent the regression estimates from Chart C, the regression equation in terms of demand, X_2, is

$$Y_c = y_1 + \frac{y_2 - y_1}{x_2 - x_1}(X_2 - x_1)$$
$$= -20 + \frac{20 - (-20)}{60 - 24}(X_2 - 24)$$
$$= -20 + \frac{40X_2 - 960}{36}$$
$$= -46 + 1.1X_2 \tag{2}$$

Using this formula, column 7 of the table is filled in, by substituting values for X_2 from column 4, and computing the corresponding value of Y_c. Thus, in year 1, $X_2 = 60$. Therefore, $Y_c = -46 + 1.1(60) = 20$, and this value is recorded at the top of column 7. Similarly, the remainder of the column is filled in, either by reading the values off the graph, or preferably by using both the formula and the graph as a check against the calculations. As a final step at this stage of the analysis, the residuals about the regression line in Chart C may also be estimated and recorded in column 8 of the table. These estimates can be made either directly from the chart, or by subtracting column 7 from column 6, which is simpler once column 7 is completed.

Forecasting (Chart D)

The analysis of the separate parts is now completed and it remains to combine the results into a meaningful whole. Basically, we are seeking an answer to the question: How can the graphic method of correlation be used in forecasting the dependent variable, price?

As signified by the word itself, the term "correlation" (or "co-relation") refers to the nature of the interdependency that exists between two or more variables. The purpose of correlation analysis is to establish this interdependency in numerical terms, that is, to quantify the relationship. Once this has been done, the problem of predicting the dependent variable is nothing more than a mechanical application or extension of the basic relationship already established.

In either method of correlation. analysis, whether mathematical or graphic, the independent variables must be predicted first, and on the basis of these predictions the dependent variable is then forecast. Thus, correlation and regression analysis does not solve entirely the problem of prediction; it merely facilitates forecasting the dependent variable once the independent variables have already been estimated for a given period in the future, and the nature of the functional relationship is known. The forecast procedure, therefore, may be accomplished as follows:

1. In column 9 of the table, record the calculated prices by combining the separate regression estimates obtained in columns 5 and 7. The calculated price figures in column 9, therefore, represent the prices that would be expected on the basis of the partial Y-X_1 relationship (with X_2 constant) and the partial Y-X_2 relationship (with X_1 constant), or simply the expected variations in price based on *both* independent variables, supply and demand. These figures, of course, can also be represented by an equation which combines the two separate regression equations derived above. Thus, letting P represent the calculated price, the two regression equations may be combined to form the single regression or predicting equation,

$$P = 31 - .8X_1 + 1.1X_2 \qquad (3)$$

Either this equation, or its numerical equivalent in column 9, or its graphic equivalent which is constructed next, may be used in forecasting the price of the commodity. In later chapters, all three are employed in the construction of models in order to facilitate comprehension of the techniques used.

2. On Chart D, plot the actual price variations of Y (column 2) as a solid line and the final calculated price variations (column 9) as a dashed line. These figures are plotted as a time series with price on the vertical axis and the observation periods or time on the horizontal. The two lines as they now stand provide a visual indication of how well we were able to estimate price as compared to the actual price variations that occurred.

3. It remains now to make a prediction of price, say for year 11, on the basis of the relationship already established. Suppose that for year 11, therefore, it was predicted that for the independent variables, X_1 would be 33 and X_2 would be 57. What price level may be expected on the basis of these supply and demand values?[4] Before answering the question, it is convenient to record the values of X_1 and X_2 at the bottom of columns 3 and 4 respectively, on a line with year 11, the forecast year. Then by referring to the predicting equation above, the estimate of P is easily obtained by substituting in the formula. Thus

---

[4] Prediction of the independent variables is a separate problem area which is taken up at various points in subsequent chapters.

$$P = 31 - .8(33) + 1.1(57)$$
$$= 68$$

This 68, representing the estimate of price based on both supply and demand, is recorded at the bottom of column 9. Alternatively, had formulas not been computed, the estimate could be obtained directly from the charts. Thus, referring to Chart B, we note that when $X_1 = 33$, the expected value of Y as estimated from the regression line (as shown by an X on that line) is about 51, and this number is written at the bottom of column 5 of the table. This is what the price is expected to be on the basis of the partial Y-X_1 regression. Similarly, on Chart C, we note that when $X_2 = 57$, the expected value of Y (as shown by the X on the regression line) is about 17, and this figure is written at the bottom of column 8. This is what the price is expected to be on the basis of the partial Y-X_2 regression. We now have two price estimates, the first based on supply with demand assumed constant, the other based on demand with supply assumed constant. To arrive at a forecast for year 11, these two estimates are brought together by recording their total, 68, at the bottom of column 9. As with the other numbers in this column, the figure 68 represents the net estimate of price based on both supply and demand. This value is then recorded on Chart D for year 11 as an X, and connected by a dashed line to the previous actual figure. This completes the forecast. In like manner, price can be predicted for any year in the future, provided of course that supply and demand can be forecast first for the same time period.

Remark. The final dashed line connects the predicted price with the last actual price, because it is the actual price that is being forecast. When year 11 is over and the actual price is realized, the latter would be connected by a solid line to the previous actual price and the forecast price connected by a dashed line to the previous estimated price.

It is possible to extend this method to include three or more independent variables in the same manner as the two used in this problem. If an additional variable were included, say X_3, the residuals in column 8 would be obtained by reading off the deviations about the regression line in Chart C, or more simply by taking column 6 minus column 7. These values are then plotted against the new variable X_3 and a new set of estimates obtained. The regression line would then represent the partial relationship between Y and X_3 with X_1 and X_2 constant, and the final price estimate would reflect the combined effect of the three independent determinants, X_1, X_2, and X_3. Stated conceptually, the general functional form would be $Y = f(X_1, X_2, X_3)$ instead of $Y = f(X_1, X_2)$ as was assumed in the problem discussed in this section. A forecast of price, therefore, would require that the three independent variables be predicted first. In practical work, typical problems can sometimes involve a half dozen or so independent variables, and sometimes as few as one or two, depending on the underlying theory. In any event, analysts are not usually concerned with obtaining a perfect fit, that is, accounting for the entire variation in the dependent variable by the independent factors included. Instead they are quite content to explain a substantial part of the total variation in the dependent variable, say about 90 per cent, and this can frequently be done by incorporating a few of the most important independent factors.

Remark 1. Statistically, a high degree of multiple correlation, that is, a nearly perfect fit, would be of no significance if obtained by too complex an analysis relative to the number of observations available, because there would be too few degrees of freedom. Accordingly, analysts usually employ straight lines or logarithmic curves based on a minimum of about twenty years of data, as will be seen in later chapters.

Remark 2. It should be noted again that in drawing a curved regression line, the best fit will be obtained with a line that does *not* pass through the means of the two series. As stated in an earlier remark, the means rule applies only for straight lines.

Further Refinements

The method of graphic correlation discussed above provides a basic outline of the procedures commonly employed in constructing models and deriving relationships among economic variables. Various modifications and improvisations are frequently necessary in practical work, depending on the particular problem, the underlying theory, the available data, and so forth. Many variations and applications of the basic ideas presented above, therefore, will be illustrated in the actual problems of later chapters. At this point, it is useful to mention that many analysts employing the graphic method of correlation also add certain refinements to the procedure in order to improve and evaluate their final estimates. Of the various refinement techniques that exist, three that may be mentioned briefly are: (1) successive approximations, (2) time trends, and (3) estimates of determination.

Successive Approximations. The method of graphic correlation is sometimes called the "method of successive approximations" because it provides a means by which the first approximation to the regression line can be progressively improved. Although the procedure in this problem employed only a first approximation because the results seemed quite adequate for the purpose at hand, the remaining steps for approximating the regression lines more accurately may be sketched briefly.

1. The vertical deviations from the regression line in Chart C are recorded as residual #2 in column 8 of the table. These deviations would then be plotted *about the regression line* in Chart B against X_1. (Colored pencils may be used so as not to confuse this new set of dots with the original ones.) The resulting dots would form a new scatter and the deviation for each observation would be directly above or below the original dot for that observation, since the same X_1 values were retained. A new regression line (the same color as the new dots) would then be drawn through this new scatter so that it passes approximately through the means

shown by the original filled-in square, and in such manner that it appears to reduce the squared deviations about itself to a minimum. This new regression line would represent an improved approximation to the partial Y-X_1 relationship.

2. The vertical deviations of the new scatter about the new regression line in Chart B would then be plotted about the regression line in Chart C against the same X_2 values, and this time a new regression line on Chart C would again be drawn through the filled-in square. This new regression line on Chart C would represent an improved approximation to the partial Y-X_2 relationship.

The above two steps may be repeated, using the latest deviations about the latest regression approximations, until no further correction seems necessary. In the illustration used here, only a first approximation was made so as to convey the basic concept and technique, and because no further approximation appeared desirable for improving forecasting accuracy as shown visually by Chart D. If the charts are published, only the last set of observations about the final regression line should be shown, since it represents the most refined estimate. The construction of Chart D would be essentially the same as before, except that actual prices would be compared to estimates based on the latest approximations.

Remark 1. Two further points may be noted. (*a*) It can be proven that the lower the intercorrelation between the independent variables the closer each approximation moves to the mathematically calculated least-square value at a very rapid rate. (*b*) The new scatter in Chart B indicates the part correlation between Y and X_1. If the intercorrelation between X_1 and X_2 is low, the part correlation will almost equal the partial correlation which shows the degree of relationship between Y and X_1 with X_2 constant.[5]

Remark 2. The use of systems of equations, or simultaneous equations, may be justified where intercorrelation is significant. This is discussed further in subsequent chapters.

Time Trend. If all of the variations in price were explained completely by the independent variables in the analysis, the dots in Chart C would have fallen along the regression line instead of around it, indicating that no further unexplained variations exist. Similarly, the dotted line in Chart D would have coincided with the solid line, and a "perfect fit" would have been obtained.

Three or four decades ago, analysts engaged in the construction of econometric models tried to achieve as nearly perfect a fit as possible by the use of a few factors. This was particularly true of certain agricultural economists during the 1920's. These men, working primarily in the area of

[5] See R. J. Foote and J. R. Ives, "The Relationship of the Method of Graphic Correlation to Least-Squares," *Statistics and Agriculture*, Vol. 1, USDA, pp. 13–18; also, F. L. Thomsen and R. J. Foote, *Agricultural Price Analysis*, and M. Ezekiel and K. Fox, *Methods of Correlation and Regression Analyses*, 3d ed.

farm prices, were among the early pioneers in applied econometrics, and it was fairly typical in the published studies of the time to encounter analyses in which it was stated that over 99 per cent of the variations in the dependent variable had been accounted for by the independent variables in the analysis. It gradually came to be realized, however, that a perfect or nearly perfect fit is not always meaningful, because (*a*) it is mathematically possible to fit a line or curve to any pattern of dots even if no real relationship between the variables actually exists, and (*b*) there may be too few degrees of freedom, that is, the curves may be too complex compared to the number of observations available. Accordingly, as stated earlier, analysts are frequently content to explain only the great majority of variations in the dependent variable, and to do this by using straight lines or logarithmic curves based on twenty years or more of economic data. Almost all of the studies in later chapters, it will be seen, have these characteristics.

Frequently, by employing the most important independent variables in a particular problem, a reasonably good fit is obtained. However, unexplained residuals still remain, such as those in column 8, for any of three reasons. (1) There may be errors in the data used, in that the estimates of price, supply, and demand obtained from published sources are not exact or perfect measures of the prices, supplies, and demands that actually occurred. (2) Certain variables which have an influence on price may have been partially or completely omitted, or in some way not completely accounted for in the analysis. Thus, supply may be measured by total output, but the rate of change of output, stocks on hand, and other supply factors may also exert an influence on price and not be included in the actual supply figures in column 3. Similarly, income may serve as an indirect measure of demand, but the prices of competing products, changing population, and other demand factors may be at work which are not completely recognized and included in the demand figures of column 4. (3) Technical errors may have been made in the interpretation of the relationships, and hence incorrect curves, time lags, and so forth, may have been employed.

All three of these conditions can be responsible for the residuals that remain in a particular analysis. If, however, the analyst is reasonably satisfied, after performing the analysis, that the remaining residuals are not due to significant errors in the data or to technical errors but to the omission of certain minor variables, he may account for these variables by the use of a *time trend*. This is done by taking the final set of residuals about the last regression line, such as residual #2 in column 8, and plotting it against "time" on a scatter diagram. The observation years in column 1, in other words, are regarded as a third independent variable, X_3, representing all factors other than supply, X_1, and demand, X_2, which may be exerting an influence on price, Y. By plotting the residuals against the time factor and then fitting a freehand regression line as was done in Charts B and C, a Y-X_3 relationship with X_1 and X_2 constant is obtained. The final fit is thereby considerably improved, because "time" has been utilized as a catchall variable for factors other than the specific variables X_1 and X_2 which may be influencing price.

The use of a time trend will be commented upon again in the next chapter. For the moment, therefore, suffice it to say that it was not used in the present example because a rather good fit was obtained by the use of the two explicit variables, supply and demand. Many of the studies in subsequent chapters, however, involve the use of a time trend as a catchall variable, and it will become evident when reading these studies how a time trend can be effectively used to improve the estimates and fits that are obtained.

Estimates of Determination. Various techniques can be employed to measure the degree of fit, thus obtaining an indication of how successful we have been in explaining the fluctuations in the dependent variable by the independent variables in the analysis. Both graphic and formula procedures may be mentioned briefly.

Chart D provides a useful graphic indication of the closeness of fit by showing visually the extent to which the dashed line approximates the solid line. Alternatively, a common procedure frequently employed by analysts is to compute the ratio of the actual to the calculated values as done in column 10, and plot these as a time series with the 1.00 or 100 per cent level near the middle of the vertical axis. Both of these devices are used extensively in later chapters.

In addition to these graphic devices for illustrating goodness of fit, a numerical measure which serves as an indication of the extent to which the dependent variable is explained by the independent variables for the years included in the analysis, may be computed. The measure obtained is called the *coefficient of multiple determination.* It is symbolized R^2 and may be computed from the formula

$$R^2 = 1 - \frac{\Sigma(d^2)}{\Sigma(Y^2) - (\overline{Y})^2 N} \geqq 0 \leqq 1$$

where

$\Sigma =$ the Greek capital letter sigma, meaning "the sum of."

$d =$ the unexplained deviations or residuals in the analysis, such as the deviations about the regression line in Chart C, or the deviations between the actual and calculated values in Chart D. The figures for d are in column 8, or may also be obtained by taking column 2 minus column 9.

$\overline{Y} =$ the mean of the Y values.

$N =$ the number of observations in the analysis.

This coefficient gives the percentage of variation in the dependent variable which is explained by the independent variables in the analysis, and hence yields a solution between 0 and 100 per cent (expressed in decimal form).

The closer the coefficient is to 1, the closer the dashed line will be to the solid line in Chart D. The coefficient of multiple determination is also of extreme practical value to management from the standpoint of investment in research. As will become apparent in later chapters, adding further independent variables to the analysis will increase the coefficient (or the marginal returns to precision) at a decreasing rate, while it may increase the costs of computation in terms of time and expense (the marginal cost of research) at an increasing rate. Hence it is not the increased accuracy alone which is a deciding factor as to whether more variables should be included in the analysis, but the *increment in gains* realized from the greater accuracy balanced against the *increment in costs* involved. Incidentally, it may also be mentioned that the square root of the coefficient of multiple determination is the *coefficient of multiple correlation*, R, which is an abstract measure and not as useful for practical purposes as is the squared form.

A second measure is called the *coefficient of partial determination* (which is the partial correlation coefficient squared) and measures the proportion of variations in the dependent variable (Y) explained by variations in another independent variable (say X_1), with the other independent variables held constant. Some graphic interpretations of this measure are presented in later studies.

Conclusion

The following concluding points may be noted.

1. The coefficient of multiple determination indicates the proportion of variation in Y due to the *combined* effects of the independent variables. Graphically, an approximate indication of this is revealed by the closeness with which the estimated (calculated) values equal the actual values, as in Chart D.

2. An approximate indication of the relative importance of the independent variables in affecting the dependent variable is also given visually, as in Charts B and C, by the amount of scatter (that is, degree of correlation) in the separate charts after completing the approximation process. Graphically, therefore, we can say that if the partial correlation between Y and X_1 is large and that between Y and X_2 is small, then in general, X_1 has a greater effect on Y and does X_2. Similarly, if the correlations appear about the same, it could be assumed that both exert about an equal effect on Y. The regression line, therefore, shows the net effect of each of the independent variables on the dependent variable.

(3) The slope of the regression line, that is, the change in the vertical distance per unit of change in the horizontal distance, or $\Delta Y/\Delta X$, where Δ (delta) means "the change in," shows the *amount* of change in the dependent variable associated with a unit change in the corresponding independent factor with the influence of the other independent factors assumed constant.

Remark. If the slope is measured in percentages, it reveals the *partial elasticity*, which is defined as the percentage change in the dependent variable resulting from a 1 per cent change in the independent variable, with the other independent variables held constant. If Charts B and C had been plotted on double logarithmic paper, these elasticities could be determined directly from the charts by measuring with a ruler the change in the vertical and horizontal distances, and computing the ratio of quantity to price, or $\Delta Q/\Delta P$. The reason for this is that, by using logarithms, the scales of the chart are automatically converted such that equal distances on both axes represent equal percentage changes, and elasticity is, after all, a measure of *relative* (rather than absolute) change between the dependent and independent variables.

This completes the discussion of the method of correlation analysis. The term "correlation" has been used here in a general sense to include not only the measurement of association between variables, but the derivation of equations of relationship which is a process referred to as "regression analysis."

As might be expected, there is considerably more to the science of correlation and regression analysis than has been presented here. And, indeed, in the discussion above, much has been omitted that might have been included, particularly the problems of correlating time series and the establishment of reliability criteria—concepts which are at least vaguely familiar even to readers who have had recent elementary courses in modern statistics. However, since this is primarily a book in applied economics, not statistics, it has been necessary to confine the statistical portion to a presentation of those basic concepts and techniques that are sufficient to comprehend the studies presented in later chapters. For those desiring a fuller and more comprehensive treatment of the general area of correlation and regression analysis, several excellent statistics books are available, one of which, M. Ezekiel and K. Fox, *Methods of Correlation and Regression Analysis* (3d ed.) is highly readable even for beginners, and has long been the "bible" in the field.

QUESTIONS

See end of next chapter.

Chapter	FORECASTING TOOLS
4	(CONTINUED)

CORRELATION ANALYSIS IN FORECASTING

Against the background of the previous chapter in which the concept and technique of correlation were developed, we turn now to a discussion of some technical considerations which should be understood before any attempt at correlation is undertaken. For correlation (including regression) analysis, it should be realized, is one of the most powerful tools available for business and economic research, especially where the objective is to establish relationships among selected variables as is the case in econometrics, forecasting, and the like. Before employing the method, however, the analyst must frequently make a number of technical decisions based on a priori knowledge or considerations. A few of the more important problems and some indications as to their resolution are sketched briefly in the paragraphs below. Throughout the discussion, as well as in later chapters, it should be kept in mind that we are using the term correlation in a broad sense to include regression analysis as well.

Selection of Analysis Period and Variables

As a first step in constructing a forecasting model, it is necessary to decide on the period of the analysis and the nature of the variables that are involved. Among the chief factors to be kept in mind are the following two.

1. The analysis period should include as many years as possible, since the object is to derive underlying and durable relationships that are both meaningful and reliable. Further, the inclusion of many years of data makes it all the more feasible for the analyst to test the model immediately, by placing the last few years "in suspension" and then seeing how close his calculated values came to the actual for those years. For many problems that are encountered in sales and in economic forecasting, fairly accurate series are available as far back as the early 1920's and this is frequently sufficient to yield good results. Often, however, data covering much shorter periods are all that can be obtained, in which case the analysis procedure or its conclusions must sometimes be modified.

Some analysts have followed the practice of omitting exceptional or unusual years which appear to depart significantly from the established pattern. Unless the omissions can be justified or explained on rational economic grounds, however, the practice can easily result in an incorrect analysis of the data and in the emergence of erroneous conclusions. Care should be taken, therefore, to account for unusual variations and swings in the data if the results are to be meaningful.

2. The identification and selection of the variables to be used in the analysis should be based on logical considerations. This means, among other things, that the variables should be chosen according to economic judgment and criteria. In studying fluctuations in commodity prices, for instance, various measures of supply and of demand may be used, and sometimes a time trend, to explain the variations in prices. In forecasting sales of consumers' durables, on the other hand, the level of purchasing power, the number of consuming units of the product (e.g., households or families), and consumer replacement rates are some of the important determining factors involved. In general, the type of product, its economic use or purpose, and the kind of market in which it is sold are the bases for deducing the information necessary as to the nature and types of variables to employ.

Choice of Equation or Curves

After the analysis period has been chosen and the essential variables have been defined and quantified, a decision as to the nature of the relationship between the variables must be made. This usually involves two classes of considerations: first, whether the model should utilize a simple or a multiple correlation, and second, whether the variables should be combined in an additive or in a multiplicative relationship.

1. A consideration of practical importance concerns the question of whether the predicting equation to be derived should be based on a simple correlation between a dependent variable, such as demand, and one independent variable, say price, or whether it should be a multiple correlation involving two or more independent variables, such as price, income, and other demand determinants as controlling factors. Simple relations have the advantage of being easier to compute; from the management standpoint they are also easier to comprehend and may be easier to manipulate, since only one controlling variable is involved. But a demand forecast or analysis involving a simple relation may be of limited application, especially if the attempt is to manipulate demand by varying this single controlling factor. The forecasting reliability of the function may also be questioned: If disposable income is the independent variable, it will be correlated with broad product groups and there may actually be little or no causal relation between it and the specific product under analysis. When price, on the other hand, is the independent variable, it will likely be a controlling factor only in the short run while other demand-determining elements are still relatively constant. Multiple correlation, however, permits the introduction of several

independent variables as controlling factors, and for many kinds of practical problems only a few such variables are necessary to explain the great majority of the variations in the dependent variable. Multiple correlation, therefore, provides for a more general demand function as compared to the results achieved by using only simple relations. But it is also more expensive and, in terms of the extra time and expense, may not always be worth the gain in precision. Each problem has its own peculiarities and characteristics, and these are the factors to be considered, in light of the time and expense limitations, in deciding on a simple versus multiple type of regression analysis.

2. The shape of the partial regression lines (i.e., whether they are curved or straight) in the separate scatter diagrams will determine the type of partial regression equations and hence the nature of the final predicting equation that is derived. What factors should be considered in deciding on the shape of the regression lines? When should the lines be straight and when should they be curved? Although the graphic correlation example in the previous chapter assumed a set of straight-line relationships, are other possibilities sometimes encountered where the separate relations are all curved, or perhaps some curved and some straight?

Graphically, the pattern of the dots on the scatter diagrams provide a visual indication of the relation between the variables. Usually, however, the dots will not indicate clearly whether a linear or curvilinear relationship exists, and, if the relationship is curvilinear, the exact nature of the curve and the number and location of its bends. These are all factors which must be decided, not so much by the scatter of the dots, but by economic theory and judgment. The choice of theoretically correct curves is particularly important, of course, if extrapolations of the regression lines are to be made beyond the range of the original data.

In deciding upon the general shape of the curves, a theoretical consideration which may be of some help is whether the separate independent variables are expected to exert an additive or multiplicative effect upon the dependent variable. For instance, the demand for a consumers' durable good, such as automobiles, is made up of two parts: a new-owner demand on the part of those who have never had the product, and a replacement demand on the part of those who are replacing their existing product for a new one. If both new-owner demand and replacement demand are each determined by a separate set of factors, the *sum* of the two demands would form the total demand variable. On the other hand, the production of an agricultural product, such as wheat, depends upon yield per acre and the number of acres. Hence the *product* of the two variables is needed to form the production variable. Thus, in each problem, the independent variables exert either an additive or multiplicative effect on the dependent variable, and should be analyzed carefully in order to see if a decision can be made as to the way in which the variables should be combined.

Most of the time it is difficult to decide on the exact nature of the relationship, because the variables do not meet the simple judgment criteria cited above. Moreover, when the dots are plotted as ordinary scatter diagrams, they often exhibit curvilinear patterns and the possibility of multiplicative rather than additive relationships. When this occurs, as it frequently does in practical problems, simple methods exist for transforming a multiplicative relationship into an additive one by using either logarithms, reciprocals, roots or powers, or logarithms of logarithms.

For example, consider the following multiplicative relationship which is the well-known compound interest function

$$Y = ab^X$$

On ordinary (arithmetic) graph paper this equation plots as a curved line. However, if the equation is plotted on logarithmic paper (or, what is the same thing, if the logarithms of the variables are scaled on arithmetic paper) the following additive relationship is obtained

$$\log Y = \log a + X \log b$$

In this form, the analysis could be run by the graphic method and straight lines used, since the equation is linear in logarithms. (The elementary mathematics of logarithms is reviewed in the next section.) Similarly, a multiplicative relationship such as

$$Y = aW^b X^c Z^d$$

can be made additive by expressing the variables in logarithms, thus resulting in

$$\log Y = \log a + b \log W + c \log X + d \log Z$$

There are many occasions in forecasting when the use of logarithms or logarithmic charts is desirable in order to transform relationships from multiplicative to additive form, thereby simplifying the analysis. Sometimes semilogarithmic charts (i.e., graph papers on which the vertical axes are logarithmic and the horizontal axes are arithmetic) are used; sometimes logarithmic charts (graph papers on which both axes are logarithmic) are employed. Examples of both types and their use in many forecasting problems are illustrated in later chapters.

When either semilogarithmic or logarithmic charts are employed, the two-point formula mentioned in the previous chapter for estimating the equation of a straight line will be different, since the data are no longer in the same form. Actually, any one of three variations of the formula may be used, depending on whether the scatter diagram is on arithmetic paper, semilogarithmic paper, or logarithmic paper. Thus, on arithmetic scales

$$Y = y_1 + \frac{y_2 - y_1}{x_2 - x_1}(X - x_1)$$

which is the same formula as the one used earlier in the illustrative problem on graphic correlation, page 52. On semilogarithmetic paper, the vertical axis is logarithmic and the horizontal axis is arithmetic. Hence the above formula becomes, for a straight line on semilogarithmic paper,

$$\log Y = \log y_1 + \frac{\log y_2 - \log y_1}{x_2 - x_1}(X - x_1)$$

On logarithmic paper, both axes are scaled logarithmically. Therefore, the above formula becomes, for a straight line on logarithmic paper,

$$\log Y = \log y_1 + \frac{\log y_2 - \log y_1}{\log x_2 - \log x_1}(\log X - \log x_1)$$

It should be mentioned again that readers with little or no knowledge of the elements of logarithms will find the explanation of logarithms at the end of this chapter a useful supplement and reference for various studies in later chapters.

The above formulas may be employed to estimate the equation for straight lines, depending on which of the three types of graph paper is used. The important points to be kept in mind are: (1) The choice of whether to use a straight line or a curve should depend as much as possible on logical economic considerations about the data, and (2) complicated curvilinear relationships can usually be transformed into linear form by using logarithms, thereby reducing greatly the amount of work involved as well as enabling management to comprehend the results more easily.

Single Equations versus Systems of Equations

For a number of years the Cowles Foundation for Research in Economics, located at Yale University, has proposed that many forecasting problems employing only single equations should be solved by using systems of equations of simultaneous equations. There are technical economic and statistical reasons for this which are better deferred to Part III of this book, dealing with aggregate econometric models, since it is in the construction of such models that the use of simultaneous equations becomes most meaningful. Accordingly, since we will be dealing only with single-equation models in Part II, Chapters 5–9, we shall confine the discussion to such equations and not dwell on the use of simultaneous equations until Chapter 10. At that time we shall be able to present a fuller and more useful treatment of the problem within a more meaningful context.

First Differences versus Actual Data

The customary method in forecasting is to employ the actual data themselves as a basis for arriving at the forecast equation. Once the equation is derived and the values for the independent variables established, the forecast itself is an automatic result by simply substituting the known independent variables in the equation and then solving for the dependent variable. For example, the analysis may result in the forecast equation:

$$\text{Sales} = a + b \text{ (income per family)} + c \text{ (advertising outlay)}$$

or in symbols, if S denotes sales, I is income per family, and A is advertising expenditures, then

$$S = a + bI + cA$$

In this equation, S is the dependent variable that is to be forecast; a, b, and c are the constants (parameters) of the equations, and the purpose of correlation analysis is to arrive at their probable values; and I and A are the independent variables which, once they are predicted, are substituted in the equation, combined with their corresponding known constants, and the result is a forecast of S. The equation can be generalized to represent any year by utilizing a subscript, t; thus,

$$S_t = a + bI_t + cA_t \qquad (1)$$

where the subscript, t, refers to the time in question and can represent any year desired.

This method is fairly typical of the forecasting procedure involved when the actual data are used. It is sometimes useful, however, to employ not the actual data, but the *absolute changes* in the data from the preceding year (called "first differences") or the *percentage changes* in the data from the preceding year (known as "link relatives"). When the first differences are used, for example, the mathematically derived function can be employed to forecast the *change* in sales rather than the level of sales. By using a lagged subscript, S_{t-1}, to represent sales in the last time period as compared to sales in the current period, S_t, the forecast change in sales (ΔS) could be expressed

$$\Delta S = S_t - S_{t-1}$$

Therefore, since

$$S_t = a + bI_t + cA_t \quad \text{(from equation 1 above)}$$

and

$$S_{t-1} = a + bI_{t-1} + cA_{t-1}$$

then

$$\Delta S = S_t - S_{t-1} = (bI_t - bI_{t-1}) + (cA_t - cA_{t-1})$$

or

$$\Delta S = b(I_t - I_{t-1}) + c(A_t - A_{t-1})$$

To forecast the change in sales, it is only necessary to insert in the last equation the required values of I and A and then solve for ΔS. The forecast of the sales level in time t would then be the sum of actual sales in the preceding time period and the forecast change in sales from time $t - 1$ to time t. This result is not the same as would have been obtained by forecasting the level of sales directly from the original equation.[1]

[1] *Cf.* R. Ferber, "Sales Forecasting by Correlation Techniques," *Journal of Marketing*, January, 1954, p. 221.

What are the bases for distinction in using the actual data for the forecast as against using the first differences? It will be remembered that the first step in the graphic correlation method was to compute the average for the dependent variable. By using actual data, the analysis was ultimately able to show the relative importance of the independent variables in causing the dependent variable to change *from its average value* for the period of the analysis. Had first differences been used instead of actual data, the analysis would have shown the relative importance of the independent variables in causing the dependent variables to change *from one year to the next*. An advantage of using first differences became especially noticeable after World War II when postwar predictions were made on the basis of interwar data.[2] The structural changes that took place during and after the war brought sharp changes in the variables from their interwar average, making postwar forecasts grossly inaccurate. Studies based on first differences, however, were generally more accurate and often required little or no long-range extrapolations since they were designed to predict one year from the previous one.

In addition to these considerations, the choice between actual data and first differences must be made in the following instances. (1) If strong growth or trend factors tend to outweigh the more immediate affects of the variables, using first differences will tend to reflect the more direct period-to-period variations. (2) If intercorrelation is higher between the independent variables when actual data are used as compared to when first differences are used, the latter procedure is preferable. (3) If the residuals from the final analysis are serially correlated when based on actual data but not when based on first differences, the latter method is again preferable. By "serial correlation" is meant that the successive observations of a single variable, such as sales, are not completely independent of one another. Sales in one year are at least partially affected by sales in a previous year and will partially affect sales in the following year. Hence, a close relationship between the dependent and an independent variable may be due as much to the serial correlation within each series as to the causal relationship itself.[3] In other words, where time series are involved, the different observations are not usually randomly distributed and hence there may be no logical basis for estimating the reliability of the correlation.

The above considerations should not be construed as meaning that

---

[2] Until World War II, most analyses were based on actual data, although Henry Moore had advocated the use of first differences and link relatives as early as 1914. (See R. Ferber, *A Study of Aggregate Consumption Functions*, NBER, Technical Paper 8, 1953, for some implications of the postwar predictions mentioned above.)

[3] A possibility suggested by Ferber is to incorporate the serial correlation directly into the equation by using last period's sales as an extra independent variable. Thus

$$S_t = a + bI_t + cA_t + dS_{t-1}$$

The use of last period's sales in this manner reflects the effects of past influences as a whole on future sales levels. (See Ferber, "Sales Forecasting," p. 227; also, Thomson and Foote, *op. cit.*, p. 286.)

actual-data analyses are always inferior to first-differences methods. The latter procedures, for instance, would be difficult to use for longer-range predictions where extrapolations must be made much beyond the analysis period for which data are available, because they are most suitable for year-to-year predictions. Both approaches have their usefulness, and the choice of either one depends on the significance of issues like those raised above.

Time Lags and Time Trend

As pointed out in previous discussions, one of the chief problems of forecasting is to secure a relationship that will remain in conformity with cyclical influences. The forecast formula may backcast excellently for the analysis period, but break down completely in predicting the future course (and particularly the turning points) of the dependent variable. One common reason for this is that the variables used in the formula all relate to the same time unit, for example, current sales are a function of current income and current advertising expenditures. The introduction of a time lag may thus improve considerably the accuracy of the predictions. Time lags are used whenever the *effect* of a given independent variable manifests itself in a later time period, as, for example, when the assumption is made that advertising this year affects sales next year because it takes the average consumer that long to adjust his buying and for the message to "soak in" and take effect. Ideally, as many time lags as possible should be used for the independent variables, thereby reducing the uncertainty inherent in predicting the latter.[4] The length of the time lag chosen, however, should be based on logical considerations, because statistically, the correct time lag to choose is not necessarily the one that makes the correlation coefficient a maximum.[5]

A second aspect of the time element in correlation problems is its customary usage by analysts as a catchall for the many factors known to change over time, such as tastes, technology, and so on, but for which data are unavailable or which, singly, would be expected to have a small effect on the dependent variable. The result of this, as stated in the previous subsection, is that "time" is often incorporated in the function as an independent variable[6]

---

[4] An approach suggested by Duesenberry and Modigliani is to lag income by its past cyclical peak, on the assumption that in forecasting consumption, it is more difficult for people to adjust their standard of living downward that it is to adjust it upward. Therefore, the future spending and savings habits of people are at least in part conditioned by their highest past level of income and their living standards at that time. (J. Duesenberry, *Income, Saving, and the Theory of Consumer Behavior*; and F. Modigliani, "Fluctuations in the Saving-Income Ratio: Problems in Economic Forecasting," in NBER, *Studies in Income and Wealth*, Vol. 11, pp. 371–443.)

[5] This may seem surprising, but is nevertheless true. See J. Marschak, "Economic Interdependence and Statistical Analysis," *Studies in Mathematical Economics and Econometrics*, pp. 135–50, especially p. 150, note 19.

[6] Assuming its regression coefficient differs significantly from zero; if not, it may be omitted from the analysis.

with the recognition that it is a substitute for other causal variables that are being omitted. Some analysts, however, use an alternative approach of excluding time from the original analysis and then checking the final residuals to see if they exhibit a time trend. If they do, either another variable can be added which explains this trend, or, if the necessary data are unavailable, "time" as such can be added as an additional variable. Hence, when a time trend is used, an attempt should be made to explain it on logical grounds, although sometimes this may also be difficult to do. Otherwise, recognition should be given to the dangers inherent in this source for making predictions.

Substitute or Proxy Variables

Economic theory, for the most part, provides the guide which is used in selecting the variables to be employed in an econometric study. It often happens, however, that the series needed is not available, hence a decision must be made by the analyst as to whether a substitute or proxy variable should be employed which would reflect the displaced series indirectly. A proxy variable is thus an index or series which is believed to have the same historical pattern as the missing variable. Sometimes a proxy series can be obtained directly from published sources; sometimes it must be specially constructed by combining several different series in a particular manner, according to the problem at hand. If a proxy variable is employed in a study, it should be based on logical considerations so that the series will continue to reflect the missing variable during the forecast period. Many examples of the use of proxy variables, and of the reasoning behind their selection, will be presented in later chapters.

Per Capita and Deflated Data: Statistical Adjustments

In demand analyses, particularly where elasticity coefficients are being estimated, there is no consistent agreement as to whether these estimations should be based on total or per capita data or on deflated or undeflated price and income series. There is, however, the obvious consideration that the several series should be consistent with one another. Thus, if consumption depends on income, and if per capita consumption data are being forecast, the independent variable, income, should also be expressed in per capita terms. The use of per capita data, however, requires some thought as to the population groups that are to be included as a divisor. In forecasting the demand for cigarettes, for example, only adults would be included in the analysis, and perhaps shifting weights could be ascribed to both men and women. Let us consider these and related problems of statistical adjustment further.

Due to the *economic* meaning of the term "demand," the measurement of it can be divided into two sorts of problems. The first is the nature of the price-quantity relation (i.e., the demand schedule or curve) on the assumption that other demand-determining factors remain constant. This type of measurement can be used, for example, as a means for determining elasticity. The second aspect of the problem is to measure changes in the intensity of demand. This type of measurement can be used in determining the nature of shifts in the demand curve. Thus, where management is contemplating a change in price and its subsequent effect on the quantity demanded, it is the first concept of demand in the schedule or curve sense that must be measured; alternatively, if price remains the same and there are changes in other demand-determining factors, such as income and advertising, it is the shifts in the demand curve as a whole that are of immediate concern. Realistically, however, in the actual work of demand measurement, these two problem areas are not regarded as mutually exclusive. Analysts are usually concerned both with the nature of the demand curve and with its shifts, for rarely is it possible to measure one without measuring the other in the same process.

Analysts have developed two different methods for making quantitative estimates of demand: one of these involves the use of time series data; the other is of a cross-sectional nature. Some comments as to both approaches are of interest.

(1) Time series data are sometimes used in which the historical changes in prices, incomes, population, and other variables affecting demand are observed and their interrelationships with demand are measured. Since a demand relation with only certain independent variables is wanted, it may be necessary to eliminate the influence of other independent variables that have a significant effect on demand. Thus, in a demand-price study where the influence of price is the only independent factor under consideration, it is often necessary to make two types of adjustments in the data.

(a) **Population Adjustment.** In order to eliminate the effect of population variations on the sale of the product, incomes and demand quantities are reduced to a per capita basis. This adjustment is usually made, however, when the data cover a number of years, since population figures do not usually show sharp fluctuations from year to year. The result of the adjustment is to enable the changes in demand to be attributed to factors other than population. Where the product being analyzed is a family good, such as an automobile or washing machine, a better demand estimate is often obtained by reducing the relevant data to a per household rather than per capita basis. In any event, it should be realized that such reductions do not, of course, adjust for changes in the age distribution, racial composition, or other elements in the population that may affect demand over the long run.

(b) **Deflation Adjustment.** A similar reduction, usually called "deflation," is to adjust for changes in the purchasing power of money, by dividing the price series in current dollars by an average price index of all goods. An example of the latter and one that is commonly used in consumer demand studies is the Consumer Price Index, since it reflects the average prices paid by consumers for most goods and services. Other indexes, of course, may be used for different kinds of problems. Although this procedure yields fairly satisfactory results, it should be kept in mind that deflation methods of this sort do not give precise measures of price changes mainly because no perfect index has yet been constructed and because the time period covered may be too long.[7]

(2) Cross-sectional analysis attempts to discover how consumption by individuals or families varies with prices, incomes, geographic differences, and the like, at the present time rather than over a period of time. This is similar in some ways to a controlled experiment, in that variations in the data are current and not historical. For example, in establishing a sales-income relationship for the purpose of measuring the *income elasticity of demand* (percentage change in demand relative to percentage change in income), the time series approach would employ past variations in the data as a basis for measurement. The cross-sectional approach, on the other hand, would compare the different levels of sales at the present time among different income groups, and the elasticity measure would be derived on the basis of these differences. But as in the time series approach, adjustments in the data may also be needed in order to eliminate the effects of other factors (in this case all factors other than income) that may affect significantly the demand for the product. In any event, the choice of either approach depends upon time and expense considerations, and the data already available. For these reasons, time series data are more commonly employed—the data being already available from published sources and company records—with minor use made of cross-sectional information when it seems appropriate.

Adjustment for Scale

It was pointed out in the discussion of graphic correlation in the previous chapter that, for linear regression lines, the coefficient of regression measures the slope of the regression line. This means that the coefficient of regression shows the change in the dependent variable resulting from a unit change in the independent variable, or in other words the average number of units increase or decrease in the dependent variable which occurs with each increase or decrease of a specified unit in the independent variable. The size of the coefficient of regression thus depends not only on the relation between the variables, which is the measure that is desired, but also on the units in which the variables are stated, the influence of which is undesired. A method that is commonly employed to eliminate the influence of the units and thus obtain a pure measure of the relation between the variables is to divide the data of each series by its own *standard deviation*. Each of the variables is then stated in units of its own standard deviation, in which form it is called β or the *beta* coefficient in the literature on correlation analysis. The English letter s, or the Greek letter σ (*sigma*) is commonly

---

[7] In addition to the population and deflation adjustments in time series analysis, other adjustments are also sometimes made, such as removal of trend, seasonal, and cyclical influences as explained in Chapter 1.

used as the symbol for the standard deviation. Thus, whereas the regression equation in original form would be of the type

$$Y = a + bX$$

in standard deviation form it becomes

$$\frac{Y}{\sigma_y} = a' + \beta \left(\frac{X}{\sigma_x} \right)$$

where σ_y and σ_x represent the standard deviation of y and x, respectively.

How is an equation of the second type interpreted? Since several predicting equations involving standard deviations will be derived in subsequent studies, a word as to their meaning is appropriate at this time.

Thus, suppose that in a particular sales forecasting problem, Y = sales in units and X = purchasing power in dollars. Also, suppose the respective standard deviations were calculated and found to be $\sigma_y = 120$, $\sigma_x = 10$, and that for *beta* $\left[\text{which is } b \left(\frac{\sigma_x}{\sigma_y} \right) \right]$ the value is $\beta = .25$. We could then say that for each increase of one standard deviation ($\$10$ of purchasing power) in X, sales increased .25 of one standard deviation. Since the standard deviation of Y is 120, this amounts to 30 units of sales for each $\$10$ of purchasing power, or a rate of 3 units for each dollar of purchasing power which is the value of the original coefficient of regression. When the standard deviations differ widely, the use of the beta coefficient is valuable because it makes the different series comparable. Many examples of this will be seen in later chapters.

Intercorrelation

Finally, of all the technical areas to be considered in a discussion of correlation analysis, perhaps none has attracted more interest, confusion, and attention than the problem of intercorrelation. In fact, it is largely because of the existence of correlation among the independent variables that the theory and techniques of partial correlation and regression have been developed. As implied in the previous chapter, the following conditions involving the dependent variable will prevail when the intercorrelation (or the simple correlation) between each of the independent variables is zero: (1) The partial regressions will equal the corresponding simple regressions; and (2) the coefficient of multiple determination will equal the sum of the several coefficients of simple determination. In reality, however, a significant amount of intercorrelation often does exist, hence the theory of partial correlation is needed.

The use of "drift lines" or "guide lines" is the graphic device for estimating the partial regression line, as was explained in one of the early remarks of the previous chapter when the first regression line was fitted in Chart B. It should be apparent, however, from the two conditions stated above, that if the intercorrelation itself could be eliminated or reduced to insignificance, the graphic method could proceed without the use of drift lines, as in the previous chapter, and the analysis would thus be less complicated and confusing. The objective, therefore, is to see what can be done about avoiding high intercorrelation.

Unfortunately, a high degree of intercorrelation has a more serious effect on the graphic method than on the mathematical method. Specialists on the subject point out that a major contribution of the graphic procedure is a simplified method whereby the first approximations of the partial regression lines or curves are progressively improved. Further, it can be shown that each successive improvement (approximation) varies inversely with the degree of intercorrelation.[8] But where the differences between two successive approximations may be unnoticeable, the graphic analysis may be terminated at too early a stage as compared to the correct regressions that would have been obtained by an equivalent mathematical procedure. In view of this, what might the analyst employing the graphic method do to avoid high intercorrelations and hence offset the possibility of incorrect regressions? One alternative, as mentioned earlier, is to use first differences or link relatives when the variables are highly intercorrelated in terms of the actual data. A second possibility, say when there are two independent variables, is to combine them as a ratio instead of using the two separate variables, if this is feasible. A third alternative is to try a substitute or proxy variable which may reflect the displaced variable indirectly. And finally, a fourth possibility is to "compute out" the intercorrelation. In later chapters, all four of these procedures, and variations of them, will be illustrated graphically and explained with application to actual forecasting problems and models. Of course, other methods may also be employed, and the analyst must try to derive those that seem most appropriate and logical for the particular problem at hand.

Conclusion: Forecasting Accuracy

Regardless of the method used, every forecast that ultimately emerges must eventually be evaluated. What criteria exist for performing this evaluation? Evidently, the criteria themselves must be quantitative in nature, and at least four simple ones that can easily be employed may be mentioned.

1. The percentage deviation of the forecast value from the actual or realized value can be computed. Where several forecasts have been made for a succession of periods, the separate percentage deviations can be combined and averaged to obtain an average percentage deviation.

2. A set of forecasts can be evaluated by comparing them with a bench mark such as a naïve model set of predictions. An example of the latter would be a prediction of next year's sales as a mere extension of this year's sales, or perhaps some multiple or fraction of this year's sales level.

[8] See Foote and Ives, *Statistics and Agriculture*, Vol. 1, pp. 13–18.

This provides an indication of the value of the present (presumably more elaborate) method compared to a more simple procedure.

3. To remove the spurious results that may be obtained by comparing levels of forecasts with actual sales, the criterion can be changed from one of comparison to one of direction of change. That is, because of the influence of serial correlation, a comparison of levels of forecasts with actual sales, as in the first standard above, will appear favorable, because sales each year have some influence on sales in the following year. By comparing directions of change rather than levels, the association between predicted and actual figures due to level is largely removed.

4. The most rigorous test, of course, is the one that measures the percentage of turning points that have been correctly forecast. However, as already mentioned, one way to gain an immediate indication of the forecasting effectiveness of a new model is to terminate the analysis a few years back, and then test the formula against the recent omitted years. If the results are satisfactory, the omitted years could then be introduced and the analysis rerun to obtain the most up-to-date formula.

APPENDIX TO CHAPTER 4: LOGARITHMS

It has already been pointed out that the use of logarithms can frequently simplify calculations and analyses that would otherwise be tedious and complicated. Accordingly, logarithmic charts and relationships come into play to a considerable extent in later chapters. Since some readers may never have been exposed to the study of logarithms, and others who have studied it may recall it only imperfectly, this section on the elements of logarithms is offered as both an introduction and review. Those who already possess a working knowledge of the subject may omit this section without loss of continuity.

Meaning of Logarithms

A logarithm is an exponent. It shows the power to which a given base must be raised to produce a given number. Thus, the expression $2^3 = 8$ states that the base 2 raised to the third power is 8. When written in this manner, the expression is said to be in *exponential form*. Some examples of other expressions in exponential form are $4^2 = 16$, $5^2 = 25$, and $6^3 = 216$.

Another way of writing these expressions is to put them in *logarithmic form*, thereby placing the emphasis on the exponent, or logarithm. Thus the equivalent of $2^3 = 8$ is the expression $\log_2 8 = 3$. This is read "the log of 8 to the base 2 is equal to 3." Similarly, the equivalent of the exponential expression $4^2 = 16$ is the logarithmic expression $\log_4 16 = 2$, and the equivalent of $5^2 = 25$ is $\log_5 25 = 2$. In general, if $b^x = N$, then $\log_b N = x$. The following pairs of equivalent statements are illustrations of this generalization.

Exponential form	*Logarithmic form*
$100^2 = 10,000$	$\log_{100} 10,000 = 2$
$2^{-3} = \dfrac{1}{2^3} = \dfrac{1}{8}$	$\log_2 \tfrac{1}{8} = -3$
$3^0 = 1$	$\log_3 1 = 0$
$2^1 = 2$	$\log_2 2 = 1$

It is apparent, therefore, that since a logarithm is an exponent, any number that can be an exponent can be a logarithm. Hence we find logarithms that are positive or negative, integral or fractional, or zero. Further, it is also apparent that a variety of numbers may be used as the base of a system of logarithms. In fact, any positive number except 1 can be used as the base of logarithms. (The number 1 is not used as a base because 1 raised to any power is still 1.) In practice, however, only two bases are widely used in all branches of applied science. These are the base 10, because 10 is the base of our number system, and the base e, an irrational number whose value is approximately 2.71828. Logarithms to the base e are called *natural logarithms* and are first encountered in the study of calculus. They will not, therefore, be of concern to us in this book. Logarithms to the base 10, on the other hand, are called *common logarithms*, and are studied in second year high school algebra. They are the type of logarithms that are employed later in this book and hence the ones that are reviewed here.

Characteristic and Mantissa

Since a logarithm is an exponent, and since we are assuming 10 as the base, the problem that now confronts us is to express numbers as powers of 10. An examination of the following table, in which the integral powers of 10 from −4 to +4 are presented, along with the corresponding logarithms to the assumed base 10, serves as a starting point.

10^4	=	10,000	log 10,000 =	4
10^3	=	1,000	log 1,000 =	3
10^2	=	100	log 100 =	2
10^1	=	10	log 10 =	1
10^0	=	1	log 1 =	0
10^{-1}	=	.1	log .1 = −1	
10^{-2}	=	.01	log .01 = −2	
10^{-3}	=	.001	log .001 = −3	
10^{-4}	=	.0001	log .0001 = −4	

It is evident from the table that only a small percentage of the positive numbers can be expressed as integral powers of 10. The remaining positive numbers are decimal powers of 10. Thus, if $10^1 = 10$, and $10^2 = 100$, it follows that the logarithm of, say, 18, is somewhere between 1 and 2, or simply 1 + some decimal. In fact, $10^{1.2553} = 18$; hence we say that log 18 = 1.2553 (where the base 10 is assumed and therefore not shown). Similarly, as can be seen from the table, the log of 300 must be somewhere between 2 and 3, since $10^2 = 100$ and $10^3 = 1,000$. Actually, as will be seen shortly, $10^{2.4771} = 300$. Hence we can write log 300 = 2.4771.

It is apparent from the above examples that a logarithm consists of two parts: an integral part to the left of the decimal point called the *characteristic*, and a fractional part to the right of the decimal point called the *mantissa*. Of course, either the characteristic or the mantissa may be zero. In the expressions $10^{2.4771} = 300$ and log 300 = 2.4771, the characteristic is 2 and the mantissa is .4771, so neither is zero. But in the expression log 100 = 2 the mantissa is zero, while in the expression log 6 = .7782 the characteristic is zero. These examples indicate that a rule may exist for discovering the characteristic of a logarithm. As a matter of fact, two simple rules do exist which may be stated as follows:

1. For any number greater than 1, the characteristic of its logarithm is *positive* and numerically *one less* than the number of digits to the left of the decimal point.

2. For any number between 0 and 1, the characteristic of its logarithm is *negative* and numerically *one more* than the number of zeros between the decimal point and the first significant digit.

The following examples are illustrations of the rule:

log 43.2 = 1 + some mantissa, because by rule 1, 43.2 is greater than 1, and there are two digits to the left of the decimal point.

log .008 = −3 + some mantissa, because by rule 2, .008 is less than 1, and there are two zeros between the decimal point and the first significant figure.

Similarly,

$$\begin{aligned} \log\ \ 6.239 &= \ \ \ 0 + \text{a certain mantissa.} \\ \log 20{,}903 &= \ \ \ 4 + \text{a certain mantissa.} \\ \log\ \ \ \ .61 &= -1 + \text{a certain mantissa.} \end{aligned}$$

The characteristic of a logarithm can always be determined, therefore, by following this simple rule. What about the mantissa? This, of course, is always positive, and as will be seen shortly, is obtained from published tables that are readily available.

Writing Negative Characteristics

The characteristic of a logarithm, as seen above, can be positive, zero, or negative. Characteristics that are positive or zero are written in a straightforward manner and create no particular difficulties; negative characteristics, however, may be written in either of two forms, called the *monomial* form and the *binomial* form. Usually, the latter form is employed in computational work, with a slight difference in notation from that which might normally be expected. The nature of these notations can be described briefly.

The monomial form of negative characteristics is simply −1, −2, etc., the minus sign being placed in front of the number as is customary when writing negative numbers. However, when the mantissa is written along with the characteristic, as is usually the case, the minus sign should be written *above* the characteristic in order to emphasize the fact that it is only the characteristic which is negative, since the mantissa, as stated above, is always positive. Thus, the preferred form is $\bar{2}.3928$ rather than −2.3928, or $\bar{1}.6973$ instead of −1.6973.

The binomial form is the one that is commonly employed when using logarithms, because it facilitates computational work. In the binomial form, the negative characteristic is converted into a different but equivalent expression, and the negative part is moved to the back of the logarithm so that the front end can become positive. Thus, if a characteristic is −3 and the mantissa is .2786, we write the characteristic in the form 7 −10 and the logarithm in the form 7.2786 −10. Similarly, if the characteristic is −4 and the mantissa is .4665, we write the logarithm in the form 6.4665 −10. Of course, this logarithm could also be written 16.4665 −20 and it would still mean the same thing. As stated above, the advantage of using the binomial form for expressing negative characteristics is that it facilitates computations with logarithms. Thus, in the following example, it is a simple matter to subtract a larger logarithm from a smaller one when the binomial form is used.

$$7.4692 - 10$$
$$6.5731 - 10$$
$$\overline{0.8961}$$

Handled in this manner, there is considerably less chance of making errors in arithmetic when working with negative characteristics. Hence, the binomial form of expression is typically employed when negative characteristics arise.

Table of Mantissas

It has already been pointed out that the characteristic of a logarithm does nothing more than reflect the position of the decimal point, while the mantissa, which is the exponent of 10, constitutes the balance of the logarithm. It follows, therefore, that given a sequence of digits with a shifting decimal point, the mantissa will remain the same but the characteristic will vary according to the changing position of the decimal point. Thus, from a table of mantissas such as appears in Table 4-1, it is possible to determine the logarithm of a number by obtaining the mantissa from the table, and then establishing the characteristic by inspection. Let us see how this is done.

The table presents the mantissas of the logarithms of numbers from 100 to 999. These mantissas are expressed as decimals correct to the fourth place, and are accurate to within $\frac{1}{2}$ of 1 per cent. Five-place tables, six-place tables, and even tables to twenty-five places are available, but for the problems encountered in economics and business, a four-place table is quite adequate. With this table it is possible to find the mantissa of the logarithm of a given number and to find the *antilogarithm*, or the number which corresponds to a given logarithm. The following examples are illustrative.

1. Find the log of 847. In the left-hand column labeled N, we look for the number 84, the first two digits of 847. We then move over to the column headed 7, and read the mantissa .9279. Applying the rule, we note the characteristic is 2, since there are three digits to the left of the decimal point. Hence, log 847 = 2.9279, which means $10^{2.9279} = 847$.

Note that when the decimal point changes position, the characteristic changes, as stated above, but the mantissa remains the same. Thus,

$$\log 847 \quad = 2.9279$$
$$\log\ 84.7 \quad = 1.9279$$
$$\log\quad 8.47 \quad = 0.9279$$
$$\log\quad .847 = \bar{1}.9279,\ \text{or } 9.9279 - 10$$
$$\log\quad .0847 = \bar{2}.9279,\ \text{or } 8.9279 - 10$$

TABLE 4–1

TABLE OF MANTISSAS

N	0	1	2	3	4	5	6	7	8	9
10	0000	0043	0086	0128	0170	0212	0253	0294	0334	0374
11	0414	0453	0492	0531	0569	0607	0645	0682	0719	0755
12	0792	0828	0864	0899	0934	0969	1004	1038	1072	1106
13	1139	1173	1206	1239	1271	1303	1335	1367	1399	1430
14	1461	1492	1523	1553	1584	1614	1644	1673	1703	1732
15	1761	1790	1818	1847	1875	1903	1931	1959	1987	2014
16	2041	2068	2095	2122	2148	2175	2201	2227	2253	2279
17	2304	2330	2355	2380	2405	2430	2455	2480	2504	2529
18	2553	2577	2601	2625	2648	2672	2695	2718	2742	2765
19	2788	2810	2833	2856	2878	2900	2923	2945	2967	2989
20	3010	3032	3054	3075	3096	3118	3139	3160	3181	3201
21	3222	3243	3263	3284	3304	3324	3345	3365	3385	3404
22	3424	3444	3464	3483	3502	3522	3541	3560	3579	3598
23	3617	3636	3655	3674	3692	3711	3729	3747	3766	3784
24	3802	3820	3838	3856	3874	3892	3909	3927	3945	3962
25	3979	3997	4014	4031	4048	4065	4082	4099	4116	4133
26	4150	4166	4183	4200	4216	4232	4249	4265	4281	4298
27	4314	4330	4346	4362	4378	4393	4409	4425	4440	4456
28	4472	4487	4502	4518	4533	4548	4564	4579	4594	4609
29	4624	4639	4654	4669	4683	4698	4713	4728	4742	4757
30	4771	4786	4800	4814	4829	4843	4857	4871	4886	4900
31	4914	4928	4942	4955	4969	4983	4997	5011	5024	5038
32	5051	5065	5079	5092	5105	5119	5132	5145	5159	5172
33	5185	5198	5211	5224	5237	5250	5263	5276	5289	5302
34	5315	5328	5340	5353	5366	5378	5391	5403	5416	5428
35	5441	5453	5465	5478	5490	5502	5514	5527	5539	5551
36	5563	5575	5587	5599	5611	5623	5635	5647	5658	5670
37	5682	5694	5705	5717	5729	5740	5752	5763	5775	5786
38	5798	5809	5821	5832	5843	5855	5866	5877	5888	5899
39	5911	5922	5933	5944	5955	5966	5977	5988	5999	6010
40	6021	6031	6042	6053	6064	6075	6085	6096	6107	6117
41	6128	6138	6149	6160	6170	6180	6191	6201	6212	6222
42	6232	6243	6253	6263	6274	6284	6294	6304	6314	6325
43	6335	6345	6355	6365	6375	6385	6395	6405	6415	6425
44	6435	6444	6454	6464	6474	6484	6493	6503	6513	6522
45	6532	6542	6551	6561	6571	6580	6590	6599	6609	6618
46	6628	6637	6646	6656	6665	6675	6684	6693	6702	6712
47	6721	6730	6739	6749	6758	6767	6776	6785	6794	6803
48	6812	6821	6830	6839	6848	6857	6866	6875	6884	6893
49	6902	6911	6920	6928	6937	6946	6955	6964	6972	6981
50	6990	6998	7007	7016	7024	7033	7042	7050	7059	7067
51	7076	7084	7093	7101	7110	7118	7126	7135	7143	7152
52	7160	7168	7177	7185	7193	7202	7210	7218	7226	7235
53	7243	7251	7259	7267	7275	7284	7292	7300	7308	7316
54	7324	7332	7340	7348	7356	7364	7372	7380	7388	7396

In like manner, the logarithms of other numbers can be found. Thus, to find the log of 92.8, we find 92 under the N column, and the mantissa under the 8 column. The answer is log 92.8 = 1.9675. Similarly, log 1.29 is obtained by finding 12 under N, and the mantissa 1106 under 9; therefore, log 1.29 = .1106. And finally, log .3 is obtained by recognizing that it and log 300 have the same mantissas, .4771. Since the number .3 is between 0 and 1, its characteristic according to the rule is negative and 1 more than the number of

TABLE 4–1—*Continued*

TABLE OF MANTISSAS

N	0	1	2	3	4	5	6	7	8	9
55	7404	7412	7419	7427	7435	7443	7451	7459	7466	7474
56	7482	7490	7497	7505	7513	7520	7528	7536	7543	7551
57	7559	7566	7574	7582	7589	7597	7604	7612	7619	7627
58	7634	7642	7649	7657	7664	7672	7679	7686	7694	7701
59	7709	7716	7723	7731	7738	7745	7752	7760	7767	7774
60	7782	7789	7796	7803	7810	7818	7825	7832	7839	7846
81	7853	7860	7868	7875	7882	7889	7896	7903	7910	7917
62	7924	7931	7938	7945	7952	7959	7966	7973	7980	7987
63	7993	8000	8007	8014	8021	8028	8035	8041	8048	8055
64	8062	8069	8075	8082	8089	8096	8102	8109	8116	8122
65	8129	8136	8142	8149	8156	8162	8169	8176	8182	8189
66	8195	8202	8209	8215	8222	8228	8235	8241	8248	8254
67	8261	8267	8274	8280	8287	8293	8299	8306	8312	8319
68	8325	8331	8338	8344	8351	8357	8363	8370	8376	8382
69	8388	8395	8401	8407	8414	8420	8426	8432	8439	8445
70	8451	8457	8463	8470	8476	8482	8488	8494	8500	8506
71	8513	8519	8525	8531	8537	8543	8549	8555	8561	8567
72	8573	8579	8585	8591	8597	8603	8609	8615	8621	8627
73	8633	8639	8645	8651	8657	8663	8669	8675	8681	8686
74	8692	8698	8704	8710	8716	8722	8727	8733	8739	8745
75	8751	8756	8762	8768	8774	8779	8785	8791	8797	8802
76	8808	8814	8820	8825	8831	8837	8842	8848	8854	8859
77	8865	8871	8876	8882	8887	8893	8899	8904	8910	8915
78	8921	8927	8932	8938	8943	8949	8954	8960	8965	8971
79	8976	8982	8987	8993	8998	9004	9009	9015	9020	9025
80	9031	9036	9042	9047	9053	9058	9063	9069	9074	9079
81	9085	9090	9096	9101	9106	9112	9117	9122	9128	9133
82	9138	9143	9149	9154	9159	9165	9170	9175	9180	9186
83	9191	9196	9201	9206	9212	9217	9222	9227	9232	9238
84	9243	9248	9253	9258	9263	9269	9274	9279	9284	9289
85	9294	9299	9304	9309	9315	9320	9325	9330	9335	9340
86	9345	9350	9355	9360	9365	9370	9375	9380	9385	9390
87	9395	9400	9405	9410	9415	9420	9425	9430	9435	9440
88	9445	9450	9455	9460	9465	9469	9474	9479	9484	9489
89	9494	9499	9504	9509	9513	9518	9523	9528	9533	9538
90	9542	9547	9552	9557	9562	9566	9571	9576	9581	9586
91	9590	9595	9600	9605	9609	9614	9619	9624	9628	9633
92	9638	9643	9647	9652	9657	9661	9666	9671	9675	9680
93	9685	9689	9694	9699	9703	9708	9713	9717	9722	9727
94	9731	9736	9741	9745	9750	9754	9759	9763	9768	9773
95	9777	9782	9786	9791	9795	9800	9805	9809	9814	9818
96	9823	9827	9832	9836	9841	9845	9850	9854	9859	9863
97	9868	9872	9877	9881	9886	9890	9894	9899	9903	9908
98	9912	9917	9921	9926	9930	9934	9939	9943	9948	9952
99	9956	9961	9965	9969	9974	9978	9983	9987	9991	9996

zeros between the decimal point and the first significant digit. Therefore, $\log .3 = \overline{1}.4771$, or $9.4771 - 10$.

2. Find the antilog of 1.1492. That is, find the number whose logarithm is 1.1492. Since the mantissa is .1492, we look for this mantissa in the table and find that it appears on the line whose N value is 14, in column 1. The sequence of digits for this mantissa, therefore, is 141. Since the position of the decimal point is determined by the characteristic, and since the

characteristic is 1, there must be *two* digits to the left of the decimal point, as stated earlier in the rule. Hence, antilog 1.1492 = 14.1. Similarly, antilog 8.3054 −10 = .0202. This is because the mantissa .3054 has the digit sequence 202 as can be seen from the table. Since the characteristic in effect is −2, and, according to the rule, numerically 1 more than the number of zeros between the decimal point and the first significant digit, the number or antilog must be .0202.

Interpolation

The table of mantissas can be used to find the logarithm of any number which does not have more than three significant digits. What if the number has four or more digits? Can the logarithm still be obtained? The answer is yes, but it must be approximated by the process of *interpolation*, as illustrated in the following examples.

1. Find the logarithm of 37.654. The first step is to disregard the decimal point for the time being, and to round off to four significant digits. The number thus becomes 3765. Looking in the table of mantissas, we note that the mantissas on each side of the number are

$$
10 \left\{ 5 \left\{ \begin{array}{l} 3760 \\ 3765 \\ 3770 \end{array} \right. \right. \qquad
\left. \begin{array}{l} .5752 \\ ? \\ .5763 \end{array} \right\} x \right\} .0011
$$

Number   Mantissa

Next, setting up the proportion:

$$\frac{5}{10} = \frac{x}{.0011}$$

and cross-multiplying, we get

$$10x = .0055$$
$$x = .00055 = .0006$$

Adding this amount to the smaller mantissa, we obtain the mantissa .5758. Referring back to the original number with its decimal, we note that the characteristic is 1. Therefore, log 37.65 = 1.5758.

2. Find the antilog of 9.8624 −10. Looking in the table, we note that the closest mantissas and their corresponding N values are

$$
1 \left\{ x \left\{ \begin{array}{l} 728 \\ ? \\ 729 \end{array} \right. \right. \qquad
\left. \begin{array}{l} 8621 \\ 8624 \\ 8627 \end{array} \right\} 3 \right\} 6
$$

Hence, setting up the indicated proportion and cross-multiplying we get,

$$\frac{x}{1} = \frac{3}{6}$$
$$6x = 3$$
$$x = \tfrac{1}{2}$$

The number, therefore, will be halfway between 728 and 729, or 728.5. Since the characteristic is −1, the correct antilog is .7285.

With a little practice, interpolations can be done mentally, thereby speeding up the process of computation where logarithms are concerned.

Operations with Logarithms

When working with logarithms, certain operations arise the nature of which must be understood. These operations are the *laws of logarithms*. In later chapters, these laws are frequently applied in the process of estimating prediction equations from charts. Since we shall assume that these operations are already familiar to the reader, they should be thoroughly mastered at this time. Basically, the operations are nothing more than the application of four laws or theorems.

I. *The logarithm of a product equals the sum of the logarithms of its factors.* That is,

$$\log MN = \log M + \log N$$

The proof of this is simple.

$$\text{Let } x = \log M, \text{ so that } 10^x = M$$
$$\text{Let } y = \log N, \text{ so that } 10^y = N$$

If we multiply these equations, we must add the exponents in accordance with the laws of multiplication. Thus, multiplying the two equations together, we get

$$10^{x+y} = MN$$

Therefore, $\log MN = x + y = \log M + \log N$. Thus, numbers can be multiplied by simply adding their logarithms, and then obtaining the antilog of the result. For example, multiply 47.2 by 3.61.

$$\text{Let } x = 47.2 \times 3.61$$
$$\text{Then } \log x = \log 47.2 + \log 3.61$$
$$\log 47.2 = 1.6739$$
$$\log 3.61 = 0.5575$$
$$\overline{\log x = 2.2314}$$
$$x = 170.4$$

II. *The logarithm of a quotient equals the logarithm of the dividend or numerator, minus the logarithm of the divisor or denominator.* In symbols,

$$\log \frac{M}{N} = \log M - \log N$$

As before, the proof is simple.

$$\text{Let } x = \log M, \text{ so that } 10^x = M$$
$$\text{Let } y = \log N, \text{ so that } 10^y = N$$

According to the laws of division, exponents are subtracted when dividing. Thus, dividing the first equation by the second,

$$10^{x-y} = \frac{M}{N}$$

Therefore, $\log \dfrac{M}{N} = x - y = \log M - \log N$

Thus, numbers can be divided by simply subtracting their logarithms, and then obtaining the antilog of the result. For example, divide 745 by 2.63.

$$\text{Let } x = 745 \div 2.63$$
$$\text{Then } \log x = \log 745 - \log 2.63$$
$$\log 745 = 2.8722$$
$$\underline{\log 2.63 = .4200}$$
$$\log x = 2.4522$$
$$x = 283.3$$

III. The logarithm of a power of a number equals the exponent of the power times the logarithm of the number. That is,

$$\log M^n = n \log M$$

Thus, numbers can be raised to a power by simply multiplying the exponent of the power by the logarithm of the number, and then obtaining the antilog of the result. For example, what is the value of 7.1632^3?

$$\text{Let } x = 7.163^3 \text{ (after rounding off)}$$
$$\text{Then } \log x = 3 \log 7.163$$
$$\log 7.163 = 0.8551$$
$$\log x = 3(0.8551) = 2.5653$$
$$x = 367.5$$

IV. The logarithm of a root of a number equals the logarithm of the number divided by the index of the root. In symbols,

$$\log \sqrt[n]{M} = \frac{1}{n}\log M$$

The proof is as follows:

Let $x = \log M$, so that $10^x = M$. Taking the nth root of both sides of the equation

$$\sqrt[n]{10^x} \quad \text{or} \quad 10^{\frac{x}{n}} = \sqrt[n]{M}$$

Thus, any root of a number can be found by simply dividing the logarithm of the number by the root, and then obtaining the antilog of the result. For example, find $\sqrt[3]{473.7}$

$$\text{Let } x = \sqrt[3]{473.7}, \text{ or } 473.7^{\frac{1}{3}}$$
$$\text{Then } \log x = \tfrac{1}{3}\log 473.7 = \tfrac{1}{3}\,2.6755$$
$$\log x = .8918$$
$$x = 7.795$$

These four laws or theorems cover all of the operations that can be performed with logarithms. Thus, multiplication, division, raising to powers, and taking roots can all be done by the use of logarithms. However, addition and subtraction *cannot* be done by logarithms.

Special Computations

In certain situations involving work with logarithms, special computations arise which require manipulation of the characteristic, in order that the binomial form of expression can be used. Three possibilities, and the ways in which they may be handled, are the following.

I. *Subtracting a numerically larger logarithm from a numerically smaller one.*

EXAMPLE 1. Subtract:

$$\begin{array}{r} 5.3421 \\ 7.4214 \end{array}$$

SOLUTION: Add 10 to the characteristic of the minuend, and subtract it at the end. Thus

$$\begin{array}{r} 15.3421 - 10 \\ 7.4214 \\ \hline 7.9207 - 10 \text{ Ans.} \end{array}$$

EXAMPLE 2. Subtract:

$$\begin{array}{r} 8.5215 - 10 \\ 9.6312 - 10 \end{array}$$

SOLUTION. Again, rewrite the minuend so that it is larger than the subtrahend. Thus,

$$\begin{array}{r} 18.5215 - 20 \\ 9.6312 - 10 \\ \hline 8.8903 - 10 \text{ Ans.} \end{array}$$

II. *Subtracting a logarithm with a negative characteristic from a logarithm with a positive characteristic.*

EXAMPLE. Subtract:

$$\begin{array}{r} 2.2038 \\ 9.3047 - 10 \end{array}$$

SOLUTION. The minuend must be rewritten so that it is larger than the subtrahend.

$$\begin{array}{r} 12.2038 - 10 \\ 9.3047 - 10 \\ \hline 2.8991 \text{ Ans.} \end{array}$$

III. *Dividing a logarithm with a negative characteristic by a number.*

EXAMPLE. Find $\sqrt[3]{.0682}$

SOLUTION. To find the cube root of .0682, we first obtain its log, and then divide by 3. Log .0682 = 8.8338 − 10. However, dividing this by 3 will create some difficulties because of the negative characteristic. Therefore, we can rewrite 8.8338 −10 in a manner such that the negative part of the characteristic gives −10 when divided by 3. Thus, 8.8338 −10 can be rewritten as 28.8338 −30. Now dividing by 3,

$$3 \overline{\smash{)}\ \begin{array}{r} 9.6113 - 10 \\ 28.8338 - 30 \end{array}}$$

Antilog 9.6113 −10 = 0.4086, ans.

If it were $\sqrt[4]{.0682}$ which we were seeking, we would have written the log as 38.8338 −40, so that the negative characteristic would give −10 when divided by 4. Thus

$$\frac{9.7084 - 10}{4\;)\;38.8338 - 40}$$

Exponential Equations

An *exponential equation* is one in which the unknown appears in the exponent. Thus $2^x = 16$ and $5^x = 125$ are examples of exponential equations. If x is a rational number, it can often be found by inspection. Thus, if

$$2^x = 8$$

we can write 8 as a power of 2.
Then

$$2^x = 2^3$$

Therefore,

$$x = 3$$

Similarly

$$3^{x+2} = 81$$
$$3^{x+2} = 3^4$$
$$x + 2 = 4$$
$$x = 2$$

By expressing both members as powers of the same base, the solution is readily obtained.

Suppose, however, that both members cannot be expressed as integral powers of the same base. In that case, or any other, the equation can always be solved by using logarithms. Thus, if

$$a^x = b$$

simply take logarithms of both sides of the equation to obtain

$$\log a^x = \log b,$$

and therefore, by the laws of logarithms discussed earlier, it follows that

$$x \log a = \log b \quad \text{(Law III)}$$

For instance, solve

$$2^x = 7$$

Taking logarithms of both sides,

$$x \log 2 = \log 7$$

Therefore,

$$x = \frac{\log 7}{\log 2} = \frac{.8451}{.3010} = 2.808$$

Note that since $2^2 = 4$ and $2^3 = 8$, we should expect for $2^x = 7$ that the answer lies somewhere between 2 and 3. Note also that $\dfrac{\log 7}{\log 2}$ is a *quotient of two logarithms*, and is *not* the same as the *logarithm of the quotient*, $\log \dfrac{7}{2}$. Therefore, the former expression must be solved by looking up the logarithms and then dividing, as was done above. The latter expression, of course, could be solved by subtracting the logarithms, since it is of the type

$$\log \frac{M}{N} = \log M - \log N$$

Therefore, the former expression could also be solved by subtracting the *logarithms of the logarithms*. That is

$$\frac{\log 7}{\log 2} = \frac{.8451}{.3010} = \log .8451 - \log .3010$$

One more example should be sufficient to fix ideas firmly in mind. Solve

$$2^x = 3^{x+1}$$

Taking logarithms of both sides

$$x \log 2 = (x + 1) \log 3$$

Therefore

$$x \log 2 - x \log 3 = \log 3$$
$$\text{or} \quad x(\log 2 - \log 3) = \log 3$$

Therefore

$$x = \frac{\log 3}{\log 2 - \log 3}$$

Using the table of mantissas,

$$x = \frac{.4771}{.3010 - .4771} = \frac{.4771}{-.1761} = -2.709$$

Conclusion

Against this background of logarithms and exponential functions, the discussions of logarithmic charts and the estimation of formulas from such charts, as developed in parts of the previous chapter, should be clear. It is suggested, therefore, that those portions of the chapter be reviewed at this time, since the following chapters will provide many instances where equations are to be estimated from arithmetic, semilogarithmic, and logarithmic charts. An understanding of these basic logarithmic concepts will help immeasurably in comprehending the graphic manipulations and interpretations to be encountered later.

QUESTIONS

1. The first section of the previous chapter deals with the statistical basis of econometrics. What fundamental concepts were brought out in this discussion? Explain.

2. In the earlier years of econometric science, the studies made dealt largely with the prices, supplies, and demands of agricultural commodities, and very rarely with manufactured goods. Why?

3. (*a*) Why is it necessary when performing a graphic correlation that the regression line, if straight, pass through the means of the two variables? (*b*) Of what practical value is this rule?

4. (*a*) What is the meaning of a set of dots which fall precisely along a regression line? (*b*) What is the meaning when the dots scatter about the regression line?

5. Suggest a graphic and a mathematical technique that can be used to indicate the degree of fit, or goodness of fit, of an econometric model.

6. (*a*) Using the formula for the coefficient of multiple determination on p. 61, compute R^2 from Table 3–1, p. 47. (*b*) In one sentence, interpret your result. (*c*) How does your computed value of R^2 relate to the dashed and solid lines in Chart D of Figure 3–1, p. 49?

7. What are the *economic* implications of adding further variables to an econometric analysis? Explain.

8. What relationship is indicated by the *slope* of a linear regression line on a scatter diagram?

9. (*a*) Explain the kind of considerations that should be kept in mind in choosing the type of equation or curve for an econometric analysis. (*b*) Can you suggest when a simultaneous-equation model might be preferred to a single-equation model?

10. (*a*) What are "first differences"? "Link relatives"? (*b*) In general, when might the use of first differences be preferred over the use of actual data?

11. Why is a time trend sometimes employed in an econometric analysis?

12. Why are per capita and deflated data used in some studies?

13. What procedures or techniques might be employed to reduce if not eliminate the significance of intercorrelation and thereby facilitate more simplified analyses?

14. (*a*) What approaches might be employed in evaluating forecasting accuracy? (*b*) How can an analyst obtain an immediate indication of the forecasting ability or durability of a newly created model?

PART II

Forecasting By Sectors

How can the sources, techniques, and tools developed in previous chapters be employed in actual forecasting? The answer to this question will occupy the core of our attention in the following chapters that comprise Part II. Emphasis is placed on the construction of "sector" models involving different types and classes of goods, as distinguished from aggregate models or models of the total economy which constitute the subject matter of Part III.

In the chapters that follow, theories and procedures are developed for forecasting prices (Chapter 5), the sale of consumers' nondurable goods (Chapter 6), the sale of consumers' durable goods (Chapter 7), the sale of capital goods (Chapter 8), and the sale of construction materials and supplies (Chapter 9). All of the procedures are developed in considerable detail using examples of actual products in all cases. Throughout the discussions and explanations, some of the points mentioned and implied both in the Preface and in the Note to Instructors, however, should be kept in mind.

1. The models are presented for discussion and for instructional purposes only, and should not necessarily be regarded as indicative of current practices either on the part of the authors or by econometricians in general.

2. Econometrics involves continuously changing processes and hypotheses, and a model which may appear acceptable at one time may soon become obsolete as new theories and methods are developed. Thus, in the following chapters, all of the models backcast favorably, and some even exquisitely. However, a few have not held up for a long enough period of time to be of much practical value, and for some the methods might even be considered "out of date" by current standards.

Why, then, do we bother to include such models? The answer is that we can try to profit from our mistakes (and from the mistakes of others). If the models, as mentioned in the Note to Instructors, are used as a springboard for critical thinking, further research, and discussion, it should be possible to construct new and improved versions, thereby furthering our knowledge of the subject and its usefulness for solving practical problems.

Chapter 5

FORECASTING PRICES

Price forecasting, particularly the forecasting of agricultural prices, is perhaps the oldest branch of modern econometrics. Henry Moore, for instance, as far back as 1914, in his *Economic Cycles; Their Law and Cause*, attempted a study of the relation of supply to price for corn, hay, oats, potatoes, and cotton. Since then, the literature of agricultural economics has abounded with price studies of specific farm products, most of them published in the professional statistical and agricultural economics journals, and in the monographs and bulletins of various university agricultural experiment stations. In this chapter we shall be concerned with the development of *general* principles and techniques which may be used to forecast prices of various kinds, including not only farm prices but the prices of raw materials and semimanufactured goods, metals and fuels prices, interest rates, and stock market prices as well.

PRICE DETERMINANTS

Many commodity prices in the United States are highly correlated with disposable income which, in turn, correlates well with three price-determining factors—consumer demand, farm wages, and wages and material costs of production. Prices also correlate very well with the ratio (or pressure index) of supply to consumption and, in fact, disposable income and this ratio together explain fairly well a large majority of variations in commodity prices. While the "explanation" does not necessarily precede prices, it points up the factors that need to be forecast in order to predict price changes. Good forecasts of the price-determining factors, therefore, can provide good forecasts of prices once a sound relationship has been established.

Rather than utilize consumer demand, farm wages, and production costs as sole price-making factors, a more general system can be constructed which attributes variations in prices to four classes of factors: supply, demand, competitive, and monetary. *Supply factors* include domestic and foreign production, available domestic and foreign stocks, unit labor costs

93

of production, other costs of production, and alternative uses of productive resources. *Demand factors* include domestic and foreign consumption, domestic and foreign speculative inventory demand, and demand for government stockpiling. *Competitive factors* include prices of principal competing products, prices of all other products, technological changes in the commodity, and technological changes in competitive products. *Monetary factors* include demand deposits plus currency in circulation, rate of turnover of deposits, rate of change of bank deposits, rate of change of foreign exchange, gold prices, and gold flows.

Are all of these factors at work in influencing particular commodity prices? The answer, of course, is no. Certain domestic commodities such as peaches or potatoes may show very little relation to gold flows, technology, or foreign exchange, while certain international commodities such as cotton might be quite sensitive to one or more of these same factors at different times. The four classes of price-determining factors, therefore, should be thought of as a "master list" from which particular items may be taken and analyzed as causes of changes in particular prices, as will be seen in subsequent sections of this chapter.

Specific Considerations

In analyzing price changes by attempting to find cause and effect relationships, certain problems and obstacles tend to arise which are more specific than the general framework of difficulties mentioned thus far. The most important specific factors ought to be recognized, therefore, before proceeding with the actual analyses and model constructions of later sections. Chief among these specific factors are the development of supply-demand relationships and the role of inflation and technological change in affecting prices. The statistical and economic implications are noted briefly in the following paragraphs.

Supply-Demand Factors: Intercorrelation. As pointed out in Chapter 4, an important technical problem occurs in the usual methods of regression analysis when there is a significant amount of intercorrelation among the independent variables in the analysis. Some common methods of overcoming this obstacle are: (1) to use only one of several intercorrelated variables, or (2) to combine the intercorrelated variables into a single weighted synthetic variable, the weights being determined by rational considerations if possible, or even by "common sense" (i.e., arbitrarily) if necessary. For example, supply and demand might be unrelated to each other in the short run, and yet be highly correlated over the long run as prices adjust to the unbalance. In price forecasting, it is this unbalance which causes price changes, and hence in analyzing the causes, the ratio of demand to supply is a better variable to use than either one employed separately. If the ratio of world consumption, a demand variable, to world stocks, a supply variable, is taken for a particular commodity, it will probably be highly correlated with domestic consumption and domestic stocks, and therefore cannot be taken as an independent variable in a regression analysis. However, if weights are constructed on the basis of average imports and exports, the ratios can be combined into a single variable and used in this manner. Thus, in this example, four variables have been combined into one before proceeding with a regression analysis of any type.

Monetary Factors. Are supply-demand ratios the only factors affecting price? The answer, of course, is no. Although good correlations are obtained when supply-demand ratios are used as an independent variable, residuals or unexplained variations still remain which must be accounted for. Some of the residuals are the result of dealers' errors of estimate of the four variables, and others are due to the competitive relation with other products, technological factors, and the changing value of money. With respect to the last factor, a high correlation between prices and unit labor costs of production has existed in the United States since the latter half of the nineteenth century. Analyses of various types of data, in fact, reveal that prior to World War II, there was a clear-cut tendency for unit labor costs in any one year to be correlated with the price level six months earlier. Thus, a price increase could be expected to yield an increase in unit labor costs several months later. During World War II this lag relationship shifted to a concurrent one, and since World War II the lag relationship has actually reversed itself, with increases in unit labor costs tending for the most part to precede increases in the price level. Unit labor cost, which is usually measured by the ratio of average hourly earnings to average output per man-hour, is thus a measure of the supply of the commodity under competitive labor conditions and the cost at which the product can be produced. Unit labor cost, therefore, in view of its high correlation both with consumer and wholesale prices, is a good measure of monetary inflation and forecaster of general prices. For even if the measure of unit labor cost, namely

$$\frac{\text{Average Hourly Earnings}}{\text{Average Output per Man-Hour}}$$

is such that the long-term trend of the numerator, due to union pressures or otherwise, increases faster than the long-term trend of the denominator (i.e., productivity), the same relative relationship between prices and unit labor cost will exist in the future just as it has in the past. Some success in forecasting the general level of prices can frequently be made, therefore, by establishing a relationship or correlation between, for example, wholesale prices and unit labor costs, and then predicting the latter by projecting the trend of its two chief determinants, the numerator and denominator in the above ratio. The result of one such forecast made in 1957 is shown in Figure 5–1A. The high correlation between unit labor cost and wholesale prices that has existed in the past is also evident from this chart.

Further refinements can be introduced, particularly with respect to commodity prices. Thus, whenever demand deposits of banks increase, the

FIGURE 5–1A

UNIT LABOR COST IN MANUFACTURING AND WHOLESALE PRICES
1947–1949 = 100

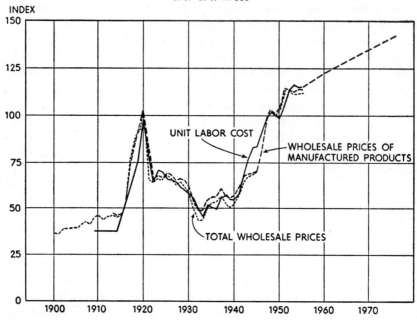

money supply and purchasing power are augmented and, other things being equal, there is an increase in demand and in prices. Speculative purchases
and withholding from the market in anticipation of higher prices is thereby
induced, with the result that there is a further increase in demand over the
short term. Conversely, a decrease in the demand deposits of banks means
a decline in the money supply and purchasing power, and a fall in demand
and prices if other factors remain constant. Speculative sales and decreases
of inventory in anticipation of still lower prices is thereby induced, which
serve to contract demand still further over the short term. A crucial variable
to observe, therefore, is the *rate of change of demand deposits*, or *money
gradient* as it is sometimes called, since it will often tend to signal an advance warning of an impending change in the trend of wholesale prices of
agricultural commodities. And as pointed out in Chapter 1, successful forecasts are most valuable at the change in trend, since it is at these turning
points that new decisions must be made and new plans must be formulated.
Figure 5–1B shows that even agricultural prices, which are extremely sensitive to economic change, have followed the money gradient at changes in
trend.

Technological Factors. The influences of technology are often impossible to predict, but some understanding of the effects of technological
change are of use in providing a better basis for explaining past develop-

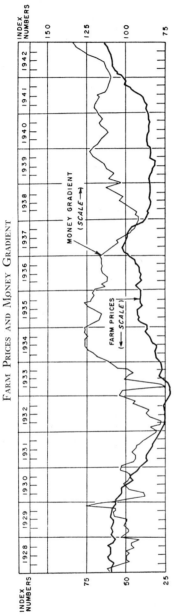

FIGURE 5-1B

FARM PRICES AND MONEY GRADIENT

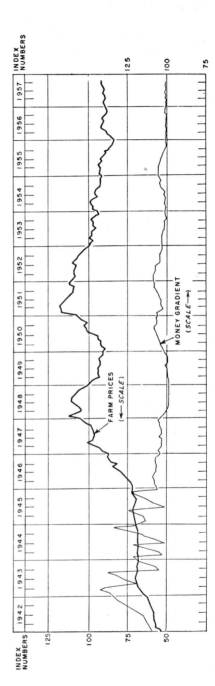

ments. In most instances, a technological development has at least two effects: (1) it increases output per man hour, and (2) it increases total output. It ultimately results, therefore, in lower unit labor costs and hence is a significant means of increasing profits. The importance of this will become more apparent in subsequent discussions, when efforts are made either to explain or evaluate the role of technology as a "variable" in a particular forecasting problem.

FARM COMMODITY PRICES

What are the forces at work that determine fluctuations in farm commodity prices? In the light of what was said in the previous section, supply, demand, and monetary factors, each weighted in the over-all relationship, should provide a reliable answer to the question. This is noteworthy because farm inventories, which have long been a problem to the industry, have in the years following World War II been even more distorted by the federal support program. Nevertheless, even with the government operating as an important factor in the market, farm prices have not shifted much from the level indicated by supply, demand, and monetary forces. This may be illustrated by the following study of general farm prices as well as the studies of specific commodity prices to be discussed afterward.

General Farm Prices

If we consider first the aggregate farm market, a comprehensive picture of farm price behavior can be established which provides a basis for analyzing the prices of particular farm commodities. Thus, as a comprehensive measure of agricultural prices, the BLS series of wholesale farm prices serves as a dependent variable since it shows the combined price movements of representative farm products such as fruits, vegetables, grains, eggs, livestock, milk, poultry, and plant and animal fibers. The remaining independent variables in the analysis are income as a measure of demand, agricultural production and stocks as a measure of supply, and foreign exchange rates as a measure of the monetary factor. The relations among these variables are explained and illustrated in the following paragraphs. First, however, it should be noted that the separate variables, listed in Table 5–1, have been plotted as a time series in Figure 5–2. It is apparent from this chart that farm prices tend to fluctuate directly with the income factor, inversely with production and stocks, and, in 1933–34, directly with foreign exchange rates. It remains for correlation analyses to reveal these relationships more clearly, as shown in Table 5–2 and the charts.

Demand Factor. Although disposable income as a measure of demand provides a good explanation of price fluctuations, a much better result is obtained by utilizing a weighted combination of disposable income and the value of consumers' new orders for semidurable goods. The reason

TABLE 5-1

WHOLESALE FARM PRICES AND RELATED DATA INDEXES
(1947–49 = 100)

Year	(1) BLS Price Index	(2) Agricultural Production	(3) Agricultural Stocks*	(4) Foreign Exchange Rates†	(5) Income Factor ‡
1928	59.1	74	79	64.9	43.1
1929	58.6	74	80	64.5	45.4
1930	49.3	72	86	63.2	42.2
1931	36.2	73	100	59.8	34.8
1932	26.9	71	109	53.0	26.6
1933	28.7	72	105	60.4	25.3
1934	36.5	71	85	68.0	28.6
1935	44.0	66	76	66.4	32.2
1936	45.2	71	74	65.5	36.5
1937	48.2	74	82	63.4	39.2
1938	38.2	76	107	61.7	36.1
1939	36.5	79	118	57.9	38.9
1940	37.8	80	121	53.9	42.0
1941	46.9	82	129	54.5	51.6
1942	59.1	90	115	54.6	64.8
1943	68.4	92	105	54.6	73.0
1944	69.0	99	117	54.7	80.7
1945	71.6	99	117	54.5	82.5
1946	83.1	97	100	54.2	87.7
1947	100.0	100	74	54.2	93.2
1948	107.3	97	79	54.2	103.3
1949	92.8	103	101	51.8	103.5
1950	97.5	99	106	47.7	113.4
1951	113.4	101	107	48.6	124.3
1952	107.0	104	109	48.5	130.3
1953	97.0	108	127	47.5	137.2
1954	95.7	109	146	45.8	139.4
1955	89.7	112	157	44.3	148.4
1956	88.4	117	169	43.9	160.0

*Col. 3: Stocks adjusted for government stocks. Average for 1947–49 of total stocks including government stocks equals 100. Military demand also excluded.

†Col. 4: Index of prices of selected foreign countries weighted according to their trade with the United States.

‡Col. 5: Income Factor = .85 disposable income *plus* .15 value of consumers' semidurable goods. See Table 5–3 for details of construction.

TABLE 5–2

CALCULATION OF FARM PRICES

Year	(1) Price Equivalent of Income	(2) Production	(3) Stocks	(4) Foreign Exchange Rates	(5) Calculated Prices (1)×(2)× (3)×(4)	(6) Actual Prices	(7) Residual Ratios (6)÷(5)
			Price Adjustments for:				
1928............	44.1	1.13	1.06	1.03	54.4	59.1	1.086
1929............	46.5	1.13	1.05	1.03	57.9	58.6	1.012
1930............	43.6	1.15	1.02	1.02	53.2	49.3	.927
1931............	35.4	1.14	.95	1.02	39.1	36.2	.926
1932............	27.0	1.16	.91	1.01	28.8	26.9	.934
1933............	25.3	1.15	.93	1.02	27.6	28.7	1.039
1934............	29.1	1.16	1.02	1.04	35.8	36.5	1.019
1935............	32.7	1.22	1.07	1.03	44.0	44.0	1.000
1936............	37.3	1.16	1.08	1.03	48.1	45.2	.940
1937............	40.2	1.13	1.04	1.02	49.1	48.2	.982
1938............	37.2	1.11	.92	1.02	38.7	38.2	.987
1939............	39.8	1.08	.87	1.02	38.1	36.5	.958
1940............	43.2	1.07	.86	1.01	40.2	37.8	.940
1941............	53.4	1.05	.83	1.01	47.0	46.9	.998
1942............	68.2	.97	.88	1.01	60.0	59.1	.985
1943............	77.0	.94	.93	1.01	68.0	68.4	1.005
1944............	85.7	.90	.88	1.01	68.6	69.0	1.006
1945............	87.6	.90	.88	1.01	70.1	71.6	1.021
1946............	93.7	.91	.95	1.01	81.8	83.1	1.016
1947............	99.1	.89	1.08	1.01	96.2	100.	1.040
1948............	110.5	.91	1.06	1.01	107.7	107.3	.968
1949............	110.5	.86	.95	1.01	91.2	92.8	1.018
1950............	121.5	.90	.93	.99	100.7	97.5	.968
1951............	134.4	.88	.92	1.00	108.8	113.4	1.042
1952............	141.0	.86	.91	1.00	111.5	107.0	.960
1953............	149.2	.83	.83	.99	101.8	97.0	.953
1954............	151.2	.82	.76	.99	94.4	95.7	1.014
1955............	161.7	.80	.72	.99	92.2	89.7	.973
1956............	174.0	.76	.68	.99	89.0	88.4	.993

FIGURE 5–2

BLS WHOLESALE FARM PRICES AND RELATED DATA

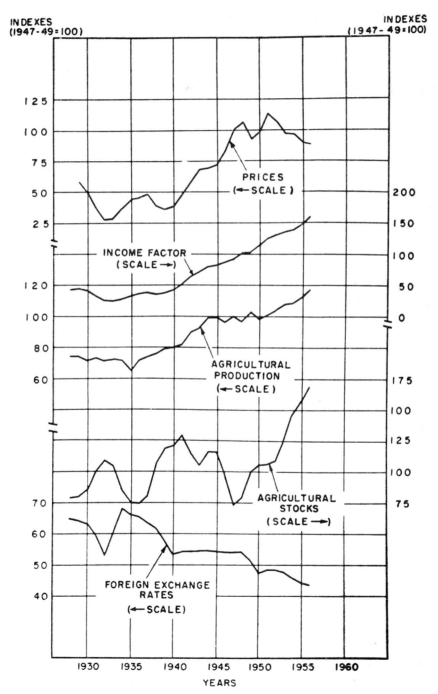

for this is that disposable income tends to be a slow-moving upward-trending series, whereas the new orders' series is more susceptible to cyclical forces in the economy. The new orders' series, therefore, by being combined with the income series, exercises a dampening effect on the latter over the long run. The procedure for combining the variables is illustrated in Table 5–3.

Figure 5–3 shows the freehand regression line or line of relationship between prices and the income factor. Since the chart is plotted on log-

TABLE 5–3

CONSTRUCTION OF VARIABLES FOR TOTAL FARM PRICES

Year	(1) Disposable Income	(2) Value of New Orders*	(3) Total Income Factor .85 (1) +.15 (2)	(4) Index of (3) (1947–49 = 100)
1928	78.8 †	12.99 †	68.95 †	43.1
1929	83.1	13.68	72.65	45.4
1930	74.4	10.84	67.43	42.2
1931	63.8	9.95	55.66	34.8
1932	48.7	7.45	42.51	26.6
1933	45.7	10.54	40.38	25.3
1934	52.0	10.38	45.76	28.6
1935	58.3	12.28	51.44	32.2
1936	66.2	13.66	58.35	36.5
1937	71.0	14.93	62.64	39.2
1938	65.7	12.30	57.65	36.1
1939	70.4	15.94	62.19	38.9
1940	76.1	15.99	67.10	42.0
1941	93.0	22.91	82.44	51.6
1942	117.5	24.61	103.59	64.8
1943	133.5	28.24	116.74	73.0
1944	146.8	27.56	128.93	80.7
1945	150.4	27.17	131.88	82.5
1946	159.2	32.80	140.22	87.7
1947	169.0	35.80	149.07	93.2
1948	187.6	37.40	165.11	103.3
1949	188.2	36.00	165.40	103.5
Avg. 1947–49			159.86	
1950	206.1	40.60	181.29	113.4
1951	226.1	43.20	198.68	124.3
1952	237.4	43.60	208.34	130.3
1953	250.2	44.70	219.41	137.2
1954	254.3	44.20	222.83	139.4
1955	270.6	47.90	237.19	148.4
1956	286.7	48.40	250.96	160.0

*Col. 2: Consumers' semidurables.
†In billions of dollars.

FIGURE 5-3

BLS WHOLESALE FARM PRODUCT PRICES VERSUS INCOME FACTOR

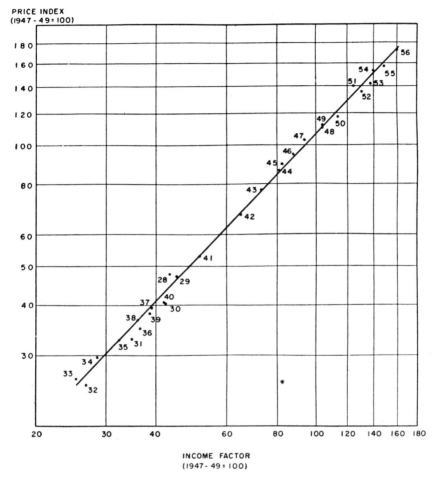

PRICE INDEX
(1947 - 49 = 100)

INCOME FACTOR
(1947 - 49 = 100)

arithmic paper, the equation for the line can be estimated from the chart (as given by the formulas on pp. 67–68):

$$\text{Price} = .91 \ (\text{Income Factor})^{1.035}$$

And since the equation is linear in the logarithms, the exponent reveals the elasticity directly. Thus, a 1 per cent change in the income factor produces, on the average, a 1.04 per cent change in farm prices, indicating an elasticity of about unity.

It is clear from the charts, especially Figure 5–2, that while the income factor accounts for the general growth in demand for farm products, it does not explain periods of price weaknesses such as the drop in prices from 1937–38 and again in 1953, nor the sudden strength in prices in the period 1933–34. These variations are explained primarily by stocks or inventories (the supply factor) and foreign exchange rates (the monetary factor). The generally low level of prices relative to income is also found to be explained by the continuing growth in agricultural production and the substantial increases in output per agricultural worker.

Supply Factor. Agricultural production and agricultural stocks are jointly involved in determining the level of supply at any given time. Since 1928, substantial technological improvements in farming and a strong growth in population have combined to produce a general increase in agricultural production. The net relationship of farm prices to farm production is illustrated in Figure 5–4. This chart is constructed by taking the devia-

FIGURE 5–4

BLS Wholesale Farm Prices versus Agricultural Production

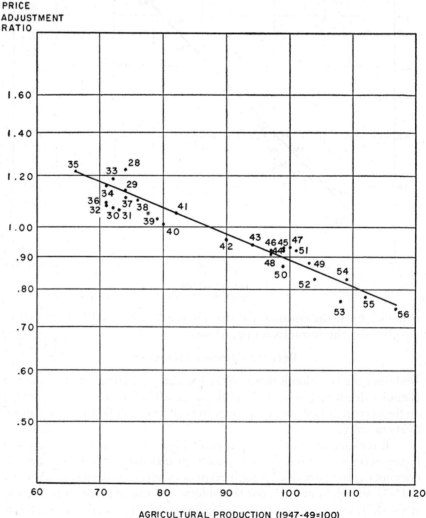

PRICE ADJUSTMENT RATIO

AGRICULTURAL PRODUCTION (1947-49=100)

tions of the dots from the regression line in the previous chart, Figure 5–3, and plotting these deviations (expressed as the ratio of actual to expected values) against the next independent variable, agricultural production. (In other words, as explained in Chapter 3, the residuals about the regression line can be expressed either in absolute amounts by noting the differences between the actual and expected values, or in ratio or percentage form by dividing the actual by the expected values.) The result is the freehand regression line in Figure 5–4. Its downward movement indicates that an inverse relationship exists between production and prices.

If the deviations (expressed as a ratio of actual to estimated values)

FIGURE 5–5

BLS Wholesale Farm Prices versus Agricultural Stocks

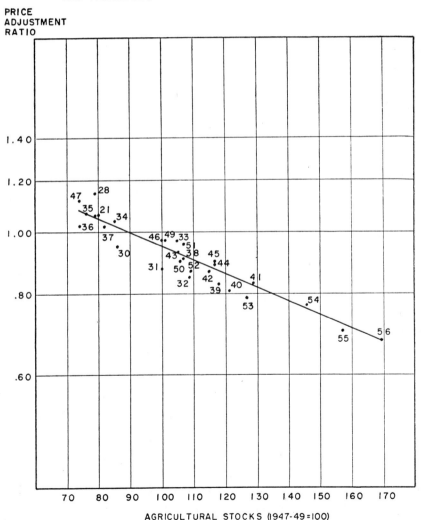

PRICE
ADJUSTMENT
RATIO

AGRICULTURAL STOCKS (1947-49=100)

are calculated from the chart, and the results are plotted against the next supply variable, agricultural stocks, the regression line in Figure 5–5 is obtained. The series on agricultural stocks consists of a weighted combination of the volume of farm products such as wheat, corn, oats, barley, cotton, poultry, and eggs, with the weights based on 1947–49 conditions. The data are also adjusted to exclude military purchases and one half of the government's holdings of farm commodities. The latter adjustment is based on some preliminary research which indicated that about half the government's stock exerts an influence on market prices.

Monetary Factor. As a measure of the relevant monetary factor, an index of foreign exchange rates relative to the dollar was used as the last independent variable in the analysis. Although of less significance now in view of the greater degree of exchange stability, changes in foreign exchange rates relative to the dollar are especially important in explaining price variations during the world-wide currency devaluation period of the 'thirties. Accordingly, when the deviations (in the form of ratios) of Figure 5–5 are plotted against the foreign exchange variable, the result obtained is the regression of Figure 5–6A. As will be seen momentarily, a better fit for the 1930's was thus achieved than might otherwise have oc-

FIGURE 5–6A

BLS WHOLESALE FARM PRICES VERSUS FOREIGN EXCHANGE RATES

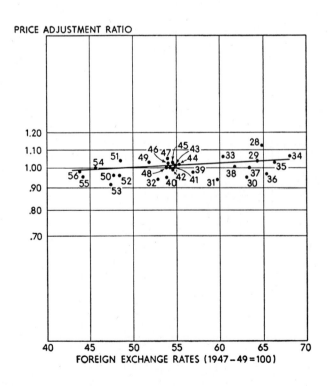

PRICE ADJUSTMENT RATIO

curred, by utilizing this variable. Since this is its chief advantage, however, it could probably be omitted from an analysis involving, for example, only post–World War II data.

Conclusion. How well have these four variables explained the fluctuations in actual farm prices? An indication is given in Figure 5–6B, where

FIGURE 5–6B

BLS WHOLESALE FARM PRICES AND TIME TREND

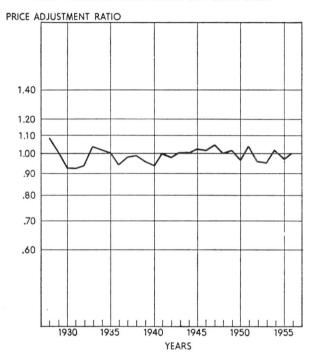

the ratio of actual prices to the product of the above factors is plotted. The ratios fluctuate closely about 1.00, indicating that the four factors have explained the major variations in farm prices. The product of these factors, therefore, yields an adequate annual calculation of farm price. A comparison of the actual and calculated farm prices is shown in Figure 5–7, the dashed line being the line that is equivalent to the product of the previous regression lines.[1] This dashed line need not be obtained by the mathematical

[1] In addition to the equation for Figure 5–3 which was already given in the text, the equations for the remaining regression lines can be estimated from the graphs as follows, using the relevant formula on pp. 67–68:

Figure 5–4: log Price = −.0038 (Production) + .330
Figure 5–5: log Price = −.0021 (Stocks) + .188
Figure 5–6A: log Price = .001 (Exchange Rates) − .052

The product of these equations (including the one for Figure 5–3) gives the final predicting equation, the geometric equivalent of which is the dashed line in Figure 5–7.

FIGURE 5-7

BLS WHOLESALE FARM PRICES ACTUAL VERSUS CALCULATED

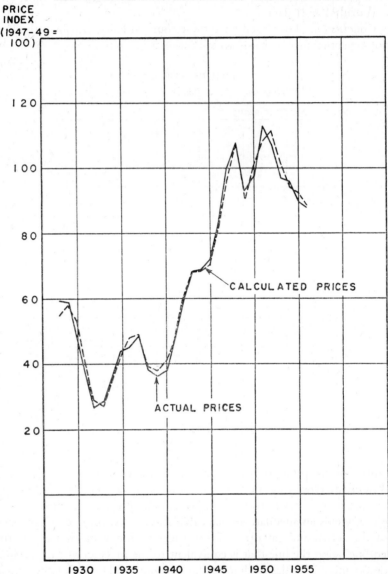

method just described in the footnote; it can also be derived by straight-forward tabular and graphic procedures as explained in Chapter 3. If, however, the separate equations are combined mathematically, they produce a formula of the type

$$\text{Price} = (\text{Income})^A \times 10^{B\ (\text{Production})} \times 10^{C\ (\text{Stocks})} \times 10^{D\ (\text{Exchange Rates})}$$

where the letters are constants whose values are determined by correlation analysis, as illustrated in the following price studies of specific commodities.

Corn Prices *

How can the general principles and procedures developed in the previous paragraphs be applied to the analysis of particular commodities? In the following paragraphs, a model of corn prices is constructed utilizing the above-mentioned concepts and techniques. Some modifications, of course, are necessary at times in order to allow for peculiarities and differences that are associated with corn prices in particular as compared to farm prices in general. However, the principles involved are basically the same as will be readily recognized.

Price Determinants. In analyzing corn prices, only demand and supply factors are needed; monetary factors of an international nature (e.g., foreign exchange rates) need not be considered because corn is primarily a domestic commodity, and because the income factor takes account of changes in domestic wage levels brought about by monetary conditions.

The demand variables entering into the analysis are : (1) an income factor (defined as cash income from meat animals plus 5 per cent of disposable income plus 10 per cent of the value of consumers' new orders for semidurable goods), and (2) animals on farms. The supply variables employed are: (1) corn production, (2) corn stocks (equal to one half of government stocks deducted from total stocks), (3) wheat production less exports, (4) wheat stocks, and (5) other feed grain production. All the data and tabular analyses are shown in Tables 5–4 through 5–8 and may be used for reference. Our attention will center mainly on the charts because they reveal more clearly the essential relationships between the variables.

Before beginning, it may be noted that each series employed in the analysis was divided by its standard deviation, thereby placing all the series on comparable scales. As explained on pp. 74–75, the reason for this is that the slope of the regression line should be influenced only by the relation between the variables and not by the units of quotation as well.

Analysis. The separate variables are plotted first as ordinary time series in Figures 5–8A and 5–8B on pp. 116 and 117, in order to observe their general behavior over the years. It is apparent from this, at least roughly, that a positive relationship exists between corn prices and both income and animals on farms, and a negative relationship between corn prices and the remaining variables. It remains for the subsequent charts, therefore, to exhibit these relationships more explicitly.

The historic record of the uses of corn reveals that about 90 per cent is fed directly to livestock, approximately 7 per cent is sold commercially of which about half is also used for livestock feed, and the remainder of commercial sales is used to manufacture either food or industrial products. On the basis of this information, the income factor was constructed as shown in Table 5–8 and at the bottom of Figure 5–9. The regression line in the diagram indicates that a positive relationship exists between corn prices and income, and that for every 1 per cent change in the income fac-

TABLE 5–4

CORN PRICES AND RELATED DATA

Crop Year Beginning August	(1) Corn Prices (Cents per Bushel)	(2) Income Factor (Billions of Dollars)	(3) Corn (Millions of Bushels) Production	(4) Corn (Millions of Bushels) Stocks	(5) Animals on Farms (Jan. 1)	(6) Wheat (Millions of Bushels) Production	(7) Wheat (Millions of Bushels) Stocks (July 1)	(8) Other Feed Grain Prod. (Mil. Tons)
1921.......	54.4	5.83	2,928	1,074	156	819	124	21.8
1922.......	73.8	6.53	2,707	875	158	847	96	23.4
1923.......	84.3	6.98	2,875	824	157	759	132	25.1
1924.......	114.7	7.36	2,225	658	151	842	137	28.3
1925.......	79.1	7.88	2,798	845	149	669	108	28.6
1926.......	79.6	7.89	2,547	812	153	832	97	24.3
1927.......	97.3	7.99	2,616	726	154	875	109	25.4
1928.......	92.9	8.49	2,666	664	153	914	113	30.9
1929.......	86.6	7.94	2,516	681	154	824	227	25.8
1930.......	69.2	6.58	2,080	576	153	887	291	28.6
1931.......	36.3	5.00	2,576	749	156	942	313	24.7
1932.......	32.0	4.37	2,930	972	160	756	375	29.0
1933.......	49.8	4.42	2,398	853	154	552	378	16.9
1934.......	84.9	5.52	1,449	551	141	526	273	12.0
1935.......	68.8	6.51	2,299	626	139	628	146	27.8
1936.......	116.2	7.42	1,506	456	138	630	140	17.0
1937.......	66.0	6.80	2,643	740	138	874	83	26.0
1938.......	48.8	7.09	2,549	910	149	920	153	25.3
1939.......	57.5	7.60	2,581	986	156	741	250	23.4
1940.......	66.7	9.02	2,457	1,080	156	815	280	29.6
1941.......	79.1	11.69	2,652	1,199	167	942	385	30.6
1942.......	94.5	14.54	3,069	1,271	192	969	631	34.6
1943.......	112.5	15.61	2,966	1,078	193	744	619	28.8
1944.......	115.1	16.00	3,088	1,070	173	861	317	29.8
1945.......	131.6	17.16	2,869	1,016	167	697	279	33.3
1946.......	172.4	19.83	3,217	1,081	160	732	101	32.8
1947.......	238.7	22.04	2,355	868	153	870	83	28.0
1948.......	146.2	21.98	3,605	1,011	159	785	196	34.2
1949.......	134.3	22.33	3,239	1,355	164	796	307	29.1
1950.......	169.0	25.59	3,075	1,429	168	643	425	35.3
1951.......	183.0	26.61	2,926	1,317	167	501	396	30.8
1952.......	162.0	26.33	3,292	1,166	159	976	254	27.3
1953.......	156.0	25.80	3,210	1,312	157	945	562	27.4
1954.......	152.0	26.29	3,058	1,396	162	700	934	37.8
1955.......	134.0	27.07	3,230	1,482	166	584	1,036	40.0
1956.......	136.4	28.47	3,451	1,626	163	646	1,033	32.7

Sources: Columns (1), (3), (4), (5), (6), (7) from U.S. Department of Agriculture. Construction of variables is presented in Table 5–8.

TABLE 5–5

CORN PRICES AND RELATED DATA
(In Units of Standard Deviations)

Crop Year Beginning August	Corn Price	Income Factor	Corn Production	Corn Stocks	Animals on Farms, Jan. 1	Wheat Production	Wheat Stocks, July 1	Other Feed Grain Production
1921......	1.16	.71	6.42	2.75	12.20	6.36	.49	3.89
1922......	1.58	.80	5.93	3.05	12.85	6.58	.38	4.18
1923......	1.81	.85	6.30	2.87	12.76	5.90	.52	4.48
1924......	2.46	.86	4.87	2.30	12.28	6.54	.54	5.05
1925......	1.69	.97	6.13	2.95	12.11	5.20	.43	5.11
1926......	1.70	.97	5.58	2.83	12.44	6.46	.38	4.34
1927......	2.08	.98	5.73	2.53	12.52	6.80	.43	4.54
1928......	1.99	1.04	5.84	2.32	12.44	7.10	.45	5.52
1929......	1.85	.97	5.52	2.38	12.52	6.40	.90	4.61
1930......	1.48	.81	4.56	2.01	12.44	6.89	1.15	5.11
1931......	.78	.61	5.65	2.61	12.68	7.32	1.24	4.41
1932......	.69	.54	6.42	3.39	13.01	5.87	1.48	5.18
1933......	1.07	.54	5.26	3.33	12.52	4.29	1.49	3.02
1934......	1.82	.68	3.18	1.92	10.65	4.09	1.08	2.14
1935......	1.47	.80	5.04	2.18	11.30	4.88	.58	4.96
1936......	2.49	.91	3.30	1.59	11.22	4.89	.55	3.04
1937......	1.41	.83	5.79	2.58	11.22	6.79	.33	4.64
1938......	1.04	.87	5.59	3.17	12.11	7.15	.60	4.52
1939......	1.23	.93	5.66	3.44	12.68	5.76	.99	4.18
1940......	1.43	1.10	5.39	3.77	12.68	6.33	1.11	5.29
1941......	1.69	1.43	5.81	4.18	13.58	7.32	1.52	5.46
1942......	2.02	1.78	6.73	4.43	15.61	7.53	2.49	6.18
1943......	2.41	1.91	6.50	3.76	15.69	5.78	2.45	5.14
1944......	2.46	1.96	6.77	3.73	14.06	6.69	1.25	5.32
1945......	2.82	2.10	6.29	3.54	13.58	5.41	1.10	5.95
1946......	3.69	2.43	7.05	3.77	13.01	5.69	.40	5.86
1947......	5.11	2.70	5.16	3.03	12.44	6.76	.33	5.00
1948......	3.13	2.69	7.90	3.53	12.93	6.10	.77	6.11
1949......	2.88	2.73	7.10	4.73	13.33	6.18	1.21	5.20
1950......	3.62	3.13	6.74	4.99	13.66	4.99	1.68	6.30
1951......	3.92	3.26	6.41	4.60	13.58	3.89	1.57	5.50
1952......	3.47	3.22	7.22	4.07	12.93	7.58	1.00	4.87
1953......	3.34	3.16	7.04	4.58	12.76	7.34	2.22	4.89
1954......	3.25	3.22	6.70	4.87	13.17	5.44	3.69	6.75
1955......	2.87	3.31	7.08	5.17	13.50	4.54	4.09	7.14
1956......	2.92	3.49	7.56	5.67	13.25	5.02	4.08	5.84

TABLE 5-6

CALCULATION OF CORN PRICES

(In Units of Standard Deviations)

Crop Year Beginning August	(1) Price Equivalent of Income	(2) Corn Production	(3) Corn Stocks	(4) Animals on Farms	(5) Wheat Production	(6) Wheat Stocks	(7) Other Feed Grain Production
				Price Adjustments for:			
1921........	1.12	.906	.848	.992	.981	1.016	1.022
1922........	1.27	.973	.959	1.050	.963	1.022	1.011
1923........	1.36	.917	.991	1.042	1.021	1.015	.999
1924........	1.38	1.057	1.095	.999	.966	1.014	.978
1925........	1.56	.932	.977	.984	1.083	1.020	.975
1926........	1.56	.985	.998	1.013	.973	1.022	1.004
1927........	1.59	.970	1.052	1.020	.945	1.020	.997
1928........	1.70	.960	1.091	1.013	.921	1.018	.960
1929........	1.58	.991	1.08	1.020	.978	.994	.994
1930........	1.28	1.090	1.153	1.013	.938	.981	.975
1931........	.96	.978	1.037	1.035	.904	.976	1.002
1932........	.81	.906	.904	1.065	1.023	.964	.972
1933........	.82	1.016	.914	1.020	1.170	.963	1.057
1934........	1.05	1.251	1.170	.866	1.191	.985	1.093
1935........	1.26	1.040	1.120	.917	1.113	1.011	.981
1936........	1.46	1.237	1.240	.910	1.113	1.013	1.056
1937........	1.32	.964	1.040	.910	.946	1.025	.993
1938........	1.39	.983	.940	.984	.918	1.010	.997
1939........	1.50	.977	.896	1.035	1.033	.989	1.011
1940........	1.81	1.003	.846	1.035	.984	.983	.969
1941........	2.42	.962	.787	1.119	.904	.962	.962
1942........	3.09	.878	.753	1.338	.889	.913	.936
1943........	3.34	.898	.847	1.348	1.031	.915	.974
1944........	3.43	.874	.852	1.168	.954	.976	.967
1945........	3.71	.917	.880	1.119	1.064	.983	.944
1946........	4.35	.851	.846	1.065	1.039	1.021	.948
1947........	4.90	1.026	.963	1.013	.949	1.025	.979
1948........	4.88	.781	.882	1.057	1.003	1.001	.939
1949........	4.97	.846	.714	1.095	.996	.978	.972
1950........	5.78	.877	.682	1.127	1.103	.953	.931
1951........	6.04	.906	.731	1.119	1.211	.959	.961
1952........	5.97	.836	.802	1.057	.885	.989	.984
1953........	5.83	.851	.733	1.042	.903	.926	.984
1954........	5.96	.881	.745	1.080	1.061	.856	.916
1955........	6.19	.848	.661	1.112	1.146	.838	.902
1956........	6.51	.808	.605	1.087	1.100	.838	.948

TABLE 5-6 (*Continued*)

Crop Year Beginning August	(8) Product of Specific Factors (1)×(2)× (3)×(4)×(5) ×(6)×(7)	(9) Residuals Including Trend (2)÷(8)	(10) Time Trend of (9)	(11) Calculated Price (8)×(10)	(12) Actual Prices	(13) Final Residual (12)÷(11)
1921	.870	1.332	1.44	1.25	1.16	.925
1922	1.238	1.269	1.37	1.70	1.58	.929
1923	1.333	1.359	1.32	1.76	1.81	1.030
1924	1.529	1.612	1.27	1.94	2.46	1.269
1925	1.506	1.125	1.22	1.83	1.69	.922
1926	1.551	1.094	1.18	1.83	1.70	.927
1927	1.592	1.309	1.14	1.81	2.08	1.148
1928	1.620	1.225	1.11	1.80	1.99	1.104
1929	1.666	1.107	1.09	1.82	1.85	1.016
1930	1.463	1.008	1.06	1.56	1.48	.951
1931	.881	.872	1.04	.92	.78	.848
1932	.677	1.023	1.03	.69	.69	.993
1933	.925	1.159	1.02	.94	1.07	1.136
1934	1.705	1.068	1.01	1.72	1.82	1.056
1935	1.481	.989	1.00	1.49	1.47	.988
1936	2.425	1.021	.99	2.40	2.49	1.037
1937	1.155	1.214	.975	1.13	1.41	1.245
1938	1.167	.885	.965	1.13	1.04	.917
1939	1.400	.870	.96	1.34	1.23	.918
1940	1.483	.960	.95	1.41	1.43	1.011
1941	1.712	.983	.94	1.62	1.69	1.046
1942	2.077	.975	.935	1.94	2.02	1.043
1943	3.146	.765	.93	2.94	2.41	.820
1944	2.685	.917	.93	2.49	2.46	.986
1945	3.304	.853	.93	3.08	2.82	.917
1946	3.346	1.101	.93	3.12	3.69	1.183
1947	4.660	1.096	.93	4.34	5.11	1.178
1948	3.343	.934	.93	3.11	3.13	1.006
1949	3.110	.927	.93	2.89	2.88	.997
1950	3.817	.950	.93	3.54	3.62	1.022
1951	4.997	.786	.93	4.64	3.92	.845
1952	3.641	.951	.93	3.39	3.47	1.023
1953	3.116	1.072	.93	2.90	3.34	1.153
1954	3.508	.925	.93	3.27	3.25	.995
1955	3.377	.857	.93	3.11	2.87	.922
1956	3.015	.965	.93	2.80	2.92	1.043

TABLE 5–7

USES OF CORN

(In Millions of Bushels)

	(1)	(2)	(3)	(4)	(5)	(6)	(7)	(8)	(9)
			Alcohol and					Ratios	
Crop Year Beginning August	Dry Processing	Wet Processing	Distilled Spirits	Seed	Livestock Feed	Exports	Total Disappearance	(5) ÷ (7)	(6) ÷ (7)
1926......	91	82	8	18	2,398	16	2,613	92	.6
1927......	96	88	6	18	2,515	19	2,742	92	.7
1928......	99	87	10	18	2,359	41	2,613	90	1.5
1929......	93	80	10	19	2,315	8	2,524	92	.3
1930......	89	67	2	20	1,874	2	2,053	91	.1
1931......	87	63	5	20	2,296	4	2,474	92	.1
1932......	84	72	6	20	2,625	8	2,814	93	.3
1933......	88	71	12	18	2,255	4	2,447	92	.2
1934......	87	55	23	18	1,575	*	1,759	90	0
1935......	89	76	35	18	1,991	*	2,209	90	0
1936......	84	67	32	17	1,519	*	1,720	88	0
1937......	84	72	18	16	2,020	140	2,349	86	5.9
1938......	86	76	18	15	2,099	34	2,327	90	1.4
1939......	87	83	20	14	2,231	44	2,478	90	1.8
1940......	90	101	26	13	2,258	15	2,501	90	.6
1941......	93	127	55	12	2,500	20	2,807	89	.7
1942......	100	128	42	13	2,909	5	3,196	91	.1
1943......	102	121	11	13	2,866	10	3,123	92	.3
1944......	102	125	38	12	2,717	17	3,010	90	.5
1945......	94	112	28	12	2,747	20	3,013	91	.7
1946......	98	144	56	12	2,671	127	3,106	86	4.1
1947......	92	110	31	12	2,263	7	2,515	90	.3
1948......	93	117	30	12	2,554	111	2,916	88	3.8
1949......	91	128	36	11	2,834	107	3,207	88	3.3
1950......	94	133	45	12	2,790	107	3,181	88	3.4
1951......	93	124	27	12	2,848	76	3,179	90	2.4
1952......	93	130	17	12	2,618	140	3,011	87	4.6
1953......	90	128	23	13	2.710	97	3,061	89	3.1
1954......	90	139	23	13	2,589	92	2,944	88	3.1
1955......	89	141	27	12	2,734	108	3.100	88	3.5

*Less than one million.

TABLE 5-8

CONSTRUCTION OF VARIABLES

	(1)	(2)	(3)	(4)	(5)	(6)	(7)	(8)	(9)	(10)
	Income Factor, Billions of Dollars				Corn Stocks, Millions of Bu.			Wheat Production, Millions of Bu.		
Crop Year Beginning August	Cash Income from Meat Animals	Dis- posable Income	Value of New* Orders	Total Income Factor (1) + .05 (2) + .10 (3)	Total Stocks	CCC† Stocks	Net Stocks (5) − .5 (6)	Pro- duction (July 1)	Ex- ports‡	Produc- tion Ex- cluding Exports (8) −.5 (9)
1921	2.02	57.6	9.27	5.83	1,074		1,074	819		
1922	2.22	64.4	10.91	6.53	875		875	847		
1923	2.30	69.3	12.12	6.98	824		824	759		
1924	2.57	71.6	12.12	7.36	658		658	842		
1925	2.83	74.9	13.03	7.88	845		845	669		
1926	2.83	76.3	12.41	7.89	812		812	832		
1927	2.88	77.4	12.41	7.99	726		726	—		
1928	3.01	82.1	13.79	8.49	664		664	—		
1929	2.75	79.7	12.12	7.94	681		681	—		
1930	2.11	68.6	10.37	6.58	576		576	—		
1931	1.45	54.6	8.22	5.00	749		749	—		
1932	1.19	44.5	9.64	4.37	972		972	—		
1933	1.35	50.0	10.14	4.42	893	81	853	—		
1934	1.68	54.7	11.10	5.52	551	—	551	—		
1935	2.09	63.1	12.71	6.51	626	—	626	—		
1936	2.31	70.0	16.10	7.42	456	—	456	—		
1937	2.27	67.2	11.67	6.80	762	45	740	—		
1938	2.23	68.0	14.57	7.09	1,039	258	910	—		
1939	2.33	73.3	16.06	7.60	1,222	471	986	—		
1940	2.81	83.3	19.97	9.02	1,281	403	1,080	—		
1941	4.00	105.4	24.21	11.69	1,298	197	1,199	942	44	942
1942	5.30	130.9	27.05	14.54	1,275	8	1,271	969	56	969
1943	5.77	140.9	27.96	15.61	1,081	6	1,078	844	106	744
1944	5.80	150.9	26.60	16.00	1,074	9	1,070	1,060	199	861
1945	6.47	152.4	30.71	17.16	1,016	—	1,016	1,108	411	697
1946	8.17	164.3	34.48	19.83	1,085	9	1,081	1,152	420	732
1947	9.33	180.1	37.13	22.04	868	—	868	1,359	489	870
1948	8.84	190.5	36.25	21.98	1,257	493	1,011	1,295	510	785
1949	8.79	195.0	37.93	22.33	1,680	650	1,355	1,099	303	796
1950	10.31	218.8	43.38	25.59	1,672	487	1,429	1,019	376	643
1951	10.74	232.2	42.56	26.61	1,470	306	1,317	988	487	501
1952	9.45	247.2	45.17	26.33	1,456	580	1,166	1,306	330	976
1953	8.83	251.9	43.71	25.80	1,680	736	1,312	1,173	228	945
1954	8.53	262.0	46.56	26.29	1,831	870	1,396	984	284	700
1955	8.22	280.4	48.35	27.07	2,007	1,050	1,482	935	351	586
1956	8.78	295.8	49.00	28.47	2,226	1,200	1,626	997	351	646

*Col. 3: Value of consumers' semidurables.

†Col. 6: Support program began in 1933.

‡Col. 9: Prewar exports were generally small, and hence not included.

FIGURE 5–8A

CORN PRICES AND RELATED DATA

(Data Adjusted for Standard Deviations)

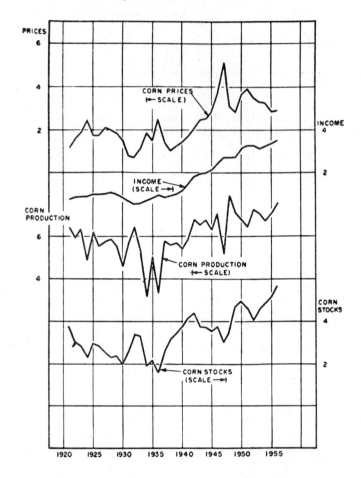

FIGURE 5-8B

CORN PRICES AND RELATED DATA

(Data Adjusted for Standard Deviations)

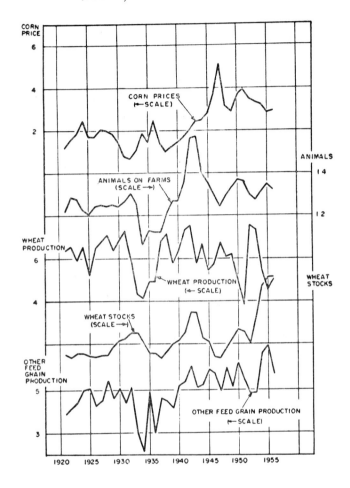

FIGURE 5-9

Corn Prices versus Income Factor

(Data Adjusted for Standard Deviations)

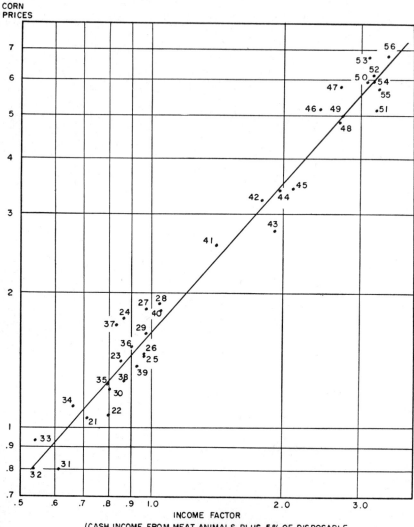

INCOME FACTOR

(CASH INCOME FROM MEAT ANIMALS PLUS 5% OF DISPOSABLE INCOME PLUS 10% OF THE VALUE OF NEW ORDERS FOR CONSUMERS' SEMI-DURABLE GOODS)

tor, prices tend to change by about 1.1 per cent in the same direction. The equation for this regression line may be estimated if desired (see pp. 67–68):

$$\text{Price} = .975 \, (\text{Income})^{1.11} \qquad (1)$$

where the exponent is the elasticity since the equation is linear in logarithms. That is, the equation may also be written log Price = log .975 + 1.11 log Income

since it is of the form $Y = ab^x$, or log Y = log a + X log b, as explained in Chapter 4, p. 67.

Corn production and corn stocks are taken into account in Figure 5–10A, B. In Figure 5–10A, the dots are obtained by calculating the actual-to-expected deviations from the previous chart (i.e., the ratio of the dots to

FIGURE 5–10A

CORN PRICES VERSUS CORN PRODUCTION

(Data Adjusted for Standard Deviations)

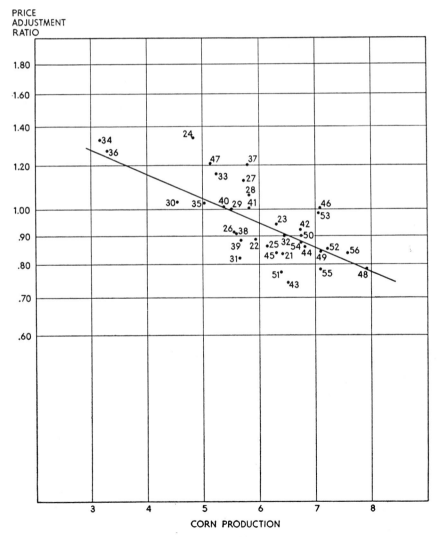

CORN PRODUCTION

FIGURE 5–10B

CORN PRICES VERSUS CORN STOCKS

(Data Adjusted for Standard Deviations)

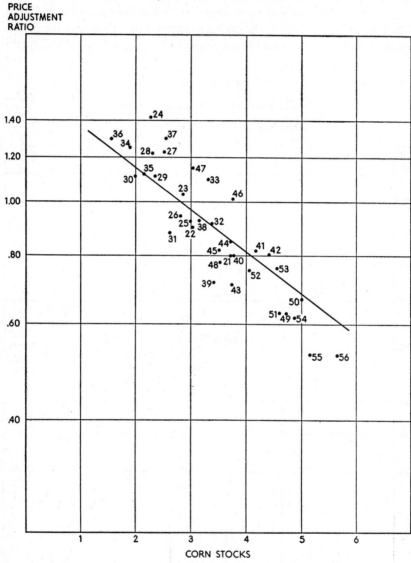

the regression line in Figure 5–9), and plotting the values, expressed as ratios, against the next independent variable, corn production. The resulting regression line, negatively sloped, indicates the inverse nature of the relationship between prices and production in that for every change of one standard deviation of production (equal to 456 million bushels), prices tend to change inversely by about 9 per cent. Unlike the previous chart which

FIGURE 5-11

CORN PRICES VERSUS ANIMALS ON FARMS

(Data Adjusted for Standard Deviations)

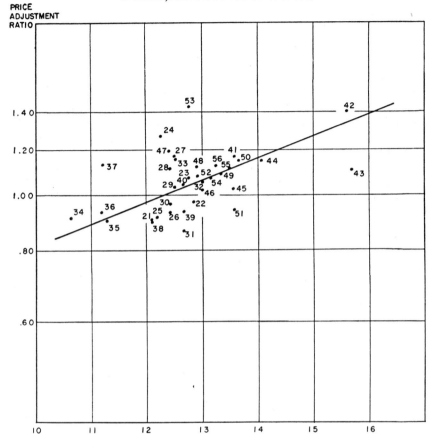

is logarithmic, this one (and the remaining ones in this study) it may be noted, is semilogarithmic. The equation for the regression line, as always, is optional in graphic analysis. It may be estimated, however, as

$$\text{Price} = 10^{[-.043 \,(\text{Corn Production}) + .235]} \tag{2}$$

or equivalently as

$$\log \text{Price} = -.043 \,(\text{Corn Production}) + .235$$

When the deviations of the dots from the regression line are calculated, and these deviations, expressed as ratios, are plotted against the corn stocks variable, the result obtained is the regression line in Figure 5–10B. According to the relationship shown, every change of one standard deviation of stocks (equal to 287 million bushels) tends to change prices inversely by 16 per cent. The equation of relationship is estimated to be

$$\text{Price} = 10^{[-.077 \text{ (Corn Stocks)} + .216]} \tag{3}$$

or equivalently

$$\log \text{Price} = -.077 \text{ (Corn Stocks)} + .216$$

Corn is consumed chiefly by hogs and to a smaller extent by horses, cattle, and poultry. The number of animals on farms, therefore, is a significant variable affecting the consumption of corn, and hence corn prices. The series, "Animals on Farms on January 1," is a combination of these animals weighted according to the average amount of grain consumed by each, and is constructed by the Department of Agriculture as are the other series used in these farm commodity studies. The ratio deviations from the previous chart are plotted against this series in Figure 5–11. According to the slope of the resulting regression line, every change of one standard devia-

FIGURE 5–12A

CORN PRICE VERSUS WHEAT PRODUCTION

(Data Adjusted for Standard Deviations)

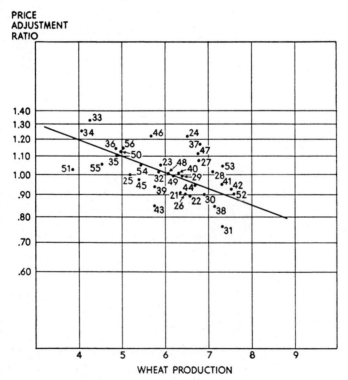

tion in animals on farms (equal to 12 million units) tends to produce a 9 per cent change in the same direction in corn prices. The regression equation is

$$\text{Price} = 10^{[.038 \,(\text{Animals}) \,+\, .018]} \tag{4}$$

or

$$\log \text{Price} = .038\,(\text{Animals}) + .018$$

The volume of wheat fed annually to livestock is often a significant part of total wheat disappearance, the proportion frequently amounting to between 5 and 30 per cent, and sometimes more. Wheat, therefore, is competitive with corn, and hence must be taken into account in an analysis of corn prices. Wheat production less wheat exports, of course, is the relevant variable to employ, since the volume of wheat exported does not compete as a domestic feed. Figure 5–12A presents the results of the relationship between corn prices and net wheat production. The vertical axis measures the ratio deviations of the dots from the regression line in the previous chart. The line of relationship obtained in Figure 5–12A indicates that for every change of one standard deviation in net wheat production (equal to 129

FIGURE 5–12B

CORN PRICES VERSUS WHEAT STOCKS

(Data Adjusted for Standard Deviations)

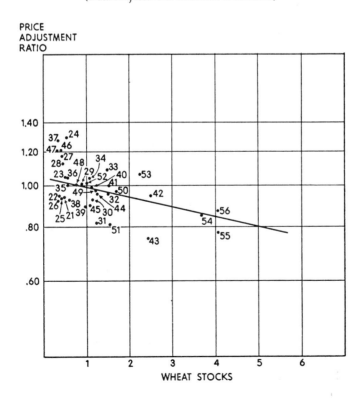

million bushels), price tends to change inversely by 8 per cent. The equation for the line may be written

$$\text{Price} = 10^{[-.037\ (\text{Wheat Production}) + .227]} \tag{5}$$

or in logarithmic form

$$\log \text{Price} = -.037\ (\text{Wheat Production}) + .227$$

Since wheat stocks are also an important source of demand for livestock feed, they must be taken into account along with wheat production. Accordingly, the ratio deviations from Figure 5–12A are plotted against wheat stocks as shown in Figure 5–12B. According to the regression line, a change of one standard deviation in wheat stocks (equal to 253 million bushels) changes prices by 5 per cent in a reverse direction. The equation for the regression line is estimated to be

$$\text{Price} = 10^{[-.023\ (\text{Wheat Stocks}) + .018]} \tag{6}$$

or

$$\log \text{Price} = -.023\ (\text{Wheat Stocks}) + .018$$

FIGURE 5–13A

CORN PRICES VERSUS OTHER FEED GRAINS

(Data Adjusted for Standard Deviations)

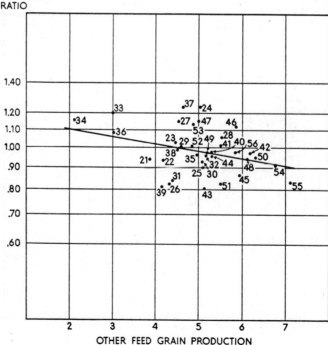

PRICE
ADJUSTMENT
RATIO

OTHER FEED GRAIN PRODUCTION

Still other grains compete with corn, but they can be adequately accounted for by treating them together as one variable. This has been done in Figure 5–13A, in which the ratio deviations from the previous chart are plotted against a weighted sum of oats, barley, and grain sorghums, shown on the horizontal axis as "other feed grain production." The regression line indicates that a change of one standard deviation produces an inverse change of 4 per cent in corn prices. The regression equation is estimated as

$$\text{Price} = 10^{\,[-.017\,(\text{Other Feed})\,+\,.075]} \tag{7}$$

or

$$\log \text{Price} = -.017\,(\text{Other Feed}) + .075$$

The deviations which now remain indicate that still other factors besides the ones included exercise an influence on corn prices. These other factors may be combined and treated as one variable under the heading of "time." That is, we take the ratio deviations of the dots from the regression line in Figure 5–13A, and plot them against "time" as shown in Figure 5–13B. Since the dots will be in chronological order, they may be connected,

FIGURE 5–13B

CORN PRICES VERSUS TIME TREND

(Data Adjusted for Standard Deviations)

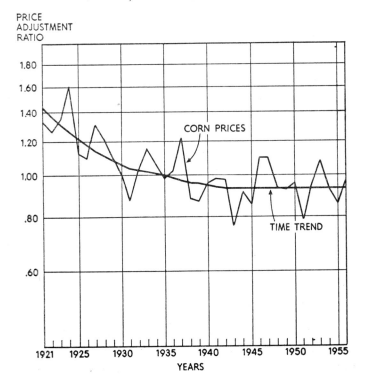

and a trend line, called a time trend, drawn through so as to represent the regression of corn prices on time after other factors (income, corn production, corn stocks, animals, wheat production, wheat stocks, and other feed) have been accounted for. Thus, the sharp relative decline in prices prior to 1940 reflects, among other things, the use of hybrid seeds, increased use of fertilizer, and improved cultural practices. None of these factors were treated separately in this analysis; all of them, however, are being allowed for by incorporating them in the analysis as a time trend. The equation for this time trend, TT, may be written

$$\text{Price} = 10^{TT} \tag{8}$$

or

$$\log \text{Price} = TT$$

Conclusion. The influence of each of the separate factors on price has now been obtained, and it remains to combine them into a unified whole. The procedure for accomplishing this can be either graphic or mathematical. The graphic method has already been explained and illustrated in Chapter 3. Briefly, it consists of combining the separate calculated values, either in an additive or multiplicative relation, directly in the work table, thereby producing a final column of calculated values of the dependent variable. These calculated values are then drawn on a final chart along with the actual values in order to facilitate visual comparison and to see how close a fit has been obtained. An example of such a chart is Figure 5–14.

The mathematical method consists, simply, of combining the equations for the separate regression lines into a single formula which then becomes the prediction equation. This equation, of course, will be the mathematical equivalent of the dashed line in Figure 5–14; hence, it is derived by either adding or multiplying the separate regression equations. Since a multiplicative relationship has been assumed here, the final predicting equation is

$$\text{Price} = .975 \, (\text{Income})^{1.11} \, 10^Z$$

where $Z =$ the sum of the exponents of 10 in equations (2) through (8) above. The calculations were presented in Tables 5–5 through 5–8 where they may be easily followed by anyone interested in mastering the procedure.

Cotton Prices

An analysis of cotton prices can be made along the same lines as corn prices, except for some modifications due to particular economic conditions which affect supply, demand, and monetary factors. Thus, the chief world sources of cotton are the United States, India, Russia, Egypt, Brazil, and China, with the United States in recent years consuming about 25 per cent of the world's total and supplying about 40 per cent of it. Hence, an analysis of cotton prices must consider not only domestic but also foreign

FIGURE 5–14

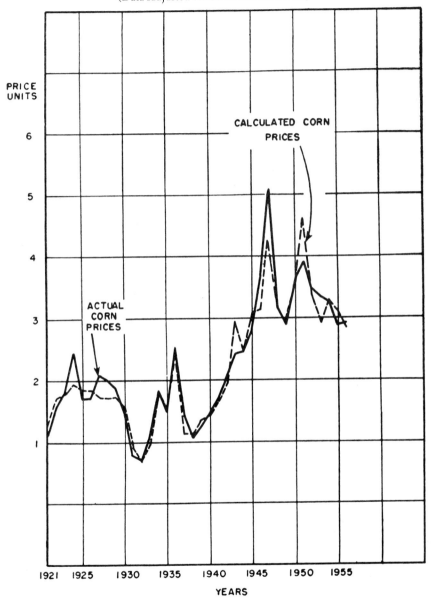

Corn Prices: Actual versus Calculated
(Data Adjusted for Standard Deviations)

factors, and these separate influences must be identified and measured in order to determine their combined effect on price.

Price Determinants. As before, three classes of forces—supply, demand, and monetary factors—are taken into account in this model of cotton prices. The supply factors include: (1) domestic cotton production plus one-half foreign production; (2) domestic stocks (adjusted to exclude one-half government stocks for reasons already explained) plus one-half foreign stocks; and (3) world production of substitutes, namely rayon, silk, wool, and noncellulosic fibers. Demand factors included in the model are: (1) world cotton consumption, and (2) an income factor (equal to 40 per cent of disposable income plus 60 per cent of the value of consumers' new orders for semidurable goods, as explained below). And finally, because of the international forces affecting cotton prices, the monetary factor chosen was the foreign exchange gradient, or the rate of change of foreign exchange, the measurement of which is also explained below.

As in the previous study, all data used in the analysis were adjusted to their respective standard deviations in order to place the series on comparable scales. Except for the series "other fiber production," which is on a calendar-year basis, each series is on a 12-month basis extending from August of one year through July of the next. The fiber production series, therefore, has a seven months' lead with respect to prices, and gives good results.

Price data used in the analysis are the averages of $15\frac{1}{16}''$ at 10 southern markets. Beginning with 1956, this series was replaced by the average price of $1''$ middling cotton in 14 markets. By means of the overlap in the two series for the years 1951–55, it was estimated that for 1956 and 1957, the price differential of $1''$ cotton averages about 1.2 cents per pound over $15\frac{1}{16}''$ cotton.

Analysis. The statistical data relevant to the analysis, and their processing, are presented in Tables 5–9 through 5–12, largely for reference purposes. Our attention may be focused on the charts since they serve as a guide in attempting to visualize relationships between variables. Thus, in Figure 5–15, the individual variables are plotted as time series as the first step in the analysis. Over-all patterns of relationship are thereby observed which are then developed more explicitly in the separate regression charts that follow. Since the statistical procedures are basically the same as in the previous study of corn prices, the analysis may be outlined briefly.

The most important variable affecting cotton prices is income. The relationship between price and income is shown in Figure 5–16. Since textiles and apparel represented about 60 per cent of consumers' new orders for semidurable goods during 1947–49, the income factor was constructed by combining 40 per cent of disposable income and 60 per cent of new orders. The regression line indicates that for every change of 1 per cent in income, cotton prices tend to change 1.1 per cent in the same direction. The formula for this line is estimated as (see pp. 67–68):

$$\text{Price} = .68 \ (\text{Income})^{1.11} \tag{1}$$

Since all of the dots do not fall on the regression line, factors other than income must be affecting cotton prices. To measure the influence of

TABLE 5-9

COTTON PRICES AND RELATED DATA

Year Beginning August	(1) Price* (Cents per Lb.)	(2) Income† Factor	(3) Cotton ‡ Production-Consumption Ratio	(4) Cotton ‡ Stocks-Consumption Ratio	(5) Other Fiber Production-Consumption Ratio	(6) Foreign Exchange Gradient
1921...........	18.39	28.6	.570	.561	80.4	102.9
1922...........	26.13	32.3	.684	.351	58.2	102.2
1923...........	30.44	35.0	.675	.232	56.3	95.9
1924...........	24.52	35.9	.837	.183	58.2	102.0
1925...........	19.98	37.8	.884	.198	57.4	100.0
1926...........	14.70	38.0	.911	.278	59.3	100.0
1927...........	20.02	38.4	.709	.320	60.8	100.0
1928...........	18.97	41.1	.792	.258	65.2	99.5
1929...........	16.24	39.2	.846	.264	70.0	98.5
1930...........	9.99	33.7	.841	.323	72.2	97.5
1931...........	6.09	26.8	.939	.381	74.1	88.5
1932...........	7.29	23.6	.749	.526	70.6	98.6
1933...........	11.00	26.1	.782	.457	71.3	121.0
1934...........	12.68	28.5	.625	.425	73.9	101.8
1935...........	11.88	32.9	.662	.291	72.6	98.9
1936...........	13.25	37.7	.757	.277	77.5	96.5
1937...........	9.09	33.9	.973	.286	88.2	98.2
1938...........	9.00	35.9	.705	.484	94.0	96.0
1939...........	10.09	39.0	.710	.442	104.7	90.1
1940...........	11.00	45.7	.778	.275	115.1	98.3
1941...........	18.31	56.7	.721	.332	129.6	100.7
1942...........	20.14	68.6	.808	.339	132.1	100.0
1943...........	20.65	73.1	.789	.457	121.2	99.9
1944...........	21.86	76.3	.800	.494	120.0	99.9
1945...........	25.96	79.4	.600	.566	94.2	99.6
1946...........	34.82	86.4	.561	.465	90.7	99.6
1947...........	34.58	94.3	.664	.264	93.1	100.0
1948...........	32.15	98.0	.779	.259	102.9	100.0
1949...........	31.83	100.8	.799	.184	103.5	91.7
1950...........	42.58	113.5	.611	.223	117.8	91.0
1951...........	39.42	118.4	.774	.217	122.9	91.5
1952...........	34.52	126.0	.761	.265	116.4	90.5
1953...........	33.55	127.0	.791	.303	124.4	89.5
1954...........	33.88	132.7	.718	.324	128.9	85.0
1955...........	34.38	141.2	.721	.342	138.1	84.0
1956...........	32.35	147.7	.680	.373	141.1	84.0

*Col. 1: 15/16" at 10 southern markets.
†Col. 2: .40 disposable income *plus* .60 value of consumers' semidurable goods new orders.
‡Col. 3; 4: Divided by trend of world cotton consumption.

TABLE 5-10

COTTON PRICES AND RELATED DATA
(All Data Adjusted for Standard Deviations) *

Year Beginning August	(1) Price	(2) Income	(3) Cotton Production	(4) Cotton Stocks	(5) Other Fiber Production	(6) Foreign Exchange Gradient
1921..........	1.80	1.50	5.82	4.09	3.08	18.15
1922..........	2.56	1.67	6.98	2.56	2.23	18.02
1923..........	2.98	1.80	6.89	1.69	2.16	16.91
1924..........	2.40	1.86	8.54	1.34	2.23	17.99
1925..........	1.96	1.95	9.02	1.45	2.20	17.64
1926..........	1.44	1.98	9.30	2.04	2.27	17.64
1927..........	1.96	2.01	7.23	2.34	2.33	17.64
1928..........	1.86	2.13	8.08	1.88	2.50	17.55
1929..........	1.59	2.07	8.63	1.93	2.68	17.37
1930..........	0.98	1.78	8.58	2.36	2.77	17.20
1931..........	0.60	1.42	9.58	2.78	2.84	15.61
1932..........	0.71	1.56	7.64	3.84	2.70	17.39
1933..........	1.08	1.30	7.98	3.34	2.73	21.34
1934..........	1.24	1.42	6.38	3.10	2.83	17.95
1935..........	1.16	1.64	6.75	2.12	2.78	17.44
1936..........	1.30	1.82	7.72	2.02	2.97	17.02
1937..........	0.89	1.75	9.92	2.09	3.38	17.32
1938..........	0.88	1.77	7.19	3.53	3.60	16.93
1939..........	1.07	1.90	7.25	3.23	4.01	15.89
1940..........	1.08	2.19	7.94	2.01	4.41	17.34
1941..........	1.79	2.74	7.36	2.42	4.97	17.76
1942..........	1.97	3.40	8.25	2.47	5.06	17.64
1943..........	2.02	3.66	8.05	3.34	4.64	17.62
1944..........	2.14	3.92	8.16	3.61	4.60	17.62
1945..........	2.54	3.96	6.12	4.13	3.61	17.57
1946..........	3.41	4.27	5.72	3.39	3.47	17.57
1947..........	3.39	4.68	6.78	1.93	3.57	17.64
1948..........	3.15	4.95	7.95	1.89	3.94	17.64
1949..........	3.12	5.06	8.15	1.34	3.97	16.17
1950..........	4.17	5.68	6.23	1.63	4.51	16.05
1951..........	3.86	6.03	7.90	1.58	4.71	16.14
1952..........	3.38	6.42	7.76	1.86	4.46	15.96
1953..........	3.29	6.54	8.07	2.21	4.77	15.78
1954..........	3.32	6.81	7.33	2.36	4.94	14.99
1955..........	3.37	7.28	7.36	2.50	5.29	14.81
1956..........	3.17	7.68	6.94	2.72	5.41	14.81

*Standard Deviations: Cotton Price = 10.2, Income = 38.5, Cotton Production Ratio = .098, Cotton Stocks Ratio = .137, Other Fiber Production Ratio = .261, Foreign Exchange Gradient = 5.7.

TABLE 5–11

CALCULATION OF COTTON PRICES

Year	(1) Price Equivalent of Income	(2) Production	(3) Stocks	(4) Foreign Exchange Gradient	(5) Other Fiber Production	(6) Time Trend	(7) Calculated Prices (1)×(2)×(3)×(4)×(5)×(6)	(8) Actual Prices	(9) Residual Ratios (8)÷(7)
1921	.95	1.360	.718	1.044	.951	1.93	1.78	1.80	1.01
1922	1.08	1.142	1.000	1.033	1.172	1.71	2.55	2.56	1.00
1923	1.19	1.158	1.196	.949	1.195	1.51	2.84	2.98	1.05
1924	1.23	.903	1.284	1.030	1.172	1.33	2.29	2.40	1.05
1925	1.29	.844	1.254	1.000	1.181	1.18	1.91	1.96	1.03
1926	1.32	.809	1.112	1.000	1.165	1.09	1.53	1.44	.94
1927	1.35	1.096	1.050	1.000	1.144	1.05	1.86	1.96	1.05
1928	1.44	.965	1.153	.992	1.100	1.03	1.80	1.86	1.03
1929	1.37	.891	1.142	.978	1.050	1.02	1.46	1.59	1.09
1930	1.17	.898	1.045	.965	1.030	1.01	1.10	.98	.89
1931	.88	.771	.958	.855	1.010	1.00	.57	.60	1.05
1932	1.00	1.036	.761	.979	1.042	1.00	.80	.71	.89
1933	.80	.977	.854	1.335	1.035	1.00	.92	1.08	1.17
1934	.89	1.250	.895	1.027	1.010	1.00	1.03	1.24	1.20
1935	1.05	1.117	1.093	.984	1.022	1.00	1.37	1.16	.85
1936	1.19	1.024	1.116	.955	.979	1.00	1.27	1.30	1.02
1937	1.14	.737	1.101	.973	.885	1.00	.80	.89	1.11
1938	1.15	1.103	.816	.950	.839	1.00	.83	.88	1.06
1939	1.26	1.096	.878	.872	.760	1.00	.81	1.07	1.32
1940	1.49	.986	1.120	.975	.688	1.00	1.11	1.08	.97
1941	1.96	1.081	1.030	1.011	.600	1.00	1.32	1.79	1.36
1942	2.57	.941	1.020	1.000	.586	1.00	1.45	1.97	1.36
1943	2.79	.968	.845	.999	.649	1.00	1.48	2.02	1.36
1944	3.04	.955	.800	.999	.655	1.00	1.52	2.14	1.41
1945	3.09	1.300	.720	.994	.836	1.00	2.37	2.54	1.07
1946	3.37	1.380	.840	.994	.862	1.00	3.35	3.41	1.02
1947	3.75	1.180	1.140	1.000	.846	1.00	4.27	3.39	.79
1948	4.02	.986	1.150	1.000	.770	1.00	3.50	3.15	.90
1949	4.16	.955	1.290	.896	.765	1.00	3.51	3.12	.89
1950	4.75	1.275	1.220	.880	.670	1.00	4.35	4.17	.96
1951	5.14	.997	1.228	.888	.638	1.00	3.57	3.86	1.08
1952	5.53	1.017	1.140	.880	.679	1.00	3.83	3.38	.88
1953	5.62	.965	1.075	.865	.628	1.00	3.18	3.29	1.03
1954	5.88	1.083	1.042	.820	.603	1.00	3.28	3.32	1.01
1955	6.37	1.080	1.018	.805	.554	1.00	3.16	3.37	1.07
1956	6.76	1.150	.962	.805	.538	1.00	3.28	3.17	.97

TABLE 5–12

CONSTRUCTION OF VARIABLES

	(1)	(2)	(3)	(4)	(5)	(6)	(7)	(8)	(9)
	Cotton Production*			Cotton Stocks*				Military Cotton	
Crop Year Beginning August	United States	Foreign	Total (1) + .5 (2)	United States	United States Government	Foreign	Total (4) −.5(5) +.5 (6)	Consumption, Estimated	Net Stocks (7) −(8)
1921	7.95	6.89	11.40	6.90	—	8.64	11.22		11.22
1922	9.76	8.33	13.94	3.32	—	7.66	7.15		7.15
1923	10.14	8.76	14.42	2.32	—	5.25	4.95		4.95
1924	13.63	10.09	18.68	1.56	—	5.06	4.09		4.09
1925	16.10	10.56	21.38	1.61	—	6.34	4.78		4.78
1926	17.98	9.77	22.87	3.54	—	6.93	7.01		7.01
1927	12.96	10.39	18.16	3.76	—	8.89	8.21		8.21
1928	14.46	11.25	20.09	2.54	—	8.00	6.54		6.54
1929	14.83	11.54	20.60	2.31	—	8.23	6.43		6.43
1930	13.93	11.50	19.68	4.53	1.31	7.36	7.55		7.55
1931	17.10	9.60	21.90	6.37	3.39	8.44	8.89		8.89
1932	13.00	10.50	18.25	9.68	2.38	8.66	12.82		12.82
1933	13.05	13.35	19.73	8.16	2.21	8.95	11.53		11.53
1934	9.64	13.47	16.38	7.74	3.04	9.80	11.14		11.14
1935	10.64	15.65	18.47	7.21	6.03	7.86	8.12		8.12
1936	12.40	18.45	21.63	5.41	3.24	8.24	7.91		7.91
1937	18.95	18.33	28.12	4.50	1.67	9.20	8.26		8.26
1938	11.94	15.84	19.86	11.53	6.96	11.17	13.64		13.64
1939	11.82	15.91	19.78	13.03	11.05	8.61	12.31		13.31
1940	12.57	16.40	20.77	10.56	8.73	9.71	11.05	3.70	7.35
1941	10.74	14.99	18.24	12.13	7.05	10.00	13.60	5.20	8.40
1942	12.82	13.05	19.35	10.64	6.66	11.94	13.28	5.10	8.10
1943	11.43	13.45	18.16	10.66	5.39	12.91	14.42	3.90	10.52
1944	12.23	11.64	18.05	10.74	6.66	14.66	14.74	3.60	11.14
1945	9.02	10.95	14.27	11.16	6.95	18.00	16.68	3.20	13.48
1946	8.64	11.53	14.29	7.33	.79	17.80	15.83	4.00	11.83
1947	11.86	11.68	17.76	2.53	.06	15.90	10.45	3.40	7.05
1948	14.88	12.8	21.28	3.08	.04	11.60	8.86	1.80	7.06
1949	16.13	14.0	23.13	5.29	3.82	9.70	8.23	2.90	5.33
1950	10.01	17.5	18.76	6.85	3.54	9.90	10.03	3.00	7.03
1951	15.15	20.0	25.15	2.28	.08	9.60	7.40		7.04
1952	15.14	20.5	25.39	2.79	.29	12.40	8.84		8.84
1953	16.47	21.7	27.32	5.61	2.00	11.70	10.46		10.46
1954	13.70	23.8	25.60	9.73	7.04	10.70	11.56		11.56
1955	14.72	23.6	26.52	11.21	8.13	10.90	12.59		12.59
1956	13.31	24.8	25.71	14.54	9.88	9.00	14.10		14.10

*Millions of bales.

TABLE 5–12 (Continued)

	(10)	(11)	(12)	(13)	(14)	(15)	(16)	(17)
							Other Fiber Production	
				Ratios			Index of	
	World Production of Other Fibers, (Mil. Lbs.)	World Cotton Consumption	3-Year Moving Average of (11) Centered	Production to Consumption (3)÷(12)	Stocks to Consumption (9)÷(12)	Index of (10)	World Cotton Consumption Trend (1947–49=100)	Ratio
Crop Year Beginning August								(15)÷(16)
1921	2,663	19.78	20.00 *	.570	.561	58.1	72.3	.804
1922	1,966	21.34	20.38	.684	.351	42.9	73.7	.582
1923	1,991	20.03	21.37	.675	.232	43.5	77.3	.563
1924	2,155	22.73	22.31	.837	.183	47.0	80.7	.582
1925	2,299	24.17	24.19	.884	.198	50.2	87.5	.574
1926	2,463	25.68	25.10	.911	.279	53.8	90.7	.593
1927	2,583	25.44	25.63	.709	.302	56.4	92.7	.608
1928	2,740	25.78	25.37	.792	.258	59.8	91.7	.652
1929	2,827	24.88	24.36	.846	.264	61.7	88.1	.700
1930	2,797	22.43	23.40	.841	.323	61.1	84.6	.722
1931	2,864	22.89	23.32	.939	.381	62.5	84.3	.741
1932	2,850	24.65	24.38	.749	.526	62.2	88.1	.706
1933	2,985	25.60	25.24	.782	.457	65.1	91.3	.713
1934	3,068	25.48	26.20	.625	.425	70.0	94.7	.739
1935	3,355	27.53	27.88	.662	.291	73.2	100.8	.726
1936	3,670	30.64	28.58	.757	.277	80.1	103.3	.775
1937	4,223	27.57	28.91	.973	.286	92.2	104.5	.882
1938	4,387	28.51	28.19	.705	.484	95.8	101.9	.940
1939	4,835	28.50	27.87	.710	.442	105.5	100.8	1.047
1940	5,093	26.60	26.71	.778	.275	111.2	96.6	1.151
1941	5,433	25.03	25.30	.721	.332	118.6	91.5	1.296
1942	5,219	24.29	23.96	.808	.339	113.9	86.2	1.321
1943	5,074	22.57	23.02	.789	.457	110.8	83.2	1.212
1944	4,478	22.20	22.55	.800	.494	97.8	81.5	1.200
1945	3,710	22.90	23.80	.600	.566	81.0	86.0	.942
1946	3,819	26.30	25.46	.561	.465	83.4	90.0	.907
1947	4,120	27.20	26.73	.664	.264	89.9	96.6	.931
1948	4,654	26.70	27.30	.779	.259	101.6	98.7	1.029
1949	4,968	28.00	28.96	.799	.184	108.4	104.7	1.035
1950	5,986	32.20	30.70	.611	.223	130.7	111.0	1.178
1951	6,616	31.90	32.50	.774	.217	144.4	117.5	1.229
1952	6,434	33.40	33.36	.761	.265	140.4	120.6	1.164
1953	7,083	34.80	34.56	.791	.303	155.4	124.9	1.244
1954	7,563	35.50	35.66	.718	.324	166.1	128.9	1.289
1955	8,368	36.70	36.80	.721	.342	183.7	133.0	1.381
1956			37.80 *	.680	.373	192.9	136.7	1.411

* = Estimate.

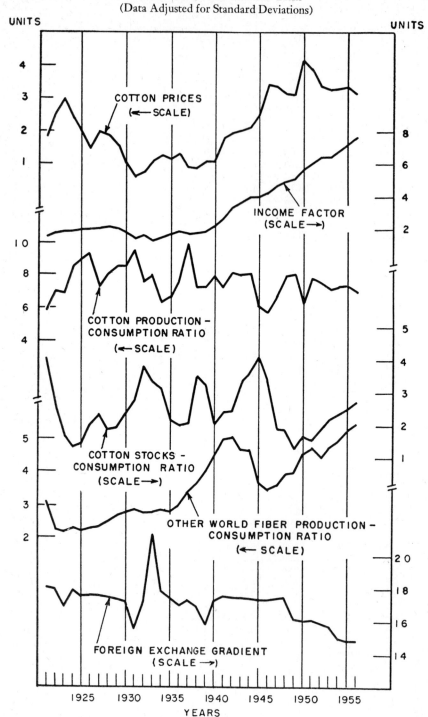

FIGURE 5–15

COTTON PRICES AND RELATED DATA
(Data Adjusted for Standard Deviations)

FIGURE 5-16

Cotton Prices versus Income Factor
(Data Adjusted for Standard Deviations)

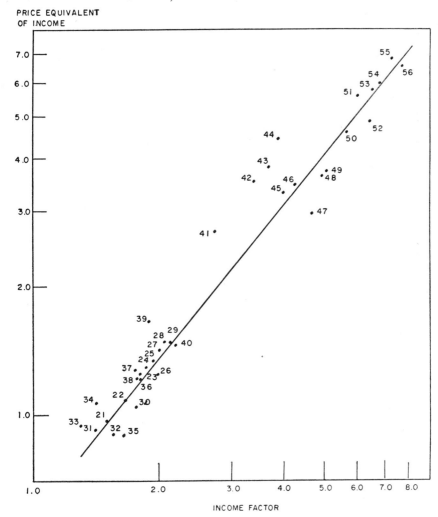

PRICE EQUIVALENT
OF INCOME

INCOME FACTOR

these factors, the deviations are expressed as ratios, and then plotted against the next variable.

The three supply factors—cotton production, cotton stocks, and fiber production—are the next variables to be utilized in the analysis. Before they can be used, however, they must be adjusted. This is necessary because a given level of production or stocks today is relatively less influential on price as compared with earlier years, and hence these variables should not be given as much weight in making current price estimates as they were in earlier years when the population was smaller and the standard of living lower. The adjustment is made in Table 5–12, pp. 132–33, by dividing the separate supply factors by a centered 3-year moving average of world cotton consumption. The resulting supply-demand *ratios* are thus employed as independent variables instead of the supply and demand factors separately.

In Figure 5–17, the ratio deviations from the previous chart are plotted against the cotton production-consumption ratio. The downward slope of the regression line indicates that a change of one standard deviation in the

FIGURE 5–17

COTTON PRICES VERSUS COTTON PRODUCTION-CONSUMPTION RATIO
(Data Adjusted for Standard Deviations)

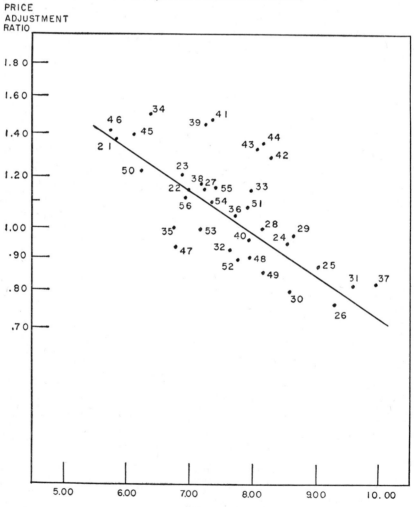

COTTON PRODUCTION–CONSUMPTION RATIO

ratio (equal to .10) causes an inverse change in price of 14 per cent. The equation for the line is estimated as

$$\text{Price} = 10^{[-.0665\,(P/C)\,+\,.5224]} \tag{2}$$

where P = world cotton production and C = world cotton consumption.
In Figure 5–18, the ratio deviations from the previous chart are plotted

FIGURE 5–18

Cotton Prices versus Cotton Stocks-Consumption Ratio

(Data Adjusted for Standard Deviations)

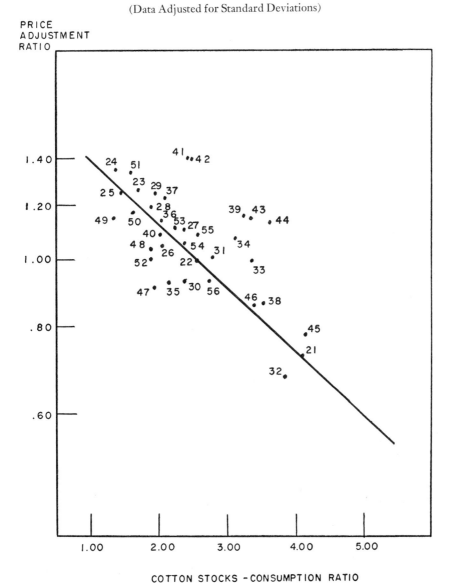

COTTON STOCKS - CONSUMPTION RATIO

FIGURE 5-19

COTTON PRICES VERSUS OTHER WORLD FIBER PRODUCTION

(Data Adjusted for Standard Deviations)

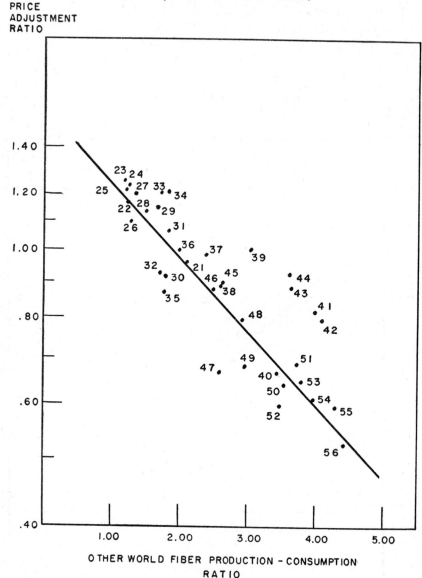

against the cotton stocks-consumption ratio. According to the relationship, a change of one standard deviation in the ratio (.137) changes prices in the opposite direction by 19 per cent. The formula for the line is

$$\text{Price} = 10^{[-.0915\,(S/C)\,+\,.2336]} \qquad (3)$$

where S = cotton stocks and C, as before, is world cotton consumption.

These deviations, expressed as ratios, are then plotted against the ratio of fiber production to consumption. The change in price resulting from a change of one standard deviation (.261) is, according to the regression line, 22 per cent. The formula is

$$\text{Price} = 10^{[-.104 \ (F/C) \ + \ .3014]} \qquad (4)$$

where F = fiber production and C = world cotton consumption.

The foreign exchange gradient is considered next. This is a measure of the weighted rate of change of an index of foreign exchange rates, and these changes exert their influence on prices by setting speculative forces in motion that could not otherwise be explained by domestic economic factors alone. After exchange rates stabilize, prices settle down once more in

FIGURE 5–20

COTTON PRICES VERSUS FOREIGN EXCHANGE GRADIENT

(Data Adjusted for Standard Deviations)

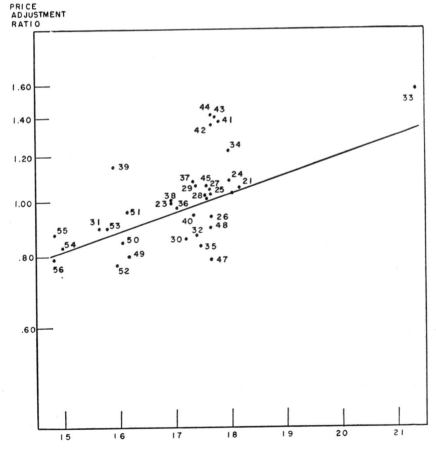

FOREIGN EXCHANGE GRADIENT

line with demand and supply, until the foreign exchange gradient becomes significant again. In Figure 5–20, the regression line is such that a change of one standard deviation in the exchange gradient (equal to 5.7 index points) causes a change of 8 per cent in cotton prices in the same direction. The formula for the regression line is

$$\text{Price} = 10^{[.033G - .5819]} \tag{5}$$

where G = the foreign exchange gradient.

A time trend may now be incorporated as the last "catchall" variable for factors other than those included thus far. If the ratio deviations of Figure 5–20 are plotted against "time," the result obtained is the jagged line of Figure 5–21. The smooth line is the time trend drawn freehand. Its downtrend until 1930 reflects declining costs of production due to improved

FIGURE 5–21

COTTON PRICES VERSUS TIME TREND

(Data Adjusted for Standard Deviations)

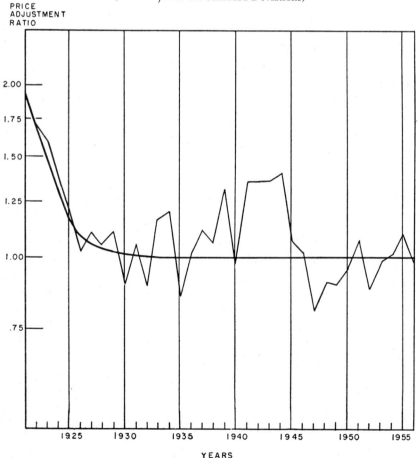

methods and the utilization of new and more fertile planting grounds. Since 1930, the effects of these factors have been fairly stable. The equation for the time trend, *TT*, may be written

$$\text{Price} = 10^{TT} \tag{6}$$

Conclusion. Calculated and actual cotton prices are shown in Figure 5–22. The equation for the dashed line can, of course, be obtained by multiplying the equations for the separate regression lines given above, as explained in the previous study. The result is then

$$\text{Price} = .68 \, (\text{Income})^{1.11} \, 10^{Z}$$

where Z = the sum of the exponents of 10 in equations (2) to (6) above.

PRICES OF RAW MATERIALS AND SEMIMANUFACTURED GOODS

The list of price-determining forces presented earlier in this chapter—supply, demand, competitive, and monetary factors—serves as a basis for constructing models of raw materials prices and prices of semimanufactured goods, as well as prices of farm commodities as shown in the previous section. Certain guides, such as leading series and pressure indexes (see Chapter 1), are often of further assistance in constructing such models. Thus, the ratio of raw materials inventories to new orders for finished goods is a useful indicator of the future trend of raw materials prices. The "operating rate," defined as the ratio of production to capacity, may be an indicator of price strength if the ratio is rising, and price weakness if the ratio is declining. (Steel production is typically quoted this way, that is, as a per cent of capacity, as is the rate of output of many other products.) And the "money gradient," or rate of change of bank deposits, is a useful measure of the rate at which money is entering or leaving the purchasing power stream. Variations in purchasing power will in turn affect general price levels and particular commodity prices as well.

What are the chief variables to employ in an analysis of raw materials prices and the prices of semimanufactured goods? Three factors—demand, supply, and unit labor costs—are involved. With respect to the first two, it may be noted that new orders received by manufacturers for finished and semifinished goods are actually a measure of manufacturers' demand for raw materials. This is because the supply of raw materials usually changes slowly, particularly at cyclical tops and bottoms; hence, changes in new orders tend to cause later changes in raw materials prices. However, imbalance between supply and demand usually affects only short-term prices; in the long run, supply and demand imbalances tend to be self-correcting, leaving the price trend to be determined by a more fundamental factor, unit labor cost. Let us examine this relation more fully by means of the following studies of print cloth and leather prices, respectively.

FIGURE 5–22

Cotton Prices: Actual versus Calculated

(Data Adjusted for Standard Deviations)

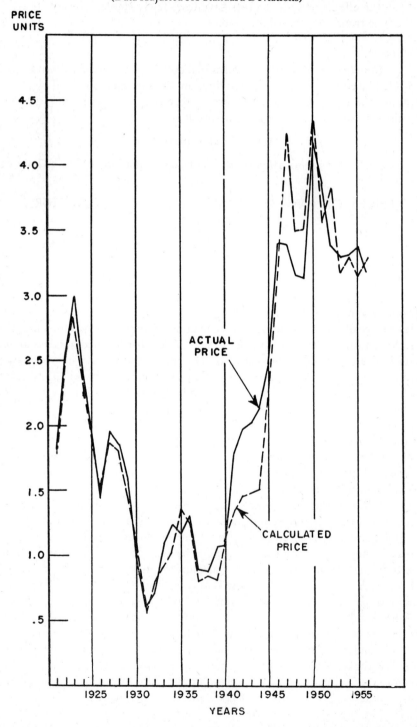

Price of Print Cloth

A model of print cloth prices may be constructed in three broad stages. First, a formula for unit labor cost is derived; second, the price of cotton is utilized as a factor affecting the total cost of print cloth production; and third, a measure of all other cost factors, called "mill balance," is established. These three elements are then combined to yield a single prediction formula. The data involved in the analysis are presented in Tables 5–13 to 5–17. Since cost data are not readily available for adequate and continuing analyses of the price structure by means of cost components, substitute or proxy variables are employed where necessary as shown in the tables. Since the relationships are revealed more clearly by the charts, we will concentrate attention on these and leave the tables for reference purposes. The charts used in this study are shown in Figures 5–23 to 5–31, with the separate variables plotted first as a time series in Figure 5–23. The explanation of the remaining charts will now be given, but the order of explanation will be somewhat different from the order in which the charts are presented, because of certain necessary calculations, as will be explained in the following paragraphs.

Unit Labor Costs. The development of a formula for unit labor costs in the broadwoven goods industry is based on changes in wage rates and in output per man-hour. In this study, a measure of unit labor cost in all manufacturing was also incorporated in the analysis, so as to reflect the total inflationary and deflationary forces in the labor market and thereby provide an aid in forecasting unit labor costs for the broadwoven goods industry.

The graphic analysis of unit labor cost in the industry is shown in Figures 5–26 to 5–29. In each, as in the previous studies, the residuals from each regression line (or from the formula for each line as shown on the respective charts) are expressed as ratios and then plotted against the next independent variable. When the separate formulas for these regression lines are combined, they produce the following equation for unit labor cost:

$$U_c = \frac{(2.704W^{.7})(.57 + .345M)}{(-9.20 + 1.05P)(91.8 + .075\,G/I)} \tag{1}$$

in which

U_c = Unit labor cost.
W = Wage in total manufacturing.
M = Mill activity as per cent of capacity.
P = Productivity rate in total manufacturing.
G = Production of broadwoven goods.
I = Total industrial production.

The equation is obviously nothing more than a weighted ratio of wages to output, and consists of the product of the separate formulas that have been written next to the regression lines in the relevant charts.

TABLE 5-13

PRINT CLOTH DATA

	(1)	(2)	(3)	(4)	(5)	(6)	(7)	(8)	(9)
					Estimated	Estimated	Man-Hours		
					No. of	Print Cloth	per Pound		Wages per
	Value		Average	Print	Man-	Product	of Print		Pound of
	of	Wages	Hourly	Cloth	Hours	(Proxy)	Cloth	Smooth	Cloth
	Product	Paid	Earnings	Price	(2)÷(3)	(1)÷(4)	(Proxy)	Trend	(3)×(8)
	($ Mil.)	($ Mil.)	(Cents)	(¢/Lb.)	(Mil.)	(Mil. Lbs.)	(5)÷(6)	of (7)	(Cents)
1925	1,714	354	33.3	44.98	1,063	3,810	.279	.2790	9.29
1926			32.6	36.65				.2704	8.82
1927	1,567	381	33.6	36.76	1,134	4,260	.266	.2618	8.80
1928			32.6	37.47				.2532	8.25
1929	1,524	324	32.7	35.94	991	4,240	.234	.2446	8.00
1930			32.1	28.27				.2360	7.58
1931	805	220	30.2	22.07	728	3,650	.199	.2274	6.87
1932			23.9	17.02				.2188	5.23
1933	861	216	27.7	25.84	780	3,330	.234	.2102	5.28
1934			37.8	32.84				.2016	7.62
1935	984	236	37.6	30.86	628	3,190	.197	.1930	7.26
1936			36.8	28.76				.1844	6.79
1937	1,296	321	41.3	29.81	777	4,350	.179	.1758	7.26
1938			39.7	22.31				.1672	6.64
1939	1,119	281	38.8	23.08	724	4,860	.149	.1586	6.15
1940			41.2	24.32				.1500	6.18
1947	4,218	888	98.2	115.99	905	3,640	.248	.2480	24.35

	(10)	(11)	(12)	(13)	(14)	(15)	(16)	(17)
	Total			Average			Index	Wages
	Broadwoven			Yearly	Wages		of Wages	per Pound
	Goods	No. of	Average	Payroll	per Yd.		per Pound	of Cloth
	Production	Production	Weekly	(11)×(12)	of Cloth	Pounds	of Cloth	(16)×
	(Mil. Lin.	Workers	Earnings	×(52.14)	(13)÷(10)	per Yd.	(14)÷(15)	(24.35)
	Yds.)	(000)	($)	($ Mil.)	(¢ per Yd.)	of Cloth	1947=100	(¢/Pound)
1947	12,371	590.2	41.52	1,278	10.3	.3070	100	24.35
1948	12,405	607.9	46.13	1,462	11.8	.3031	116	28.25
1949	10,923	532.7	44.58	1,235	11.3	.3066	110	26.79
1950	13,091	558.8	49.28	1,436	11.0	.3046	108	26.30
1951	12,887	548.3	51.74	1,479	11.5	.3173	108	26.30
1952	12,160	508.6	51.99	1,379	11.3	.3263	103	25.08
1953	12,946	500.6	52.80	1,378	10.6	.3126	101	24.59
1954	12,518	443.6	50.69	1,172	9.4	.3015	93	22.65
1955	13,123	439.6	54.27	1,244	9.5	.3084	92	22.40
1956	12,859	430.0	56.28	1,262	9.8	.2980	98	23.86

TABLE 5–14

PRINT CLOTH DATA
(Cents per Pound)

Year	(1) Print Cloth Price	(2) Cost of Raw Cotton	(3) Print Cloth Mill Margin (1) − (2)	(4) Wage Cost	(5) Mill Balance (3) − (4)
1926............	36.65	18.17	18.48	8.82	9.66
1927............	36.76	18.46	18.30	8.80	9.50
1928............	37.47	20.28	17.19	8.25	8.94
1929............	35.94	19.66	16.28	8.00	8.28
1930............	28.27	14.20	14.07	7.58	6.49
1931............	22.07	8.98	13.09	6.87	6.22
1932............	17.02	6.76	10.26	5.23	5.03
1933............	25.84	10.73	15.11	5.28	9.29
1934............	32.84	17.13	15.71	7.62	8.09
1935............	30.86	16.85	14.01	7.26	6.75
1936............	28.76	13.19	15.57	6.79	8.78
1937............	29.81	12.65	17.16	7.26	9.90
1938............	22.31	9.60	12.71	6.64	6.07
1939............	23.08	9.82	13.26	6.15	7.11
1940............	24.32	10.65	13.67	6.18	7.49
1947............	115.99	35.16	80.83	24.35	56.48
1948............	93.68	35.01	58.67	28.25	30.42
1949............	70.05	32.74	37.31	26.79	10.52
1950............	86.82	37.92	48.90	26.30	22.60
1951............	88.15	42.66	45.49	26.30	19.19
1952............	73.59	40.39	33.20	25.08	8.12
1953............	75.14	35.02	40.12	24.59	15.53
1954............	67.43	36.42	31.01	22.65	8.36
1955............	69.38	36.71	32.67	22.40	10.27
1956............	70.19	36.09	34.10	23.86	10.24

TABLE 5–15

PRINT CLOTH DATA

Year	(1) Mill Activity as a Per Cent of Capacity	(2) 1.3 ×(1)	(3) (2)×.0238	(4) Time Trend (Figure 5–25)	(5) Calculated Mill Balance (3)×(4)
1929	104.6	422.1	10.05	.79	7.94
1930	82.0	307.5	7.32	.85	6.22
1931	86.2	328.3	7.81	.90	7.03
1932	79.7	296.5	7.06	.94	6.64
1933	64.4	224.7	5.35	.98	5.24
1934	59.4	202.2	4.81	1.01	4.86
1935	61.3	210.8	5.02	1.04	5.22
1936	78.3	289.7	6.89	1.06	7.30
1937	85.8	326.3	7.77	1.08	8.39
1938	70.5	252.7	6.01	1.09	6.55
1939	96.0	377.6	8.99	1.10	9.89
1940	96.5	380.0	9.04	1.11	10.03
1947	125.0	532.1	12.66	1.94	24.56
1948	125.7	535.8	12.75	1.55	19.76
1949	107.6	438.0	10.42	1.28	13.34
1950	132.8	575.7	13.70	1.10	15.07
1951	133.2	578.0	13.76	.96	13.20
1952	124.6	529.9	12.61	.86	10.84
1953	132.0	571.2	13.59	.74	10.74
1954	124.7	530.3	12.62	.74	9.33
1955	136.3	596.3	14.19	.71	10.07
1956	136.5	596.5	14.20	.69	9.86

TABLE 5–16

PRINT CLOTH DATA

Year	(1) W Wages*	(2) $(W)^{.7}$ $(1)^{.7}$	(3) $(2) \times$ 2.704	(4) Mill Activity as a Per Cent of Capacity	(5) $(4) \times$ .345	(6) $(5) +$ .57	(7) $(3) \times (6)$	(8) Trend of Residual	(9) $(7) \times (8)$
1947	49.97	15.45	41.78	125.0	43.13	43.70	1825.79	1.080	1971.9
1948	59.33	17.43	47.13	125.7	43.37	43.94	2070.89	1.060	2159.1
1949	54.92	16.51	44.64	107.6	37.12	37.69	1682.48	1.045	1758.2
1950	54.14	16.35	44.21	132.8	45.82	46.39	2050.90	1.025	2102.2
1951	64.71	18.52	50.08	133.2	45.94	46.52	2329.72	1.005	2341.4
1952	67.97	19.17	51.84	124.6	42.99	43.56	2258.15	.990	2235.6
1953	71.69	19.90	53.81	132.0	45.54	46.11	2481.18	.970	2406.7
1954	71.86	19.94	53.92	124.7	43.02	43.59	2350.37	.960	2256.4
1955	76.52	20.83	56.32	136.3	47.02	47.59	2680.27	.940	2519.5
1956	80.19	21.52	58.19	136.5	47.09	47.66	2773.34	.920	2551.5

Year	(10) † $P \div \sigma$	(11) $(10) \times$ 1.05	(12) $(11) -$ 9.20	(13) ‡ $BWG \div FRB$	(14) $(13) \times$ .075	(15) $(14) +$ 91.8	(16) $(15) \times (12)$	(17) $(9) \div (16)$	(18) Calculated Wage Cost per Pound $(17) \times 25$ (¢ per Lb.)
1947	25.3	26.6	17.4	123.7	9.28	101.1	1759.1	1.1210	28.02
1948	26.4	27.7	18.5	120.4	9.03	100.8	1864.8	1.1771	29.43
1949	27.9	29.3	20.1	112.6	8.45	100.3	2016.0	.8721	21.80
1950	29.6	31.1	21.9	116.9	8.77	100.6	2203.1	.9542	23.86
1951	29.5	31.0	21.8	107.4	8.06	99.9	2177.8	1.0751	26.88
1952	30.6	32.1	22.9	98.1	7.36	99.2	2271.7	.9841	24.60
1953	31.7	33.3	24.1	96.6	7.25	99.1	2388.3	1.0077	25.19
1954	33.2	34.4	25.2	100.1	7.51	99.3	2502.4	.9017	22.54
1955	34.4	36.1	26.9	94.4	7.08	98.9	2660.5	.9470	23.68
1956	35.3	37.1	27.9	89.9	6.74	98.5	2748.2	.9248	23.21

*Col. (1): Average weekly wage rates in all manufacturing industries, symbolized W.

†Col. (10): Index of output per man-hour (productivity) in all manufacturing industries ÷ its standard deviation.

‡Col. (13): Broadwoven goods production ÷ FRB index of total industrial production.

TABLE 5-17

PRINT CLOTH DATA

(In Cents per Pound)

Year	(1) Cost of Raw Cotton	(2) Calculated Wage Cost	(3) Calculated Mill Balance	(4) (1)+(2)+(3)	(5) Residual (Actual Price ÷(4))	(6) Trend of (5)	(7) Calculated Price: (4)×(6)	(8) Actual Price	(9) Ratio: (8)÷(7)
1929	19.66	8.00	7.94	35.60	1.010	1.00	35.60	35.94	1.010
1930	14.20	7.58	6.22	28.00	1.010	1.00	28.00	28.27	1.010
1931	8.98	6.87	7.03	22.88	.964	1.00	22.88	22.07	.964
1932	6.76	5.23	6.64	18.63	.914	1.00	18.63	17.02	.914
1933	10.73	5.28	5.24	21.25	1.216	1.00	21.25	25.84	1.216
1934	17.13	7.62	4.86	29.61	1.109	1.00	29.61	32.84	1.109
1935	16.85	7.26	5.22	29.33	1.052	1.00	29.33	30.86	1.052
1936	13.19	6.79	7.30	27.28	1.054	1.00	27.28	28.76	1.054
1937	12.65	7.26	8.39	28.30	1.053	1.00	28.30	29.81	1.053
1938	9.60	6.64	6.55	22.79	.979	1.00	22.79	22.31	.979
1939	9.82	6.15	9.89	25.86	.892	1.00	25.86	23.08	.892
1940	10.65	6.18	10.03	26.86	.905	1.00	26.86	24.32	.905
1947	35.16	28.02	24.56	87.74	1.322	1.245	109.24	115.99	1.06
1948	35.01	29.43	19.76	84.20	1.112	1.125	94.72	93.68	.99
1949	32.74	21.80	13.34	67.88	1.032	1.055	71.61	70.05	.98
1950	37.92	23.86	15.07	76.85	1.130	1.020	78.39	86.82	1.11
1951	42.66	26.88	13.20	82.74	1.065	1.005	83.15	88.15	1.06
1952	40.39	24.60	10.84	75.83	.970	1.000	75.83	73.59	.97
1953	35.02	25.19	10.74	70.95	1.059	1.000	70.95	75.14	1.06
1954	36.42	22.54	9.33	68.29	.987	1.000	68.29	67.43	.99
1955	36.71	23.68	10.07	70.46	.985	1.000	70.46	69.38	.99
1956	36.09	23.21	9.86	69.16	1.015	1.000	69.16	70.19	1.02

FIGURE 5–23

PRINT CLOTH DATA—CHART I

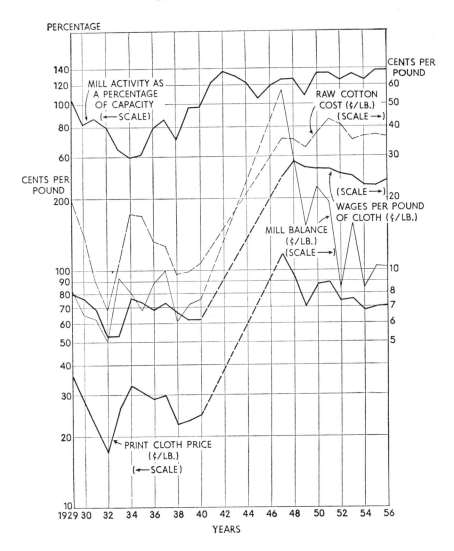

FIGURE 5-24

PRINT CLOTH DATA—CHART II

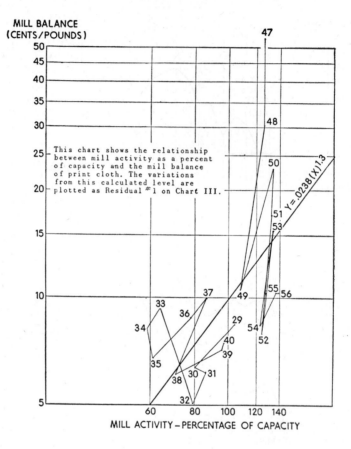

This chart shows the relationship between mill activity as a percent of capacity and the mill balance of print cloth. The variations from this calculated level are plotted as Residual #1 on Chart III.

$Y = .0238(X)^{1.3}$

MILL ACTIVITY—PERCENTAGE OF CAPACITY

FIGURE 5–25

Print Cloth Data—Chart III

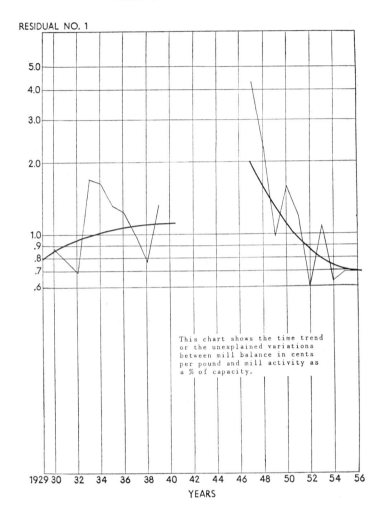

RESIDUAL NO. 1

This chart shows the time trend
or the unexplained variations
between mill balance in cents
per pound and mill activity as
a % of capacity.

YEARS

FIGURE 5-26

Print Cloth Data—Chart IV

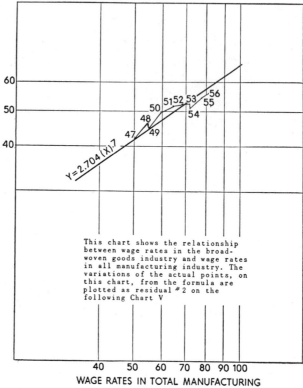

WAGE RATES IN
BROADWOVEN
GOODS INDUSTRY

This chart shows the relationship
between wage rates in the broadwoven goods industry and wage rates
in all manufacturing industry. The
variations of the actual points, on
this chart, from the formula are
plotted as residual #2 on the
following Chart V

WAGE RATES IN TOTAL MANUFACTURING

FIGURE 5–27

Print Cloth Data—Chart V

RESIDUAL NO. 2

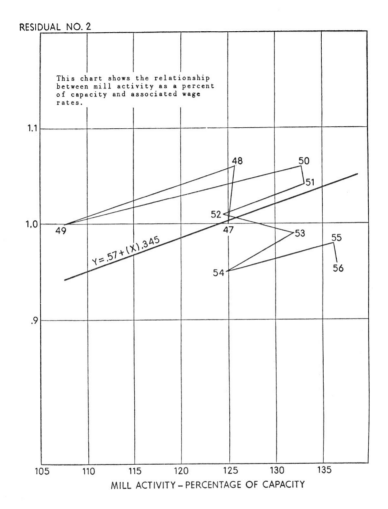

This chart shows the relationship
between mill activity as a percent
of capacity and associated wage
rates.

MILL ACTIVITY – PERCENTAGE OF CAPACITY

FIGURE 5–28

PRINT CLOTH DATA—CHART VI

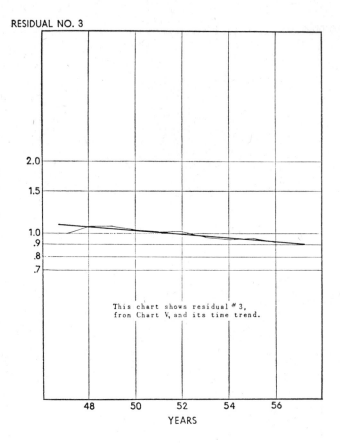

RESIDUAL NO. 3

This chart shows residual #3, from Chart V, and its time trend.

YEARS

FIGURE 5–29

PRINT CLOTH DATA—CHART VII

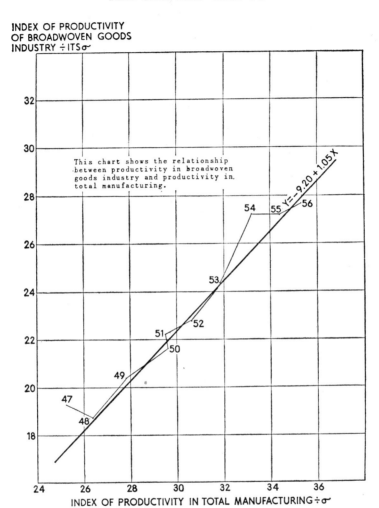

INDEX OF PRODUCTIVITY
OF BROADWOVEN GOODS
INDUSTRY ÷ ITSσ

This chart shows the relationship
between productivity in broadwoven
goods industry and productivity in.
total manufacturing.

Y=-9.20+1.05X

INDEX OF PRODUCTIVITY IN TOTAL MANUFACTURING÷σ

FIGURE 5–30

PRINT CLOTH DATA—CHART VIII

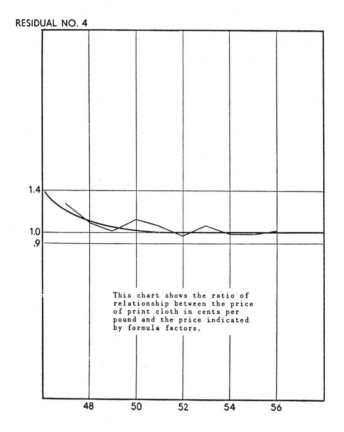

RESIDUAL NO. 4

1.4

1.0
.9

This chart shows the ratio of relationship between the price of print cloth in cents per pound and the price indicated by formula factors.

48   50   52   54   56

Cotton Prices. The price of cotton represents the second important factor affecting the cost of producing print cloth. The forecasting of cotton prices has already been discussed in the previous section. Hence, its predicted value may be incorporated directly in the forecasting equation for print cloth as shown below.

Mill Balance. When the costs of direct labor and of raw cotton are deducted from the price of print cloth, the difference represents all other cost factors. This difference is referred to in the industry as "mill balance." In general, the mill balance tends to be high when a large proportion of the industry's mill capacity is in use, because of the operation of less efficient mills and less efficient processes in order to meet demand. When demand declines, the percentage of mill capacity in use declines, and the mill balance tends to decline. The relationship between mill balance, Y, and per cent of capacity, X, is shown in Figure 5–24. The deviations, expressed as ratios,

FIGURE 5-31

PRINT CLOTH DATA—CHART IX

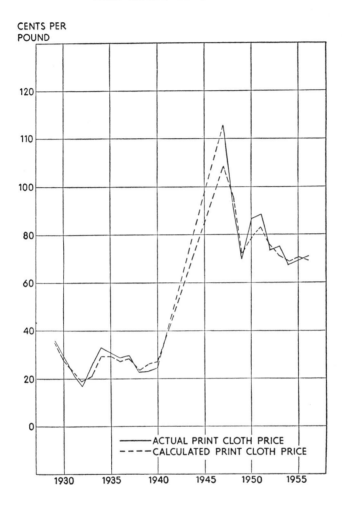

CENTS PER POUND

are plotted as a time series in Figure 5–25, with the war and postwar years excluded. The heavy line is a time trend, *TT*, and measures the influence of factors other than mill activity in affecting mill balance. The formula combining both regressions, therefore, is

$$Y = .0238X^{1.3}TT \qquad (2)$$

Conclusion. Combining the above concepts and formulas, we obtain a final predicting equation for the price of print cloth:

$$P_c = (C + 25U_c + .0238M^{1.3}TT) \, TT$$

FIGURE 5–32

Leather Price Data—Chart I

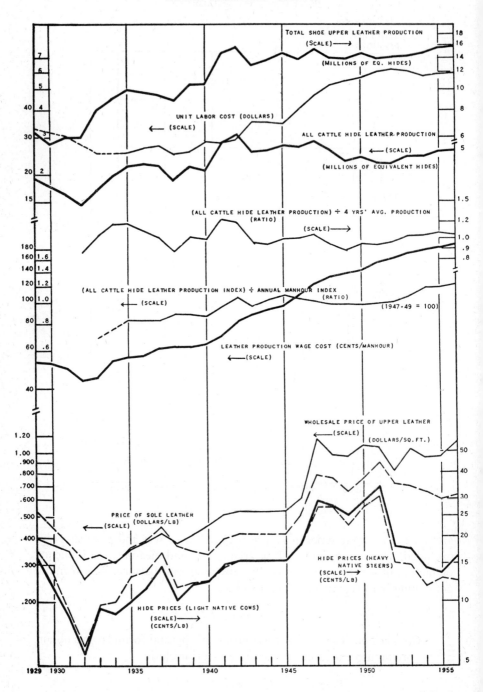

where

P_c = Price of print cloth in cents per pound.
C = Price of raw cotton in cents per pound.
U_c = Unit labor cost, the formula for which is given above in equation (1).
M = Mill activity as per cent of capacity.
TT = Time trend, a measure of the influence of factors not otherwise included in the formula.

The graphic equivalent of this formula is the dashed line in Figure 5–31. It can, of course, be derived independently of the equations as explained in Chapter 3.

Leather Prices

A study of the price of leather can be conducted along the same basic lines as the study of print cloth prices, but with certain modifications due to the particular economic differences between the products. Thus, the price of leather is significantly affected not only by unit labor costs in manufacturing, but also by the price of hides. Hides are a by-product of beef production, and the production of hides reflects the growth pattern of cattle slaughter as well as certain pressures from various synthetic substitutes which have tended to reduce the demand for leather and leather prices. Since leather is primarily used by the shoe industry, the relatively small gain in per capita demand for shoes has also restricted the growth potential for leather demand. In fact, the main area of relative strength has occurred in the demand for upper leather, as seen in Figure 5–32, especially in the production of men's shoes. This is due to the increasing competition of synthetic materials, especially in the sole market for men's work shoes. The price impact of synthetic materials in the sole market is indicated by the lower position of sole leather prices relative to the price for upper leather. It is apparent from the chart that the price divergency has existed since 1929, and has become especially severe since 1952.

Analysis. Based on the data in Table 5-18, the graphic portion of the analysis may be outlined briefly.

In Figure 5–33, prices of leather are plotted against changes in unit labor cost. On the average, as shown by the regression line, a 1 per cent change in unit labor cost has resulted in a 1 per cent change in the price of leather. The equation for the line is

$$Y = .863X$$

where X = index of unit labor cost (1947–49 = 100) in the leather industry, and Y = price of leather in cents per square foot.

This equation, or its corresponding regression line, expresses the price of leather as a function of unit labor cost. We now want to find a relation between the price of leather and the price of hides, without the influence

TABLE 5–18

LEATHER PRICE DATA

Year	(1) Unit Labor Costs (1947–49 =100)	(2) .863(X)	(3) Cattle Hide Price (Cents per Pound)	(4) .460(1).85	(5) (3)÷(4)	(6) 1.022(5).5	(7) Cattle Hide Leather Production ÷Capacity
1929........	64.6	55.7	15.6	15.80	.987	1.016	
1930........			11.7				
1931........	59.5	51.3	8.5	14.83	.573	.774	
1932........			5.7				.864
1933........	49.0	42.3	9.3	12.57	.740	.879	1.043
1934........			8.8				1.172
1935........	49.4	42.6	10.0	12.66	.790	.908	1.197
1936........	51.8	44.7	11.5	13.18	.873	.955	1.113
1937........	53.3	46.0	14.6	13.51	1.081	1.063	1.032
1938........	48.8	42.1	10.2	12.53	.814	.922	.884
1939........	50.0	43.1	12.0	12.79	.938	.991	1.028
1940........	55.4	47.8	12.4	13.96	.888	.963	1.000
1941........	54.7	47.2	14.8	14.02	1.056	1.051	1.243
1942........	57.2	49.4	15.5	14.34	1.081	1.063	1.208
1943........	68.5	59.1	15.5	16.72	.927	.984	.973
1944........	68.3	58.9	15.5	16.67	.930	.986	.946
1945........	67.9	58.6	15.5	16.59	.934	.987	1.000
1946........	78.6	67.8	18.6	18.78	.990	1.017	1.015
1947........	91.8	79.2	29.1	21.44	1.357	1.190	1.051
1948........	102.1	88.1	28.1	23.46	1,198	1.119	.953
1949........	106.0	91.5	25.2	24.22	1.040	1.042	.886
1950........	110.3	95.2	29.3	25.05	1.170	1.105	.953
1951........	116.9	95.5	34.0	26.33	1.291	1.161	.942
1952........	120.2	103.7	18.0	26.96	.668	.835	.974
1953........	119.8	103.4	17.8	26.88	.662	.832	1.026
1954........	112.6	97.2	14.3	25.50	.561	.765	1.034
1955........	115.0	99.2	13.6	25.96	.524	.740	1.066
1956........	116.1	100.2	16.0	26.18	.611	.799	1.036

TABLE 5-18 *(Continued)*

Year	(8) 1.837(7) −.768	(9) (2)×(6)×(8)	(10) Actual Price of Leather (Cents per Sq. Ft.)	(11) Ratio: (10)÷(9)	(12) Time Trend of (11)	(13) Calculated Price of Leather (9)×(12) (Cents per Sq. Ft.)	(14) Residual: (10)÷(13)
1929........			39.5				
1930........			37.2				
1931........			34.5				
1932........			25.9				
1933........	1.448	42.7	30.2	.707	.600	25.6	1.18
1934........	1.385		30.7				
1935........	1.431	55.4	35.2	.635	.675	37.4	.94
1936........	1.277	54.5	38.0	.697	.715	39.0	.97
1937........	1.128	55.2	42.1	.763	.755	41.7	1.01
1938........	.856	33.2	37.6	1.132	.800	26.6	1.41
1939........	1.120	47.8	41.0	.858	.845	40.4	1.01
1940........	1.069	49.2	45.8	.931	.895	44.0	1.04
1941........	1.515	75.1	50.7	.675	.710	53.3	.95
1942........	1.451	76.2	53.0	.696	.755	57.5	.92
1943........	1.019	59.3	52.9	.892	.800	47.4	1.12
1944........	.970	56.4	52.9	.938	.840	47.4	1.12
1945........	1.069	62.1	52.9	.852	.890	55.3	.96
1946........	1.097	75.6	60.5	.800	.940	71.1	.85
1947........	1.163	109.6	116.5	1.063	.995	109.1	1.07
1948........	.983	96.9	98.6	1.018	1.050	101.7	.97
1949........	.860	82.0	94.8	1.156	1.120	91.8	1.03
1950........	.983	103.4	106.9	1.034	.86	88.9	1.20
1951........	.962	106.7	105.1	.985	.910	97.1	1.08
1952........	1.021	88.5	82.1	.928	.960	85.0	.97
1953........	1.117	96.1	103.4	1.076	1.020	98.0	1.06
1954........	1.131	84.1	94.2	1.120	1.080	90.8	1.04
1955........	1.190	87.4	95.3	1.090	1.140	99.6	.96
1956........	1.135	90.5	109.7	1.212	1.210	109.5	1.00

Source: Tanners' Council of America, Inc., and Department of Agriculture.

of unit labor cost on the latter. That is, hide prices and unit labor costs are themselves intercorrelated, and this intercorrelation must be removed if the effect of hide prices on leather prices is to be determined. This step is accomplished in Figure 5–34. Cattle hide prices are plotted against unit labor costs, producing a regression line with the equation

$$Y = .460X^{.85}$$

FIGURE 5–33

LEATHER PRICE DATA—CHART II

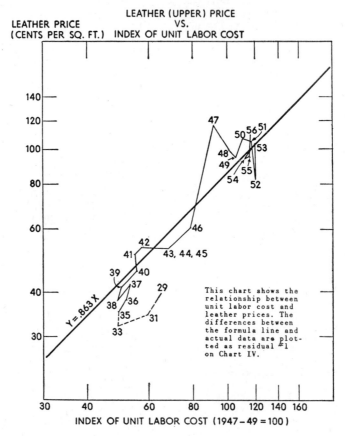

LEATHER (UPPER) PRICE
LEATHER PRICE   VS.
(CENTS PER SQ. FT.)   INDEX OF UNIT LABOR COST

INDEX OF UNIT LABOR COST (1947–49 = 100)

This chart shows the relationship between unit labor cost and leather prices. The differences between the formula line and actual data are plotted as residual #1 on Chart IV.

where Y represents cattle hide prices in cents per pound, and X is an index of unit labor cost in the leather industry.

We now have two relationships and therefore two sets of residuals: The first set of residuals, called #1, is derived from Figure 5–33, and represents the influence of factors other than unit labor cost on leather prices; the second set, #2, comes from Figure 5–34, and represents the influence

FIGURE 5-34

LEATHER PRICE DATA—CHART III

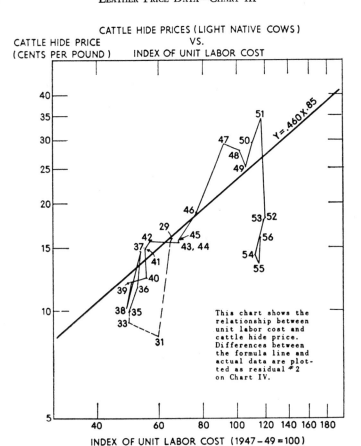

CATTLE HIDE PRICES (LIGHT NATIVE COWS)
VS.
INDEX OF UNIT LABOR COST

CATTLE HIDE PRICE
(CENTS PER POUND)

$Y = 460X^{.85}$

This chart shows the relationship between unit labor cost and cattle hide price. Differences between the formula line and actual data are plotted as residual #2 on Chart IV.

INDEX OF UNIT LABOR COST (1947-49 = 100)

of factors other than unit labor cost on hide prices. These residuals are then plotted against each other in Figure 5–35. The resulting regression line expresses the relation between leather prices and hide prices after the intercorrelation between hide prices and unit labor cost has been removed. The equation for the line is

$$Y = 1.022X^{.5}$$

where Y denotes the price of leather in cents per square foot, and X is the price of hides after removing the intercorrelation with unit labor cost.

The demand for leather relative to productive capacity creates another pressure on leather prices and hence should be accounted for in the analysis. Since data on tanning capacity are not available, a proxy variable may be employed. In the present study, the proxy variable chosen as a measure of capacity is the arithmetic average of production for the pre-

FIGURE 5-35

LEATHER PRICE DATA—CHART IV

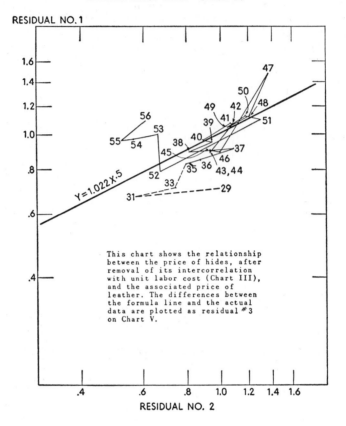

This chart shows the relationship between the price of hides, after removal of its intercorrelation with unit labor cost (Chart III), and the associated price of leather. The differences between the formula line and the actual data are plotted as residual #3 on Chart V.

ceding four years. The ratio of actual production to this proxy capacity variable, therefore, gives an indication of the pressure of overhead costs on prices. The relation between leather prices and per cent of capacity is shown in Figure 5–36. The formula for this relationship is

$$Y = 1.837X - .768$$

where Y = leather prices and X = annual production of leather as a per cent of capacity.

The final step in the analysis is the incorporation of a time trend in order to account for the remaining forces that may be influencing leather prices. This is done by plotting the residuals from the last regression line against "time," as in the upper panel of Figure 5–37. (This step can also be accomplished by taking the formula value below, exclusive of the time trend, TT, and dividing it into the annual average price of leather. The residual pattern shown in the upper panel of Figure 5–37 results.) This

FIGURE 5-36

LEATHER PRICE DATA—CHART V

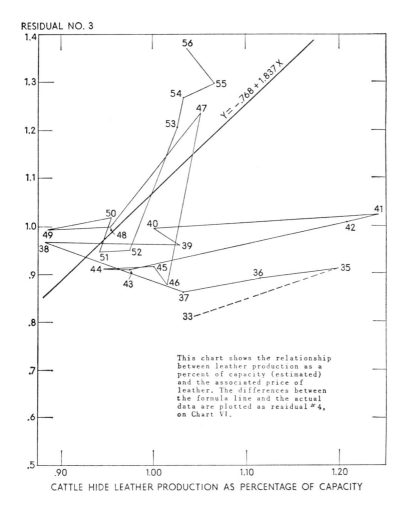

RESIDUAL NO. 3

$Y = -.768 + 1.837 X$

This chart shows the relationship between leather production as a percent of capacity (estimated) and the associated price of leather. The differences between the formula line and the actual data are plotted as residual #4, on Chart VI.

CATTLE HIDE LEATHER PRODUCTION AS PERCENTAGE OF CAPACITY

residual pattern has three distinct time trends: the first, from 1935 to 1940; the second, from the beginning of World War II to the outbreak of the Korean War; and the third, from the Korean period to 1956. These three trends are also shown in the chart, and the adjusted residual after including these time trends is shown in the lower panel of Figure 5–37.

Conclusion. When the above formulas are combined, they produce the final predicting equation:

$$P_l = .863U \left(\frac{1.022 P_h^{.5}}{.460 U^{.85}} \right) (1.837S - .768) \, TT$$

FIGURE 5-37

LEATHER PRICE DATA—CHART VI

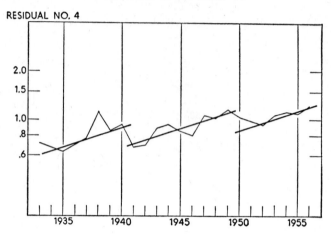

RATIO OF ACTUAL PRICE TO CALCULATED PRICE—CHART VII

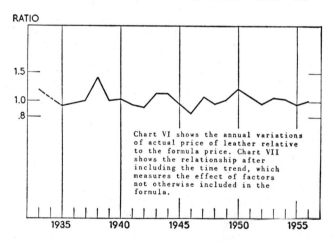

Chart VI shows the annual variations of actual price of leather relative to the formula price. Chart VII shows the relationship after including the time trend, which measures the effect of factors not otherwise included in the formula.

in which

P_l = Calculated price of leather in cents per square foot.
U = Index of unit labor cost, 1947–49 = 100.
P_h = Price of cattle hide.
S = Annual production of leather as a per cent of capacity.
TT = Time trend, a measure of factors not otherwise included in the formula.

Figure 5–38 shows the graphic counterpart of the formula, and compares the actual with the calculated values. The dashed line, of course, can be

FIGURE 5-38

LEATHER PRICE DATA—CHART VIII

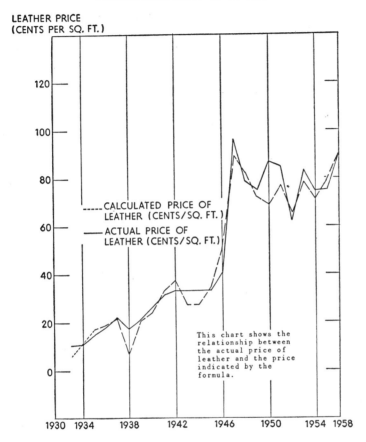

This chart shows the relationship between the actual price of leather and the price indicated by the formula.

constructed either from the formula or from the table, as explained in Chapter 3.

Summary

In the long run, prices of industrial raw materials and semimanufactured goods are determined by unit labor cost; in the short run, these trends may be modified by supply and demand imbalances. Unfortunately, cost data are generally not available for adequate and continuing analyses of the price structure by means of cost components. Therefore, proxy variables must frequently be employed, depending on the information available. The construction of forecasting models is thus dependent on the ability of the analyst to integrate economic ideas with statistical technique. To some extent this has already become apparent from the previous material. It will become increasingly evident in the sections and chapters that follow, as more models are introduced involving various intricacies and complexities.

PRICES OF METALS AND FUELS

Are prices of metals and fuels determined by forces similar to those described in previous studies? To some extent, yes. Unit labor cost is still the most important causal factor, although it is highly correlated with other business costs such as transportation, insurance, power, depreciation, interest, taxes, and profits. The last two, taxes and profits, must be treated as business costs for purposes of forecasting, even though the practice may violate certain established principles of economic theory. The reason for this is that businessmen themselves regard these items as costs, and make their decisions accordingly. Thus, a tax on payrolls is an added wage cost; a tax on real estate is simply a capital charge like interest; and a tax on profits is often treated, for decision purposes, as a percentage of selling price, the price then being increased by an amount sufficient to accommodate the tax.

It follows that while unit labor cost is still a prime determinant of general as well as industry prices, other factors specific to the industry must be considered, particularly in the short run. These factors include: (1) production and stocks of the commodity and of related commodities, (2) consumption patterns of the relevant commodities, (3) exports, imports, and foreign exchange rates of principal producing and consuming countries, (4) prices and costs of the commodities involved, and (5) speculative influences resulting from strikes, disaster, new laws, and so forth, leading to inventory buying or liquidation. These factors, of course, are the same supply, demand, and related forces listed at the beginning of this chapter as price determinants. Let us see how they may be applied, therefore, to actual price studies of metals and fuels.

Metals and Metal Products

Changes in the wholesale price index of metals and metal products are closely associated with (1) changes in unit labor cost in the metal and metal products industry, (2) changes in expenditures for durable goods, and (3) changes in the ratio of steel production to rated capacity. The evidence of this is presented in Figures 5–39 and 5–40. The predicting equation, corresponding to the dashed line in Figure 5–40B, is

$$Y = \frac{U^{1.063} E^{.256} S^{.271}}{.579}$$

where

Y = Calculated price of metals and metal products.
U = Unit labor cost in the manufacture of metals and metal products.
E = Index of expenditures for all durable goods (producers' and consumers').
S = Ratio of steel production to rated capacity.

As can be seen from the charts, the regression lines are each linear in the logarithms, and hence the exponents of the above equation reveal the elasticities or weights directly. Thus, for every 10 per cent change in unit labor cost there is a 10.6 per cent change in the price of metals and metal products (Figure 5–39A). Similarly, a 10 per cent change in expenditures for durable goods is associated with a 2.6 per cent change in the price of metals and metal products (Figure 5–39B). And finally, a 10 per cent change in the ratio of steel production to rated capacity implies a change of 2.7 per cent in the price of metals and metal products (Figure 5–40A).

FIGURE 5–39

A	B
PRICES OF METALS AND METAL PRODUCTS VERSUS UNIT LABOR COST IN METALS AND METAL PRODUCTS INDUSTRIES	PRICES OF METALS AND METAL PRODUCTS VERSUS EXPENDITURES FOR DURABLE GOODS

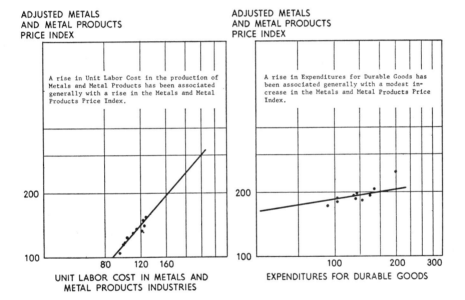

A forecast of the metals and metal products price index is thus contingent upon a forecast of each of the independent variables. How can these variables be predicted? Can results be obtained that will make the model useful for actual forecasting purposes? The following paragraphs indicate the answers to these questions.

1. A forecast of unit labor cost in the metals and metal products' industry can be determined from a forecast of average hourly earnings and production per man-hour in the industry. Changes in hourly earnings are dependent primarily on (*a*) changes in productivity in the preceding year, (*b*) changes in the cost of living over the preceding year, and (*c*) unemployment in excess of about 6 per cent, because a figure significantly less

FIGURE 5–40

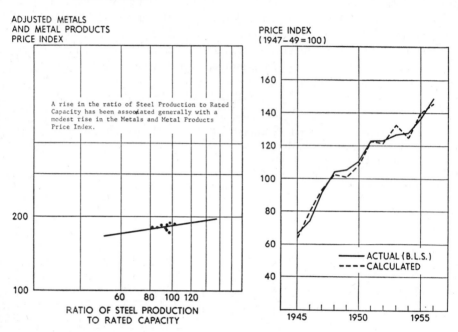

A

PRICES OF METALS AND METAL PRODUCTS
VERSUS RATIO OF STEEL PRODUCTION TO
RATED CAPACITY

B

PRICES OF METALS AND METAL PRODUCTS:
ACTUAL AND CALCULATED

ADJUSTED METALS
AND METAL PRODUCTS
PRICE INDEX

A rise in the ratio of Steel Production to Rated
Capacity has been associated generally with a
modest rise in the Metals and Metal Products
Price Index.

200

100

60   80   100 120
RATIO OF STEEL PRODUCTION
TO RATED CAPACITY

PRICE INDEX
(1947–49 = 100)

160

140

120

100

80

60

40

ACTUAL (B.L.S.)
CALCULATED

1945   1950   1955

than this is indicative of a labor shortage in the industry with a consequent effect on wages.

2. A forecast of expenditures for durable goods can be made by combining separate forecasts of expenditures on consumer durable goods and on capital goods. Techniques of forecasting the former are explained and illustrated in Chapter 7, and will be seen to involve such factors as consumers' purchasing power, consumers' inventories, relative prices, and replacement pressures. Forecasts of the latter are treated in Chapter 8, and employ variables such as corporate purchasing power, relative prices, and long-term interest rates. In making a short-term forecast of the metals and metal products' price index, a weighted index of new orders for consumer durables and new orders for capital goods may be constructed, and this index then used in place of actual expenditures for the products. The reason for this is that new orders normally lead changes in prices and changes in actual spending, thereby offering a useful pressure index for predicting these factors.

3. The ratio of steel production to rated capacity can be forecast on the basis of the outlook for steel demand and the steel industry's projections of expected steel capacity, published weekly.

Specific Metals

Price forecasts for specific metals must take into account additional factors peculiar to that metal. Unit labor cost, however, continues to be a key variable, and when combined with average unit costs of main raw materials (in an index with equal weights for each), a reasonably good explanation of price variations for individual commodities is obtained. Fortunately, the securing of data on employment and earnings, arranged by industry groups and subgroups, has been facilitated since World War II as a result of periodic publications along these lines by the Bureau of Labor Statistics. Unit labor cost data can thus be derived for a great many industries, and can be incorporated as an independent variable in price studies for these industries.

In using unit labor cost data, a distinction should be made between (1) unit labor cost, and (2) production worker payrolls per unit of output. The former is a concept; the latter is the most common measure of the concept. Since it is a payroll series for production workers, it excludes wages and salaries of nonproduction workers, and also fringe benefits. The series, payrolls per unit of output, can be determined by the ratio of payrolls to production, or specifically by the ratio of average hourly earnings to output per man-hour. The payrolls per unit of output series should then be combined with an average unit cost of raw materials series in order to obtain a comprehensive measure of the most significant cost factors affecting the price of specific metals. The following products may be cited as examples.

Finished Steel Prices. In Figure 5–41, it is apparent that the price of finished steel has fluctuated only slightly more than iron ore prices, and to a closer degree with unit labor cost in the industry. An analysis of steel prices and unit labor cost reveals that a 10 per cent change in the latter produces about a 12 per cent change in the former. The slightly steeper rise in steel prices relative to unit labor cost reflects in part the exclusion of labor fringe benefits from the measure of unit labor cost, and the continuous effort of the industry to utilize an increasing amount of capital equipment relative to labor in order to expand its proportion of finished products relative to crude items. The purpose of the latter has been to stabilize, to an increasing degree, the industry's production and sales mix.

Forecasts of finished steel prices can thus be made, based on unit labor cost and raw materials prices. Unit labor cost is the ratio of hourly earnings to production per man-hour, and hence the trend of unit labor cost will be affected directly by the trends of its two determinants, and indirectly by other factors such as increasing fringe benefits, the ratio of production to capacity, and the supply of durable goods production workers relative to the population. With respect to raw materials, their prices are likely to rise as less accessible iron mines are opened and as poorer grades of coal and iron ore are extracted from existing mines. On both counts, therefore, it

FIGURE 5–41

<small>FINISHED STEEL PRICES</small>

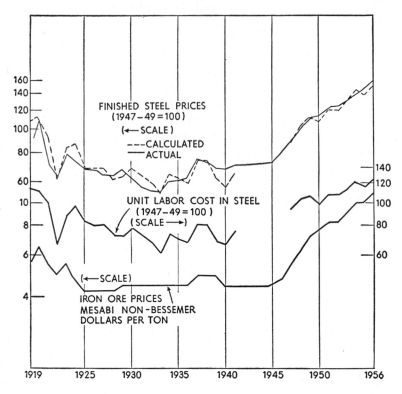

appears that the long-run price trend for finished steel will be upward in the years to come. This conclusion is further supported in the discussion of scrap prices below.

Scrap Iron and Steel Prices. In Figure 5–42, most of the fluctuations in scrap prices, it can be seen, were explained by changes in the price of pig iron and in the rate of steel operations. The reason for the relationship between the price of pig iron and the price of iron and steel scrap is that steel may be made from scrap as well as from pig iron. Steel manufacturers have considerable leeway in the proportion of scrap and pig iron that they can use. The ratio of scrap consumption to total steel production has remained remarkably stable since 1919, averaging about 62 per cent. Hence the prices of scrap iron and steel, and pig iron, with few exceptions, have tended to remain approximately in line with one another during most of the three and a half decades shown on the chart. As for the rate of steel operations, it is included as a variable because, as already noted in previous sections, significant positive correlations tend to exist in many industries between operating rates and prices. A good explanation of scrap prices is thus obtained which serves as a useful model for forecasting.

FIGURE 5-42

PRICE OF IRON AND STEEL SCRAP

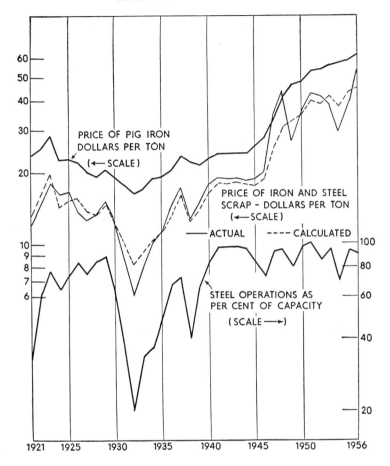

Zinc Prices. What important factors are at work in determining zinc prices? The largest consumers of zinc are the construction materials and consumers' durable goods industries which together use between one half and two thirds of total refined zinc. The construction materials industry absorbs somewhat over 30 per cent of the total zinc supply, primarily in galvanizing, while the second largest user, consumer durable goods, utilizes a little under 30 per cent of which about 75 per cent goes into automobiles. As shown in Figure 5-43, most of the changes in zinc prices can be attributed to, or explained by, changes in industrial prices, shipments to domestic consumers, and a time trend in the postwar years which allows for government policy changes and their influence on the free market.

The rise in zinc prices over the period shown has about equaled the rise in price of industrial commodities, as measured by the Bureau of Labor Statistics wholesale commodity price index, excluding farm products and

FIGURE 5-43

ZINC PRICES

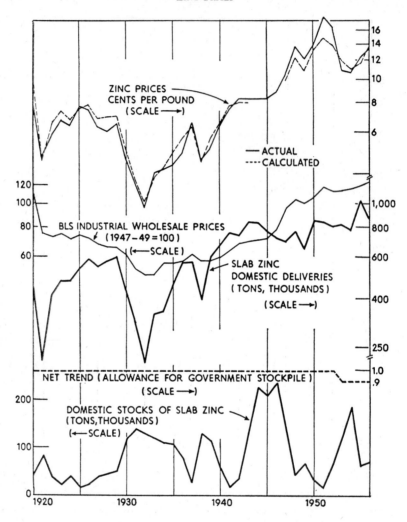

food. Variations in zinc prices that are not related to changes in the BLS index can be explained by fluctuations in domestic deliveries of zinc. In general, a 10 per cent variation in domestic deliveries has been associated with a 5 per cent fluctuation in zinc prices after allowing for changes in industrial wholesale prices.

Whereas in some price studies it is possible to use a measure of industrial production, such as the Federal Reserve Board index, as a general demand factor, this is not possible in the case of zinc, for at least two reasons. (1) Zinc has experienced a long-term decline in competitive position, being replaced by products like aluminum, plastics, or copper in such uses as tubes, pipes, fittings, wire, and wire rope. Since almost half the use of zinc is as a galvanizing metal, the long-term growth prospects of steel production are likely to provide the greatest strength to the market for zinc. (2) Beginning in the postwar years, the government's strategic stockpiling program exerted an increasing influence on zinc prices, although the stockpiling program became more stable in later years after the minimum requirements were filled, and subsequent government purchases were ostensibly aimed at stabilizing the industry. A time trend was thus included to measure the effect of stockpiling by American and foreign governments. The decline in the trend after 1952 indicates that the stockpiling effect has ceased to influence prices, and will not exert an influence unless it is liquidated and sold in world markets.

Copper Prices. In Figure 5–44, a good explanation of copper prices is obtained by merely using world copper consumption and a time trend as

FIGURE 5–44

Copper Prices

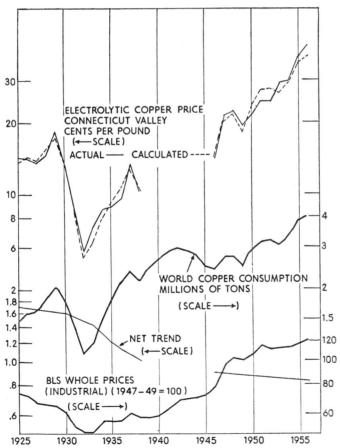

independent variables. The time trend takes into account the influence of indirect factors, such as discovery of new foreign sources, depletion of domestic sources, technological improvements, shifts in the general price level, and copper's loss of market position. The influence of both monetary conditions and unit labor costs may also be included. A proxy variable that serves as an adequate measure of these factors is the BLS wholesale price index of industrial commodities (that is, the all-commodity index minus farm products and foods).

The United States, it may be noted, accounts for about one half of world copper consumption, and copper demand in the United States is correlated with new orders for durable goods. The relative uses of copper have been declining since World War II, however, due to the encroachment of aluminum, zinc, and several new metals in a market that was traditionally supplied by copper. Of the combined world market for copper and aluminum, for example, copper has declined from a market share of 90 per cent in the mid-1930's to 75 per cent by the mid-forties, and to somewhat over 50 per cent by the late 1950's. Recent reports indicate that aluminum will continue to take an increasing share of the copper market, implying that new uses of copper will need to be developed in order to absorb the increasing supply of the product over the long run at prices that are reasonably profitable.

Prices of Fuels

Unit labor cost in the industry, combined with certain price factors that are relevant to the particular product in question, provide the variables that are needed for a study of fuel prices. Two specific examples, one dealing with bituminous coal and the other with distillate fuel oil, may be cited briefly.

Bituminous Coal Prices. Over the long run the level of bituminous coal prices has been determined principally by three factors: (1) unit labor cost in bituminous coal mining; (2) the ratio of bituminous coal stocks to total coal demand (specifically, the ratio of year-end stocks to one twelfth of the following year's total coal consumption); and (3) fuel oil prices.

These three factors determine rather well the price of bituminous coal, as shown in Figure 5–45 where the final results of the analysis are presented. The calculated price, or dashed line on the chart, was derived from the formula

$$Y = .404U^{.458} S^{-.006} P^{.437}$$

where

Y = Calculated wholesale price of bituminous coal (BLS index).
U = Unit labor cost in the bituminous coal industry.
S = Ratio of bituminous coal stocks at year-end to one twelfth of total coal consumption (plus domestic export) in the year following.
P = Price of #2 distillate fuel oil.

FIGURE 5–45

PRICES OF BITUMINOUS COAL, ACTUAL AND CALCULATED

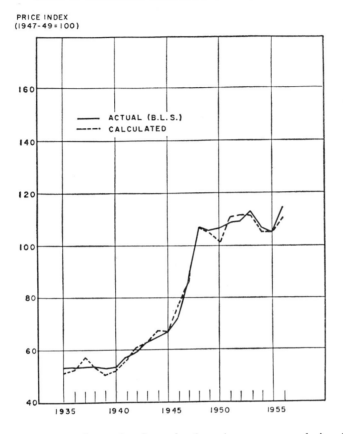

PRICE INDEX
(1947-49=100)

It is apparent from the formula that the separate relationships or regression lines, though not shown graphically, are linear in logarithms. Hence the exponents are the elasticities and may be interpreted accordingly. As for the independent variables, unit labor cost, U, was determined by dividing total bituminous coal production by average annual wages, including welfare charges, paid to production and related workers in this industry. The stocks factor, S, while of relatively small importance according to the elasticity, can have a significant short-run influence on coal price. The reason for this is that short-term variations in the ratio, such as the ratio of stocks on a given date to potential demand in the month following, can vary widely, with changes of 20 or 30 per cent or more occurring quite frequently. Finally, fuel price, P, has been almost equal to unit labor cost in its effect on the price of bituminous coal, as shown by the exponents, that is, elasticities. This has been borne out by the increasing utilization of diesel fuel oil for locomotive use during the past thirty years, with a consequent decline in coal consumption by railroads during the same period.

Distillate Fuel Oil Prices. Distillate fuel oil is used mainly for home heating and in diesel engines. It is one of the intermediate fractions in the refining process and includes fuel oil grades 1, 2, 3, and 4. At present it amounts to about 20 per cent of total refined petroleum products production.

An analysis of the price of distillate fuel oil #2 is presented in Figures 5–46 and 5–47. The analysis was run just as in previous studies, by plotting the price of fuel oil against the first independent variable, obtaining a relationship in the form of a regression line, then plotting the residuals (expressed as ratio deviations) against the next independent variable, and so forth. The final fit is shown in Figure 5–47B. The predicting equation is:

$$Y = .592 C^{.518} S^{-.033} P^{.541}$$

where

Y = Calculated price of distillate fuel oil #2, in cents per gallon.
C = Crude oil price, in dollars per barrel.
S = Ratio of stocks of distillate fuel oils and gas oils at year-end to domestic consumption of distillate fuel oil in the following year.
P = Average yield of gas oil and distillates, per barrel of crude oil.

Since the regression lines, as can be seen, are linear on logarithmic charts, the formula must also be linear in logarithms, and hence the ex-

FIGURE 5–46

FUEL OIL ANALYSIS

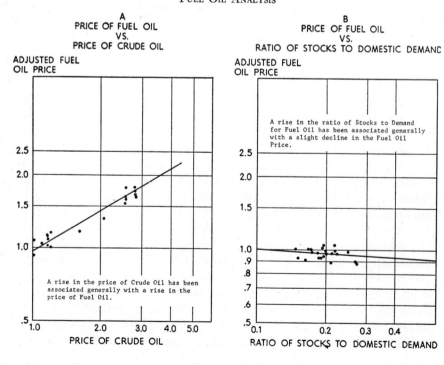

A
PRICE OF FUEL OIL
VS.
PRICE OF CRUDE OIL

ADJUSTED FUEL
OIL PRICE

A rise in the price of Crude Oil has been associated generally with a rise in the price of Fuel Oil.

PRICE OF CRUDE OIL

B
PRICE OF FUEL OIL
VS.
RATIO OF STOCKS TO DOMESTIC DEMAND

ADJUSTED FUEL
OIL PRICE

A rise in the ratio of Stocks to Demand for Fuel Oil has been associated generally with a slight decline in the Fuel Oil Price.

RATIO OF STOCKS TO DOMESTIC DEMAND

ponents reveal the elasticities directly. The price of crude oil, C, and the average yield, P, appear to have the highest elasticity effect on the calculated price, Y, while the stock-demand ratio, S, is of relatively little importance in the long run but can be of considerable significance in its short-term effects on price, as pointed out in the previous study.

What is the explanation for the unusual peak in price in 1948, and consequent drop in 1949 and 1950, as shown in Figure 5–47B? Since the calculated values do not seem to account for this erratic pattern, an explanation is in order. Actually, the explanation lies in the fact that there was an unusually large demand for fuel oil in 1948 and 1949 as the number of diesel locomotives rose, first by 40 per cent and then by 35 per cent. This new demand put pressure on existing supplies of fuel oil, thereby creating a temporary situation of scarcities and higher prices that was finally corrected by 1950.

Is there an absence of a demand factor for fuel oil in this analysis? The answer is that the demand for fuel oil is reflected indirectly by a proxy variable—the price of crude oil. This price represents in a sense the forces of demand and supply for petroleum products in general, and hence has been used as an explaining variable for the price of fuel oil. In this way,

FIGURE 5–47

FUEL OIL ANALYSIS

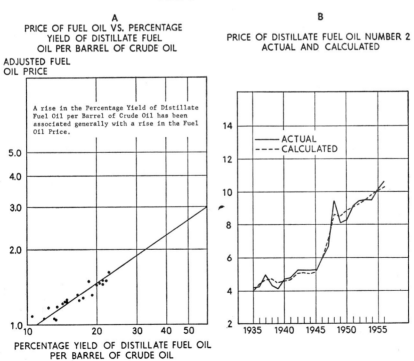

A
PRICE OF FUEL OIL VS. PERCENTAGE
YIELD OF DISTILLATE FUEL
OIL PER BARREL OF CRUDE OIL

B
PRICE OF DISTILLATE FUEL OIL NUMBER 2
ACTUAL AND CALCULATED

shifts in fuel oil demand relative to supply are left to be encompassed by the stocks-demand ratio, S.

Summary

Prices of metals and fuels can be analyzed in terms of such variables as (1) unit labor cost, (2) expenditures for durable goods, (3) ratios of stocks to demand, or of production to capacity, (4) prices of related products, and (5) yields in output, such as fuel oil per barrel of crude. Early turning indicators, such as new orders, can be employed to forecast short-term price pressures about the levels calculated from the basic determining factors. Different variables may thus be employed, depending on the particular product, the information that is available, and the analyst's imagination combined with his knowledge of economic principles as evidenced by his understanding of economic relationships.

INTEREST RATES

Interest is the price paid for the use of loanable funds. Hence, interest is (1) an economic connecting link between the present and future value of money, (2) a significant factor affecting investment decisions, and (3) an important element in the price of real and of financial assets.

Like any price, interest is affected by forces of supply and demand. Therefore, since interest is a price, it serves to allocate the scarce supply of a commodity—in this case loanable funds—among alternative uses or demands. The way in which it accomplishes this task is the subject of monetary theory and related fields of economics, while the measurement and prediction of the factors which cause it to change are of concern to us here. The following paragraphs, therefore, describe some principles and techniques that may be used to construct econometric models of interest rates.

Aaa Corporate Bond Yields

Figure 5–48 illustrates the results of a study of Moody's Aaa (high grade) corporate bond yields. The line called "criterion" on the chart represents the calculated or estimated values, and appears to be an extraordinarily good fit. An examination of the formula for the bond yield criterion, particularly the nature of the independent variables, reveals the reasons why:

$$\text{Aaa Yield} = .304\left(\frac{\text{Government Securities Held by Banks}}{\text{Liquidity Assets}}\right) + .632\left(\frac{\text{Business and Real Estate Loans}}{\text{Liquidity Assets}}\right)$$

$$+ .449\left(\frac{\text{Security Loans of Banks}}{\text{Liquidity Assets}}\right) + .046\left(\frac{\text{Bills Discounted}}{\text{Liquidity Assets}}\right)$$

FIGURE 5-48

Aaa Corporate Bond Yields

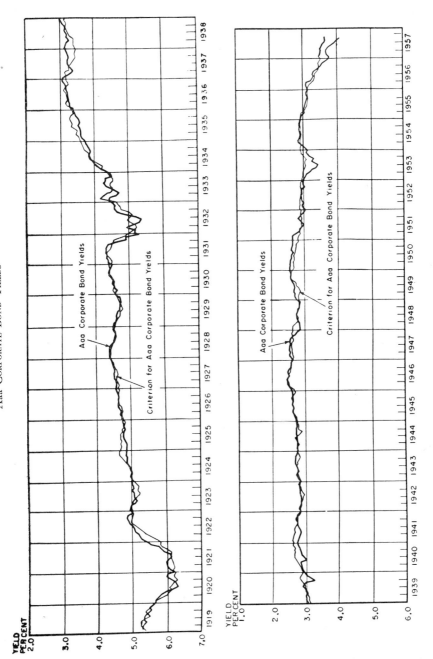

$$-.350\left(\frac{\text{Excess Reserves}}{\text{Liquidity Assets}}\right) + .127\left(\frac{\text{Total Debt}}{\text{Liquidity Assets}}\right)$$

$$+.577\left(\frac{\text{Long-Term Debt}}{\text{Total Debt}}\right) + .788\left(\frac{\text{Insurance and}}{\text{Pension Reserves}}{\text{Total Debt}}\right)$$

$$-\left(\frac{\text{Yield on 3–5 Year Governments}}{\text{Yield on Long-Term Governments,}}\atop{\text{10 Years Earlier}}\right) + (\text{Time Trend})$$

The first five factors in this equation, along with a time trend, were the variables used to explain Aaa bond yields until 1938, as shown by the upper panel of Figure 5–48. Systematic residuals between actual and criterion yields began to develop during the 1930's, however, thereby indicating that other forces were exercising an influence on yields. To account for these other forces, new variables were added to the formula to serve as measures of (1) the changing importance of debt in the economy, (2) the

FIGURE 5–49

Aaa Utility Bond Yields Plotted with Aaa Utility Criterion

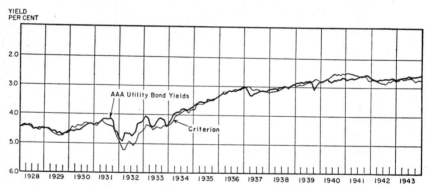

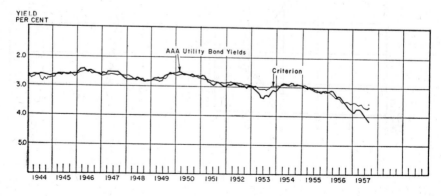

increasing significance of insurance and pension reserves, and (3) relative yields on government bonds. The result of adding these new factors is shown in the lower panel of the chart. Although deviations still exist, they appear to be more random than systematic, and are to be expected in any econometric study since all causal factors (economic, political, etc.) can never be taken completely into account.

It will be noted that the prediction or criterion formula above is actually made up of weighted ratios representing the demand for funds on the part of consumers, businesses, and banks, relative to the supply of funds on the part of businesses, banks, and government. Thus there is a bank demand for government securities, a demand for business, real estate, consumer and security loans, and a bank demand for rediscounts and reserves. On the supply side, insurance and pension reserves, or liquidity assets generally, are major forces at work in affecting the availability of funds. Many other specific demand and supply factors could be mentioned, but they were not included directly in the formula. They are accounted for, however, by the variables that were actually included, on the assumption that the latter are also substitute or proxy variables and thus provide an indirect but satisfactory measure of the real factors affecting interest rates.

Aaa Utility Bond Yields

The Aaa utility bond yield criterion reflects the typical relation between yields on these bonds and the average yield on Aaa corporate bonds. Some relation between the indexes of yields is to be expected, of course, since five of the fifteen bonds making up the corporate average are utility bonds. The ratio of the Aaa utility bond yield to the Aaa corporate bond yield has, however, ranged between .95 and 1.025 (annual average) since 1930. This ratio has been slightly greater than unity in several recent years, probably reflecting the increased amount of financing done by public utilities in the postwar period. Since changes in the ratio are small from one year to the next, a satisfactory criterion value for Aaa utility bonds can be constructed once the Aaa corporate criterion has been determined. Thus, in the late 1950's, a ratio of 1.010 was used to compute the expected spread between the corporate and utility yields.

Figure 5–49 shows the correspondence between the criterion and actual values of Aaa utility bond yields. (Note that the vertical axis, as in the previous chart, is scaled to increase downward rather than upward. This is not necessary, but is sometimes done in order to facilitate an estimate of the price trend, since bond prices and yields are inversely related). With few exceptions, the residuals are random rather than systematic, hence the criterion fits the actual quite closely. Those periods in which systematic deviations occurred can be explained by an examination of the supply and demand factors of the time, since the utility yield is correlated to the corporate yield and follows a pattern similar to the previous chart.

U.S. Government Taxable Bond Yields

Experience with government taxable bond yields has been relatively short, dating from 1942 when the first fully taxable Treasury bonds were issued. Moreover, during nine years of this period—from 1942 to March, 1951—the government bond market was pegged by the Treasury and the Federal Reserve System. The period of free market rates since then has

FIGURE 5–50

SPREAD IN BASIS POINTS BETWEEN U.S. GOVERNMENT TAXABLE BOND YIELDS
AND Aaa CORPORATE BOND YIELDS[a]

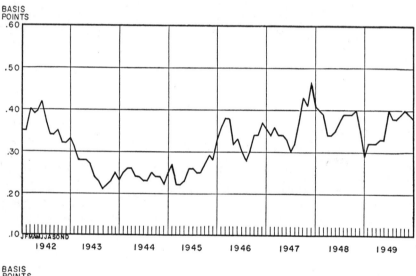

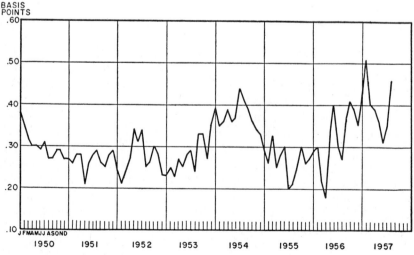

[a] Moody's Averages.

been somewhat shorter than the time usually required to establish characteristic relationships between government taxable yields and other variables.
Nevertheless, a basic relation between government taxable bond yields and
Aaa corporate bond yields (the latter having continuously enjoyed a free
market) can be derived, and an explanation provided of the variations in
spread between the two.

Figure 5–50 shows the spread in basis points between Treasury taxable bonds (Moody's averages) and Aaa corporate bond yields by months.
The spread, it can be seen, has generally ranged between 20 and 40 basis
points, occasionally going beyond these limits, depending on the state of
the money market. Thus, when the money market is easy, the spread between Treasury taxables and Aaa corporates tends to narrow to about 25
basis points or perhaps less. When the money market is tight, the spread
tends to widen, probably because the government bonds are more closely
connected to the banking system than are the Aaa corporates. (Federal
bonds are often used as collateral for bank loans, and, of course, the Federal
Reserve banks themselves buy and sell government bonds.) The spread also
tends to widen when there is a strong upward pressure on the yields of Aaa

FIGURE 5–51

GOVERNMENT TAXABLE BOND YIELDS PLOTTED WITH GOVERNMENT
TAXABLES CRITERION

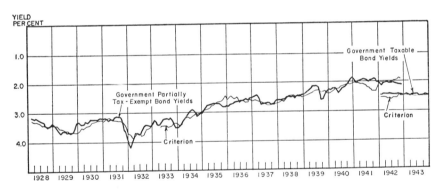

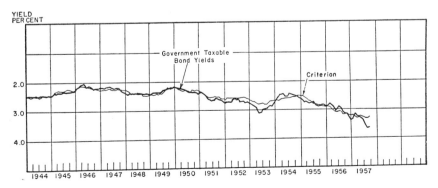

corporates, as may occur from a large volume of new corporate security offerings.

In view of these factors, how can forecasts of the criterion for government taxable bonds be made? Two variables must be predicted: (1) the Aaa corporate bond yield criterion, and (2) the probable spread between government taxables and Aaa corporates based on the considerations stated above. The performance of the government taxable bond criterion and the actual yields on these bonds is presented in Figure 5–51.

High-Grade Municipal Bond Yields

A difference in yields tends to exist between high-grade municipal bonds and Aaa corporate bonds. What are the factors responsible for this difference? Over the long run, using annual data, the differences, or ratios as expressed here, have been directly correlated with a weighted average of tax rates applicable to holders of municipal bonds, and a supply factor. That is, changes in the ratio of municipal yields to Aaa corporate yields have accompanied changes in the tax rate and supply factors, as shown in the charts.

Thus, in Figure 5–52, the ratio of municipal bond yields, M, to Aaa corporate bond yields, C, is plotted against the average tax rate, T, and a

FIGURE 5–52

RATIO OF HIGH-GRADE MUNICIPAL BOND YIELDS TO Aaa CORPORATE BOND YIELD CRITERION VERSUS AVERAGE TAX RATE APPLICABLE TO PURCHASERS OF MUNICIPAL BONDS

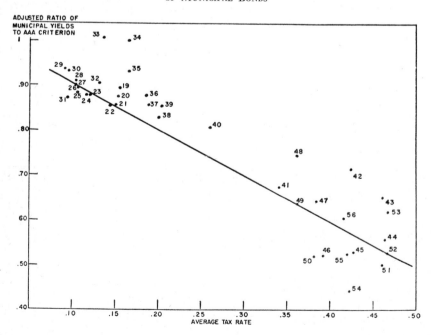

freehand regression line is drawn through the scatter. The formula for this regression line may be estimated from the chart as

$$y = 1.008 - 1.030T$$

The residuals from this formula or regression line are expressed as ratios, and then plotted in Figure 5–53 against the supply factor, municipal bond

FIGURE 5-53

RATIO OF HIGH-GRADE MUNICIPAL BOND YIELDS TO Aaa CORPORATE BOND YIELD CRITERION VERSUS NEW ISSUES OF STATE AND LOCAL BONDS

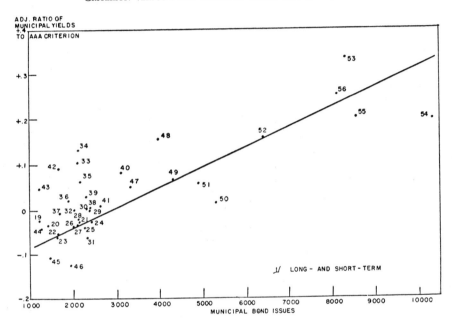

issues. A freehand regression line is again fitted, for which the formula as estimated from the chart is

$$y = -.128 + .0444S$$

where S is the supply of new issues of state and local bonds.

Combining the two formulas we obtain

$$\frac{M}{C} = (1.008 - 1.030T) + (-.128 + .0444S)$$

and multiplying both sides by the yields on Aaa corporates, C, the yields on municipals, M, is found to be

$$M = C\left[(1.088 - 1.030T) + (-.128 + .0444S)\right]$$

The graphic counterpart of this equation is shown as the criterion in Figure 5–54.

FIGURE 5-54

HIGH-GRADE MUNICIPAL BOND YIELDS PLOTTED WITH HIGH-GRADE
MUNICIPAL CRITERION

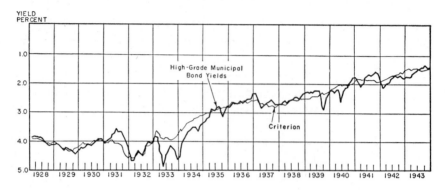

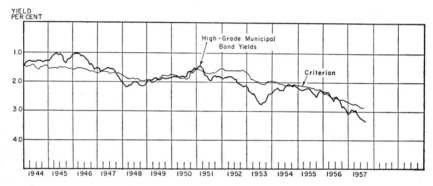

What economic considerations underlie the choice of these variables? Can an explanation be provided of the procedures involved in calculating the two new independent variables—the average tax rate (T) and the supply of new municipals (S)? The answers to both of these questions may be given briefly.

1. Since municipal bonds are tax exempt whereas other securities are subject to federal income taxes, it seems that the average tax rate ought to be a significant factor affecting the demand for municipal issues. It is necessary, therefore, to estimate the average annual tax rate that is applicable to holders of municipal bonds. This can be done by examining the *Annual Report* of the Secretary of the Treasury in order to determine the distribution of ownership of state and municipal bonds. For 1956, for example, it was found that one group composed of corporations, financial institutions, and other private organizations subject to the 52 per cent corporate income tax constituted about half of all municipal bondholders, while a second group consisting of individuals, partnerships, trust accounts, and other units subject to the personal income tax made up the other half. Hence, the 52 per cent corporate rate could be combined with the average personal in-

come tax rate, provided the latter was first estimated. This was done by constructing a frequency distribution of adjusted gross income for incomes over $10,000 annually, from data in the Treasury's *Statistics of Income— Individual Income Tax Returns*. The average tax rate for each income class in the distribution was estimated from tax tables, and the mean of the distribution as a whole was computed. This mean, found to be 31 per cent, was then averaged with the 52 per cent figure (both given equal weight because each group represented about half the market for bonds after excluding all governmental purchases as explained above). The resulting overall average tax rate was 41.5 per cent, which was the estimate used in this study.

2. The supply factor used in the calculation is represented by the volume of long- and short-term state and municipal obligations floated during the year. It can be forecast fairly easily on the basis of changes in population, school requirements, highway programs, and so forth. Of course, short-term fluctuation about the average supply level will occur during the year, thereby contributing to short-term deviations between actual and calculated yields. These deviations, however, will be due to seasonal factors and to the decisions of local authorities on the timing of offerings, and hence pose no difficulties for establishing either short-term (within one year) or long-term (annual) forecasts.

Referring back to the final formula, it may be noticed that the equation was chosen so as to show that: (1) some municipal bonds are bought for reasons other than taxes, and (2) some of the supply does not affect yields. Consequently, the two sets of parentheses inside the brackets of the equation were connected by a plus sign, that is, they were combined in an additive rather than multiplicative relationship. It is probable that in the future as more people become tax conscious, a multiplicative relationship will produce a better fit.

Baa Corporate Bond Prices

The concepts employed in the study of Aaa and municipal bonds are much the same as those used to analyze the prices of Baa (lower medium grade) bonds. The criteria for Baa bond prices are based on: (1) the Aaa bond yield criterion, which tends to precede the actual Aaa yields that affect the Baa yields, and (2) current earnings available for fixed charges of companies included in the Baa bond yield averages. The results of an analysis of utility, railroad, and industrial bonds utilizing these variables are shown in Figure 5–55. It may be noted that a lead characteristic on the part of the criterion or calculated values has appeared at various cyclical tops and bottoms, thereby facilitating the use of these estimates for prediction purposes. Beyond this, the analysis and interpretation of the relationships follow the same pattern as in previous studies, and hence need not be discussed again.

FIGURE 5–55

Baa CORPORATE BOND PRICES

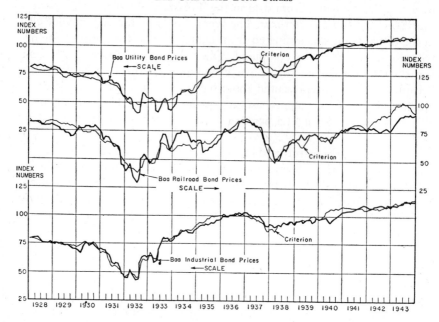

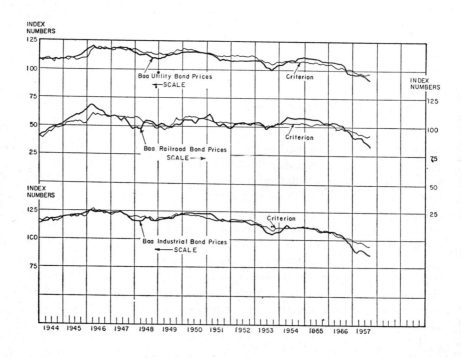

Short-Term Money Rates

All theoretical money rates can be computed from: (1) weighted averages of the basic factors upon which the Aaa corporate criterion rests, and (2) particular factors that are peculiar to the rate. Thus, the following paragraphs illustrate a study of the commercial paper rate and the Treasury bill rate, both utilizing the Aaa corporate bond yield as one of the variables.

FIGURE 5–56

COMMERCIAL PAPER RATE VERSUS Aaa CORPORATE BOND YIELD

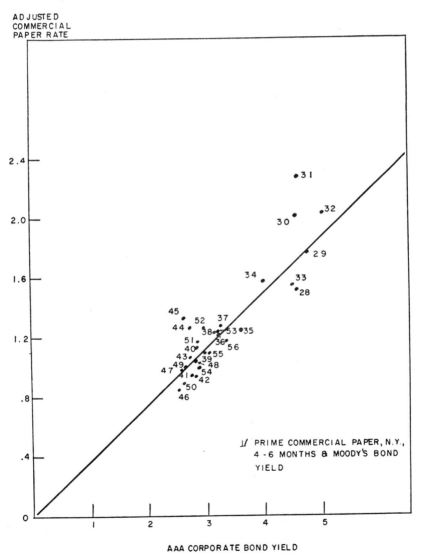

AAA CORPORATE BOND YIELD

The other variables introduced are the effects of changes in the discount rate of the New York Federal Reserve Bank, and the ratio of the supply of commercial paper to the supply of money (essentially a long-term factor). Changes in the former react on commercial paper rates within a very short time.

The analysis of commercial paper rates is presented in Figures 5–56 to 5–60. In the first chart, the commercial paper rate is plotted against Aaa

FIGURE 5–57

COMMERCIAL PAPER RATE VERSUS REDISCOUNT RATE
OF NEW YORK FEDERAL RESERVE BANK

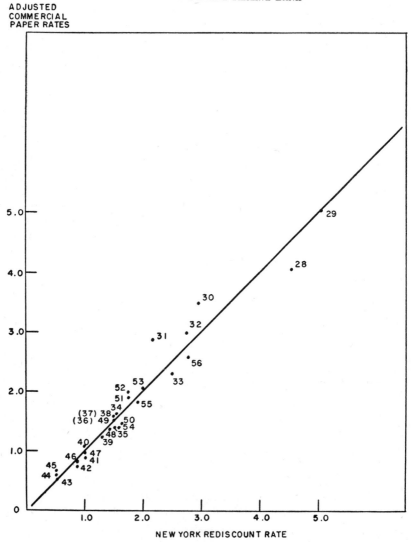

FIGURE 5-58

COMMERCIAL PAPER RATE VERSUS MONEY GRADIENT

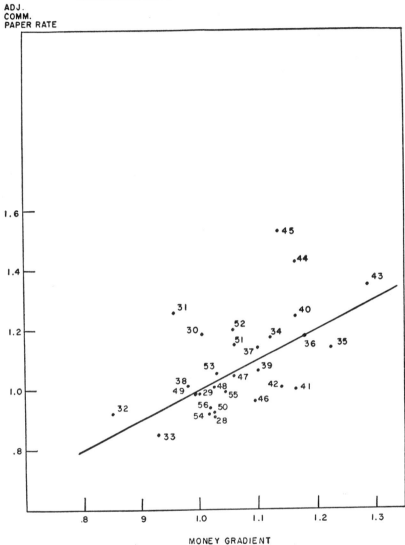

MONEY GRADIENT

yields. Except for the year 1931 when rates shot up sharply due to an out-flow of gold from the United States because the United Kingdom went off the gold standard, a fairly well defined positive relationship between commercial paper rates and Aaa bond yields has prevailed.

The residuals from the freehand regression line are plotted against the next variable, the New York rediscount rate, and another freehand regression line is fitted. The rediscount rate is used by the Federal Reserve,

FIGURE 5–59

TIME TREND FOR COMMERCIAL PAPER RATES

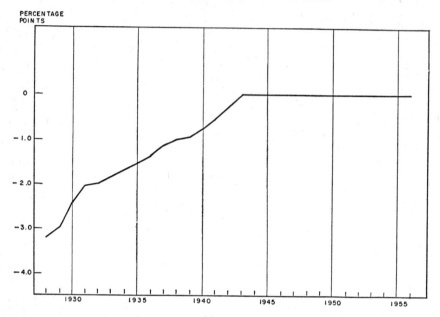

along with other devices, as a means of controlling an unhealthy credit expansion and inflation. Since it usually makes little difference to a businessman whether he pays 3 per cent or 4 per cent for a short-term inventory loan, and since government is going to borrow—irrespective of interest rates—when expenditures exceed revenues, an increase in the rediscount rate and a consequent increase in commercial paper rates are not apt to check expansion in the demand for bank credit. However, changes in short-term money conditions usually affect long-term money rates, which in turn affect long-term business expectations and business investment. To this extent the inclusion of the rediscount rate is an important variable in an analysis of this type.

The residuals from the regression line are again expressed as ratios and then plotted against the next variable, the money gradient or rate of change of bank deposits. This serves as a measure of changes in the money supply and is thus included in the analysis along with the previous demand factors. A freehand regression line is drawn through the scatter, and again the residuals are collected. These residuals are plotted against the next and final variable, "time." The resulting time trend is a measure of the average influence of all factors other than Aaa bond yields, the rediscount rate, and the money gradient in affecting commercial paper rates. The graphic fit is shown in Figure 5–60, for which the formula is

$$
\begin{array}{c}
\text{Commercial} \\
\text{Paper Rate} \\
\text{Criterion}
\end{array} = .68 \left\{ .55 \left(\begin{array}{c} \text{Aaa} \\ \text{Bond} \\ \text{Yield} \end{array} \right) \left(\begin{array}{c} \text{N.Y. Re-} \\ \text{discount} \\ \text{Rate} \end{array} \right) \left(\begin{array}{c} \text{Money} \\ \text{gradient} \end{array} \right) \right\} + \begin{array}{c} \text{Time} \\ \text{Trend} \end{array}
$$

where the commercial paper rate criterion refers to the rate on prime commercial paper, 4-to-6 months, in the New York money market.

The criterion for the Treasury bill rate is determined by the same factors as the commercial paper rate, but different weights or constants are involved. The result of a study of the Treasury new bill rate is shown in Figure 5–61.

COMMON STOCK PRICES

The late British economist John Maynard Keynes, observing that most buyers and sellers in the stock market base their decisions to trade on

FIGURE 5–60

COMMERCIAL PAPER RATES AND THE CRITERION FOR COMMERCIAL PAPER RATES

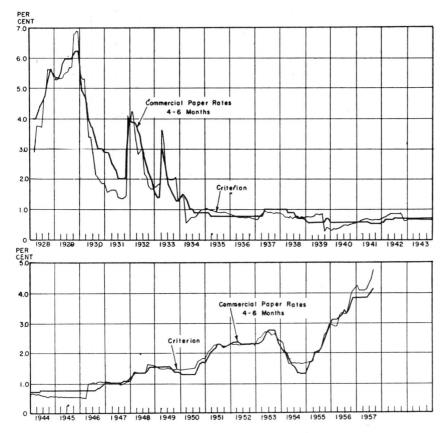

FIGURE 5-61

TREASURY NEW BILL RATE AND THE CRITERION FOR TREASURY NEW BILL RATE

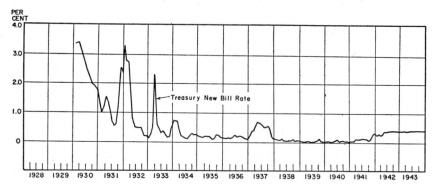

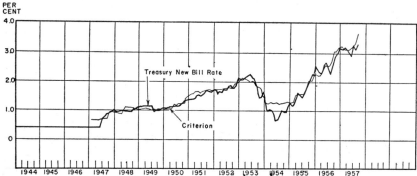

uninformed guesses and hunches, was led to write in his well-known *General Theory* (p. 155) that stock market trading was like a "game of Snap, of Old Maid, of Musical Chairs—a pastime in which he is victor who says Snap neither too soon nor too late, who passes the Old Maid to his neighbor before the game is over, who secures a chair for himself when the music stops."

Statements of this and a similar nature have led many analysts to believe that the pattern of stock prices is basically random, reflecting the hopes and fears of the mass of investors as these are modified by outside shocks such as wars, political upheavals, strikes, and various random events. Extensive research along these lines (some results of which are illustrated below) indicates, however, that the pattern of stock prices is not random, and that the pattern is not likely to have arisen from the cumulation or summation of a random series. Indeed, the pattern of stock prices has been found to have a nonrandom structure on hourly, weekly, and annual bases, thus implying that there ought to be a rational explanation of past price movements which would serve as a basis for predicting their future. Let us see if this is so.

If the majority of traders in common stocks actually know very little about their stocks or why prices should go up or down, why is the pattern of stock prices not random? The answer is that the real trend of stock prices is determined by an informed minority rather than an uninformed majority. Thus, suppose there are 1,000 equal traders in a particular stock, and that a majority, say 900, are not informed about the underlying economic forces at work in affecting this stock. This majority will then decide to buy or sell on the basis of their largely unfounded hunches or guesses, and the effect will be the same as if they tossed coins. That is, their average expectations will be zero, and the real market trend will be determined by the confident few who base their decisions on knowledge of the underlying causes. Thus, suppose the minority of 100 are informed as to conditions and act accordingly. Then if conditions are improving, we should expect about 550 buyers (that is, half of the majority plus all of the minority) and 450 sellers; hence share prices will rise. Alternatively, if conditions are deteriorating, we should expect about 550 sellers and 450 buyers; therefore the trend of prices will be downward.

Of course, the actual balance would not be as precise as this, since there would usually be chance deviations from the average expectation. Moreover, there would be occasional undercurrents of bias as when large traders influence short-term price trends, and the market at times is subjected to external impacts which serve to bias the decisions of the guessers. At best, therefore, only the long- and intermediate-term trends of common stock prices can be evaluated, by relating the essential variables that are involved. In the following paragraphs, therefore, the use of the term "investors" refers to the informed or minority group, since its actions are responsible for determining the real trends of common stock prices.

Essential Variables

What are the factors that prompt investors to purchase common stocks? Five major classes of motives may be cited: (1) to secure income, (2) to obtain capital appreciation, (3) to own property in liquid form, (4) to protect savings against inflation, and (5) to gain managerial control of enterprises. There may be other reasons as well, but these are by far the most important for purposes of intermediate- and long-run analysis. The problem, of course, is to quantify these motivating forces, sometimes by combining separate measures into a single synthetic variable, and sometimes by employing substitute or proxy variables where direct measures are unobtainable. Both of these techniques have been employed in this study.

Income. Assuming that income is the sole force motivating investors to buy common stocks, what income factors should we look for in making an analysis? Dividend yield, or the annual rate of dividends divided by the price, is clearly significant since it serves as a measure of the rate of return on the investment. Further, it is probably correct to assume that investors compare dividend yields with the rate of return on relatively "sound" investments, such as the yields on Aaa corporate bonds, before making a decision to buy common stocks. If after making the comparison it is found that the dividend yield exceeds the Aaa bond yield, and if there is reason to believe that the current dividend will be maintained, investors probably buy the common shares. The trend of earnings of a company is obviously an important variable for determining whether the dividend is likely to be maintained over the short term, since directors generally gear dividend policy to past earnings. Three variables—(1) *dividends*, (2) *earnings*, and (3) *yields on Aaa corporate bonds*—are therefore important as income measures for purposes of evaluating common stock prices. Good indexes of the first two, dividends and earnings, are readily available from published sources such as Standard and Poor, and good indexes of bond yields can be obtained from Moody's Investors Service. School and public libraries, brokers' offices, and many other organizations have these publications on file. If, along with these three variables, other measures of investors' assets and incomes could be obtained—measures such as (*a*) cash holdings and deposits, (*b*) incomes, and (*c*) borrowings for common stock purchases—their inclusion in the analysis would provide the essential ingredients of investors' purchasing power and hence serve as the demand factor in the model. Fortunately, such measures, or good substitutes for them, do exist and have been incorporated in the present study of common stock prices. Their nature, therefore, may be outlined briefly.

1. Data on investors' cash and deposits are not available directly. However, data on personal holdings of currency and deposits do exist. Hence, in addition to the above three variables, we may include (4) *personal holdings of currency and deposits* as a reasonably good proxy variable for investors' cash and deposits; this measure is also considerably improved if we add a reasonable estimate of (5) *cash position of institutional investors.*

2. Data pertaining to investors' income are also incomplete. However, in recent years a series showing (6) *the per cent changes in the disposable income of the top 1 per cent of the nonfarm population* has become available from the National Bureau of Economic Research, and has been found to serve as a good proxy variable for the disposable income of investors. In addition, an increasing volume of data on (7) *the income of pension funds*, and on (8) *the flow of funds to investment trusts* has become available. A good measure of investors' income can be obtained from these variables, therefore, by combining them in the way in which they seem to affect common stock prices most significantly. In the present study, preliminary research indicated that the best measure of investors' income was obtained by combining (6) with the ratio of half of both (7) plus (8) to total disposable personal income. The use of half rather than all represents the approximate proportion attributed to common stock purchases.

3. Loans for the purchase of common stocks involve two major vari-

ables for consideration: one is the volume of bank loans for the purchase of common stocks; the other is the ratio of the dividend yield to the short-term loan rate on securities. No data are available on the first, but the series (9) *net customer balances of member firms of the New York Stock Exchange*, must be closely correlated with it and, therefore, seems to be a satisfactory proxy variable for the true variable, loans for the purchase of common stocks. Hence it is used as a measure of such loans in this study.

The series (4) to (9) above are all parts, or measures of parts, of investors' disposable purchasing power. Data for (4) currency and deposit holdings, and (5) investors' cash position, measure the liquidity status of the investor, while series (6) to (8) represent income flows which are available for stock market investment, and (9) measures investors' willingness to incur debt for the purchase of common stocks. These series are not purported to be complete measures of the variables they represent, for clearly there are many other measures that could be introduced to yield still greater refinements. However, as will be seen below, the measures chosen have produced consistently good results for more than thirty years, indicating that they are probably the most important factors at work.

Capital Appreciation. The series (4) to (9) outlined above are, of course, also applicable to investors who buy for capital growth or appreciation. These investors also study earnings and dividends, but with a different emphasis. Being interested primarily in capital gains, they are apt to attach a greater weight to earnings than to dividends, and hence look primarily for situations in which earnings have increased substantially for a period of more than a year. The series (10) *rate of change of earnings with respect to time*, thus becomes an additional significant variable.

It should be worth noting that while the capital gains investor gives special attention to the *trend* of earnings, he cannot completely ignore either the dividend or the long-term interest rate. If he does, he may find himself paying absurdly high prices for a growth stock; for what he is really buying is the *present value of future earnings* which, according to the hypothesis, has been increasing at a known rate. This present value necessarily changes with the long-term interest rate. To pay thirty times earnings when the long-term interest rate is 3 per cent does not require nearly so much faith in the future as when the interest rate is 4 per cent.

Market Liquidity. The liquidity of stocks becomes particularly apparent at tops and bottoms of cyclical movements in stock prices. Near the top, the market is relatively more active and large blocks of stocks are traded without significantly affecting prices. The average investor is confident that, if he did make a mistake, the market is sufficiently fluid to enable him to sell to someone else; that is, he can call "Snap" or "Old Maid," as described earlier. At the bottom, however, trades are fewer, and it may become more difficult to sell, let us say, a thousand-share lot without significantly affecting the price. There are fewer interested buyers, hence the average investor is aware that he may not be able to rectify a mistake as easily as in the previous instance. Such changes in liquidity at tops and bottoms take place both for individual stocks and for the market average.

Inflationary Hedge. Prices of common stocks are highly correlated with prices of industrial commodities. This fact has led many students of the stock market to the conclusion that investors buy and sell common stocks primarily as a hedge against changes in commodity prices. Thus, when the investor believes that commodity prices are going to rise, he buys stocks on balance, and when he anticipates a decline in commodity prices, he sells stocks. Although this explanation on the surface sounds plausible, it should be noted that there are actually significant differences between commodity prices and stock prices, and it appears more likely that there is a common set of factors affecting both, with differences due to the peculiarities of each series. Thus, the key to the explanation of the correlation between stock prices and commodity prices is that commodity prices are highly correlated with unit labor cost as established earlier in this chapter, and that the long-term interest rate can be expressed as a function of commodity prices (as proposed by Irving Fisher as early as 1907), or more completely by relating it to the rate of change of bank deposits.

Whenever bank deposits are changing, liquid assets of individuals as well as business sales are likely to be changing in the same direction. Hence, the rate of change of bank deposits measures with some difference in timing (a short lead or lag) at least the following five variables in the list of ten selected above to explain stock prices: (1) corporate earnings, (2) corporate dividends, (4) personal holdings of currency and deposits, (5) cash position of institutional investors, and (10) the rate of change of earnings. In addition, the rate of change of bank deposits bears some relation to (3) the long-term interest rate, and to (9) the net customers' balances of member firms of the New York Stock Exchange. It happens, therefore, just as would be expected, that the rate of change of bank deposits indicates changes in the prices of common stocks, the latter advancing during periods of rising demand deposits or money supply, and declining during periods of falling money supply.

Managerial Control. Financially able groups from time to time contend with each other for managerial control of an enterprise. Although the reasons for these fights vary, they usually rest on differences of opinion with respect to the effects of current policies on future earnings, dividends, and managerial capabilities. An outside group seeking control may plan to change substantially the character of the business by merger or even liquidation, or it may wish to increase the financial strength of the enterprise so as to enable it to enter new fields of production and new markets. In every fight for control of an enterprise there is always a motive other than the normal motive of buying for income, appreciation, owning property in a liquid form, or protection against inflation. Therefore, in contests for control, prices of a stock may deviate considerably from levels indicated by the major normal factors.

A Stock Price Criterion

How important are the various factors mentioned above in affecting stock prices? Figure 5–62 shows a stock price criterion constructed from a weighted average of our ten factors. The statistical weights, or parameters, were determined by using annual data, and the resulting annual regression equation was then converted to a monthly criterion by substituting inter-polating series for data not available monthly. For example, earnings and dividends are only available quarterly and then several months after the fact; but industrial production times prices of finished goods less variable costs is available monthly and is highly correlated with earnings. Hence it can serve as a satisfactory proxy variable until (and if ever) the better series is made available at sufficiently early dates to be utilized directly.

Data showing the personal holdings of currency and deposits are only reported annually and must therefore be estimated between reporting dates. And the data on changes in disposable income of the upper 1 per cent have not been kept up to date since their development in 1953 in a work by Simon Kuznets, *Shares of Upper Income Groups in Income and Savings.* However, quarterly and annual data on income appear frequently in vari-ous Commerce Department publications (such as the *Survey of Current Business* and the July National Income Number) from which current esti-mates of investors' income can be made.

Conclusion

Some definitions and interpretations of the variables employed in the stock price analysis, Figure 5–62, are in order before concluding this sec-tion. The four series shown on the chart, with their associated code num-bers used in the study, are as follows: (58)—*Industrial Net Earnings.* This series shows profits after taxes of the 200 largest manufacturing corpora-tions, as reported by the Federal Reserve Board. Prior to 1939 it is the series formerly reported by the Board, but has been adjusted here to the one currently reported. (69)—*Industrial Dividends.* This represents the divi-dends after taxes paid by the same 200 corporations in the previous series. It is also reported by the Board and has been statistically adjusted in the same way as the above series. (70)—*Industrial Stock Prices.* This is Standard & Poor's daily stock price index of 50 industrials, plotted to show weekly and monthly high, low, and closing prices. The data are on a 1926 = 100 base. (71)—*Criterion for Industrial Stock Prices.* This index is a weighted average of (1) capitalized current industrial earnings, (2) capitalized cur-rent industrial dividends, (3) capitalized past industrial earnings, (4) capi-talized past industrial dividends, (5) brokers' loans for the account of others, and (6) the income and liquid assets of investors. The capitalization factor

FIGURE 5–62

INDUSTRIAL COMMON STOCK PRICES

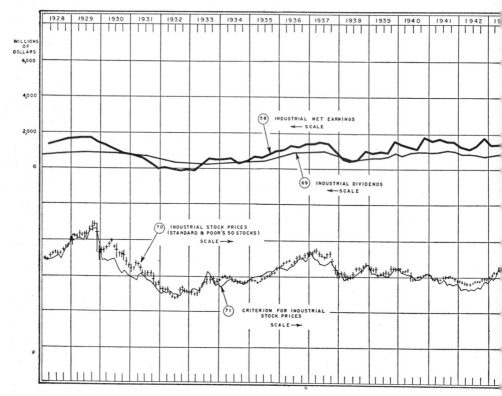

is based on the yields of Aaa long-term corporate bonds and an assumption of infinite life of producing property except during war years. In war periods, increments in earnings and dividends over the average earnings and dividends for the five years immediately preceding the war are capitalized on the basis of two and a half years' life. Current earnings are estimated, and the yield of Aaa bonds is replaced in the correlation formula by the "Criterion for Aaa Corporate Bond Yields" computed earlier in this chapter on pp. 180–83.

Finally, it may be of interest to note that a short-term relationship has long existed between common stock prices and an index of new orders for consumers' nondurable goods such as textiles and clothing. This new orders index is a good measure of what the merchant and small business-man, as part of the general investing public, think the course of business will be, because many businessmen in the nondurable goods field are active in the stock market, and retailers, who cause the changes in new orders, are often regarded as business seers in their home towns. New orders, there-fore, since they precede both earnings and dividends, may have some pre-

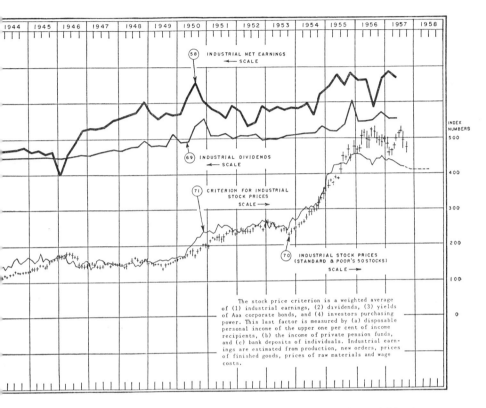

dictive value for stock prices. The lead time, however, is variable, hence new orders should be used in combination with information on price, tax, and monetary changes to obtain useful results.

While short-term stock price movements are often influenced by the short-term trend of new orders for consumers' nondurable goods, long-term stock price movements are more closely geared to new orders for capital goods. This new order index has turned down decisively before the stock market at the tops of cycles and, while lagging at the bottom, has turned up decisively before the active phases of bull markets have gotten under way.

QUESTIONS

1. Outline briefly the "master list" of factors that are primarily responsible for causing changes in commodity prices.
2. In addition to the general factors outlined above, what sort of specific considerations should be made in accounting for price changes? Explain.

204 · *BUSINESS AND ECONOMIC FORECASTING*

3. In the light of your answer to question 2, what statistical measures of price, demand, supply, and monetary factors were actually employed in the study of general farm commodity prices? Explain why.

4. In general, how did the study of farm commodity prices facilitate the study of specific commodity prices, namely corn and cotton prices?

5. (*a*) In the study of the price of print cloth, why was a measure of unit labor cost derived? (*b*) Basically, what is the nature of this labor cost formula, that is, its components?

6. (*a*) In general, what sort of factors are involved in determining the prices of metals and fuels. (*b*) Are these factors related at all to the price-determining variables discussed earlier in the chapter where other products were concerned?

7. What sort of demand and supply factors determine the yields on Aaa corporate bonds?

8. What is the role of Aaa bond yields in the study of money rates?

9. Explain the fundamental theory underlying the stock price study, that is, the forces that determine the trend of stock prices. What are the implications of this from a forecasting standpoint?

10. What are the chief motives prompting investors to purchase common stocks? Explain.

INSTRUCTORS: As a project, students may be asked to bring one or more of these models up to date, using either graphic or mathematical methods, depending on previous training. (See the Note to Instructors at the front of this book for further suggestions.)

Chapter 6

FORECASTING SALES OF CONSUMERS' NONDURABLE GOODS

Against the background of price forecasting procedures discussed in the previous chapter, we turn our attention now to the area of sales forecasting. The topics to be covered are important because sales forecasting is one of the chief activities of business economists employed in industry, and as a science it is gaining the increasing attention of accountants, financial analysts, and marketing researchers, all of whom are interested in budgeting and planning.

The basic procedure followed in this and subsequent chapters is to approach the problem of sales forecasting by what might be called the "product group" method. The technique consists of taking the Federal Reserve "Index of Industrial Production," the components of which are regularly published in the *Federal Reserve Bulletin*, the *Survey of Current Business*, and other sources, and to arrange these components in economically homogeneous groups. The problem is then one of forecasting sales within each of these groups, as will be shown in this and the chapters immediately following. Particular sales forecasts for individual firms can then be established from these product-group forecasts, by the use of market share or other devices to be discussed subsequently.

The product-group breakdown that is employed here, and the one that has proven itself reliable for arriving at successful predictions, is the following:

1. CONSUMERS' NONDURABLE GOODS (including consumer perishable and semidurable goods)
   Examples: Meats, processed and canned goods, alcoholic beverages, tobacco products, gasoline, newsprint, soap, drugs, textiles, clothing, shoes, and other consumers' leather and rubber products.

2. CONSUMERS' DURABLE GOODS
   Examples: Automobiles, appliances such as radios, television sets, and refrigerators, household furnishings, furniture, and books.

3. CAPITAL GOODS
   Examples: Machinery, machine tools, engines and turbines, electrical apparatus and equipment (other than electrical appliances), trucks,

buses, agricultural equipment, railroad equipment, and, in general, those goods that are used for the production of other goods or services, or for war purposes (such as tanks, planes, and other ordnance materials).

4. CONSTRUCTION MATERIALS

Examples: Stone, clay, glass, lumber, paints, portions of iron and steel production, and, in general, materials used in residential, industrial, commercial utility, and public construction.

5. FUELS, RAW MATERIALS, AND SUPPLIES

Examples: Petroleum and petroleum refining exclusive of gasoline, bituminous and anthracite coal, gas, and other fuels used throughout industry; also, portions of stone, clay and glass products, paper, metal mining, printing and publishing, and most important, chemicals.

Forecasting the first four categories will be the subject of our attention in this and the three chapters that follow, since the fifth classification was largely treated in the previous chapter and hence need be given only incidental attention in subsequent discussions.

DEMAND DETERMINANTS

A distinction between consumers' durable and nondurable goods is often necessary in most types of consumer demand problems. In this chapter we are concerned with consumers' nondurables, a classification which, for forecasting purposes as stated above, includes both consumers' perishable goods and consumers' semidurable goods.

What are the chief factors affecting the demand for consumers' nondurable goods? There are three basic factors which, when they are defined and measured in different ways according to the specific nondurable good involved, can be employed in actual forecasting. They are: (1) buying power, (2) demography, and (3) price. An explanation of each will help clarify their significance.

Buying Power

A series that is readily available and frequently employed as a measure of buying power is disposable personal income, or simply disposable income. It is equal to personal income less direct taxes, and represents the amount of money available to individuals to spend for goods and services or for saving. The series, as mentioned in Chapter 2, is published in the *Survey of Current Business* as well as other statistical sources. Although the use of disposable income as a measure of purchasing power will often yield good results for forecasting purposes, it has been criticized on the grounds that it does not represent "free" purchasing power. That is, it includes income that must be spent in order to maintain essential living standards, and hence is not a measure of the income actually available to people for discretionary spending. A more useful index of spending ability, therefore, would be a series that measures this "free" purchasing power. Such an index now exists, and is known as *supernumerary* or *discretionary income*, as described in Chapter 2. Both of these terms are used interchangeably throughout this book.

Discretionary income, it will be recalled from Chapter 2, is the flow of money available to individuals over and above their necessary expenditures. The National Industrial Conference Board, which now computes the index, does so by starting with the Commerce Department's figures on disposable income, and subtracting: (1) imputed income and income in kind, such as imputed rent on owner-occupied homes, imputed interest, and food, lodging, and clothing furnished to employees by employers; (2) major fixed outlay payments such as mortgage debt, consumer instalment debt, insurance and pension payments, homeowner taxes, and tenant rent; and (3) essential expenditures on food, clothing, medical facilities, household utilities, and local transportation. The resulting figure is what is now known as "discretionary income";[1] it is a more accurate measure of consumer purchasing power, and hence a more refined measure for consumption goods forecasting even though disposable income is often satisfactory.

Demography

The sale of every product depends upon certain population characteristics. These characteristics are referred to as the demographic factor. This factor does not necessarily relate to human populations, but rather to characteristics that are peculiar to the particular product being investigated. Thus, in a study of the demand for food, the demographic factor determining demand might be the number of children; in the demand for gasoline discussed below, it is the number of cars, trucks, and busses in use; and in the study of the demand for women's outerwear, which is also discussed below, it is the number of females grouped both by age and marital status.

The employment of a demographic factor in forecasting sales of consumer nondurable goods is thus nothing more than a recognition of the need to distinguish between total market demand on the one hand, and *market segments* on the other, where the latter refers to the carving up of a total market into homogeneous subgroups according to similar demand characteristics. Such segments may be established in terms of income, social status, sex, age, educational level, geographic location, nationality, religion, and numerous other dimensions. The object is to identify and then construct one or more segments that are believed to be important elements affecting the sale of the product. The segment, when it is quantified, becomes an independent variable in a predicting equation, and is referred to here as a demographic factor.

[1] The Econometric Institute, Inc. has also prepared estimates of discretionary income, but its results differ somewhat from those of the Conference Board. The Institute, for instance, adds to disposable income (1) cash stocks on hand, and (2) consumer credit.

Price

A price or product substitution factor may be included as a third variable affecting the sale of most consumer nondurables. Various direct and indirect influences of price on sales may be employed, such as price differences and price ratios between the product concerned and competing or complementary products. In this way the relationships between the more relevant prices are brought into the predicting equation, thereby enhancing management control as well as forecasting accuracy. Various measures of elasticity such as the *price elasticity of demand* and the *cross elasticity of demand* can thus be established, showing the percentage change in the dependent variable, quantity demanded (or perhaps sales), resulting from 1 per cent change in the independent variable, such as the price of the product in the former instance, or the price of a competing or complementary product in the latter instance. Illustrations of these will be given in various studies discussed below.

Basic Equation

By employing the appropriate forms of relevant variables, sales (S) can be forecast by combining in an additive or multiplicative relationship the three factors, buying power (B), demography (D), and price (P), as shown by the formulas

$$S = B + D + P, \quad \text{or} \quad S = BDP.$$

The use of these formulas to forecast sales of specific types of nondurable goods involves three basic steps: (1) the relevant variables affecting the sale of the product must be identified; (2) the data, or reasonable proxies, must be collected to represent the variables; and (3) the data must be subjected to a statistical analysis in order to determine the most probable constants or weights of the variables. Various case studies utilizing these and related concepts are presented in the sections that follow. It should be noted that for each product studied, different measures of buying power, demography, and price were employed. The choice often depends on a variety of factors, such as the availability of relevant data, economic analysis and judgment of the relationship between the variables, and the inclusion of variables that seem to fit the data best, provided that they can be supported by economic reasoning.

Finally, a word as to statistical method before proceeding with actual case studies of sales forecasting. In this and the following chapters, just as in the previous chapter, all of the studies were done graphically rather than mathematically, meaning that the various regression lines were fitted freehand. As pointed out in Chapter 4, the slope of a regression line shows the average number of units change in the dependent variable resulting from a unit change in the independent variable. The slope, therefore, depends not only upon the relation between the variables but also on the units in which each is stated. In order to adjust for the influence of the latter, therefore, and thus obtain a measure of slope which is based only on the relation between the variables, the separate series are frequently divided by their respective *standard deviation*. Each variable is thus reduced to a different form, by stating it in units of its own standard deviation (as first explained on pp. 74–75), as was done in several studies in the previous chapter.

DEMAND FOR MOTOR FUEL (GASOLINE)

What are the controlling forces affecting the sale of gasoline? Total sales of gasoline may be expressed as a function of three classes of factors: (1) the number of gasoline consuming units in use, which includes passenger cars, trucks, airplanes, buses, tractors, and other miscellaneous sources; (2) the average number of miles per consuming unit, which in turn depends upon the composition of motor vehicles in use, changes in discretionary income, and gasoline prices; and (3) the average number of miles per gallon. A fourth variable, a time trend which serves as a proxy variable, may also be used as a measure of the influence of other variables not included in the above three. This embraces the average of all other miscellaneous influences that affect average mileage. The forecast equation for the sale of gasoline, as will be seen below, is then given by the formula:

$$G = \{1.66T + [C + 5.5B][.458(3.15I)^{.165}] 4.74P^{-.52}\} 17TT$$

where

> G = Gasoline consumption in millions of barrels per calendar year.
> T = Trucks in use July 1.
> C = Cars in use July 1.
> B = Buses in use July 1.
> I = Discretionary or supernumerary income in billions of dollars per calendar year.
> P = Price of gasoline in cents per gallon (average per calendar year).
> TT = Time trend, which is a proxy variable serving as a measure of those factors not included in the formula.

How is this equation derived? The answer is given in the analysis of Table 6–1, or in Figures 6–1 to 6–6. We shall concentrate attention on the diagrams since they are easier to follow, and leave the tables for reference purposes. Thus, the first step in the analysis is to plot the variables over time, as in Figure 6–1, thereby facilitating a visual comparison of their rates of change, especially since the series are plotted on semilogarithmic paper.

Analysis

The independent variables or demand factors in the above equation are the subject matter of this particular study. Hence they are discussed separately below in the order in which they appear in the equation, al-

TABLE 6-1

MOTOR FUEL DATA

Year	(1) Cars in Use (Mil.)	(2) Buses in Use (Mil.)	(3) Cars and Buses in Use, Weighted 5.5×(2)+(1) (Mil.)	(4) Trucks in Use (Mil.)	(5) (4)×28.22	(6) Total Gasoline Consumption (Millions of Barrels)	(7) (6)−(5) (Millions of Barrels)	(8) 17×(3)	(9) Residual No. 1 (7)÷(8)	(10) Super-numerary Income ($ Billion)	(11) 3.15×(10)
1929	20.9	.076	21.3	3.0	84.7	378.0	293.3	362.1	.810	49.6	156.2
1930	21.4	.082	21.9	3.1	87.6	394.8	307.2	372.3	.825	42.1	129.8
1931	20.8	.094	21.3	3.1	87.6	403.4	315.8	362.1	.872	33.2	104.6
1932	19.3	.102	19.9	3.0	84.5	373.9	289.4	338.3	.855	20.9	65.8
1933	18.5	.101	19.1	3.0	84.5	377.0	292.5	324.7	.901	19.1	60.8
1934	19.8	.101	20.4	3.1	87.6	410.3	322.7	346.8	.931	24.2	76.2
1935	20.8	.104	21.4	3.3	93.2	434.8	341.6	363.8	.939	29.6	93.2
1936	22.3	.110	22.9	3.5	98.8	481.6	382.8	389.3	.983	36.7	115.6
1937	23.8	.114	24.4	3.7	104.4	519.4	415.0	414.8	1.000	40.2	126.6
1938	23.5	.118	24.2	3.9	110.0	523.0	413.0	411.4	1.004	35.1	110.6
1939	24.5	.122	25.2	4.0	112.9	555.5	442.6	428.4	1.033	39.9	125.7
1940	25.6	.127	26.3	4.1	115.6	589.5	473.9	447.1	1.060	44.8	141.1
1941	27.7	.131	28.4	4.4	124.1	667.5	543.4	482.8	1.126	59.5	187.4
1942	26.6	.135	27.3	4.5	127.0	589.1	462.1	464.1	.996	79.0	248.9
1943	25.3	.145	26.1	4.4	124.1	568.2	444.1	443.7	1.001	91.1	287.0
1944	24.0	.152	24.8	4.4	124.1	632.5	508.4	421.6	1.206	102.8	323.8
1945	24.0	.157	24.9	4.8	135.5	696.3	560.8	423.3	1.325	104.5	329.2
1946	25.1	.168	26.0	5.1	144.0	735.4	591.4	442.0	1.338	108.3	341.2
1947	27.5	.181	28.5	5.9	166.4	795.0	628.6	484.5	1.297	109.0	343.4
1948	30.0	.193	31.1	6.6	186.3	871.3	685.0	528.7	1.296	120.9	380.8
1949	32.7	.203	33.8	7.1	200.4	913.7	713.3	574.6	1.241	120.2	378.6
1950	35.9	.216	37.1	7.6	214.5	994.3	779.8	630.7	1.236	135.4	426.5
1951	38.5	.227	39.8	8.1	228.7	1,089.6	860.9	676.6	1.272	147.6	464.9
1952	39.8	.235	41.1	8.4	237.0	1,143.0	906.0	698.7	1.297	154.7	487.3
1953	42.2	.242	43.5	8.7	245.5	1,205.8	960.3	739.5	1.299	164.8	519.1
1954	44.4	.246	45.8	8.8	248.4	1,230.6	982.2	778.6	1.261	166.2	523.5
1955	47.4	.252	48.8	9.2	259.6	1,321.7	1,062.1	829.6	1.280	179.6	565.7
1956	49.8	.255	51.2	9.5	268.1	1,371.9	1,103.8	870.4	1.268	192.7	607.0

TABLE 6-1 (Continued)

Year	(12) (11)^.165	(13) .458×(12)	(14) Residual No. 2 (9)÷(13)	(15) Average Price of Gasoline (Cents/Gal.)	(16) (15)^-.52	(17) 4.74×(16)	(18) (9)×(13)×(17) (Mil. Bbl.)	(19) (5)+(18) (Mil. Bbl.)	(20) Residual No. 3 (6)÷(19)	(21) Time Trend of Residual No. 3	(22) Calculated Motor Fuel Consumption (19)×(21)	(23) Actual Consumption ÷ Calculated Consumption
1929	2.301	1.054	.769	21.42	.2033	.964	367.9	452.6	.835	.82	371.1	1.019
1930	2.232	1.022	.807	19.95	.2107	.999	380.1	467.1	.844	.87	406.9	.970
1931	2.154	.987	.883	17.00	.2202	1.044	373.1	460.7	.876	.90	414.6	.973
1932	1.995	.914	.935	17.93	.2231	1.057	326.8	411.3	.909	.92	378.4	1.066
1933	1.969	.902	.999	17.82	.2242	1.063	311.3	395.8	.953	.94	372.1	1.013
1934	2.044	.936	.994	18.85	.2169	1.028	333.7	421.3	.974	.96	404.4	1.026
1935	2.113	.968	.970	18.84	.2174	1.032	363.4	456.6	.952	.97	442.9	.982
1936	2.190	1.003	.980	19.45	.2137	1.017	397.1	495.9	.971	.98	486.0	.991
1937	2.223	1.018	.982	19.09	.2157	1.027	433.7	538.1	.965	.99	532.7	.975
1938	2.174	.996	1.008	19.51	.2134	1.012	414.7	524.7	.997	.99	519.5	1.007
1939	2.220	1.017	1.016	18.75	.2175	1.031	449.2	562.1	.988	.99	562.1	.988
1940	2.263	1.036	1.023	18.41	.2139	1.014	469.7	585.3	1.007	1.00	585.3	1.007
1941	2.371	1.086	1.037	19.23	.2151	1.020	534.8	658.9	1.013	1.01	665.5	1.003
1942	2.485	1.138	.875	20.43	.2048	.988	521.8	648.8	.908	1.02	661.8	.890
1943	2.545	1.166	.858	20.53	.2079	.985	509.6	633.7	.897	1.04	659.0	.862
1944	2.595	1.189	1.014	20.59	.2074	.983	492.8	616.9	1.025	1.06	653.9	.967
1945	2.602	1.192	1.115	20.50	.2079	.985	496.9	632.4	1.101	1.10	695.6	1.001
1946	2.617	1.199	1.116	20.77	.2064	.978	518.3	662.3	1.110	1.12	741.8	.991
1947	2.620	1.200	1.081	23.11	.1954	.926	538.4	704.8	1.128	1.14	803.5	.989
1948	2.666	1.221	1.061	25.88	.1841	.872	562.9	749.2	1.163	1.15	861.6	1.011
1949	2.663	1.220	1.017	26.79	.1809	.857	600.8	801.2	1.140	1.15	921.4	.992
1950	2.716	1.244	.994	26.76	.1809	.857	672.4	886.9	1.121	1.15	1,019.9	.975
1951	2.755	1.262	1.008	27.15	.1795	.851	725.8	954.5	1.142	1.15	1,097.7	.992
1952	2.776	1.271	1.020	27.56	.1781	.844	749.5	986.5	1.159	1.15	1,134.5	1.008
1953	2.805	1.285	1.011	28.69	.1746	.828	786.8	1,032.3	1.168	1.15	1,187.1	.978
1954	2.808	1.286	.981	29.09	.1736	.823	824.1	1,072.5	1.147	1.15	1,233.4	.998
1955	2.845	1.303	.982	29.07	.1733	.821	887.5	1,147.1	1.152	1.15	1,319.2	1.002
1956	2.878	1.318	.962	29.93	.1708	.810	929.2	1,197.3	1.146	1.15	1,376.9	.996

Source: Automobile Manufacturers Association, Inc., Automobile Facts and Figures (published annually).

FIGURE 6–1

MOTOR FUEL DATA

CHART I

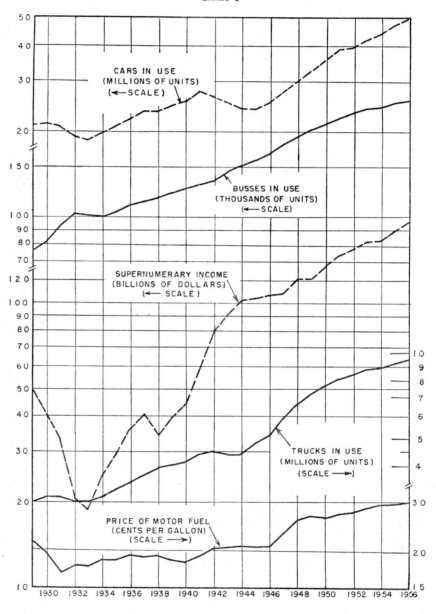

FIGURE 6–2

MOTOR FUEL DATA

CHART II—MOTOR FUEL CONSUMPTION VERSUS CARS + (BUSSES × 5.5) IN USE

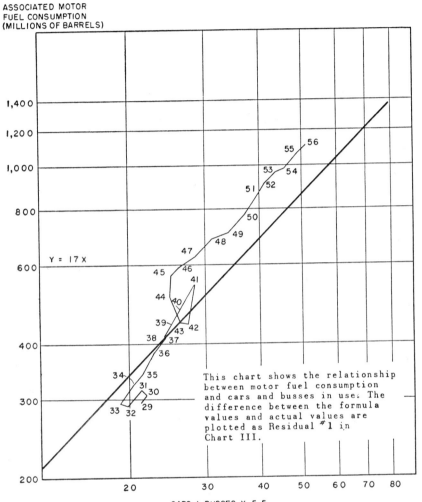

This chart shows the relationship between motor fuel consumption and cars and busses in use. The difference between the formula values and actual values are plotted as Residual #1 in Chart III.

FIGURE 6-3

MOTOR FUEL DATA

CHART III—RESIDUAL #1 VERSUS SUPERNUMERARY INCOME

RESIDUAL #1
1.400
1.200
1.000
.800
.600
.500
.400
.300
.200
20
30
40
60
80
100
120
140
160
180
200
$Y = .458 \times (I \times 3.15)^{.165}$
This chart shows the relationship between the rate of change in supernumerary income and the associated consumption of motor fuel. The differences between actual data and formula data are plotted as Residual # 2 in Chart IV.

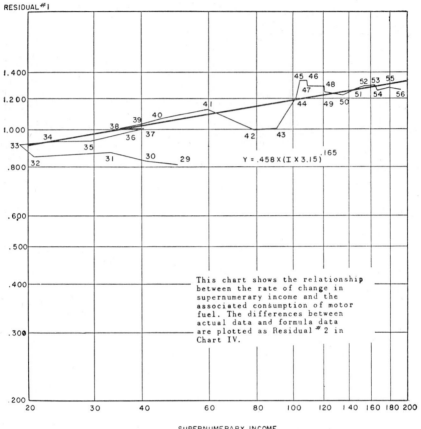

SUPERNUMERARY INCOME
(BILLIONS OF DOLLARS)

FIGURE 6–4

MOTOR FUEL DATA

CHART IV—RESIDUAL #2 VERSUS PRICE OF GASOLINE IN CENTS PER GALLON

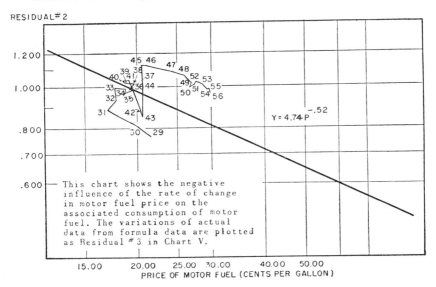

This chart shows the negative
influence of the rate of change
in motor fuel price on the
associated consumption of motor
fuel. The variations of actual
data from formula data are plotted
as Residual #3 in Chart V.

FIGURE 6–5

MOTOR FUEL DATA

CHART V

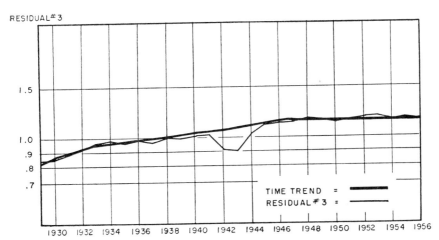

FIGURE 6–6

MOTOR FUEL DATA

CHART VI—ACTUAL AND CALCULATED MOTOR FUEL CONSUMPTION

(In Millions of Barrels)

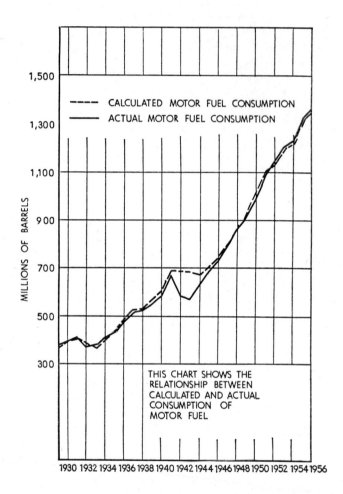

though this is not the actual sequence of volume consumption. Before beginning the analysis, it may be noted that the regression lines on the various scatter diagrams are plotted on logarithmic or ratio paper, that the formulas for the separate relationships or regression lines are combined in a multiplicative manner in the above equation, and that the data are plotted on equal scales without expressing each unit in terms of its standard deviation. These factors contrast with several subsequent studies where such conditions are not present.

The significance of each of the independent variables as demand-controlling factors may be outlined as follows.

Trucks. Truck consumption of gasoline, the first term in the equation, can fluctuate by varying the average consumption of gasoline per truck, the number of trucks, or both. It was found, however, that truck consumption of gasoline was relatively insensitive both to changes in gasoline prices and to changes in general business conditions. That is, average consumption per truck and average mileage per truck remained fairly stable, indicating that truck operators tend to take some trucks out of operation when business declines. Therefore, the rate of truck consumption of gasoline can be readily computed from the number of trucks in use, although average consumption has increased with the size and type of truck. Diesel trucks and buses have also grown in importance, but at present their combined production is under 2 per cent of the total. In developing the formula, the number of trucks was multiplied by 1.66 and the product was then subtracted from total annual gasoline consumption.

Passenger Cars and Buses. The average bus consumption of gasoline exceeds average car consumption, hence a weighted total of the two was computed. The difference between total gasoline consumption and truck consumption was then plotted against this weighted total, as shown in Figure 6–2. The spread between car and bus consumption is narrowing because of the gain in the proportion of school buses in use which, on the average, consume less gasoline than commercial buses. The increasing proportion of school buses is due in turn to two factors: the rapidly increasing number of school-age children and the trend to suburban living. The formula treats this difference in gasoline consumption as a constant and the changes become one of the factors in the time trend. Thus the equation of the relationship between gasoline consumption and the weighted average of cars and buses in use, shown in Figure 6–2 and estimated graphically by the formulas given in Chapter 4, pp. 67–68, is

$$Y = 17X$$

where

Y = Volume of gasoline consumption.
X = Weighted number of cars and buses in use.

Income. One of the interesting things revealed by this analysis was the tendency for total gasoline consumption to have a cyclical relation to purchasing power, the latter measured by supernumerary income. Thus, the total amount of driving depends upon the working and living habits of people. These habits are strongly enough entrenched so that small variations in purchasing power exercise only slight effects on gasoline consumption per car, the result being that there is a tendency for short-term fluctuations in gasoline consumption to be dampened. But when large fluctuations in purchasing power occur, as in the early 'thirties, two consequences become apparent: (1) many persons are unable to operate their cars, and (2) those that continue to operate their cars reduce their consumption of gasoline, but not in proportion to the fall in income. In other words, a sharp drop in purchasing power reduces considerably the number of cars in operation, but reduces only slightly the average consumption of gasoline per car. Therefore, as long as supernumerary income has exhibited a generally rising trend as during the past decade, gasoline consumption for cars and buses could be reasonably well forecast without the use of this variable. But in periods of wide economic fluctuation, supernumerary income turns out to be quite important for improving the accuracy of forecasts.

The result of this step in the analysis is shown in Figure 6–3. Graphically, the estimated relationship between gasoline consumption (Y) and the rate of change of supernumerary income (I), derived by plotting the ratio residuals from the previous regression line against the next independent variable (in this case supernumerary income) was found to be

$$Y = .458 \, (3.15I)^{.165}$$

Prices. With respect to gasoline prices, the influence of these on sales was not very large. The degree of elasticity varied somewhat in different regions of the country, with the greatest sensitivity to price changes in the low-income regions as is to be expected. The graphic result of this step, with the ratio residuals from the previous chart now plotted against gasoline prices, is shown in Figure 6–4. The graphically estimated formula for the regression line, representing the rate of change of gasoline consumption (Y) as a function of the rate of change in gasoline prices (P) is

$$Y = 4.74P^{-.52}$$

In this case, unlike the previous ones, the regression line as seen on the chart is negatively inclined. This is to be expected, since we know from economic theory that price exerts a negative influence on demand and that demand curves, therefore, slope downward from left to right.

Time. There still remain certain factors, other than those stated above, that may affect gasoline consumption. What are these "other" factors? They include the weight of vehicles, types of engines, the increasing use of diesel engines, highway mileage and maintenance, and trends in aviation and tractor gasoline requirements, to mention the most common ones. How are these demand-determining factors to be handled? Should they each be measured and incorporated in the analysis? The answer is that it is not necessary to treat them separately because the gain in accuracy that would result would not be warranted in view of the extra time and expense involved. Hence they may be grouped together as residual factors and represented as a net residual or time trend which changes slowly with time. In other words, "time" is incorporated in the analysis as a catchall, representing the influence of all factors other than the specific ones discussed in previous paragraphs that may affect gasoline consumption. In a complete analysis, which is impractical and usually impossible, there would be no "residual" to be explained by a growth or time trend, because all relevant factors would be included in the predicting equation. But as already stated several times in earlier discussions, forecasters are content to explain most of the variations in the dependent variable rather than all, so that the use of a time trend is both feasible and economical. Figure 6–5 reveals the results of this step. The ratio residuals about the previous regression line were plotted against time expressed in years, and a trend was fitted to the result as shown by the heavy line on the chart.

Conclusion

What can be stated in regard to the accuracy and the durability of this analysis for forecasting purposes? An indication is revealed graphically in Figure 6–6. Published originally in 1942 and based on data beginning with the year 1929, the analysis has withstood the test of time most admirably. With the exception of the war years when gasoline was rationed, the dashed line which is "calculated" gasoline consumption and represents the graphic equivalent of the predicting equation given at the beginning of this section, corresponded very closely with the solid line representing actual gasoline consumption. It is unlikely that any other method of analysis, as discussed in Chapter 1, could have produced results as accurate and as durable as has this econometric study of the factors determining the sale of gasoline.

But what about the application of the analysis to actual forecasting? As pointed out in Chapter 4, the prediction equation that is ultimately derived requires, if it is to be used for prediction, that the independent variables be forecast first. Then these separate forecasts are put into the equation to arrive at a forecast of the dependent variable. The formula, in other words, appears to be an excellent forecasting tool, provided that we can make reasonably good forecasts of its component parts, namely, the independent variables. Can such forecasts be made? The answer is yes, for reasons that can be stated briefly at this point.

1. Purchasing power, such as supernumerary income which was used in this study, can be estimated in advance because it occupies an "intermediate" position in the business cycle. That is, it is generally preceded several months by new orders, production, and the per cent of the labor force employed, and preceded as much as a year by changes in the cost of living and wage rates. These and related factors and their effect on the total economy, were discussed more fully in Chapter 5.

2. The number of gasoline consuming variables—trucks, cars, buses, and so on—can be predicted reasonably well for a year in advance by a simple naïve forecast: that is, by predicting that next year's production of these vehicles will be the same as this year's, taking into account the use of *survival tables* for durable goods. This method, crude as it may seem,

actually yields substantially good results as will become more evident in the following chapter dealing with the demand for consumer durables.

3. Price, the final important variable, can be handled in a sort of trial-and-error—or more accurately, iterative—manner, by calculating gasoline demand requirements on the assumption that price remains constant. If the demand estimate is in substantial error, the price is altered and the demand is recalculated. Only one or two such "approximations" are all that are usually necessary, except for those relatively infrequent occasions where price must be modified to account for significant changes in supply.

DEMAND FOR BEER

The basic demand equation for consumer nondurable goods, which was given in the first section of this chapter, expressed demand or sales as a function of three variables: buying power, demography, and a price or substitution factor. In the study to be discussed now dealing with the demand for beer, the measures employed for these three variables were: (1) for buying power, real disposable income; (2) for the demographic factor, the civilian population in the 18 to 44 age group; and (3) for the price or substitution factor, the consumption of beer substitutes. The rationale behind the choice of these variables and the interpretations of the results follow.

Analysis

The beer industry uses beer withdrawals (in physical volume of barrels) as the most important measure of beer sales. The problem, therefore, is to construct a formula for forecasting beer withdrawals (in barrels). As in the previous study, the first step is to plot all the relevant variables as time series on the same chart, as in Figure 6–7. This step will frequently provide an indication as to whether the variables are in some degree related. Note that here, just as in Figure 6–1, the data are plotted on semilogarithmic paper so that the relative change of the variables over time may be compared.

Real Disposable Income. Disposable income is equal to personal income less all direct taxes, and real disposable income is simply the resulting figure deflated by the consumer's price index. The purpose of this deflation is to convert the income data into constant dollars of a past period, in this case 1947–49, so that the effect of price changes on income is eliminated. Actually, the income series should be adjusted for changes in the price of beer, but no suitable price data for beer are available prior to 1947. Therefore, the Consumers' Price Index was used as a proxy or substitute variable.

Real disposable income was used in this study, rather than supernumerary income which includes consumer credit, because beer sales are predominantly cash sales and do not depend on the purchaser's decision to expand or contract his income commitments. The analysis is developed in Table 6–2 and in Figures 6–7 to 6–13. It may be noted that in this study, unlike the previous one on motor fuel, each variate was expressed in units of its standard deviation (sigma, σ) so as to place the series on comparable scales. The rationale has already been given both in this chapter and in Chapter 4, and hence requires no further explanation. In Figure 6–7, the variables are plotted over time, and in Figure 6–8 the first regression line is developed showing the average response of beer sales (Y) to changes in income (X). The equation for the relationship, estimated graphically, is

$$Y = 1.79X^{.7}$$

and the exponent, since the function is linear in logarithms, gives the elasticity directly. Thus, on the average, a 1 per cent change in real disposable income is associated with a .7 per cent change in beer sales; a 10 per cent change in real disposable income is associated with a 7 per cent change in beer sales. Although real disposable income was in a rising trend during most of the 23-year period of the analysis, beer sales have not kept up with this growth trend and have actually declined relative to income since 1947, as can be seen from the chart. This can be largely accounted for by the two remaining variables discussed next.

Population. It is believed in the beer industry, and supported by statistical evidence, that people in the 18 to 44 age group constitute the major purchasers of beer from civilian sources. Hence the per cent of the total civilian population in this age group was taken as the second independent variable—a measure of the demographic factor in the basic equation for consumer nondurables.

The problem now is to relate (1) the ratio of income-expected sales to actual sales, obtained from Figure 6–8, to (2) the population factor. This is done in Figure 6–9. It may be noted in Figure 6–7, however, that the population factor does not exhibit a smooth trend, but instead falls sharply during World War II because of the large number of men in the armed forces, then rises sharply immediately after the war as men were discharged, and finally declines steadily for the remaining ten years. It is because of this uneven trend that the analysis was started with the income factor as a sales determinant. Thus, in the following study on women's outerwear, the population factor that is used exhibits a smooth trend, and hence is employed before the income factor in arriving at a prediction formula.

Figure 6–9 reveals the resulting regression line between sales and population at this stage of the analysis. Note the decreasing demand for beer associated with the decreasing population factor. The formula for the line of relationship between beer withdrawals (Y) and the percentage of the population in the 18 to 44 age group (X) is, according to the graph, estimated to be

$$\log Y = .0066X + (9.8750 - 10)$$

or

$$Y = 10^{(.0066X - .1250)}$$

TABLE 6-2
BEER DATA

Year	(1) Income Factor* $I \div \sigma$	(2) Log (1)	(3) (2)×.7	(4) Antilog (3)	(5) Sales Factor† (4)×1.79	(6) Population Factor‡ $P \div \sigma$	(7) (6)×.0066	(8) (7)+9.8750 −10	(9) Substitution Factor§ $C \div \sigma$	(10) (9)×−.02
1934	1.93	.2856	.1999	1.584	2.835	18.47	.1219	9.9969 −10	1.26	−.0252
1935	2.11	.3243	.2270	1.687	3.020	18.51	.1222	9.9972 −10	1.89	−.0378
1936	2.49	.3962	.2773	1.893	3.388	18.51	.1222	9.9972 −10	2.54	−.0507
1937	2.48	.3945	.2761	1.888	3.379	18.56	.1225	9.9975 −10	2.82	−.0564
1938	2.32	.3655	.2559	1.833	3.227	18.56	.1225	9.9975 −10	2.70	−.0540
1939	2.52	.4014	.2810	1.910	3.419	18.60	.1228	9.9978 −10	2.94	−.0588
1940	2.71	.4330	.3031	2.009	3.596	18.56	.1225	9.9975 −10	3.27	−.0654
1941	3.13	.4955	.3440	2.208	3.952	18.34	.1210	9.9960 −10	3.48	−.0696
1942	3.58	.5539	.3877	2.442	4.371	17.90	.1181	9.9931 −10	4.22	−.0844
1943	3.83	.5832	.4082	2.560	4.582	16.98	.1121	9.9871 −10	3.26	−.0652
1944	4.18	.6212	.4348	2.721	4.871	16.29	.1075	9.9825 −10	3.70	−.0740
1945	4.06	.6085	.4260	2.667	4.774	16.07	.1061	9.9811 −10	3.96	−.0790
1946	4.04	.6064	.4245	2.653	4.758	17.90	.1181	9.9931 −10	5.17	−.1034
1947	3.78	.5775	.4043	2.537	4.541	17.94	.1184	9.9934 −10	3.88	−.0776
1948	3.92	.5933	.4153	2.602	4.658	17.77	.1173	9.9923 −10	4.09	−.0818
1949	3.93	.5944	.4161	2.607	4.667	17.55	.1158	9.9908 −10	4.21	−.0842
1950	4.29	.6325	.4428	2.771	4.960	17.46	.1152	9.9902 −10	4.60	−.0920
1951	4.36	.6395	.4477	2.803	5.017	16.90	.1115	9.9865 −10	4.46	−.0892
1952	4.48	.6513	.4559	2.857	5.114	16.55	.1092	9.9842 −10	4.48	−.0896
1953	4.68	.6702	.4691	2.945	5.272	16.29	.1075	9.9825 −10	4.67	−.0934
1954	4.74	.6758	.4731	2.973	5.322	16.07	.1060	9.9810 −10	4.62	−.0924
1955	5.06	.7042	.4929	3.111	5.569	15.89	.1049	9.9799 −10	4.79	−.0958
1956	5.28	.7226	.5058	3.205	5.737	15.67	.1034	9.9784 −10	5.05	−.1010

*Col. (1): Real disposable personal income ÷ σ.

†Col. (5): Beer withdrawal equivalent of income.

‡Col. (6): Population 18 to 44 years as per cent of civilian population.

§Col. (9): Consumption of wines and distilled spirits ÷ σ.

TABLE 6-2 (Continued)

Year	(11) (10)+.1080	(12) Equivalent Sales* (11)+(8)	(13) Antilog (12)	(14) (13)×(5)	(15)† (14)×σ	(16) Actual Sales	(17) (16)÷(15) Residual No. 3	(18) Trend of (17)	(19) (15)×(18) Calculated Sales	(20) Ratio § (16)÷(19) Residual No. 4
1934	.0828	.0797	1.201	3.405	53.6	40.0	.74	.775	41.5	.96
1935	.0702	.0674	1.168	3.527	55.5	45.1	.81	.80	44.4	1.02
1936	.0572	.0544	1.133	3.839	60.4	53.0	.88	.82	49.5	1.07
1937	.0516	.0491	1.119	3.781	59.5	55.7	.94	.84	50.0	1.11
1938	.0540	.0515	1.126	3.634	57.2	51.4	.90	.865	49.5	1.04
1939	.0492	.0470	1.114	3.809	60.0	52.8	.88	.89	53.4	.99
1940	.0426	.0401	1.096	3.941	62.0	51.8	.84	.91	56.4	.92
1941	.0384	.0333	1.080	4.268	67.2	57.4	.85	.94	63.2	.91
1942	.0236	.0167	1.040	4.546	71.6	64.6	.90	.965	69.1	.93
1943	.0428	.0299	1.071	4.907	77.2	72.7	.94	.995	76.8	.95
1944	.0340	.0165	1.039	5.061	79.7	79.5	1.00	1.02	81.3	.98
1945	.0288	.0099	1.023	4.884	76.9	81.8	1.06	1.045	80.4	1.02
1946	.0046	9.9977 −10	.995	4.734	74.5	79.5	1.07	1.075	80.1	.99
1947	.0304	.0238	1.056	4.800	75.6	87.2	1.15	1.14	86.2	1.01
1948	.0262	.0185	1.043	4.858	76.5	85.1	1.11	1.12	85.7	.99
1949	.0238	.0146	1.034	4.826	76.0	84.6	1.10	1.10	83.6	1.01
1950	.0160	.0062	1.014	5.929	79.2	82.8	1.05	1.08	85.5	.97
1951	.0188	.0053	1.013	5.082	80.0	83.8	1.05	1.065	85.2	.98
1952	.0184	.0026	1.006	5.145	81.0	84.8	1.05	1.05	85.1	.99
1953	.0146	9.9971 −10	.993	5.235	82.4	86.0	1.04	1.035	85.3	1.01
1954	.0156	9.9966 −10	.992	5.279	83.1	83.3	1.00	1.02	84.8	.98
1955	.0122	9.9921 −10	.982	5.469	86.1	85.0	.99	.995	85.7	.99
1956	.0070	9.9854 −10	.967	5.548	87.3	85.3	.98	.975	85.1	1.00

*Col. (12): Beer-withdrawal equivalent of population and consumption of wines and distilled spirits.

†Col. (15): Col. (14) × standard deviation of beer sales (15.74).

§Col. (20): Ratio of actual sales to calculated sales.

FIGURE 6–7

BEER DATA—CHART I

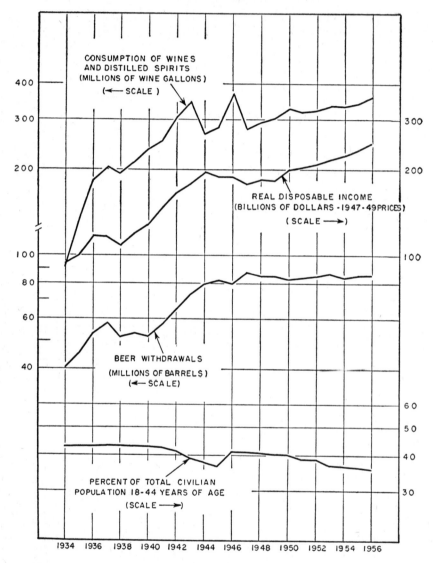

FIGURE 6–8

B<small>EER</small> D<small>ATA</small>—C<small>HART</small> II

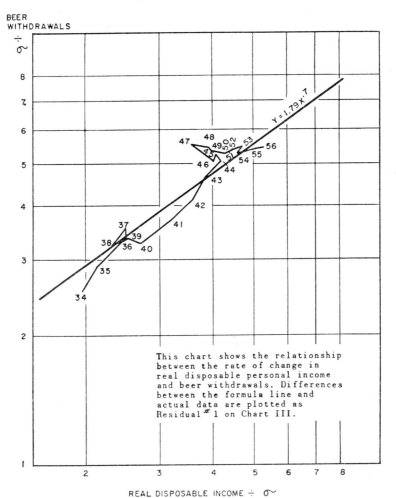

BEER
WITHDRAWALS
÷
σ~

REAL DISPOSABLE INCOME ÷ σ~

$Y = 1.79 x^{.7}$

This chart shows the relationship
between the rate of change in
real disposable personal income
and beer withdrawals. Differences
between the formula line and
actual data are plotted as
Residual # 1 on Chart III.

FIGURE 6–9

BEER DATA—CHART III

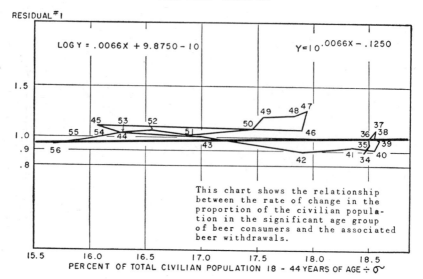

This chart shows the relationship
between the rate of change in the
proportion of the civilian population in the significant age group
of beer consumers and the associated
beer withdrawals.

FIGURE 6–10

BEER DATA—CHART IV

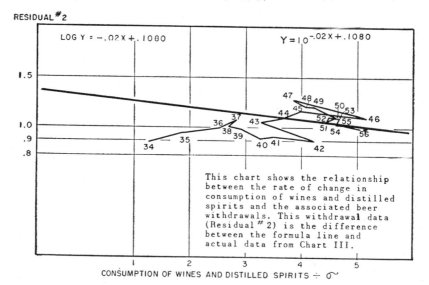

This chart shows the relationship
between the rate of change in
consumption of wines and distilled
spirits and the associated beer
withdrawals. This withdrawal data
(Residual #2) is the difference
between the formula line and
actual data from Chart III.

FIGURE 6–11

BEER DATA—CHART V

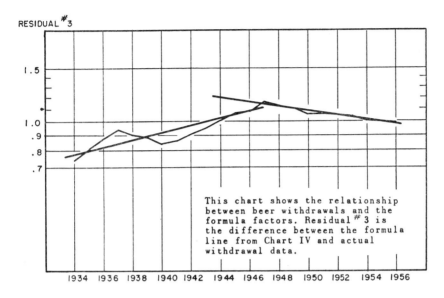

This chart shows the relationship
between beer withdrawals and the
formula factors. Residual #3 is
the difference between the formula
line from Chart IV and actual
withdrawal data.

FIGURE 6–12

BEER DATA—CHART VI

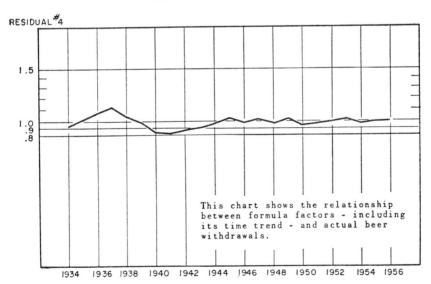

This chart shows the relationship
between formula factors - including
its time trend - and actual beer
withdrawals.

FIGURE 6–13

BEER DATA—CHART VII

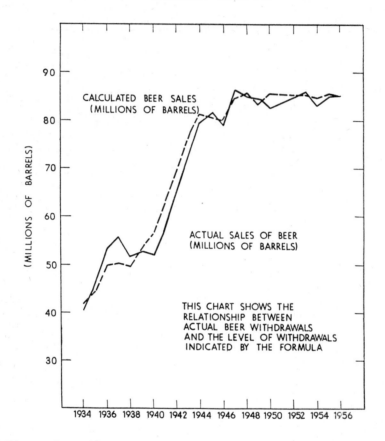

Observe from this chart that the fluctuations in actual data have been considerably reduced after the inclusion of the population factor, as compared to the previous chart when income was the only variable considered.

Substitutes. As stated in the discussion of demand determinants in the first section of this chapter, a third independent variable to employ in the basic equation is a price or a substitution factor. In this analysis the latter was selected and was defined as the consumption of wines and distilled spirits. Many of the fluctuations in actual beer sales, still apparent in Figure 6–9, can be attributed to the increasing competition between beer and other alcoholic beverages. To determine the nature of this competitive influence, the ratio residuals in Figure 6–9 are plotted against the substitute factor and a line of relationship is drawn as in Figure 6–10. The data, it can be seen, tended to cluster about the line for the period 1945–56. The estimated formula for the line is

$$\log Y = -.020X + .1080$$

or

$$Y = 10^{(-.020X + .1080)}$$

where Y represents beer withdrawals and X is the consumption of wines and distilled spirits.

Time Trend. The above three sets of equations could now be combined to produce a fairly effective prediction formula. If this were done, the resulting forecast would be the one shown below, except that the last term (TT), representing a time trend, would not be included. However, by incorporating a time trend which allows for the influence of "all other" factors affecting beer sales, a considerable improvement in forecasting accuracy can be attained. This step is accomplished in Figure 6–11, where the yearly data, plotted in time sequence, are the ratios of actual sales to calculated sales, the latter values obtained from the formula below, exclusive of the time trend, or simply the ratio residuals from Figure 6–10 plotted over time. These values, which measure the influence on sales of all nonformula factors (that is, all variables other than the income, population, and substitution factors already considered) are then represented by two regression or trend lines as shown in the chart. (Two trend lines are used instead of one, because there appears to have been a definite change between prewar and postwar patterns as shown by the chart, Figure 6–11.) The trend values are next multiplied by the calculated or formula values shown below, exclusive of the time trend TT, producing the final calculated beer sales and the final forecasting formula presented in the equation below. All of these steps, of course, could have been done directly from the tables without using formulas, as explained in Chapter 3.

Conclusion

One way of illustrating the final results of the analysis is to compute the actual sales figures as a percentage of the calculated values, the latter obtained either from the final prediction equation or from the tables as shown in Chapter 3. This has been done and the results are shown in Figure 6–12, with the residual ratios plotted in sequence over the period 1934–56. The actual values are close to the calculated values as evidenced by variations about the 100 per cent line. Alternatively, the actual and calculated values can be plotted as a time series, as done in Figure 6–13. The dashed curve, which represents the calculated values, is the graphic equivalent of the final prediction formula, which is derived by combining the separate formulas previously developed. Thus, the final prediction formula is

$$S = 1.79 \left(\frac{I}{\sigma I}\right)^{.7} 10^{\left[.0066\left(\frac{P}{\sigma P}\right) - .1250\right] + \left[-.020\left(\frac{C}{\sigma C}\right) + .1080\right]} (\sigma S)(TT)$$

where

$S =$ Beer sales, in millions of barrels annually.

$I =$ Real disposable personal income, in billions of dollars per year (1947–49 prices).

$P =$ The 18–44 age group as a percentage of the population.

$C =$ Consumption of wines and distilled spirits, in millions of gallons.

$TT =$ Time trend.

As for the predictability of the independent variables, each, it may be noted, can be forecast successfully. Thus, disposable income forecasts can be made with reasonable accuracy as mentioned earlier; the population factor is easily forecast except in war periods; and the cost of living changes slowly, usually in the direction of the ratio of hourly earnings to output per manhour, as expressed in the previous chapter. The formula, therefore, provides an excellent tool for forecasting the sale of beer.

DEMAND FOR WOMEN'S OUTERWEAR

A forecasting model involving the sale of women's outerwear can be constructed in a manner somewhat similar to the previous two studies, except for a few different techniques that are needed because of the peculiarities of the product concerned.

Total sales of a broad product group such as substitutable outerwear (women's dresses, blouses, skirts, and sportswear) are determined by external factors such as purchasing power and population characteristics. But the sales of individual apparel lines within the group are, though they also depend upon particular economic and demographic factors, a function of a third factor as well—style. A formula that attempts to forecast the sale of women's dresses, therefore, must involve the use of directly substitutable garments, particularly women's blouses, skirts, and sportswear. The approach taken in this study to arrive at a forecast of the sale of dresses was to forecast the index of combined sales of the outerwear group as a whole and then to evaluate the style trends separately.

Analysis

Combined sales of women's outerwear were found to be a function of: (1) consumer purchasing power, a series composed of disposable income plus net changes in short- and intermediate-term consumer credit, and (2) a population factor, consisting of (*a*) the ratio of females 14 to 54 years of age to total population, and (*b*) the ratio of unmarried females (consisting of single, divorced, and widowed) to total females over 14 years of age. When these determinants are correctly combined, they produce a calculated sales level around which actual sales have fluctuated within narrow limits.

From the data in Table 6–3, the variables are first plotted on a semilogarithmic chart (Figure 6–14) in order to note their comparative change

FIGURE 6–14

DRESSES DATA—CHART I

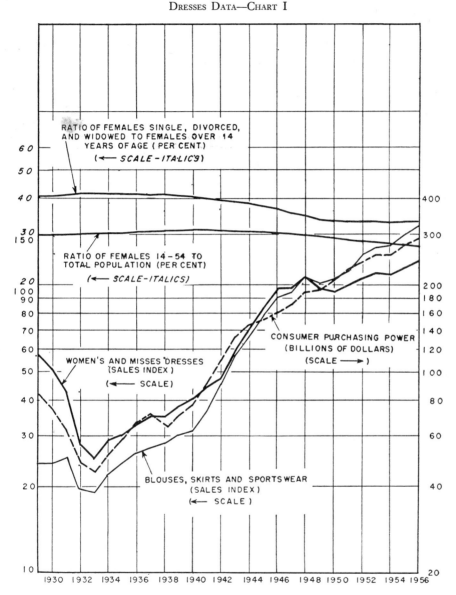

over the years. Since the population factors in the analysis exhibited a relatively smooth trend, as can be seen from the chart, their influence was removed from the composite sales index. This adjustment was made by calculating a combined population index (1947–49 = 100) with a weight of 1 assigned to the ratio of females 14 to 54 years of age to total population, and a weight of 5 assigned to the ratio of unmarried females to total females

TABLE 6-3

WOMEN'S DRESS DATA

Year	(1) Ratio of Females 14-54 to Population (Per Cent)	(2) Ratio of Females* (Per Cent)	(3) Women's and Misses' Dresses Sales Index, 1947-49=100	(4) Blouses, Skirts, and Sportswear Sales Index, 1947-49=100	(5) Consumer Purchasing Power Raw Data (Billions of Dollars)	(6) Sales Factor† $\frac{S}{\sigma_s}$	(7) Weighted Population Factor $\frac{P_1+5P_2}{6}$
1929	29.7	40.3	57	24	84.1	1.13	38.5
1930	29.9	40.3	51	24	74.8	1.04	38.6
1931	29.9	41.0	43	25	63.7	.93	39.2
1932	30.0	41.5	28	19	48.6	.64	39.6
1933	30.2	41.7	25	18	45.1	.58	39.8
1934	30.3	41.7	29	22	52.1	.68	39.8
1935	30.4	40.5	30	24	58.5	.74	38.8
1936	30.6	40.5	33	26	66.7	.79	38.9
1937	30.7	41.0	35	27	71.9	.84	39.3
1938	30.8	41.3	35	28	65.3	.85	38.7
1939	30.9	40.5	38	30	70.8	.92	38.9
1940	31.0	40.2	40	31	76.5	.95	38.7
1941	31.0	39.8	44	36	91.8	1.08	38.3
1942	30.9	39.1	47	45	111.9	1.23	38.1
1943	30.7	38.6	59	57	132.1	1.54	37.3
1944	30.6	38.2	70	66	145.8	1.81	36.9
1945	30.5	37.7	83	78	151.1	2.16	36.5
1946	30.3	36.8	97	90	160.4	2.49	35.7
1947	30.0	35.5	97	94	171.2	2.52	34.6
1948	29.8	34.9	106	106	189.2	2.81	34.0
1949	29.4	33.5	97	101	191.1	2.62	32.8
1950	29.0	33.5	95	104	207.1	2.62	32.8
1951	28.7	33.1	100	112	225.9	2.79	32.4
1952	?8.4	33.1	105	126	240.1	3.02	32.3
1953	28.1	33.0	109	134	255.7	3.18	32.2
1954	27.8	32.9	108	136	254.5	3.18	32.0
1955	27.5	33.0	114	148	274.9	3.41	32.1
1956	27.3	33.1	120	159	288.8	3.63	32.1

*Col. (2): Ratio of females, single, divorced, and widowed, to females over 14 years of age.

†Col. (6): Combined outerwear sales divided by its standard deviation.

TABLE 6–3 (Continued)

Year	(8) Population Adjustment,‡ $\dfrac{P_1+5P_2}{6} \div \sigma$	(9) Purchasing Power Adjustment § $\dfrac{1}{\sigma_I}$	(10) $\left(\dfrac{I}{\sigma_I}\right)^{1.1}$	(11) $.0856 \times (10)$	(12) $(11) \times (8)$	(13) Calculated Sales, $(12) \times \sigma_s$	(14) Actual Sales	(15) Residual $(14) \div (13)$
1929	12.6	1.03	1.033	.088	1.11	41.8	42.6	1.02
1930	12.6	.92	.912	.078	.98	36.9	39.2	1.06
1931	12.8	.78	.761	.065	.83	31.3	35.2	1.12
1932	12.9	.60	.570	.049	.63	23.8	24.1	1.01
1933	13.0	.55	.518	.044	.57	21.5	21.9	1.02
1934	13.0	.64	.612	.052	.68	25.5	26.0	1.02
1935	12.7	.72	.697	.060	.76	28.7	27.4	.95
1936	12.7	.82	.793	.068	.86	32.4	29.9	.92
1937	12.9	.88	.869	.074	.95	35.8	31.5	.88
1938	12.7	.80	.782	.067	.85	32.0	31.9	1.00
1939	12.7	.87	.858	.073	.93	35.0	34.5	.99
1940	12.7	.94	.934	.080	1.02	38.4	35.8	.93
1941	12.5	1.13	1.132	.097	1.21	45.6	40.6	.89
1942	12.5	1.38	1.425	.122	1.53	57.7	46.2	.80
1943	12.2	1.62	1.700	.146	1.78	67.1	58.1	.87
1944	12.1	1.79	1.898	.162	1.96	73.9	68.3	.92
1945	11.9	1.86	1.979	.169	2.01	75.8	81.3	1.07
1946	11.7	1.97	2.109	.181	2.12	79.9	94.0	1.17
1947	11.3	2.10	2.261	.194	2.19	82.6	94.9	1.15
1948	11.1	2.33	2.536	.217	2.41	90.9	106.0	1.17
1949	10.7	2.35	2.560	.219	2.34	88.2	98.7	1.12
1950	10.7	2.54	2.788	.239	2.56	96.5	98.9	1.02
1951	10.6	2.78	3.079	.264	2.80	105.6	105.2	1.00
1952	10.6	2.95	3.287	.281	2.98	112.3	114.1	1.02
1953	10.5	3.12	3.496	.299	3.14	118.4	119.9	1.01
1954	10.5	3.13	3.509	.300	3.15	118.8	120.2	1.01
1955	10.5	3.38	3.818	.327	3.43	129.3	128.6	.99
1956	10.5	3.45	4.029	.345	3.62	136.5	137.0	1.00

‡Col. (8): Weighted population factor: Col. (7) divided by its standard deviation.

§Col. (9): Purchasing power divided by its standard deviation.

over 14 years of age. The composite sales index, also on a 1947–49 base, was then divided by the population index in order to obtain a series of "sales per population," or simply sales adjusted for the population factor.

This resulting series was then plotted against the purchasing power variable, producing the upward sloping regression line in Figure 6–15. The equation for the line, expressing the relationship between apparel sales (Y) and purchasing power (X) is estimated from the graph to be

$$Y = .0856X^{1.1}$$

with the exponent revealing the elasticity directly (since the equation, as explained earlier, is linear in logarithms).

FIGURE 6–15

DRESSES DATA—CHART II

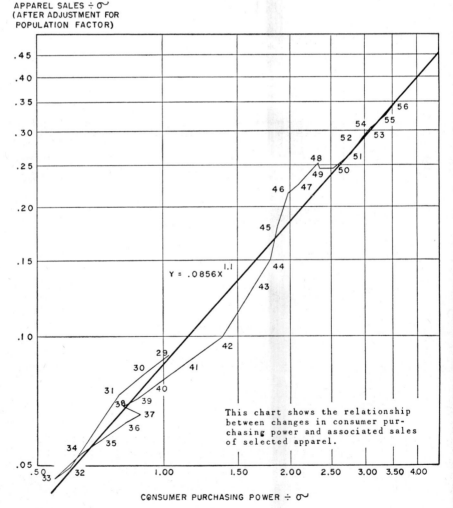

APPAREL SALES ÷ σ
(AFTER ADJUSTMENT FOR
POPULATION FACTOR)

$Y = .0856X^{1.1}$

This chart shows the relationship between changes in consumer purchasing power and associated sales of selected apparel.

CONSUMER PURCHASING POWER ÷ σ

The next step was to take the ratio residuals from this chart, or, in other words, the actual sales as a percentage of the calculated sales, and plot them around the 100 per cent line as shown in Figure 6–16. This step completes the approximation procedure, and only the conclusion remains to be formulated.

FIGURE 6–16

Dresses Data—Chart III

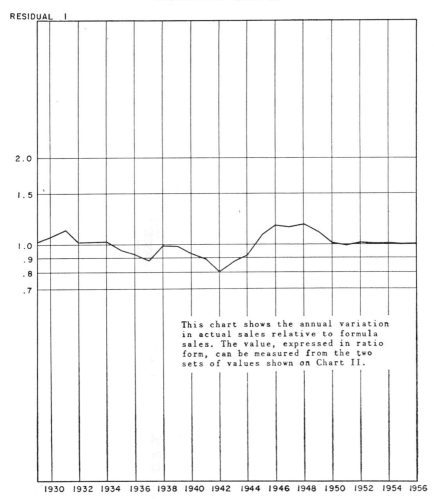

RESIDUAL

This chart shows the annual variation in actual sales relative to formula sales. The value, expressed in ratio form, can be measured from the two sets of values shown on Chart II.

Conclusion

The graphic outcome of the analysis revealing the closeness of fit between the actual and calculated sales index is presented in Figure 6–17. The final formula (that is, the formula for the dashed line) can be constructed from the tables and charts, and is seen to be

FIGURE 6–17

DRESSES DATA—CHART IV

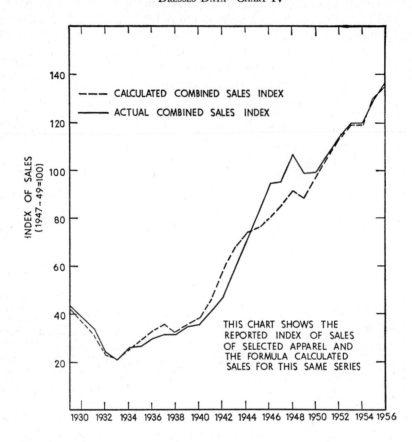

THIS CHART SHOWS THE REPORTED INDEX OF SALES OF SELECTED APPAREL AND THE FORMULA CALCULATED SALES FOR THIS SAME SERIES

$$S = \left[\frac{\frac{1}{6}(P_1 + 5P_2)}{\sigma\frac{1}{6}(P_1 + 5P_2)} \right] \left[.0856 \left(\frac{I}{\sigma I} \right)^{1.1} \right] (\sigma S)$$

where

S = Annual sales index.
I = Consumer purchasing power in billions of dollars per year.
P_1 = Ratio of females 14 to 54 years of age to total population.
P_2 = Ratio of unmarried females to total females over 14 years of age.

As can be seen from the chart, actual sales corresponded closely to calculated sales from 1929 through 1940. During the war period actual sales fell below the calculated level due to merchandise shortages, while the reverse disparity occurred during the postwar adjustment period. By 1950, however, the adjustment was completed and actual sales have since fluctuated around the calculated level within a 2 per cent range.

What about the effect of the style factor in this study? The answer

FIGURE 6–18

DRESSES DATA—CHART V

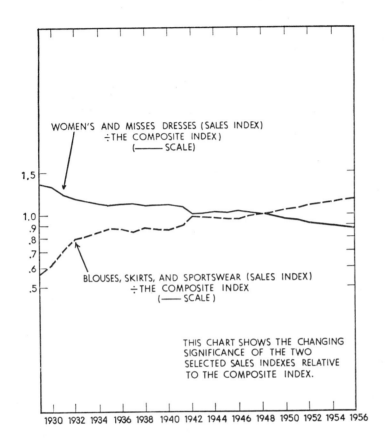

THIS CHART SHOWS THE CHANGING SIGNIFICANCE OF THE TWO SELECTED SALES INDEXES RELATIVE TO THE COMPOSITE INDEX.

is given in Figure 6–18 where the two separate indexes are plotted relative to the composite index. Casual wear (blouses, skirts, and sportswear) gained continuously relative to more formal wear (dresses) since 1930. By the year 1948 they were equal in importance, and since then the trend has continued with a greater relative share going to casual clothing. With increasing attention being given to informal (suburban) living, it is reasonable to predict that this trend will continue for some years to come.

SUMMARY AND CONCLUSION

This chapter has been concerned with the development of a set of principles and techniques for forecasting the sales of consumer's nondurable goods (including consumer's perishable and semidurable goods). Examples of products that are included in this category are foods, beverages, tobacco products, gasoline, soap, drugs, textiles, and clothing. A number of other products, of course, could also be mentioned.

The point of view taken is that most goods can be placed in one of several categories each of which has a particular set of demand determinants. Thus, the most important demand determinants for consumer's nondurable goods are: (1) buying power, (2) demography or the chief consuming unit of the product, and (3) price or a substitution factor. The problem in forecasting is to obtain statistical series that will serve as reliable measures of these variables. Thus, disposable income, supernumerary income, or some similar index may be used as a measure of buying power. The number of consuming units of the product may serve as a measure of the demographic factor. And the price of the product, or the importance of substitutes, may serve as a measure of the price or substitution factor. Since direct measures of the relevant variables are not always possible to obtain, the analyst will frequently have to select a substitute or "proxy" variable for which data are available, and which reflects the displaced variable indirectly. A knowledge of economic analysis as well as statistical techniques is necessary, therefore, if the forecaster is to interpret intelligently the significance of the variables and his reasons for their selection.

The final step consists of weighting, by statistical procedures, the variables selected, so that the final result is a predicting equation. The variables may be combined in either an additive or multiplicative relationship, depending on logical considerations and on which form produces the best fit. The statistical process employed is that of correlation analysis and it may be done either graphically or mathematically at the discretion of the analyst.

In the following chapters, further illustrative studies are presented. Some are relatively simple; others are quite complicated and elaborate. All, however, serve to illustrate the types of research that can be done, depending on time and expense considerations, the availability of data, and the technical competence of the analyst.

QUESTIONS

1. (*a*) Outline briefly the nature of the product breakdown employed here for forecasting purposes? (*b*) Why was this breakdown used?
2. What is the basic equation of demand for consumers' nondurable goods?
3. Explain the nature of the variables which you have cited in your answer to question 2.
4. Using examples from the chapter (or from other sources) as you deem necessary, discuss the general philosophy underlying the scope and method of analysis developed in this chapter. Write an essay on the subject and deliver it in class.

Chapter 7

FORECASTING SALES OF CONSUMERS' DURABLE GOODS

A distinction between consumers' nondurables and consumers' durables is necessary because, usually, different sets of economic factors determine the sales of goods in each group. Consumers' durable goods, it will be recalled, include such products as automobiles, appliances, household furnishings, furniture, and books. As in the previous chapter, we may begin by outlining the theoretical principles that serve as a guide for measurement, and then devote the remaining sections of the chapter to an examination of several empirical studies. The discussion should be instructive in view of the various approaches and techniques that have been employed by analysts in forecasting the sale of consumers' durable goods.

DEMAND DETERMINANTS

What are the more important economic factors determining the demand for consumers' durable goods? In other words, can a set of demand characteristics be established which will guide analysts who are interested in deriving quantitative relationships between essential variables and in interpreting numerical results? The answer is yes. Considerable progress has been made in recent years toward establishing a theoretical framework that can serve as a useful guide for forecasting sales of consumer durables. Basically, this framework consists of (1) a set of purchase characteristics which defines the consumption environment, and (2) a growth model or basic equation of the relationship between new demand, replacement demand, and total demand for the particular durable good. The combination of both factors, the purchase characteristics and the growth model, provide a basis for deriving a predicting equation, as will be illustrated in subsequent sections of this chapter. The purchase characteristics and the growth model (or basic equation), however, must be explained first.

Purchase Characteristics

There are three so-called "purchase characteristics" that are particularly applicable to the sale of consumer durable goods. They may be distinguished as (1) time-use characteristics, (2) use-facilities characteristics, and (3) demographic characteristics. The economic meaning and significance of each is clarified in the following paragraphs.

Time-Use Characteristics. Consumer durables, precisely because they are durable, are not consumed in a single act as are foods, for instance, but instead dole out their services or are consumed over a period of time. This time-use characteristic raises a particular problem for forecasting purposes: because the good is durable, the consumer has to make a decision between (1) using the good longer by repairing it if necessary, or (2) disposing of it and replacing it with a new one. The significance of the former alternative was well illustrated during World War II, when the scrappage rate on automobiles and other hard-to-get durables dropped sharply. The choice of the second alternative involves a decision to be made between three further alternatives: whether to (*a*) scrap the good; (*b*) trade it in; or (*c*) sell it used. Whatever the decision, it may depend as much on noneconomic factors such as one's social status and desire for prestige, as on economic factors which include product obsolescence, income, and other conditions to be discussed below.

Use-Facilities Characteristics. Durable goods usually require special facilities for their consumption. This use-facilities characteristic is exemplified by the need for roads and gas stations for the consumption of automobiles, wired homes for the consumption of electrical appliances, wired homes plus leisure time for the consumption of television sets, and dock facilities plus leisure time for the consumption of yachts. Similar examples can be cited of use-facilities characteristics that are necessary for the consumption of other types of durable goods. As will be seen subsequently, these are some of the important factors that will condition the sale of a particular durable good, hence they must often be taken into account in arriving at a meaningful sales forecast.

Demographic Characteristics. Just as with consumer nondurables, demographic factors frequently play an important role in influencing the sale of consumer durable goods. Thus, consumer durables are generally consumed by more than one person, as with a family consuming an automobile, refrigerator, or television set. The decision to purchase, therefore, may be influenced as much by family characteristics such as the size of families and the age distribution of adults and children, as by price, income, and other considerations. Further, it should be noted again that the term "demographic characteristics" need not refer exclusively to human populations. In a study of the demand for automobiles, for instance, the number of miles of paved highway was used as one of the independent variables. Similarly, a recent forecast of the sale of commercial jet airliners utilized the number of commercial airports with jet facilities as both a use-facilities characteristic and a demographic characteristic in deriving the predicting equation. Thus, the three purchase characteristics may sometimes be treated independently, and sometimes in combination, depending on the product and the economic judgment of the analyst.

The above characteristics give rise to a particular type of market structure with respect to durable goods. Thus, the total demand for a durable good is really the sum of two demands: (1) a *new-owner demand* which serves to expand the existing stock of the good in consumers' inventories, and (2) a *replacement demand* which bears a particular relationship to both the existing stock of the good at any given time and to the size of the stock over a period of time. The significance of replacement demand should not be underestimated, as is a frequent tendency on the part of many managements that think solely in terms of finding new markets as a means of expanding sales. For long-established products, such as refrigerators and automobiles, the replacement market may represent as much as half, and sometimes well over half, the total market for the product. And even for less-established products, replacement demand may nevertheless constitute a substantial proportion of total sales in many instances.

The replacement demand for consumer durables tends to grow with consumers' stocks. For certain well-established products, especially automobiles, refrigerators, and radios, some analysts have constructed life expectancy tables and survival curves which they apply to consumers' stocks in order to estimate average replacement rates. The automobile companies have derived such data at various times, based on scrappage rates, registration figures, and the like, a notable example of which appears in the study of automobile demand discussed later in this chapter. In general, it has been found that actual scrapping rates tend to depend mainly on purchasing power and production, and to a lesser extent on physical construction and operating costs. Thus, when purchasing power is increasing, scrapping rates tend to exceed theoretical expectations, and when purchasing power is declining, scrappage falls short of theoretical values. Also, when sales significantly exceed production, scrappage is less than the expected rate, but as production catches up with sales the scrappage rate tends to increase.

Basic Equation

In light of the above, the basic demand or sales equation for durable goods may be written

$$S = N + R$$

where S represents total sales of the good, N is new-owner demand or the increase in the existing stock, and R is replacement demand as measured by the scrappage of old units. Each of the independent variables may be forecast separately as explained below.

1. Replacement demand, or scrappage amounts, can be estimated by the use of life expectancy tables or survival curves. This is often necessary because the required data on replacement are not usually available from published sources, as compared to sales data, for example, which are frequently obtainable from trade associations, trade magazines, and sometimes

government publications, depending on the particular product. Of course, a well-constructed consumer survey can yield necessary data from which scrappage estimates can be made, but this procedure can involve considerable time and expense which might be avoided if good survival functions were available instead. In view of this, the studies in this chapter will incorporate the use of survival functions in order to illustrate their principles and applications. In other words, *scrappage estimates serve as a proxy variable for the measurement of replacement, because data on the latter are not usually available.*

2. New-owner demand, the remaining independent variable in the basic equation, represents the change in consumer stocks of the product with respect to a unit change in time. That is

$$\text{New-Owner Demand} = \frac{\text{Change in Consumer Stocks}}{\text{Change in Time}}$$

Alternatively, the same relationship is expressed more conveniently in symbols. Letting Δy represent the change in consumer stocks, and Δt the change in time, then new-owner demand, N, is

$$N = \frac{\Delta y}{\Delta t}$$

This, in turn, depends on other conditions which may be analyzed as follows.

Growth Model. At any given time, there exists in the economy a set of economic and cultural conditions which, in combination, determine an upper limit toward which consumers are continually adjusting their stock of a durable good. This upper limit may be defined as the *maximum* or *optimum ownership level.* It is "maximum" in the sense that it serves as an approximate demand ceiling for a durable good; it is "optimum" in that it is a level toward which the actual volume of consumer stocks of a particular good is continually gravitating. Statistically, the maximum ownership level depends, for most consumer durables, on such factors as purchasing power (for example, supernumerary income), number of families, and perhaps other factors, according to the product. Thus, for radios, it might also include some proportion of the number of automobiles, and for refrigerators the number of wired homes.

The concept of maximum ownership level applied to automobiles is portrayed graphically in Figure 7–1. In Chart A, which is theoretical, there are three such levels, indicated by M_1, M_2, and M_3, each one being static until sufficient pressures are built up by its controlling independent variables to cause a change. Accordingly, for each M-level, there is a corresponding y-curve representing actual stocks in use, such as y_1, y_2, and y_3. Note that each of these stock curves tends to approach its corresponding maximum ownership level as shown by the dashed lines, but changes in the level cause shifts in the actual stock curve as well. It is evident, too, that the

FIGURE 7–1

MAXIMUM OWNERSHIP LEVEL FOR AUTOMOBILES, 1919–38

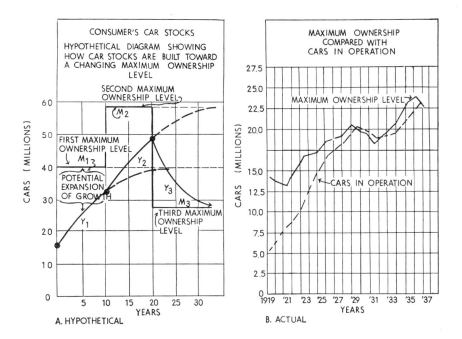

Source: Adapted from the *Dynamics of Automobile Demand* (General Motors Corporation, 1938), p. 37.

difference between M and y always represents the *potential expansion of growth* as shown on the chart. Finally, in Chart B, an empirical study for automobiles is given for the period 1919–38, indicating how the actual stock of cars is continually tending toward a changing maximum ownership level over time. The latter curve was derived from an equation in which the number of families, real supernumerary income per capita, and an index of replacement cost were the independent variables.

The rate of change of new-owner demand, N, which equals $\Delta y/\Delta t$, is dependent, therefore, on the potential expansion of growth. That is, the difference between the maximum ownership level and the actual stock of the product in use is $M - y$. But it is logical to suppose, as will become more evident later, that this difference in itself is in some way proportional to the existing stock, y, already in use. Therefore, the equation for N may be written

$$N = \Delta y/\Delta t = ay \, (M - y)$$

where a represents a constant or parameter with respect to time, t, and it is the purpose of correlation analysis, as will be seen shortly, to determine this value of *a* in arriving at a demand equation.[1]

Conclusion

An attempt was made in this section to develop the framework of a theory of demand for consumers' durable goods. Since a chief function of theory is to serve as a guide for measurement, we shall see in the discussions that follow the extent to which the theory is verified by statistical studies.

In examining these studies, it will be noted that all of them were conducted within the framework of the theory outlined here, and all produced reasonably good fits, that is, the calculated values came close to the actual ones. This serves to emphasize the point that *the theory should explain or account for the correlations found, as well as the correlations verifying and confirming the theory.* When both of these conditions are realized, the theory becomes an explanation of reality, and the statistical measures that are derived become a test of the theory. The significance of this statement will become increasingly evident throughout the following sections and chapters.

DEMAND FOR AUTOMOBILES

If we were to classify the various kinds of consumers' durable goods according to their economic importance, automobiles as a product group would surely rank at or near the top of the list. The demand for automobiles has, for several decades, exercised at least an indirect effect on the nation's level of income and employment. The fortunes of numerous industries, large and small, are closely linked with automobiles, as are the employment of millions of workers and billions of dollars of capital. It is logical, therefore, to include in a study of the demand for durable goods a discussion of the demand for automobiles, with particular emphasis on the forecasting aspects.

One of the most elaborate demand studies ever made of a consumer durable good was an analysis of the demand for automobiles done in 1938 by Charles F. Roos and Victor von Szeliski.[2] In depth and scope, it paralleled the monumental research done by Henry Schultz in the field of agri-

---

[1] Since M is assumed to be a dynamic, continuous function of time, the equation may more appropriately be written

$$\Delta y/\Delta t = ay\,[M(t) - y]$$

or: *rate of growth = a function of potential expansion of growth.*
If both sides of the equation are divided by y,

$$\frac{\Delta y/\Delta t}{y} = a\,[M(t) - y]$$

or: *percentage rate of growth = a function of percentage expansion of growth.*

[2] *The Dynamics of Automobile Demand* (General Motors Corporation, 1939).

cultural economics,[3] and hence occupies the position of a classic in econometrics, forecasting, and related areas of economic science. It is appropriate, therefore, to begin the discussion of empirical studies with a survey of this important work.

The Problem

The depression of the thirties gave rise to the problem of industrial pricing practices. Both in industry and in academic circles, businessmen and economists were questioning the effect of price changes on demand, and the further effects on production and employment. The contention was made, for example, that the price elasticity of demand for automobiles was considerably greater than unity—perhaps around 3.0—so that a small cut in price would produce a significant increase in the sale of cars.[4] This proposal gained wide enough currency to disturb the automobile manufacturers. Accordingly, in 1938 General Motors employed the services of the noted econometrician, Charles F. Roos, to conduct a study of the general effect of price changes upon the total volume of automobile sales. The following features of this study are of greatest significance.

1. *The Concept of Demand.* The notion of demand in economic theory is typically that of a simple price-quantity relation. This study, however, contributed to a broadening of the concept of demand from one of simple relations to one of multiple relations. Thus, it emphasized the fact that the quantity purchased of a product depends not only upon its price, but upon other factors as well, such as income, living standards, substitutes, and perhaps other variables. Further, it placed stress on the quantitative measurement and weighting of these demand determinants so that they might be incorporated effectively in the construction of predicting equations.

2. *Formulation of a Hypothesis.* A chief contribution of the study was its development of a hypothesis guided by criteria of mathematical consistency and economic theory. Thus, it was necessary to formulate precise definitions of significant factors, an over-all picture of the mechanism of which they are parts, and the method of interconnection of the parts. For in most scientific investigations, as mentioned earlier, *a coherent and consistent body of theory is needed to explain and account for the correlations found, as well as the correlations verifying or confirming the theory.* Thus, many statistical formulas were developed which represented the data with equal goodness of fit, and hence statistical tests of goodness of fit failed to reveal whether certain relationships were purely empirical covariations or whether there really was a significant cause and effect relationship at work. The formulas finally adopted, however, were those that seemed to integrate

---

[3] See his *Theory and Measurement of Demand* (University of Chicago Press, 1938).

[4] See for instance the study by P. DeWolff in *Econometrica* (April, 1938).

best the logical implications of the relationships with sound economic principles. Thus, supernumerary income as a more precise measure of buying power was employed, rather than national income or disposable income. With respect to price, it was decided that the best measure was an index of low-priced cars rather than a price index of all cars, because low-priced cars were typically those that were freely available in volume both in new and used markets, and sales variations were wide enough to obtain good statistical estimates. And a new variable, the consumers' car stock, was introduced and shown to be of great significance.

a) *Consumers' Car Stock.* The guiding concept and, indeed, one of the connecting threads throughout the entire analysis was the notion that what consumers consume is not new cars, but transportation service from a car stock that is continually varying. Thus the sale of new cars represents a derived demand: the primary objective of consumers is to vary—usually to build up—their car stock, and the sale of new cars is a means of achieving the objective. The most important factor determining the level toward which consumers are continually adjusting their stock of cars is the *maximum ownership level*, and this level itself varies depending upon such factors as income, population, replacement costs and price.

3. *Statistical Results.* The elaborate nature of the statistical findings that were obtained are impossible to present within the limits of this section. Enough can be shown, however, to convey the framework of the analysis and make it clear just what sort of relationships were actually derived. The statistical results may be grouped and discussed under the following five separate headings, each representing in a conceptual sense an important section of the study.

a) *Maximum Ownership Level.* The concept of a variable maximum ownership level, illustrated earlier in Figure 7–1, was found to be of considerable importance in this study of automobile demand, and has since been successfully employed in numerous other studies involving the sale of durable goods. Three formulas for the maximum ownership level, M, were derived. The first, M_1, was based on population and per capita real supernumerary income. It took the form:

$$M_1 = \text{Population}\left[.087 + .000252\left(\frac{\text{Real Supernumerary}}{\text{Income per Capita}}\right)\right]$$

The second, M_2, took price and durability (that is, replacement cost) of cars into account, and used the number of families in place of population. The formula obtained was

$$M_2 = \text{Families}\left[.378 + .00068\left(\frac{\text{Real Supernumerary}}{\text{Income per Capita}}\right)\right]\left(\frac{\text{Replacement}}{\text{Cost}}\right)^{-.3}$$

and was found to be more satisfactory; it was derived from the new-owner sales. The third, M_3, was derived from the total sales equation (which is presented later), and was found to be useful in studying the price elasticity of demand for automobiles. The formula was

$$M_3 = \text{Families}\left[.500 + .000544 \left(\frac{\text{Real Supernumerary}}{\text{Income per Capita}}\right)\right](\text{Durability})^{.3}$$

None of these equations, it should be noted, included specifically the important factor of operating costs. Also, note that these equations, despite their seemingly complicated appearance, are really nothing more than "weighted" straight lines, with the straight-line formulas enclosed in brackets.

The second formula, M_2, was used to calculate the maximum ownership level presented earlier in Figure 7–1B, p. 243. The last term in the equation, replacement cost, is derived from the ratio p/d in which p is an index of car prices and d is a durability index based on the average age of cars at retirement.[5] At the time this study was made, the quality of automobiles, measured here by durability and operating costs, seemed to be more important than price alone in influencing sales.

The difference between the maximum ownership level, M, and the current size of consumer stocks, symbolized now by the letter C, is $M - C$ and represents potential new demand, N. That is, $N = M - C$. The value of N has usually been particularly sensitive to changes in national income, especially when the current stock has been built up close to the maximum ownership level. When this occurs, the market for the product is said to be "saturated." This concept is treated more fully at a later point in this chapter.

b) *The Income Factor.* A unique feature of this study was the development and use of supernumerary income as a measure of consumer buying power for commodities in the nonnecessity class. In the predicting equation derived (see below) the income factor appears in two places: in the maximum ownership term, and as a multiplier. It thus is assumed to have a compound effect—first, in raising or lowering the goal toward which consumers build their car stock, and second, in increasing or decreasing the speed toward the objective. A convenient method of summarizing the influence of income is in terms of income elasticity. These coefficients, computed annually for the period 1919 to 1938 from the retail sales equation given below, rose continually from 1.6 in 1919 to 2.6 in 1930, then declined steadily to 2.2 in 1934, and then increased again to reach 2.6 in 1938. Thus, income elasticity varied with the degree of market saturation, being relatively high when the latter was high, and relatively low when the latter was low.

[5] The base of d was 7.4 years. Thus, if age at retirement is 8 years, the value of d is 114 (i.e., $100 \times 8.0 \div 7.04 = 114$); if the price is 90, the index of replacement cost is $90 \div 114 = 80$. With both price and durability at 100, the number of cars maintained per family is [.378 + .00068 (real supernumerary income per capita)].

c) Replacement Sales. How does the pressure for replacement affect the sale of new cars? In order to answer this question, it was necessary to define and measure the factors that determine replacement sales of automobiles. Economic factors in combination with scrapping data had to be utilized in arriving at a formula for replacement sales. This was because the actual scrapping rate tended to exceed the theoretically expected rate in times of prosperity, and to fall short of the theoretically expected rate during periods of depression. The following formula for replacement sales, S_R, by incorporating per capita supernumerary income, j, and price, p, in conjunction with theoretical scrapping data, accounted fairly well for this variation:

$$S_R = .92j^{1.07}\, p^{-.74}\, (\text{Theoretical Scrapping})^{1.10}$$

The exponent for supernumerary income in this formula is 1.07, meaning that the change in replacement sales may be expected to be a little greater than unity for a 1 per cent change in income, other factors remaining constant. The exponent, in other words, reveals the elasticity directly, and hence the remaining exponents can be interpreted in a similar manner.

d) New-Owner Sales. New-owner sales, S_N, or net additions to the car population were found to be fairly well represented by an equation which incorporated supernumerary income per capita, j, price, p, the mid-year number of cars in operation, C^1, and the second maximum ownership level discussed above, M_2. The formula derived was

$$S_N = j^{1.5}\, p^{-.9}\, .040C^1\, (M_2 - C^1)$$

Both this formula and the previous one for replacement sales yielded good fits to the actual data. And when the sum of calculated new-owner sales, N, and replacement sales, R, was taken, a reasonably good approximation to retail sales was obtained (as discussed in the previous section with reference to the basic equation for durable goods: $S = N + R$). The graphic sum of N and R, for the analysis period, is shown in Figure 7–2.

e) Retail Sales. The two formulas presented above for replacement sales and new-owner sales, respectively, were not suggested as the best demand functions, mainly because there was some theoretical basis for doubting the complete independence of the replacement and new-owner markets. Thus, if replacement sales are large, consumers will not add as many cars to their stock or inventory as they would if few replacements were needed. If replacement requirements are small, some car owners may go on a two-car basis, or at least they may spend the money not needed for replacements in such a way that others can become new-car owners. Therefore, in the equation for total sales, new-owner sales and replacement sales were not expressed separately as such; however, a replacement pressure term was included in the formula on a par with the new-owners' term.

Combining the relevant factors, the problem was to fit the demand function

FIGURE 7–2

ACTUAL SALES COMPARED WITH SUM OF CALCULATED NEW OWNER
AND REPLACEMENT SALES

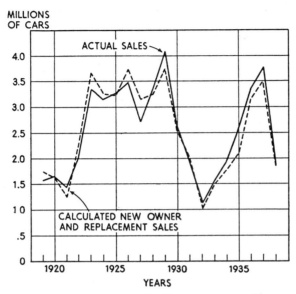

Source: *Dynamics of Automobile Demand*, p. 59.

Sales = (Income) (Price) [Car Stock (Maximum Ownership — Car Stock)
+ Replacement Pressure]

to the data. Fitting the formula, the equation derived was

$$S = j^{1.2}\, p^{-.65}\, [.03C\,(M_3 - C) + .65X]$$

where

     S = New car sales at retail.

     j = Supernumerary income per capita.

     p = Index of car prices.

     C = Number of cars in use during the year.

    M_3 = Maximum ownership level as discussed earlier.

     X = Replacement pressure, which was calculated by applying a shifting
mortality table to the age distribution of automobiles.

The graphic result of this equation is shown in Figure 7–3. Note how
closely it compares with the graph in Figure 7–2.

4. *Price Elasticity.* The primary purpose of this study was to determine the price elasticity for automobiles. The approach that was finally
decided upon was, first, to solve the problem of total demand by deriving
a satisfactory demand function for passenger cars, and second, to determine
the effect of price as a by-product of this relationship.

FIGURE 7–3

PASSENGER CAR SALES

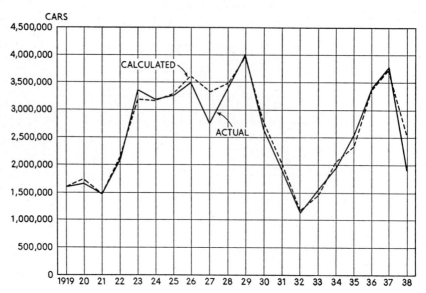

Source: *Dynamics of Automobile Demand*, p. 60.

The negative exponents of price in the equations above would seem to indicate a price elasticity of less than unity. However, by using different price series and different methods of calculation, it became evident that the exponents or elasticities could not be determined accurately. There were at least two reasons for this indeterminateness: (1) the price trend was generally downward for the analysis period and did not undergo many wide or frequent swings; and (2) the price elasticity could be expected to have a fairly high correlation with national income and with the cost of living, and the separate effects of each would be difficult to evaluate. After considering alternative calculation methods, price series, and so forth, the conclusion finally arrived at was that the elasticity of automobile sales with respect to price was probably in the vicinity of 1.5, but possibly as high as 2.0 and as low as 1.0, and perhaps even moderately beyond these limits.

Conclusion

It appears, therefore, that the price elasticity of demand for new automobiles is not very high, at least as compared with other consumer durables, especially "luxury" goods. What reasons may be offered to account for this relatively low elasticity? There are several that may be suggested: (1) The durable nature of automobiles makes it possible for consumers to run their existing cars longer, even at the cost of higher repair bills if necessary, rather than purchase a new car. (2) Consumers have access to a sufficiently large supply of adequate used cars so that they need not purchase only new cars if they require transportation. (3) The price of a car is only one of its costs, the remainder being composed of other nonoperating as well as operating costs. Automobile sales are probably more affected by style and improved operating characteristics than by price cuts. (4) Automobiles are probably not a luxury good to the extent that certain other consumer durables may be, and hence their price elasticity will not be as high. (5) Finally, dealers tend to stimulate new car sales during prosperity periods by offering better terms for used cars in trade, and depress new car sales during recession by selling off their stocks of used cars. These dealer policies, combined with the tendency for income to outweigh price in its effect on sales, exert a reinforcing downward pressure on price elasticity.

The Roos-von Szeliski study was published in 1938. Since that time several other studies of automobile demand have been made by researchers in industry, government, and universities. In general, these studies produced about equally good statistical fits as the Roos-von Szeliski work, but they were far simpler and were done with a considerably smaller expenditure of time and money. What implications does this have for the planning of future research activities? Does it mean, for instance, that time and expense considerations on the one hand, and accuracy on the other, should be the chief considerations in deciding on a forecasting study? The answer basically is yes, but certain implications are involved which must be recognized.

In economics generally, and in econometrics particularly, *the coherence and persuasiveness of a theory are absolutely vital—so much so that it can be said that the theory accounts for, illumines, and gives significance to the correlations found, rather than that the correlations verify or confirm the theory. Thus, many statistical formulas could be developed which would represent the data with substantially equal goodness of fit. But, since statistical tests of goodness of fit will not distinguish between those made up of purely empirical covariations and those which are causally significant formulations, it is evident that the logical implications of the formula and economic theory are marks of the best formula.* And the best formula, it appears, is not only the one that shows a good fit, but the one that is most durable as well. A formula may backcast beautifully, but break down completely when used to forecast for any period beyond a very short range.

What will determine the durability of a formula? The answer, of course, is the theory on which it is based. In this connection, the Roos-von Szeliski study, done in 1938, was the first study of a consumers' durable good to be supported by such a well-developed, coherent, and persuasive theory as the concept of maximum ownership level. Since then, other analyses of durable goods have appeared, but many of them have amounted to hardly more than correlations of important variables such as income, households, and prices, with relatively little dependence on a well-structured theory such as exists in the maximum ownership concept.[6] In view of its successful application, therefore, the maximum ownership principle is employed consistently in the remaining studies of consumers' durable goods discussed in this chapter.

DEMAND FOR REFRIGERATORS

Against the background of the Roos-von Szeliski automobile analysis, we turn our attention now to further studies of the demand for consumer durables. The basic theory supporting these studies, that is, the maximum ownership concept, is the same here as in the previous work. However, the studies discussed here and in the next section are, in contrast to the previous section, run by graphic rather than mathematical methods, and hence should be more palatable for the nonmathematical reader.

Before proceeding with the analysis, let us recapitulate briefly some essential principles that have already been discussed or implied in earlier sections. This should help in fixing certain ideas that form the basis of the empirical studies that follow.

First, it should be recalled that there exists a set of theoretical equations which express the demand for consumers' durable goods, and that these equations provide a guide to what it is that needs to be measured when analyzing the demand for a specific durable good. The form of the equation, in other words, is known, and the problem is to find the necessary parameters. The method usually employed for this is correlation analysis. The problem, however, is complicated by the fact that some of the parameters are constants only for a limited number of years; that is, they depend upon certain economic variables that cannot be included in the final estimating or predicting equation.

Second, the basic equations of the demand for consumers' durable goods, developed earlier in the discussion relevant to footnote 1, p. 244, may be noted briefly:

$$S = N + R \tag{1}$$

$$N = \Delta y / \Delta t = ay\,[M(t) - y] \tag{2}$$

where

$S =$ Total sales of the good.

$N =$ New-owner demand, or the increase in the total stock in use.

$R =$ Replacement demand, that is, replacement of the existing stock as measured by the scrappage of old units.

[6] Some possible exceptions are some recent studies of durable goods, such as the one by Daniel Suits, "The Demand for New Automobiles in The United States 1929–56," *The Review of Economics and Statistics* (August, 1958), as well as other studies of durable goods which have appeared lately, based on different theoretical formulations. The maximum ownership approach, however, has probably had the longest history of success in predicting turning points.

y = Number in use at beginning of each period.

t = Time.

$M(t)$ = Total number of units of the good that would probably be used under the specific economic and cultural conditions of the period. This is the *maximum ownership level* and might depend on such factors as the number of wired households in a study of electrical appliances, and the volume of purchasing power, the latter measured by income, credit, and prices. The symbol $M(t)$ is read "M of t" and means that M is a function of t.

These relationships provide a general framework for the analysis of any consumers' durable goods. Refrigerators are treated in this section with a fairly detailed explanation of the procedures and techniques involved in the construction of a forecasting model. The analysis is essentially graphic rather than mathematical so as to enhance the visualization of relationships.

Raw Data

The electric refrigerator is a well-established product and hence fairly accurate data on manufacturers' sales are available from a business magazine such as *Electrical Merchandising*. These figures are not the same as consumers' sales but over a period of several years, manufacturers' sales would of course be equal to consumers' sales. However, because of changes of inventories in the channels of distribution, manufacturers' sales probably show greater cyclical fluctuation than retail sales of the same commodity. Further, as seen in Table 7–1 or Figure 7–4, cyclical changes in sales have increased over time. This is due to the product's increasing saturation of the market over the years, the effect being that the impact of sales due to increased acceptance of the product has diminished, while changes in sales due to changes in consumers' purchasing power have become more important.

A useful source of statistical data (in addition to those discussed in Chapter 2) when electrical products of various kinds are concerned, is the magazine *Electrical Merchandising*. An examination of this and other sources, however, revealed no information on the scrappage of refrigerators, and relatively little on the number of refrigerators in use. With respect to the latter, it provided data for certain years on the number of wired homes that have at least one refrigerator. But, unfortunately, this figure tends to understate the total number actually in use, because many dwelling units have more than one refrigerator, and many household-type refrigerators are used in small business establishments such as restaurants, drugstores, and bakeries. Consequently, some other method had to be found for estimating the number of refrigerators in use, and the data provided by *Electrical Merchandising* could serve only as a check against the results obtained.

Estimate of Refrigerators in Use

The method used to calculate consumer's inventory of refrigerators, that is, the number of refrigerators in use, was based on theoretical survival

TABLE 7-1

FACTORS DETERMINING REFRIGERATOR DEMAND

	(1)	(2)	(3)	(4)	(5)	(6)	(7)	(8)	(9)
	Sales, Thousands of Units				Super-numerary Income, Billions of 1947–49 Dollars	Net Credit Extension (Except Autos) $ Billions	Price Index of House Furnishings, 1947–49 =100	Consumers' Real Purchasing Power (1947–49 Prices), $ Billions	Wired Homes, Millions
	Actual Total	Replacement	New Owner	Inventory					
Year	S	R	$N_1 = S-R$	y	I	C	P	$I+\dfrac{3C}{P}$	H_w
1925	75	5	70	272	56.3		73.5	56.3	14.7
1926	205	6	199	342	58.9		73.2	58.9	15.7
1927	375	6	369	541	58.9		73.7	58.9	16.8
1928	535	10	525	910	64.9		69.8	64.9	18.1
1929	778	13	765	1,435	72.9		68.0	72.9	19.3
1930	791	15	776	2,200	63.5	−.066	64.9	63.2	20.1
1931	906	20	886	2,976	57.6	−.178	57.6	56.8	20.5
1932	797	24	772	3,862	41.3	−.358	50.6	39.1	20.4
1933	1016	34	982	4,634	39.3	−.07	48.6	38.9	19.8
1934	1283	49	1,234	5,616	47.5	+.16	50.9	48.5	20.0
1935	1568	68	1,500	6,850	59.2	.45	50.0	62.0	20.6
1936	1996	106	1,890	8,350	72.2	.54	50.8	75.4	21.2
1937	2310	159	2,153	10,240	73.1	.27	55.0	74.5	22.0
1938	1240	237	1,003	12,393	64.4	.07	54.5	64.8	22.9
1939	1900	311	1,589	13,396	74.7	.41	53.4	77.0	23.6
1940	2600	411	2,189	14,985	84.5	.44	53.0	87.0	24.6
1941	3500	529	2,971	17,174	105.1	.19	56.6	106.2	25.0
1942				20,145	122.7				
1946	2100	898	1,202	19,516	129.1	1.18	83.9	133.4	29.4
1947	3400	1,040	2,361	20,718	112.1	1.58	97.2	117.0	31.2
1948	4766	1,187	3,579	23,079	117.1	1.21	103.2	120.6	33.1
1949	4450	1,350	3,100	26,658	120.7	1.06	99.6	123.9	35.2
1950	6200	1,505	4,695	29,758	134.9	1.59	100.3	139.8	37.2
1951	4075	1,656	2,419	34,453	132.7	.69	111.2	134.6	39.1
1952	3570	1,777	1,793	36,872	142.6	2.35	108.5	149.0	40.9
1953	3650	1,874	1,776	38,665	152.7	1.50	107.9	156.9	42.4
1954	3600	1,937	1,663	40,441	156.5	.59	106.1	158.2	43.6
1955	4200	1,990	2,210	42,104	172.7	1.79	104.1	177.7	44.8
1956	3700	2,061	1,638	44,314	186.7	1.56	103.0	191.3	46.1

Source:

Col. 1: *Electrical Merchandising.*
Cols. 2, 3, 4: calculated from the cumulative life table, Table 7–4.
Col. 5: The Econometric Institute, Inc.
Col. 6: *Federal Reserve Bulletin* (credit extended minus credit repaid).
Col. 7: Bureau of Labor Statistics, *Monthly Labor Review.*
Col. 8: calculated from cols. 5, 6, and 7, as shown by formula.
Col. 9: Edison Electric Institute.

functions.[7] The assumption was made that refrigerators had a 25-year maximum life and that they were repaired rather than scrapped during the war period 1942–45 because new models were unavailable. Consumer inventory was then computed as follows:

[7] Survival functions are "life tables" very much like insurance life tables, and hence can also be derived from sample surveys, as compared to the method used in this study.

FIGURE 7-4

REFRIGERATOR DATA—CHART 1A

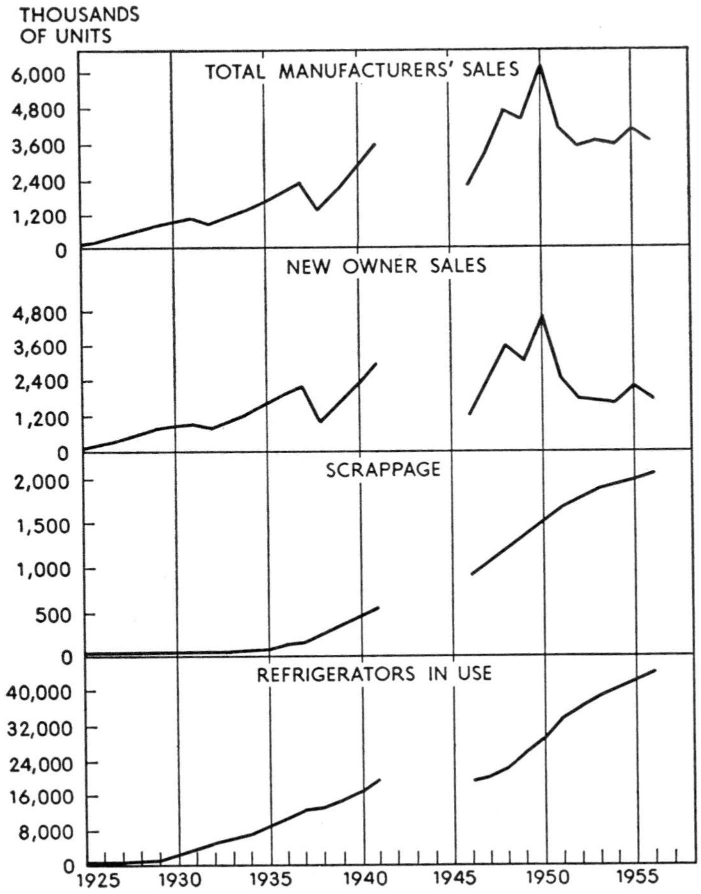

REFRIGERATOR DATA—CHART 1B

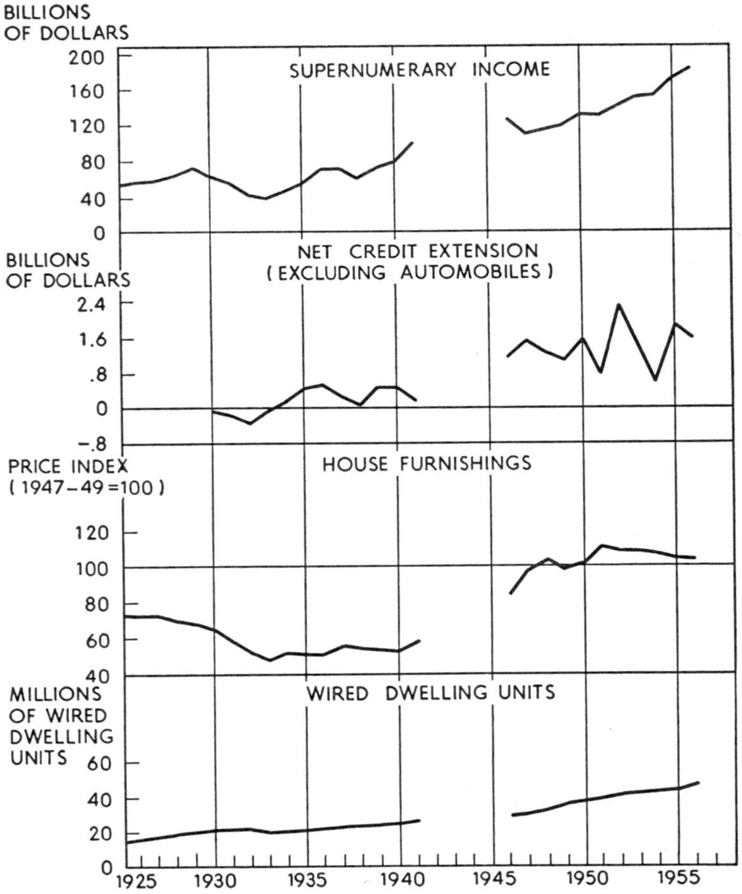

TABLE 7–2

DURABLE GOODS SURVIVAL COEFFICIENTS

Age in Years	6-Year Life	11-Year Life	14-Year Life	20-Year Life	25-Year Life
1............	1.000	1.000	1.000	1.000	1.000
2............	.996	.9995	1.000	.9998	1.000
3............	.908	.9946	.998	.9992	.9999
4............	.500	.9656	.989	.9965	.9997
5............	.092	.8621	.957	.9878	.9989
6............	.000	.6406	.874	.9641	.9965
7............		.3594	.716	.9115	.9904
8............		.1379	.500	.8159	.9762
9............		.0344	.284	.6736	.9474
10............		.0054	.126	.5000	.8962
11............		.0000	.043	.3264	.8159
12............			.011	.1841	.7054
13............			.002	.0885	.5714
14............			.000	.0359	.4286
15............				.0122	.2946
16............				.0035	.1841
17............				.0008	.1038
18............				.0002	.0526
19............				.0000	.0238
20............				.0000	.0096
21............					.0035
22............					.0011
23............					.0003
24............					.0001
25............					.0000

Source: Calculated from Bradford Kimball, "A System of Life Tables For Physical Property Based on the Truncated Normal Distribution," *Econometrica*, October, 1947.

1. A survival or life table for durable goods was calculated, the results of which appear in Table 7–2. The heading at the top of each column represents the maximum estimated life (which is equal to about twice the average estimated life), the column at the extreme left gives the age of the product expressed in years of actual life, and the body of the table reveals the calculated percentages or survival coefficients of the products surviving. Thus, given a 25-year life, what percentage of refrigerators produced in any given year may be expected to be in use 10 years later? Starting in the extreme left column with year 10, move horizontally to the extreme right column the heading of which is "25-year life." The answer is 89.62 per cent. Similarly, 29.46 per cent of the number of refrigerators manufactured in a given year may be expected to be in use 15 years later, since the survival coefficient, as can be seen from the table, is .2946.

2. The next step was the construction of an actual refrigerator survival table as shown in Table 7–3. This table was derived as follows: first, the sales data were posted at the left alongside the corresponding years; second, the years were again listed horizontally across the top of the table; and third, the number of refrigerators produced in any year that would survive to a later year was calculated by multiplying (*a*) the number pro-

duced in the given year by (b) the corresponding survival coefficient in Table 7–2, and recording the result in the body of the table under the appropriate year. Thus, referring to Table 7–3, 791,000 refrigerators were produced in 1930. According to the survival coefficient in Table 7–2, 89.62 per cent will still be in existence 10 years later, assuming a 25-year maximum life. Therefore, since 89.62 per cent of 791,000 is 708,894 or approximately 709,000, this figure is recorded on the horizontal line for the year 1930, under the column headed 1940. The remaining figures in the table are obtained in the same manner, with each figure as of January 1 of that year.

3. The final step at this stage of the analysis is to calculate the consumers' inventory of refrigerators for any given year. This is done in Table 7–4. The consumer inventory for any year is shown in boldface type, and represents the year at the top of its column. Each of these boldface inventory figures consists of (a) sales during the previous year as given in the two columns at the extreme left, plus (b) the inventory surviving from previous periods as shown in italics immediately above the numbers in boldface. Thus, on January 1, 1927, the consumer inventory was 541,000, consisting of sales in 1926 of 205,000 plus surviving inventory of 336,000. Similarly, on January 1, 1940, the consumer inventory was 14,985,000. This was made up of 1939 sales of 1,900,000 and a surviving inventory of 13,085,000.

It should be evident, therefore, that each inventory survival figure given in italics in Table 7–4 under a given year is actually the sum of all numbers except the bottom one appearing in the corresponding column of Table 7–3. For instance, in Table 7–4, the inventory surviving to January 1, 1927 is the number in italics, *336*. This is the total of all the numbers except the bottom one appearing in the 1927 column of Table 7–3. Similarly with the other figures representing the amount of inventory survival. They are the accumulations of the estimates first developed in Table 7–3.

Scrappage and New-Owner Sales

The refrigerator inventory schedule of Table 7–4 can also be used to calculate the scrappage volume for any year. The procedure is to subtract the number of units surviving to a given year from the total inventory in the previous year. To illustrate, the refrigerator inventory on January 1, 1955 was 42,104,000 units. Of these, 40,114,000 units survived to January 1, 1956. The difference, 1,990,000 units, is the calculated or theoretical number of refrigerators scrapped during 1955, shown in Table 7–1, col. 2, p. 254.

How does scrappage relate to new-owner sales? As implied at several earlier points in this chapter, new-owner sales represent the difference between total sales and replacement sales in the basic equation $S = N + R$, since replacement is measured by the scrappage of old units. That is, $N = S - R$. Over a period of several years, new-owner sales as calculated here would equal actual sales to new owners, but in any one year the actual figure may be greater or less than the calculated value. The figures analyzed in this study, therefore, are actually true new-owner sales plus the short-

TABLE 7-3

REFRIGERATOR SURVIVAL TABLE
As of January 1
Maximum Life: 25 Years
(All data in thousands of units)

Year	Sales	1925	1926	1927	1928	1929	1930	1931	1932	1933	1934	1935	1936	1937	1938	1939	1940	1941
1912–24	275	272	267	261	255	245	232	217	199	179	155	128	101	74	49	19	9	4
1925	75		75	75	75	75	75	75	74	73	71	67	61	53	43	32	22	14
1926	205			205	205	205	205	205	204	203	200	193	184	167	145	117	88	60
1927	375				375	375	375	375	375	374	371	366	355	336	306	265	214	161
1928	535					535	635	535	535	534	533	530	522	507	479	437	377	306
1929	778						778	778	778	778	777	775	771	759	737	697	635	540
1930	791							791	791	791	791	790	788	783	772	749	709	645
1931	906								906	906	906	906	905	903	897	884	858	812
1932	796									796	796	796	796	795	793	788	777	754
1933	1016										1016	1016	1016	1016	1015	1012	1006	992
1934	1283											1283	1283	1283	1283	1282	1279	1271
1935	1568												1568	1568	1568	1568	1566	1563
1936	1996													1996	1996	1996	1995	1994
1937	2310														2310	2310	2310	2309
1938	1240															1240	1240	1240
1939	1900																1900	1900
1940	2600																	2600
1941	3500																	
1942	520																	
1943	—																	
1944	—																	
1945	264																	
1946	2100																	
1947	3400																	
1948	4766																	
1949	4450																	
1950	6200																	
1951	4075																	
1952	3570																	
1953	3650																	
1954	3600																	
1955	4200																	
1956	3700																	

TABLE 7-3 (Continued)

Year	Sales	1942	1943	1944	1945	1946	1947	1948	1949	1950	1951	1952	1953	1954	1955	1956	1957	1958	1959	1960	1961
1912-24	275	1	1																		
1925	75	8	8	8	4	2	1														
1926	205	38	38	38	21	11	5	2	1												
1927	375	110	110	110	69	39	20	9	4	1											
1928	535	229	229	229	158	98	56	28	13	5	2										
1929	778	445	445	445	333	229	143	81	41	19	7	3									
1930	791	558	558	558	452	339	233	146	82	42	19	8	3	1							
1931	906	739	739	739	639	518	388	267	167	94	48	22	9	3	1						
1932	796	713	713	713	649	561	455	341	235	147	83	42	19	8	3	1					
1933	1016	963	963	963	911	829	717	581	435	299	187	105	53	24	10	4	1				
1934	1283	1252	1252	1252	1216	1150	1047	905	733	550	378	236	133	67	31	12	4	1			
*	1568	1553	1553	1553	1531	1486	1405	1279	1106	896	672	462	289	163	82	37	15	5	2		
1935	1996	1989	1989	1989	1977	1949	1891	1789	1629	1408	1141	885	588	367	207	105	48	19	7	2	1
1936	2310	2307	2307	2307	2302	2288	2255	2188	2070	1885	1629	1320	990	681	425	240	122	55	22	8	3
1937	1240	1240	1240	1240	1239	1236	1228	1210	1175	1111	1012	875	709	531	365	228	129	65	30	12	4
1938	1900	1900	1900	1900	1899	1898	1893	1882	1855	1800	1703	1550	1340	1086	814	560	350	197	100	45	18
1939	2600	2600	2600	2600	2600	2599	2597	2591	2575	2538	2463	2330	2121	1834	1486	1114	766	479	270	137	62
1940	3500	3500	3500	3500	3500	3500	3500	3496	3488	3466	3417	3316	3137	2856	2469	2000	1500	1031	644	363	174
1941	520		520	520	520	520	520	520	519	518	515	508	493	466	424	367	297	223	153	96	54
1942	—																				
1943	—																				
1944	264					264	264	264	264	264	263	261	258	250	237	215	186	151	113	78	49
1945	2100					2100	2100	2100	2100	2099	2098	2093	2080	2050	1990	1882	1713	1481	1200	900	619
1946	3400					3400	3400	3400	3400	3400	3400	3396	3388	3367	3319	3221	3047	2774	2398	1943	1457
1947	4766						4766	4766	4766	4766	4766	4765	4761	4749	4720	4653	4515	4271	3889	3362	2723
1948	4450							4450	4450	4450	4450	4450	4449	4445	4434	4407	4344	4216	3988	3631	3139
1949	6200								6200	6200	6200	6200	6199	6198	6193	6178	6140	6052	5874	5556	5059
1950	4075									4075	4075	4075	4075	4075	4074	4071	4061	4036	3978	3861	3652
1951	3570										3570	3570	3570	3570	3570	3569	3566	3558	3536	3485	3382
1952	3650											3650	3650	3650	3650	3650	3649	3646	3637	3615	3536
1953	3600												3600	3600	3600	3600	3600	3599	3596	3587	3565
1954	4200													4200	4200	4200	4200	4200	4199	4195	4185
1955	3700														3700	3700	3700	3700	3700	3699	3696
1956																					

Source: Calculated from Table 7.2.

TABLE 7-4

CONSUMERS' REFRIGERATOR INVENTORY—LIFE TABLE, CUMULATIVE

As of January 1

Maximum Life: 25 Years

(All data in thousands of units)

Year	Sales	1925	1926	1927	1928	1929	1930	1931	1932	1933	1934	1935	1936	1937	1938	1939	1940	1941
1912–24																		
1925	75	**272**	267	261	255	245	232	217	199	179	155	128	101	74	49	19	9	4
1926	205		**342**	336	330	320	307	292	273	252	226	195	162	127	92	51	31	18
1927	375			**541**	535	525	512	497	477	455	426	388	346	294	237	168	119	78
1928	535				**910**	900	887	875	852	829	797	754	701	630	543	433	333	239
1929	778					**1435**	1422	1407	1387	1363	1330	1284	1223	1137	1022	870	710	545
1930	791						**2200**	2185	2165	2141	2107	2059	1994	1896	1759	1567	1345	1094
1931	906							**2976**	2956	2932	2898	2849	2782	2679	2531	2316	2054	1739
1932	796								**3862**	3838	3804	3755	3687	3582	3428	3200	2912	2551
1933	1016									**4634**	4600	4551	4483	4377	4421	3988	3689	3305
1934	1283										**5616**	5567	5499	5393	5236	5000	4615	4297
1935	1568											**6850**	6782	6676	6519	6282	5974	5568
1936	1996												**8350**	8244	8087	7850	7540	7131
1937	2310													**10240**	10083	9846	9535	9125
1938	1240														**12393**	12156	11845	11434
1939	1900															**13396**	13085	12674
1940	2600																**14985**	14574
1941	3500																	**17174**
1942	520																	
1943	—																	
1944	—																	
1945	264																	
1946	2100																	
1947	3400																	
1948	4766																	
1949	4450																	
1950	6200																	
1951	4075																	
1952	3570																	
1953	3650																	
1954	3600																	
1955	4200																	
1956	3700																	
1957																		

TABLE 7-4 (Continued)

Year	Sales	1942	1943	1944	1945	1946	1947	1948	1949	1950	1951	1952	1953	1954	1955	1956	1957	1958
1912–24	275																	
1925	75	1	1															
1926	205	9	9	8	4	2	1											
1927	375	47	47	46	25	13	6	2	1									
1928	535	157	157	156	94	52	26	11	5	1								
1929	778	386	386	385	252	150	82	39	18	6	2							
1930	791	831	831	830	585	379	225	120	59	25	9	3	1					
1931	906	1389	1389	1388	1037	718	458	266	141	67	28	11	4	1				
1932	796	2128	2128	2127	1676	1236	846	533	308	161	76	33	13	4	1			
1933	1016	2841	2841	2840	2325	1797	1301	874	543	308	159	75	32	12	4	1		
1934	1283	3804	3804	3803	3236	2626	2018	1455	978	607	346	180	85	36	14	5	1	
1935	1568	5056	5056	5055	4452	3776	3056	2360	1711	1157	724	416	218	103	45	17	5	
1936	1996	6609	6609	6608	5983	5262	4470	3639	2817	2053	1396	878	507	266	127	54	20	
1937	2310	8598	8598	8597	7960	7211	6361	5428	4446	3461	2537	1733	1095	633	334	159	68	
1938	1240	10905	10905	10904	10262	9499	8616	7617	6516	5346	4166	3053	2085	1314	759	399	190	
1939	1900	12145	12145	12144	11501	10735	9844	8826	7691	6457	5178	3928	2794	1845	1124	627	319	
1940	2600	14045	14045	14044	13400	12633	11737	10708	9546	8257	6881	5478	4134	2931	1938	1187	669	
1941	3500	16645	16645	16644	16000	15232	14334	13299	12121	10795	9344	7808	6255	4765	3424	2301	1435	
1942	520	**20145**	20145	20144	19500	18732	17834	16795	15609	14261	12761	11124	9392	7621	5893	4301	2935	
1943	—		**20665**	20664	20020	19252	18354	17315	16128	14779	13276	11632	9885	8087	6317	4668	3232	
1944	264			**20664**	20020	19252	18354	17315	16128	14779	13276	11632	9885	8087	6317	4668	3232	
1945	2100				**20020**	19252	18354	17315	16128	14779	13276	11632	9885	8087	6317	4668	3232	
1946	3400					**19516**	18618	17579	16392	15043	13539	11893	10143	8337	6554	4883	3418	
1947	4766						**20718**	19679	18492	17142	15637	13986	12223	10387	8544	6765	5131	
1948	4450							**23079**	21892	20542	19037	17382	15611	13754	11863	9986	8178	
1949	6200								**26658**	25308	23803	22147	20372	18503	16583	14639	12693	
1950	4075									**29758**	28253	26597	24821	22984	21017	19046	17037	
1951	3570										**34453**	32797	31020	29146	27210	25224	23177	
1952	3650											**36872**	35095	33221	31284	29295	27238	
1953	3600												**38665**	36791	34854	32864	30804	
1954	4200													**40441**	38504	36514	34453	
1955	3700														**42104**	40114	38053	
1956																**44314**	42253	43759
1957																	**45953**	**48738**

Source: Calculated from Tables 7-2 and 7-3.

term or cyclical difference between actual scrapping and calculated scrapping. In this way, the cyclical component of the scrapping figure is included in the analysis. Thus, in prosperity periods when income is high, scrapping rates should tend to be somewhat above normal, and this would show up in the study as a greater-than-normal new-owner demand. Conversely, in recession periods when income is low, scrapping rates are retarded and the result is that there is a lower-than-normal new-owner demand. Hence, the new-owner figure analyzed below contains all the cyclical components of the total sales figure. Until scrapping figures become available, there is no way of making a true separation of the variables. However, this separation, it will be seen, is not necessary.

First Correlation: Percentage Increase in Consumers' Inventory versus Consumers' Inventory

The first section of this chapter was devoted to the development of a theory of demand for consumers' durable goods. An essential part of the theory was the proposition that for any consumers' durable good, the percentage increase in the number of units in use is directly proportional to the number in use. The first step in a demand analysis, therefore, is to find this factor of proportionality. To accomplish this we first assume that the maximum ownership level, $M(t)$, has an upper limit and hence within specified time periods may be expressed as a constant, M. It follows from the earlier equation (2), p. 252, therefore, that the *change* in units in use, or new-owner sales, is

$$\Delta y / \Delta t = ay \, (M - y) \tag{2a}$$

and that the *percentage change* in units in use, obtained by dividing both sides of the equation by y is

$$\frac{\Delta y / \Delta t}{y} = aM - ay, \text{ or simply } M_0 - ay \tag{3}$$

since a and M are both constants within each time period and may be combined into the single constant M_0.

What does this equation tell us? Essentially, it states that the percentage change in the number of units in use (the left side of the equation) is related to or dependent upon the number in use (right side) as shown by y. Further, although it may not be readily apparent at first, the equation, though slightly disguised, is actually the equation of a straight line whose slope is $-a$ and whose intercept at $y = 0$ is M_0. Hence, the relation between the two variables is linear, and the graphic analysis done below produces the straight line that expresses this relationship.

If M were actually a constant throughout the entire analysis period, the required line of relationship could be found by the traditional method of *least squares* because this method produces a line such that the sum of the squares of the deviations of the points about it are less than from any other line. This procedure is well known, has wide application, and is the method commonly taught in elementary statistics courses. It is not applied in this problem, however, because *M*, in reality, is not a constant but instead varies with economic conditions. A somewhat novel graphic approach is employed, therefore, to help solve the problem. Starting with Table 7–5, most of which is filled in as the analysis progresses, the first step is to derive and interpret the regression in Figure 7–5. This regression is unique in that it incorporates the known movements of the economy over time in determining the proper relationship. Hence it warrants a separate discussion.

FIGURE 7–5

REFRIGERATORS: PERCENTAGE CHANGE IN CONSUMERS' INVENTORIES
VERSUS CONSUMERS' INVENTORIES

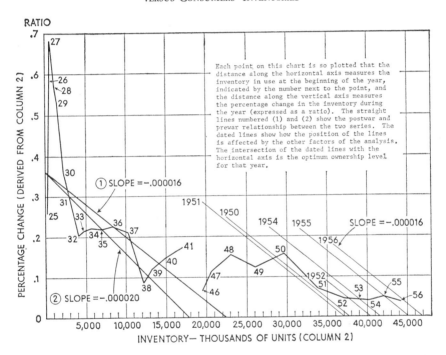

First Regression. In the scatter diagram of Figure 7–5, the percentage change in refrigerators in use is measured vertically, and the number in use, calculated from the life table, is shown horizontally. The former, therefore, is derived directly from the latter. For example, referring to the life table, Table 7–4, the figure at the bottom of the 1932 column indicates that there were 3,862,000 refrigerators in use at the beginning of 1932, and that during the year the inventory increased to 4,634,000 at the beginning of 1933, or by about 20 per cent. Hence a point labeled "32," representing 1932, is plotted at the intersection of the 20 per cent line with the 1932 inventory line in Figure 7–5. The remaining dots are plotted in the same

TABLE 7-5

Analysis of New-Owner Refrigerator Demand

Year	(1) New-Owner Sales $\Delta y/\Delta t$ From Table 7-1	(2) Inventory y From Table 7-1	(3) First Adjustment for Inventory $a_1y = -.00002(y)$ $a_1 = -.00002$ from Fig. 7-5	(4) First Adjustment for Inventory $a_2y = -.000016(y)$ $a_2 = -.000016$ from Fig. 7-5	(5) Pct. Change in Inventory Adjusted for Inventory Levels (Ratio) $\frac{\Delta y}{\Delta t \cdot y} + a_1y$ $(1)\div(2)+(3)$	(6) Pct. Change in Inventory Adjusted for Inventory Levels (Ratio) $\frac{\Delta y}{\Delta t \cdot y} + a_2y$ $(1)\div(2)+(4)$	(7) Real Purchasing Power (1947–49 Prices) $I + \frac{3C}{P}$ Billions of Dollars From Table 7-1	(8) Trend of Real Purchasing Power $f(t) = 10^{.02109T+1.0855}$ From Fig. 7-8	(9) Deviations of Real Purchasing Power from Its Trend (Ratio) $\frac{I+\frac{3C}{P}}{f(t)}=x$ $(7)/(8)$
1925	70	272	.0054		.2624		56.3	37.83	1.488
1926	199	342	.0068		.5888		58.9	39.76	1.481
1927	369	541	.0108		.6928		58.9	41.79	1.409
1928	525	910	.0182		.5952		64.9	43.93	1.477
1929	765	1,435	.0287		.5617		72.9	46.18	1.579
1930	776	2,200	.0440		.3970		63.2	48.55	1.302
1931	886	2,976	.0595		.3575		56.8	51.04	1.113
1932	772	3,862	.0772		.2772		39.1	53.69	.728
1933	982	4,634	.0927		.3047		38.9	56.40	.690
1934	1,234	5,616	.1123		.3323		48.5	59.29	.818
1935	1,500	6,850	.1370		.3560		62.0	62.33	.995
1936	1,890	8,350	.1670		.3930		75.4	65.51	1.151
1937	2,153	10,240	.2048		.4148		74.5	68.87	1.082
1938	1,003	12,393	.2479		.3369		64.8	72.40	.895
1939	1,589	13,396	.2679		.3869		77.0	76.10	1.012
1940	2,189	14,985	.2997		.4457		87.0	80.00	1.088
1941	2,971	17,174	.3435		.5165		106.2	84.10	1.263
1946*	1,202	19,516		.3123		.374	133.4	107.9	1.236
1947	2,361	20,718		.3319		.446	117.0	113.4	1.032
1948	3,579	23,079		.3693		.524	120.6	119.3	1.011
1949	3,100	26,658		.4265		.543	123.9	125.4	.988
1950	4,695	29,758		.4761		.643	139.8	131.8	1.061
1951	2,419	34,453		.5512		.639	134.6	138.2	.974
1952	1,793	36,872		.5900		.665	149.0	145.6	1.023
1953	1,776	38,665		.5186		.688	156.9	153.1	1.025
1954	1,663	40,441		.6471		.726	158.2	161.0	.983
1955	2,210	42,104		.6737		.746	177.9	169.2	1.051
1956	1,638	45,323		.7090			191.3	177.8	1.076

TABLE 7-5 (Continued)

Year	(10)	(11)	(12)	(13)	(14)	(15)	(16)	(17)	(18)	(19)	(20)
	Adjustment for Income		Wired Dwelling Units	$aM(t)$ or $M_0(t)$	Relative Increase in Inventory	Calculated New-Owner Demand	Unexplained Variation of New-Owner Demand	Calculated Scrappage	Calculated Total Demand	Actual Total Sales	Unexplained Variation of Total Demand
	Ratio		Millions	Ratio	Ratio	Thousands	Ratio		Thousands of Units		Ratio
	$y_c = .0095x + .0078$	$y_c = .011x + .0045$	H_w	$\dfrac{aM(t)}{\text{or } M_0(t)}$	$aM(t) - ay$	$N = (\Delta y/\Delta t)_c = y[aM(t) - ay]$ or $ayM(t) - ay^2$ or $ay[M(t) - y]$	$\dfrac{\Delta y/\Delta t}{(\Delta y/\Delta t)_c}$	R	$S_c = N + R$	S	$\dfrac{S}{S_c}$
	$x =$ col. (9)	$x =$ col. (9)	From Table 7-1	(12)×(11)	(13)−(3), (4)	(14)×(2)	(1)/(15)	From Table 7-1	(15)+(17)	From Table 7-1	(19)/(18)
1925	.0219		14.7	.322	.3166	86	.814	5	91	75	.824
1926	.0219		15.7	.344	.3372	115	1.730	6	121	205	1.694
1927	.0212		16.8	.356	.2480	134	2.753	6	140	375	2.679
1928	.0218		18.1	.400	.3818	347	1.513	10	357	535	1.499
1929	.0228		19.3	.440	.4113	590	1.297	13	603	778	1.290
1930	.2202		20.1	.406	.3620	796	.975	15	811	791	.975
1931	.0184		20.5	.377	.3175	945	.938	20	965	906	.939
1932	.0147		20.4	.300	.2228	860	.898	24	884	796	.900
1933	.0144		19.8	.285	.1923	891	1.102	34	925	1,016	1.098
1934	.0156		20.0	.312	.1997	1,122	1.100	49	1,171	1,283	1.096
1935	.0173		20.6	.356	.2190	1,500	1.000	68	1,568	1,568	1.000
1936	.0187		21.2	.396	.2290	1,912	.988	106	2,018	1,996	.989
1937	.0181		22.0	.398	.1932	1,978	1.088	159	2,137	2,310	1.081
1938	.0163		22.9	.373	.1251	1,550	.647	237	1,787	1,240	.694
1939	.0174		23.6	.411	.1431	1,917	.829	311	2,228	1,900	.853
1940	.0181		24.6	.445	.1453	2,177	1.006	411	2,598	2,600	1.005
1941	.0199		25.6	.509	.1655	2,842	1.045	529	3,371	3,500	1.038
1946*		.0181	29.4	.552	.2197	4,288	2.803	898	5,186	2,100	.405
1947		.0159	31.2	.496	.1641	3,400	.694	1,040	4,440	3,400	.767
1948		.0156	33.1	.516	.1467	3,386	1.056	1,187	4,573	4,766	1.042
1949		.0154	35.2	.542	.1155	3,079	1.007	1,350	4,429	4,450	1.005
1950		.0162	37.2	.604	.1279	3,806	1.234	1,505	5,311	6,200	1.167
1951		.0152	39.1	.594	.0428	1,475	1.640	1,656	3,131	4,075	1.302
1952		.0158	40.9	.646	.0560	2,065	.868	1,777	3,842	3,570	.929
1953		.0158	42.4	.670	.0514	1,987	.894	1,874	3,861	3,650	.945
1954		.0153	43.6	.667	.0199	805	2.065	1,937	2,742	3,600	1.313
1955		.0161	44.8	.721	.0473	1,992	1.109	1,990	3,982	4,200	1.055
1956		.0163	46.1	.751	.0420	1,861	.880	2,061	3,922	3,700	.943

*No refrigerators produced during 1942–45 period.

manner, and then connected in chronological order as shown by the jagged line in the diagram.

What interpretation can be drawn from the chart, even at this early stage of the analysis? Two important characteristics are immediately evident: (1) The percentage change in units in use is greatly influenced by business conditions, as evidenced by the lows for the recession years 1932, 1938, and 1949; and (2) the rate of increase has been diminishing over time. The latter characteristic is revealed more clearly in Figure 7–6, where the

FIGURE 7–6

REFRIGERATORS: PERCENTAGE CHANGE IN CONSUMERS' INVENTORIES

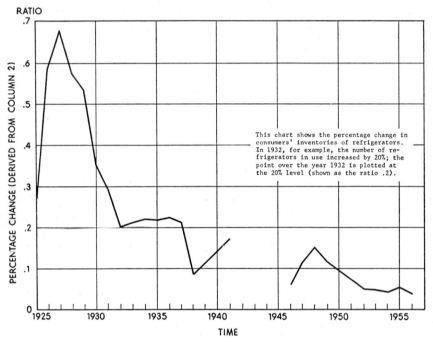

This chart shows the percentage change in consumers' inventories of refrigerators. In 1932, for example, the number of refrigerators in use increased by 20%; the point over the year 1932 is plotted at the 20% level (shown as the ratio .2).

percentage change in inventories is plotted as a simple time series. Note that the trend of this series in recent years is toward some level slightly above zero, probably around 4 per cent or so. This is a characteristic of many other consumers' durable goods series and will be accounted for at a later point in this section.

It is necessary now to choose a regression line for Figure 7–5, keeping in mind that the line of relationship selected must, as stated above, reflect both the secular growth and the cyclical swings for the period as a whole. The task is further complicated by the fact that the maximum ownership level for refrigerators, since it is determined to a large extent by general economic conditions, was considerably higher in the postwar as compared to the prewar period. Evidently, a typical least-squares line will not do, since it would only average out the swings of all the points on the chart. Instead, a line must be found that will average out the *swings of the cycles*. The line selected as a first approximation for this purpose is line (1), the slope of which, determined directly from the chart, is −.000016. The line was chosen because it seemed to average out the fluctuations for the period 1930–41, that is, the prewar period.[8]

Referring back to formula (3), note that M_0 in the formula represents the point where the line intersects the vertical axis. If M_0 now reverts to $aM(t)$, then each point M_0 identifies a separate line with the same slope as, or parallel to, line (1). Any of these lines will intersect the vertical axis at $M_0 = aM(t)$, and the horizontal axis at the maximum ownership level, $M(t)$. (When new-owner sales, N, equal zero, formula (3) becomes $aM - ay = 0$, or $y = M$.) Expressed in words rather than symbols, what this means is as follows. Other things being equal, line (1) indicates that the rate of growth of inventory should move down line (1) toward the maximum ownership level of 22,500,000 units, indicated by the intersection of line (1) with the horizontal axis. At this point, the rate of growth would be zero. But other things are not equal, for the factors determining the maximum ownership level, such as wired homes and purchasing power, have been increasing, thereby causing the maximum ownership level to rise as well. The result is that line (1) shifts to the right while retaining the same slope, as shown by the dated lines in the chart. The intersection of each of these dated lines with the horizontal axis reveals the maximum ownership level for that year.

Second Correlation: Finding the Maximum Ownership Level

The maximum ownership level, symbolized above as $M(t)$, represents the number of potential owners of a product. For each product the factors determining the maximum ownership level will vary, so the problem of the analyst is to identify these factors and then measure them. For refrigerators, as for most electrical appliances, four variables were selected which, according to economic judgment, were believed to be most significant: (1) the number of wired dwelling units; (2) the level of supernumerary income; (3) the net extension of instalment credit excluding automobile credit; and (4) a price index of household furnishings.

The first of these variables, wired households, is a use-facilities characteristic as described at the beginning of this chapter: it is a condition which determines the physical possibility of using the product, and since it has exhibited very little cyclical variation over the past thirty years, its inclusion in the analysis will explain only the general upward movement in the maximum ownership level during the period. The remaining three variables—income, credit, and price—are reflections of purchasing power.

[8] The period prior to 1930 is omitted from the graphic analysis because the data were unreliable, and because it was not until the end of the 1920's that the initial rapid accumulation of refrigerator inventories in the hands of wholesalers and dealers finally reached more normal rates.

They, unlike the wired households series, have had wide cyclical variations, and their use in the analysis will help explain the cyclical changes in the rate of increase of the maximum ownership level.

All of the variables are to some extent intercorrelated, and hence will have to be adjusted if the ultimate prediction model is to be meaningful. How is this adjustment accomplished? As mentioned in Chapter 4, one of the methods employed to eliminate the effect of intercorrelation between variables is to combine the separate variables into a single synthetic variable. This is the approach adopted here, the result being that the four variables are combined into two: (1) the number of wired households or dwelling units, which serves as a physical determinant of sales, and (2) some function of income, credit, and price, which forms purchasing power and serves as an economic determinant of sales. The steps involved in the analysis are discussed further in the following paragraphs and the techniques illustrated graphically in the accompanying charts.

Effect of Wired Households. If we let $M_0(t)$, which is also equal to $aM(t)$, represent the intersection of a regression line with the vertical axis, equation (3) may, in view of the previous discussion, be rewritten

$$\frac{\Delta y / \Delta t}{y} + ay = M_0(t) \tag{4}$$

The left side of this equation represents the percentage change in consumers' inventories adjusted for inventory levels, and is derived in columns 2 through 6 of Table 7–5. Note that the derivation consists of multiplying the slope of the regression line by the inventory level, recording the products in columns 3 and 4, and then adding these to the percentage changes (column 1 ÷ column 2) to obtain columns 5 and 6. (As will be explained later, regression line (2) in Figure 7–5, which may be disregarded for the time being, is a second approximation to the slope of the prewar regression line, and is equal to $-.00002$.)

The problem is to combine the two classes of variables, wired households on the one hand and purchasing power (that is, income, credit, and price) on the other, into a relationship that will explain the variations in $M_0(t)$. The assumption will be made that the two independent variables enter the complete formula in a multiplicative manner. However, since there will be some intercorrelation between the two variables, it will have to be removed before the second variable is introduced.

Figure 7–7, in which the left side of equation (4) is scaled vertically and the number of wired homes horizontally, illustrates the procedure. Excluding the 1925–29 period, the two series apparently expand at about the same rate, as evidenced by the freehand regression line. Since we know that $M_0(t)$ is partly explained by the number of wired households because an electric refrigerator cannot be used in an unwired home, we can introduce the wired homes variable, H_w, to the number of explained variables, and put it on the left side of the equation. Equation (4) then becomes

$$\frac{\frac{\Delta y / \Delta t}{y} + ay}{H_w} = M_1(t) \tag{5}$$

where $M_1(t)$ represents the other variables (that is, "buying power," composed of income, credit, and price). The left side of the equation now represents the percentage change in consumers' inventories adjusted for inventories and wired households. In other words, the general equation to be solved is

FIGURE 7–7

PERCENTAGE CHANGE IN CONSUMERS' INVENTORIES ADJUSTED FOR INVENTORY
VERSUS NUMBER OF WIRED DWELLING UNITS

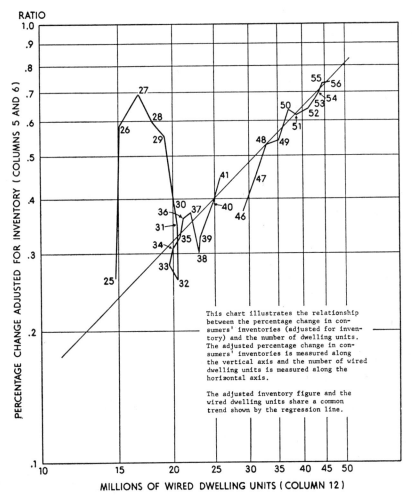

This chart illustrates the relationship between the percentage change in consumers' inventories (adjusted for inventory) and the number of dwelling units. The adjusted percentage change in consumers' inventories is measured along the vertical axis and the number of wired dwelling units is measured along the horizontal axis.

The adjusted inventory figure and the wired dwelling units share a common trend shown by the regression line.

$$\frac{\Delta y/\Delta t}{y} + ay = aM(t) = f(H_w, I, C, P)$$

where H_w = wired households, I = income, C = credit, and P = price. The last three, I, C, and P, determine buying power and are discussed next.

Effect of Income, Credit, and Price. The three remaining variables that affect $M_0(t)$ are income (measured by supernumerary income), credit (measured by net credit extension exclusive of automobiles), and price (measured by a price index of house furnishings, 1947–49 = 100). Since they are significantly intercorrelated, they are combined into a single synthetic variable and serve as a measure of purchasing power.

How is the synthetic variable constructed? Since supernumerary income and credit are both in dollar figures, they can be combined. However, one dollar of credit extension has a considerably greater effect on refrigerator sales than does one dollar of supernumerary income, as is evident when one compares these series with a series on consumer expenditures for durable goods other than autos. Such expenditures, it appears, are about three times the net extension of instalment credit. Hence a weighted measure of total purchasing power can be devised, which is equal to supernumerary income, I, expressed in 1947–49 dollars, plus three times the net extension of consumer credit, C, deflated by a price index of house furnishings, P. The resulting variable, $I + \frac{3C}{P}$, represents purchasing power in 1947–49 prices and is shown in column 7 of Table 7–5.

Third Correlation

The purchasing power variable is highly correlated with the wired households variable in that both have a pronounced upward secular trend. The trend, therefore, must be moved from the purchasing power variable before it can be introduced in the analysis. The procedure for accomplishing this is shown in the semilog chart of Figure 7–8, with purchasing power measured vertically and "time" horizontally. A trend line is then fitted freehand, the equation for which is

$$\log\left(I + \frac{3C}{P}\right) = .02169T + 1.0355 \tag{6}$$

or equivalently

$$\left(I + \frac{3C}{P}\right) = 10^{.02169T + 1.0355} \tag{6a}$$

where T, the independent variable, is "time," and represents the given year with the origin at 1900, and the subscript, c, denotes the calculated values.

The trend values are next recorded in column 8 of Table 7–5. They indicate that, on the average, the real purchasing power series has grown by about 5.2 per cent per year for the period 1925–56. In order to remove the trend from the real purchasing power variable, the latter is divided by the former (that is, column 7 ÷ column 8) and the resulting ratio residuals

FIGURE 7–8

REAL PURCHASING POWER, 1925–1956

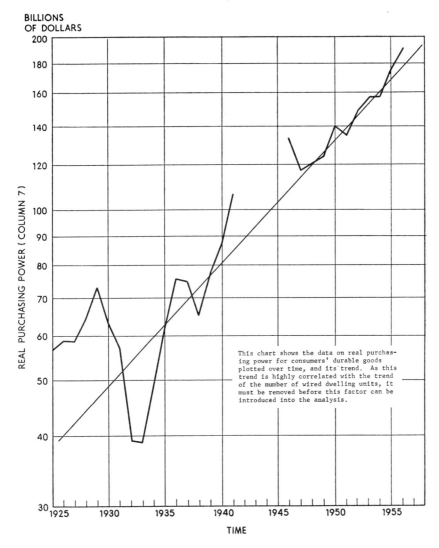

This chart shows the data on real purchasing power for consumers' durable goods plotted over time, and its trend. As this trend is highly correlated with the trend of the number of wired dwelling units, it must be removed before this factor can be introduced into the analysis.

or cyclical fluctuations of the real purchasing power series about its trend are recorded in column 9. Thus, column 9 shows that in 1925, real purchasing power was 148.8 per cent of its trend (or about 49 per cent above its trend), and in 1954 it was 98.3 per cent of its trend (or about 2 per cent below its trend).

When the series on percentage change in inventories adjusted for inventory (columns 5 and 6) is divided by the wired homes series (column 12) the result is the left side of equation (5). These ratios, plotted against

FIGURE 7–9

PERCENTAGE CHANGE IN CONSUMERS' INVENTORIES ADJUSTED FOR INVENTORY
AND WIRED DWELLING UNITS VERSUS DEVIATIONS OF REAL
PURCHASING POWER FROM ITS TREND
1925–1956

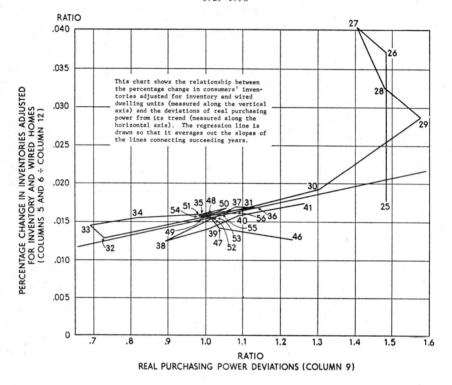

the real purchasing power deviations (column 9) in the form of a scatter diagram, produce the results shown in Figure 7–9. If we let d represent the deviations in column 9, the formula for the regression line in the diagram is

$$y_c = .0045 + .011d$$

Check on First Correlation

The value initially established for parameter a was the slope of line (1), estimated at $-.000016$. It is now necessary to inquire whether this estimate is the best one that could have been established. If it is, then the analysis is completed; if it is not, some further work remains to be done.

To test the parameter, all of the known factors are collected into one variable and then plotted against the inventory, as in Figure 7–10. The vertical axis of the chart measures the percentage increase in refrigerators in use adjusted for wired households, income, and prices, as denoted by the left side of the equation:

FIGURE 7–10

CHECK ON FIRST INVENTORY ADJUSTMENT FACTOR

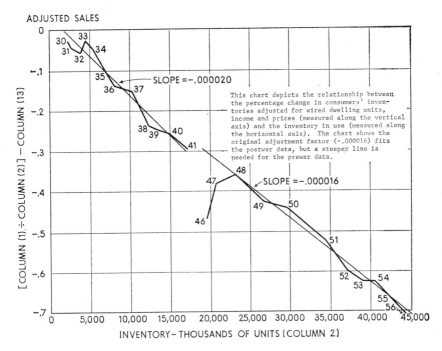

$$\frac{\Delta y / \Delta t}{y} - M_0(t) = -ay \text{ [see equation (4)]}$$

where

$$M_0(t) = H_w \frac{I + 3C/P}{10^{.02169T} + 1.0355}$$

Figure 7–10 shows that in the postwar period the value −.000016 yields a good fit, but in the prewar period a somewhat steeper slope is necessary. The fit in the prewar period indicates that a regression line with the slope −.000020 yields better results.

What is the reason for this change in slope? An explanation may be found in the different patterns of income distribution for the prewar and postwar periods. The steeper slope in the prewar period means that a given level of consumers' purchasing power was able to support a lower maximum ownership level than in the postwar period. With the leveling out of income distribution since the 1930's, an increasing proportion of households during the postwar period became potential refrigerator owners.

This change in income distribution could have been handled in the early postwar period by the use of a time trend. In other words, if only prewar data had been available, a steeper line would have originally been chosen. The deviations in Figure 7–9 would then have been about a higher level in the postwar period than in the prewar period, and a temporary trend could have been drawn. Then, as more data became available, it would have been possible to fix the constant a at its present value. Thus the graphic technique permits a great deal of flexibility in meeting changing economic conditions, provided the analyst knows how to utilize the information available.

Figure 7–11 shows the relationship between (1) the prewar new-owner sales of refrigerators, adjusted by the prewar inventory adjustment factor and the number of wired homes, and (2) the deviations, d, of real

FIGURE 7–11

PERCENTAGE CHANGE IN CONSUMERS' INVENTORIES ADJUSTED FOR INVENTORY
AND WIRED DWELLING UNITS VERSUS DEVIATIONS OF REAL
PURCHASING POWER FROM ITS TREND—1925–1941

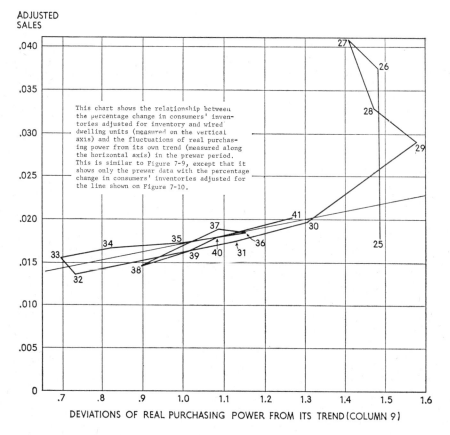

DEVIATIONS OF REAL PURCHASING POWER FROM ITS TREND (COLUMN 9)

FIGURE 7–12

Consumers' Inventories Adjusted for Inventory and Real Purchasing
Power and Wired Dwelling Units

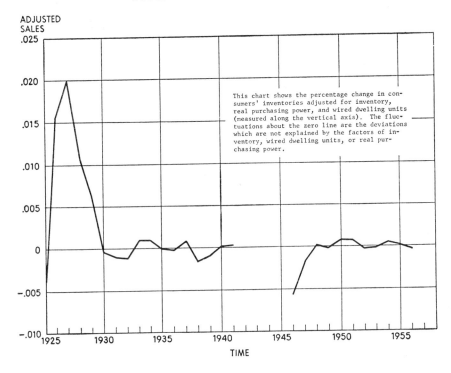

This chart shows the percentage change in consumers' inventories adjusted for inventory,
real purchasing power, and wired dwelling units
(measured along the vertical axis). The fluctuations about the zero line are the deviations
which are not explained by the factors of inventory, wired dwelling units, or real purchasing power.

TIME

purchasing power from its trend. The equation for the regression line, estimated directly from the graph (see pp. 67–68), is

$$y_c = .0078 + .0095d$$

Evidently, the slope is somewhat shallower than that indicated by the postwar experience.

Final Results

It remains now to test the equation. In Figure 7–12 are plotted the
variations in $M(t)$ that are not explained by the various factors in the formula. Note that again with the exception of 1925–29, the fluctuations are
close to the zero line for the entire period. The lows of 1946 and 1947 are
easily explained by the shortage of refrigerators at that time, for demand,
which is the criterion being measured, exceeded supply. The chart also
reveals that there was no systematic variation in the unexplained data.

Putting all the constants and relationships together, a formula for
calculated prewar new sales, N', and postwar new sales, N'', is obtained:

FIGURE 7–13

REFRIGERATORS: MANUFACTURERS' SALES AND DEMAND

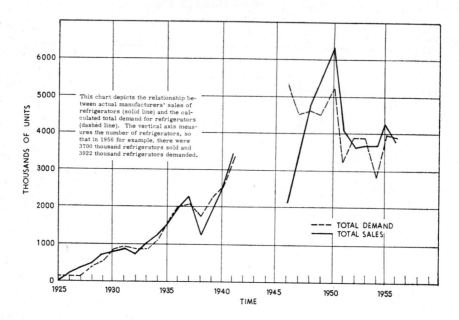

This chart depicts the relationship between actual manufacturers' sales of refrigerators (solid line) and the calculated total demand for refrigerators (dashed line). The vertical axis measures the number of refrigerators, so that in 1956 for example, there were 3700 thousand refrigerators sold and 3922 thousand refrigerators demanded.

FIGURE 7–14

DEMAND FOR REFRIGERATORS: UNEXPLAINED VARIATION

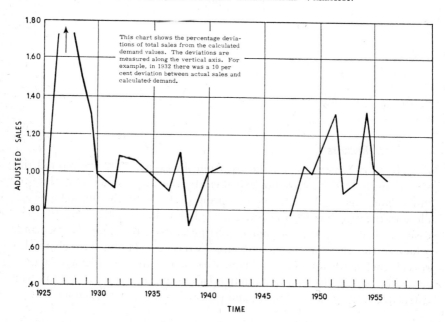

This chart shows the percentage deviations of total sales from the calculated demand values. The deviations are measured along the vertical axis. For example, in 1932 there was a 10 per cent deviation between actual sales and calculated demand.

$$N' = (\Delta y/\Delta t)_c = y \left\{ H_w \left[.0078 + .0095 \left(\frac{1 + 3C/P}{10^{.02169T} + 1.0355} \right) \right] - .00002y \right\}$$

$$N'' = (\Delta y/\Delta t)_c = y \left\{ H_w \left[.0045 + .011 \left(\frac{1 + 3C/P}{10^{.02169T} + 1.0355} \right) \right] - .000016y \right\}$$

How well has the analysis succeeded in explaining the actual sales of refrigerators? A visual illustration is given in Figure 7–13, the dashed lines of which are the calculated values, and the mathematical equivalents of these dashed lines are the two equations given above. If the actual or total sales figures for each year are now computed as a percentage of the calculated values for that year, the results when plotted reveal the deviations in Figure 7–14. The large deviation of 1938 was due probably to the recession at that time; the 1950–51 surge, on the other hand, resulted from the impact of the Korean conflict and the consequent fear of shortages, while the lower levels of 1952–53 reflected the reaction to this overbuying by tending to balance somewhat the previous peak.

Market Saturation. As for the 1954 experience, this is more difficult to explain. What appears to have happened is that sales in that year remained at the 1953 level, but purchasing power fell below its trend value. This caused a decline in the maximum ownership level which in turn brought a decline in the percentage growth from about 5 per cent to 2 per cent. With the refrigerator market as saturated as it presently is, any forecast percentage increase should be checked against the trend of percentage increases in new owners, as shown by Figure 7–6. Since the trend of the percentage increases in the consumer inventory appears to be leveling off, it will probably stabilize at around the 1 per cent line by the year 1962 or thereabouts. At that rate the unit increase in sales will be about equal to the increase in the number of wired homes. Of course, the unit increase in sales would be greater if a trend toward multiple ownership could be developed, but refrigerators, unlike automobiles, which were discussed earlier, or television sets, to be discussed next, are not readily adaptable to multiple-ownership promotion. At the same time, just as a ceiling on the annual requirements for refrigerators has emerged, a floor is also developing. The scrappage rate at the time of this study (late 1950's) was a little over 2 million units per year, and has been rising gradually to a level of about 3 million in the early 1960's.

Finally, what about the growing market for home freezers? Some analysts have contended that it will tend to retard the obsolescence rate for refrigerators because it may serve to reverse the trend toward freezer-refrigerator combinations. Even if this is true, however, it seems unlikely that it will extend the maximum life of refrigerators beyond the 25-year mark that was originally supposed.

Conclusion: Forecasting

The emphasis until now has been placed on the actual construction of the prediction model. Having completed the model, it is necessary to consider its applications, particularly to the practical problems of forecasting. This can be accomplished most conveniently by distinguishing between long- and short-range forecasts.

Long-Range Forecasts. In the present study, the formula is so constructed that it is necessary to compute demand for each year in the forecast period; and, of course, it is necessary to establish the inventory at the beginning of each year to find the base for applying the percentage growth expected. Once the independent variables have been forecast for a particular year in the future, they may be "plugged" into the formula to arrive at a prediction of refrigerator sales. The procedure, specifically, is as follows.

First, the forecast variables for each year are applied to the formula, the percentage growth is computed, and this percentage is then multiplied by the beginning-year consumers' inventory. The result is the new-owner growth. Second, this new-owner growth figure is entered in the appropriate place in the life table, and the survival figure is computed. From the life table the normal scrappage can also be calculated. The scrappage figure plus the new-owner demand is the total demand likely in the specific year. The same calculations are then repeated for each succeeding year, each time using the new inventory figure as the base. When these calculations are done for the 1960's, they indicate that total refrigerator sales will be in a slight upward trend during the period, starting with about 4 million per year at the beginning of the decade.

Establishing long-range industry goals such as these is an important step toward the establishment of long-range company goals. In such analyses, however, it is necessary to ascertain first the position of the company in its industry. The most widely used method for this purpose is the market-share approach, whereby the trend of the company's sales as a percentage of the industry's is calculated. As an alternative to plotting the actual market-share figures over time and then passing a trend through the data, it is often instructive to plot the company's sales against the industry's in the form of a scatter diagram. Either approach, however, is of value, and serves to indicate how the company moves in relation to the industry and to cyclical upswings and downswings in the economy as a whole. Sales strategies (including advertising and promotion) can thus be established for the future, depending upon the relationships and patterns that are revealed by the demand model.

Short-Range Forecasts. In contrast to long-range forecasts, that is, projections beyond one year, short-range or intrayear forecasts are also needed to facilitate the establishment of production schedules, advertising and promotional strategies, sales effort, and a host of other managerial functions that are forward looking in nature. Short-range forecasts, therefore, require demand forecasts for each of the coming months, or quarters. At least two aspects of the subject pose problems that should be mentioned here: one involves the seasonal pattern; the other is the changes in inventory. Both affect sales and must be accounted for.

The demand for refrigerators, like the demand for most consumers' durable goods, has shown a definite seasonal pattern over the years. Refrigerator sales tend to be relatively high in the first half of the year and low in the second half. This is due partly to the seasonal influence and partly to the introduction of new models. One way of adjusting the data, therefore, is to modify the standard method of calculating the seasonal variation by considering as the first month of each year the time of model introduction, rather than the month of January. An alternative approach is to analyze the impact of the new model separately, remove its influence from the data, and then obtain a pure seasonal pattern. The total seasonal for any month would then be the sum of the pure seasonal and the model introduction effect.

The level of inventories of the product in the hands of distributors and retailers must be considered because of its direct effect on sales, as well as the inventory level on the part of manufacturers because of its immediate bearing on production schedules and its indirect effect on sales. With respect to refrigerators, data are available from the trade association on the level of inventories held by distributors and dealers. The excess of these inventories must be subtracted, in total or in part, from the potential sales likely in the forecast period. It may often be possible to work out definite short-term relationships between (1) the level of inventories in the channels of distribution, and (2) the deviations of actual from expected sales. More likely, however, a qualitative estimate of the impact of the specific level of inventories can be made, leading to a percentage adjustment in the sales forecast.

DEMAND FOR TELEVISION SETS

An analysis of the demand for television sets may be conducted along the same lines as that for refrigerators. The specific problems encountered, however, involve certain differences and similarities. As to the important differences: (1) television is a relatively new industry which made its significant commercial beginning in 1946; and (2) not until 1950 when 14-inch and 16-inch screen sets were priced to fit most budgets was television fully accepted and a definite break with past relationships established. As to the similarities with refrigerators: (1) Data are available on only a unit rather than dollar basis, thereby requiring that the study be carried out in physical units instead of dollar sales; (2) manufacturers' instead of retail sales are used, thereby making it necessary to deal with the problem of inventory changes at the wholesale and retail level; and (3) scrappage rates must be estimated in order to calculate replacement demand. However, since very little information about scrappage is actually available, a television life table can be constructed similar to that done for refrigerators. Briefly, the procedure, and the steps leading to it, are as follows.

First, all of the relevant data are collected as done in Table 7–6, and

TABLE 7-6

FACTORS DETERMINING TELEVISION DEMAND

Year	(1) Sales, Thousands of Units — Actual Total	(2) Replacement	(3) New Owner	(4) Inventory	(5) Supernumerary Income, Billions of 1947–49 Dollars	(6) Net Credit Extension (Except Auto), $ Billions	(7) Price Index of House Furnishings, 1947–49=100	(8) Consumers' Real Purchasing Power (1947–49 Prices), $ Billions	(9) Wired Homes, Millions
	S	R	$N_1 = S - R$	y	I	C	P	$I + \dfrac{3C}{P}$	H_w
1947	179	5	174	12	112.1	1.58	97.2	117.0	31.2
1948	975	2	973	186	117.1	1.21	103.2	120.6	33.1
1949	3,000	21	2,979	1,159	120.7	1.06	99.6	123.9	35.2
1950	7,464	163	7,301	4,138	134.1	1.59	100.3	139.8	37.2
1951	5,385	491	4,894	11,439	132.7	.69	111.2	134.6	39.1
1952	6,096	539	5,557	16,333	142.6	2.35	108.5	149.0	40.9
1953	7,216	609	6,607	21,890	152.7	1.50	107.9	156.9	42.4
1954	6,347	1,665	5,682	28,497	156.5	.59	106.1	158.2	43.6
1955	7,757	3,272	4,485	34,179	172.7	1.79	104.1	177.9	44.8
1956	7,200	4,834	2,366	38,664	186.7	1.56	103.0	191.3	46.1

Source:

Col. 1: *Electrical Merchandising.*

Cols. 2, 3, 4: Calculated from the cumulative life table, Table 7–8.

Col. 5: The Econometric Institute, Inc.

Col. 6: *Federal Reserve Bulletin.*

Col. 7: Bureau of Labor Statistics.

Col. 8: Calculated from cols. 5, 6, and 7, as shown by formula.

Col. 9: Edison Electric Institute.

TABLE 7-7

TELEVISION SURVIVAL TABLE
As of January 1
1946–48, Maximum Life: 6 Years
1949–57, Maximum Life: 11 Years
(All data in thousands of units)

Year	Sales	1947	1948	1949	1950	1951	1952	1953	1954	1955	1956	1957
1946	7	7	7	6	4	1						
1947	179		179	178	163	90	16	1				
1948	975			975	971	885	488	90	39			
1949	3,000				3,000	2,999	2,984	2,897	2,586	1,922	1,078	414
1950	7,464					7,464	7,460	7,424	7,207	6,435	4,781	2,683
1951	5,385						5,385	5,382	5,356	5,200	4,642	3,450
1952	6,096							6,096	6,093	6,063	5,886	5,255
1953	7,216								7,216	7,212	7,177	6,968
1954	7,347									7,347	7,343	7,307
1955	7,757										7,757	7,753
1956	7,200											7,200

Source: Calculated from Table 7–2.

TABLE 7-8

CONSUMERS' TELEVISION INVENTORY—LIFE TABLE, CUMULATIVE

As of January 1
1946-48, Maximum Life: 6 Years
1949-57, Maximum Life: 11 Years
(All data in thousands of units)

Year	Sales	1947	1948	1949	1950	1951	1952	1953	1954	1955	1956	1957
1946	7*	**12**	7	6	4	1						
1947	179*		**186**	184	167	91	16	1				
1948	975*			**1,159**	1,138	976	504	91	39			
1949	3,000				**4,138**	3,975	3,488	2,988	2,625	1,922	1,078	414
1950	7,464					**11,439**	10,948	10,412	9,832	8,357	5,859	3,097
1951	5,385						**16,333**	15,794	15,188	13,557	10,501	6,547
1952	6,096							**21,890**	21,281	19,620	16,387	11,802
1953	7,216								**28,497**	26,832	23,564	18,710
1954	7,347									**34,179**	30,907	26,077
1955	7,757										**38,664**	33,830
1956	7,200											**41,030**

*Average life—3 years.

Source: Calculated from Tables 7-2 and 7-7.

TABLE 7-9

ANALYSIS OF NEW-OWNER TELEVISION DEMAND

Year	(1) New Owner Sales $\Delta y/\Delta t$ From Table 7-6	(2) Inventory y From Table 7-6	(3) First Adjustment for Inventory $a_1 y = -.00175(y)$ $a_1 = -.00175$ from Fig. 7-16	(4) $a_2 y = -.00001667(y)$ $a_2 = -.00001667$ from Fig. 7-16	(5) Percentage Change in Inventory Adjusted for Inventory Levels $\frac{\Delta y}{\Delta t} + a_1 y$ $(1) \div (2) \div (3)$	(6) $\frac{\Delta y}{\Delta t} + a_2 y$ $(1) \div (2) \div (4)$	(7) Real Purchasing Power (1947–49 Prices) $I + \frac{3C}{P}$ From Table 7-6	(8) Trend of Real Purchasing Power $f(t) = 10^{.02169T + 1.0855}$ From Fig. 7-8	(9) Deviations of Real Purchasing Power from its Trend $\frac{I + \frac{3C}{P}}{f(t)} = x$ $(7)/(8)$
	Thousands of Units				*Ratio*		*Billions of Dollars*		*Ratio*
1947	174	12	.021		14.52		117.0	113.4	1.032
1948	973	186	.326		5.557		102.6	119.3	1.011
1949	2,979	1,159	2.208		4.598		123.9	125.4	.988
1950	7,301	4,138	7.241		9.005		139.8	131.8	1.061
1951	4,894	11,439		.1907		.6187	134.6	138.2	.974
1952	5,557	16,333		.2723		.6123	149.0	145.6	1.023
1953	6,607	21,890		.3649		.6669	156.9	153.1	1.025
1954	5,682	28,497		.4750		.6740	158.2	161.0	.983
1955	4,485	34,179		.5698		.7008	177.9	169.2	1.051
1956	2,366	38,664		.6445		.6506	191.3	177.8	1.076

TABLE 7-9 (Continued)

	(10)	(11)	(12)	(13)	(14)	(15)	(16)	(17)	(18)	(19)	(20)
	Adjustment for Income		Wired Dwelling Units	$aM(t)$	Relative Increase in Inventory	Calculated New-Owner Demand	Unexplained Variation of New-Owner Demand	Calculated Scrappage	Calculated Total Demand	Actual Total Sales	Unexplained Variation of Total Demand
	Ratio		Thousands	Ratio	Ratio	Thousands	Ratio	Thousands of Units	Thousands of Units	Thousands of Units	Ratio
	$y_c =$ $1.500x - 1.35$	$y_c =$ $.0037x$ $+.01165$	H_w		$\varepsilon M(t) - ay$	$N =$ $(\Delta y/\Delta t)_o =$ $y[aM(t) - ay]$ or $ayM(t) - ay^2$ or $ay[M(t) - y]$	$\dfrac{\Delta y/\Delta t}{(\Delta y/\Delta t)_o}$	R	$S_o = N + R$	S	$\dfrac{S}{S_o}$
Year	$x =$ col. (9)	$x =$ col. (9)	From Table 7-6	$(12) \times (11)$	$(13) - (3), (4)$	$(14) \times (2)$	$(1)/(15)$	From Table 7-6	$(15) + (17)$	From Table 7-1	$(19)/(18)$
1947	.198		31.2	6.178	6.157	74	2.35	5	79	179	2.27
1948	.1665		33.1	5.511	5.185	964	1.01	2	966	975	1.01
1949	.1320		35.2	4.646	2.438	2,826	1.05	21	2,847	3,000	1.05
1950	.2415		37.2	8.984	1.743	7,213	1.01	163	7,376	7,464	1.01
1951		.01525	39.1	.6084	.4177	4,778	1.024	491	5,269	5,385	1.022
1952		.01544	40.9	.6315	.3592	5,867	.947	539	6,406	6,069	.952
1953		.01544	42.4	.6547	.2898	6,337	1.043	609	6,946	7,216	1.039
1954		.01529	43.6	.6666	.1916	5,460	1.041	1,665	7,125	7,347	1.031
1955		.01554	44.8	.6962	.1264	4,320	1.038	3,272	7,592	7,757	1.022
1956		.01563	46.1	.7205	.0760	2,938	.805	4,834	7,772	7,200	.926

then the initial graphs of the variables are sketched as in Figure 7–15. A survival table for television sets is then constructed as shown in Table 7–7. This and Table 7–8, the latter representing the consumer inventory of television sets, are derived in the same way as Tables 7–3 and 7–4 in the refrigerator study, namely, from the survival coefficients presented earlier in Table 7–2. For television sets, the assumption made was a maximum life of six years for the period 1946–48, and a maximum life of eleven years for the remainder of the analysis period 1949–57. In other words, the sets produced in 1946, 1947, and 1948 had an average life of three years, while those produced in subsequent years have lasted an average of five and a half years.

FIGURE 7–15

TELEVISION DATA

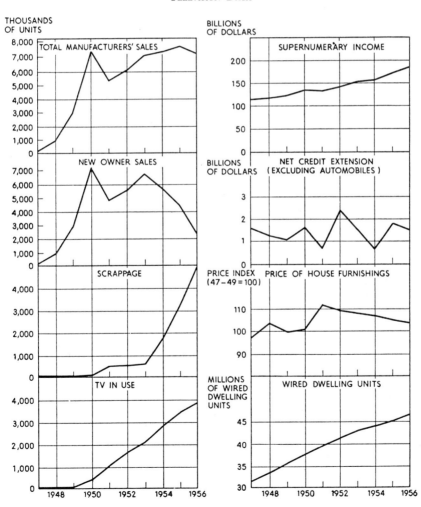

Graphic Analysis

The steps involved in arriving at the predicting equation are basically the same as in the refrigerator study. Since the refrigerator analysis was explained in considerable detail, the television study may be covered briefly by outlining the final results and eliminating the intermediate steps.

Figure 7–16 shows the relationship between (1) the percentage growth in television sets in use, and (2) the total number of sets in use. The slopes of the regression line originally chosen were shallower than the final lines, but the method of successive approximation employed in the refrigerator study established the validity of the lines finally chosen. Note the definite break in the 1947–50 relationship as compared to the 1951–56 regression. This means that a forecast of the demand for television sets based on the 1947–50 experience would have resulted in an overestimation of the percentage increase of sets in use. After 1951, however, a reasonable estimate of the percentage increase in 1952 could have been made simply on a trend

FIGURE 7–16

TELEVISION: PERCENTAGE CHANGE IN SETS IN USE VERSUS TOTAL SETS IN USE

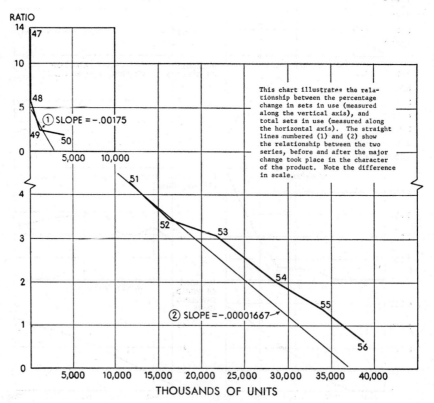

This chart illustrates the relationship between the percentage change in sets in use (measured along the vertical axis), and total sets in use (measured along the horizontal axis). The straight lines numbered (1) and (2) show the relationship between the two series, before and after the major change took place in the character of the product. Note the difference in scale.

THOUSANDS OF UNITS

basis, and after 1952 a fairly good relationship could have been established. Just as with refrigerators, other factors, namely income, credit, prices, and wired homes, are at work and tend to shift the regression line to the right each year. The result of this is that a different maximum ownership level is established with each particular set of economic conditons. In 1956, for example, the maximum ownership level was 43 million sets, and in 1955 it was 42 million sets.

FIGURE 7–17

PERCENTAGE CHANGE IN SETS IN USE ADJUSTED FOR TOTAL SETS IN USE
VERSUS NUMBER OF WIRED DWELLING UNITS

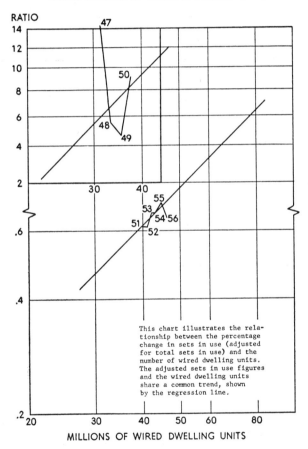

MILLIONS OF WIRED DWELLING UNITS

In Figure 7–17, the percentage change in sets in use, adjusted for consumers' inventory, is plotted against the wired homes series. Even with the relatively few years of data available, the common trend between the two series is quite evident. In this example, the first two factors appear to explain a good part of the total variations in new-owner sales.

In Figure 7–18 is shown the relationship between (1) the percentage change in sets in use adjusted for the consumer inventory level and the number of wired households, and (2) the deviations of real supernumerary income (as defined in the refrigerator study) from its trend. This relation-

FIGURE 7–18

PERCENTAGE CHANGE IN SETS IN USE ADJUSTED FOR TOTAL SETS IN USE
AND WIRED DWELLING UNITS VERSUS DEVIATIONS OF REAL PURCHASING
POWER FROM ITS TREND

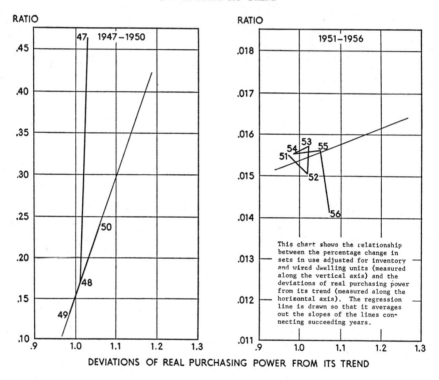

DEVIATIONS OF REAL PURCHASING POWER FROM ITS TREND

ship is then tested in Figure 7–19. Here all the known variables except the slope of the line in Figure 7–16 are grouped together and plotted against sets in use. The income factor appears at first glance to have only a relatively small impact upon new-owner demand, but this appearance is misleading. The income term influences the first term in the difference $M_0(t) - ay$, so that even relatively small numerical changes in income exert a large percentage effect upon the final difference.

Conclusion: Forecasting

How well have we been able to explain the actual variations in both new-owner and total television sales? Can this study be used as a guide for management in establishing forecasts of the sale of television sets in the

FIGURE 7–19

CHECK ON INVENTORY ADJUSTMENT FACTOR

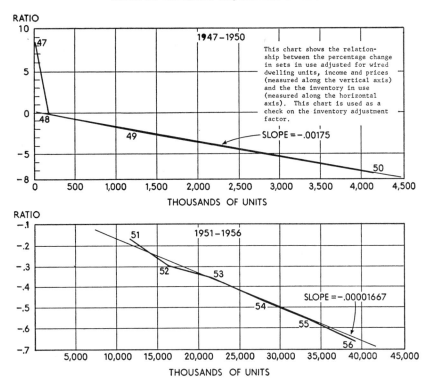

This chart shows the relationship between the percentage change in sets in use adjusted for wired dwelling units, income and prices (measured along the vertical axis) and the the inventory in use (measured along the horizontal axis). This chart is used as a check on the inventory adjustment factor.

SLOPE = −.00175

SLOPE = −.00001667

1960's? The answers to both questions are of considerable importance if any value is to be placed on the usefulness of the analysis.

In answer to the first question, Figure 7–20 summarizes the results of the study by showing visually the closeness of fit between new-owner actual and calculated sales levels, and total actual and calculated sales levels. As is to be expected, replacement sales are becoming increasingly important in affecting total sales, as evidenced by the widening gap between the two sets of lines. This leads us into an answer to the second question. Thus, given the basic equation $S = N + R$, the problem is to predict total sales by predicting the two components, new-owner sales and replacement sales. New-owner sales, at even the present number of sets per household, will probably be in the vicinity of a million sets per year in the 1960's. As for replacement sales or scrappage, a chief problem is to estimate the future average age of sets in use. The 1956 and 1957 experience indicate that this average is increasing, but it is still too early to be certain. If the average life continues to remain at 5½ years as it was in the late 1950's, a stock of 50 million sets in use in the early 1960's would build up to a scrappage rate of

FIGURE 7-20

TELEVISION: MANUFACTURERS NEW-OWNER SALES AND TOTAL SALES
TOTAL DEMAND AND NEW-OWNER DEMAND

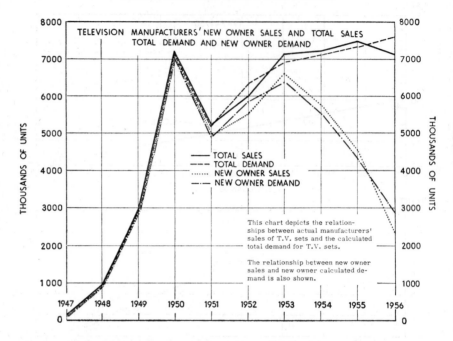

50/5.5 = 9 million sets per year, approximately, or about 18 per cent of 50 million. On the other hand, should the average life rise to as much as 7 years, the scrappage rate would build up to 50/7 = 7 million sets annually, approximately, or about 14 per cent of 50 million. This indicates that the total demand for television sets in the early 1960's will be in the range of 8 to 10 million sets per year, which is substantially above the level thus far achieved.

FORECASTING CONSUMER DEMAND: SUMMARY AND CONCLUSIONS

Classical economists, writing at a time when the analysis of demand was largely concerned with consumer perishable and semidurable goods, focused on price as the most important variable affecting demand. But in the present-day economy, price is often insufficient as a controlling variable; other factors must usually be included if the explanation of change in the dependent variable is to be reliable from the standpoint of economic theory as well as statistical analysis. Since different variables and different combinations of variables will often produce an equally satisfactory goodness of fit, it follows that statistical goodness of fit should not be a sole criterion of adequacy. An economic theory is needed which will account for, explain, and justify the relationships found, as well as the relationships serving as a test of the theory. In short, theory and measurement should not be regarded as mutually exclusive, but rather as inseparable, each one serving to support and enhance the other.

With respect to consumers' goods, it was recognized in the previous chapter that this category was too large to be treated as an entity for forecasting purposes. The forces that appear to be most important in affecting the sale of food are not the same as those affecting the sale of washing machines. Accordingly, the category called consumer goods may be broken into two reasonably homogeneous subgroups, consumer nondurable goods and consumer durable goods. The forces affecting the sale of each of these groups are then treated separately, resulting in what is in effect two independent and self-contained theories.

With regard to consumers' nondurable goods, the most important factors affecting demand are (1) buying power, (2) demography, and (3) price or a substitute product. Each of these factors may be measured in different ways and by the use of different statistical series, depending on the information available and the product group under consideration. Thus, disposable income or supernumerary income may serve as a measure of buying power, depending upon whether total buying power or "free" buying power (that is, purchasing power in excess of living costs) is the measure desired. Population, or some classification of population by age groups, sex, and so forth, may be employed as a demographic measure, in accordance with what is believed to be the chief consuming group for the product in question. And the price of the product in dollars and cents, or its "alternative" price in the form of a substitute product that might have been purchased instead, may serve as a measure of the price or substitution factor. By employing the appropriate forms of relevant variables, sales can be forecast by combining the three controlling factors in an additive or multiplicative arrangement.

As for consumers' durable goods, the total demand for them is actually the sum of two separate demands, a new-owner demand and a replacement demand. The former represents the expansion in the existing stock of consumers' inventories; the latter bears a definite relationship to both the existing stock of the good at any given time and to the size of the stock over a period of time. The problem, therefore, reduces itself to forecasting (1) new-owner demand, defined as the change in consumers' stocks per unit change in time, and (2) replacement demand. New-owner demand is forecast by relating it to the maximum ownership level, which in turn is a function of such factors as the consuming unit of the product (such as the number of families or wired households), the price of the product, and the level of income. Replacement demand, measured by scrappage, is estimated directly from life expectancy tables that are specifically constructed for the purpose. The two estimates, new-owner demand and replacement demand, when added together, produce the total sales estimate that is needed.

QUESTIONS

1. Explain the meaning of the so-called "purchase characteristics" of consumers' durable goods.
2. Of what significance are the purchase characteristics outlined in your answer to question 1?
3. State and explain the basic equation of demand for consumers' durables.
4. Explain the meaning of "maximum ownership level."
5. Is it necessary to employ the maximum ownership approach in doing a study of the demand for a consumer durable? How else might such a study be done?
6. Which is more important, a "good theory" or a "good fit"? Discuss.
7. What was the chief purpose of the automobile study? Why? What was the chief finding of the study?
8. What was the purpose of constructing a refrigerator survival table in the refrigerator study?
9. How may industry forecasts be "translated" into company forecasts?
10. Compare and contrast the basic philosophies underlying the demand for consumers' nondurable and durable goods.

INSTRUCTORS: The models in this and the previous chapter provide a strong basis for special student projects on sales forecasting, demand studies, and the like. (See the Note to Instructors at the beginning of the book for suggestions that have been found useful by many teachers.)

Chapter 8 : FORECASTING SALES OF CAPITAL GOODS

Capital goods, or producers' goods as they are also called, are produced means of further production. These goods are not desired for themselves, but rather because they are used to produce consumer goods or services, or other capital goods which in turn will be used for the production of consumer goods or services. Examples of capital goods include machines, tools, locomotives, electronic computers, and factory buildings. Strictly speaking, neat classifications are not always possible, for sometimes a capital good may also be a consumer good, depending upon its use, as when a jeep is used on a farm for work purposes and as a means of transportation for pleasure purposes. It appears, therefore, that if such overlappings are possible, difficulties of measurement will arise. Can these difficulties at least be minimized if not entirely eliminated?

The best approach, at least from a forecasting standpoint, is to emphasize certain features of the generally accepted concept of capital goods. That is, a definition may be constructed which is basically in accord with what economists would accept as the meaning of capital goods, but the definition would place greater stress on a certain aspect of the concept. Thus, the definition used here is that capital goods are produced means of further production, used in *place of labor* for the primary purpose of facilitating the production of another good to be sold for profit. The words in italics are particularly important, for by framing the concept in this way, prices of consumer goods as a whole can be compared to prices of machinery and equipment, thereby yielding a measure of the pressure of wage costs on the demand for newer, more efficient equipment and plant. This point is discussed and further clarified in the following section.

DEMAND DETERMINANTS

The approaches employed in analyzing the demand for capital goods must be divided into two parts: (1) aggregate demand, which deals with the major economic forces affecting the demand for capital goods in general, and (2) particular demand, which is concerned with the factors determining the sale of specific capital goods. This type of separation is necessary because different sets of demand determining forces are involved, hence the analysis in each instance must proceed along somewhat different lines.

Aggregate Demand

What are the most important factors determining the over-all demand for capital goods? Do changes in the demand for consumers' goods cause changes in the demand for capital goods so that the latter may be said to be derived from the former? If the demand for capital goods really is a derived demand as economic theory suggests, what is the nature of its relationship with consumer goods demand and is this relationship the same in both the upswing and downswing of a business cycle? These and similar questions have been asked by business cycle theorists and econometricians for decades, and complete answers have yet to be provided. An indication of some successful research in this direction, however, may be discussed briefly.

In 1955, C. F. Roos published the results of a study of producers' demand for durable equipment.[1] The relationship obtained was

$$E(t) = .017I \, (t-3) - 74.49 \, (P_1/iP_2)_{t-6} + 2200$$

where

$E(t) =$ Demand for capital goods, as measured by producers' expenditures in millions of dollars during the year t.

$I(t) =$ Corporate purchasing power, defined as the sum of corporate profits retained + new financing + depreciation and obsolescence.

$P_1 =$ Bureau of Labor Statistics (BLS) price index of manufactured goods.

$P_2 =$ BLS price index of metals and metal products.

$i =$ Long-term interest rate as measured by Moody's yield for high grade (Aaa) bonds. (See pp. 180ff.)

$t-6 =$ Time interval six months previous.

The formula yielded an extremely good fit with actual producers' expenditures for the analysis period, with the exception of 1928 when corporations were using funds for call loans, World War II when actual expenditures were held below the desired demand due to wartime controls, and the postwar period 1946–47 when steel shortages were still acute. This formula was successfully used, for example, in the summer of 1956 to forecast: (1) a decline in domestic new orders for capital goods, (2) a decline in total capital goods production in early 1957, and (3) a decline in industrial production as a whole in 1957—all this at a time when opinion polls

[1] See his "Survey of Economic Forecasting Techniques," *Econometrica* (October, 1955), especially pp. 391–94. For the background of the work leading up to this and the earlier formulations of his estimating equations, see Roos and von Szeliski, "The Demand for Durable Goods," *Econometrica* (1943), pp. 97–122, and Roos, "The Demand for Investment Goods," *American Economic Review* (1948), pp. 311–20.

on producers' expenditures were optimistic, and most professional forecasters both in industry and government were predicting rising production in 1957.

What are the implications of this analysis with respect to further studies of capital goods demand? The following essential points may be noted as an indication of the direction in which future thinking on the subject ought to progress.

1. In all industries, a relationship tends to exist between profits, capital outlays, and the demand for the products of the industry. When demand increases, profits rise and capital outlay expenditures relative to their average increases; when demand decreases, profits fall and capital outlay expenditures decline relative to the average. This accounts for the ability to anticipate capital expenditures industry by industry on the basis of: (*a*) an index of retained corporate profits, new financing, depreciation and obsolescence; (*b*) long-term interest rates; and (*c*) the ratio of prices of consumer goods to prices of machinery and equipment. The last factor, the price ratio, measures the relative pressure of wage costs on the demand for newer, more efficient plant and equipment, since wages are a significant determinant of commodity prices as shown in Chapter 5.

2. It appears, therefore, that the key to changes in several of the variables—retained earnings, new financing, and to some extent obsolescence—is corporate profits. Thus: (*a*) changes in corporate profits are usually reflected first in retained earnings, since corporations generally try to maintain their established dividend rates; (*b*) in other than recession periods, corporate profits generally exceed normal or even accelerated depreciation; and (*c*) corporate profits affect the prices of common stocks and of second- and lower-grade bonds, and hence the ease of new financing. On all three counts, therefore, corporate profits are of primary importance in arriving at a reliable forecast.

3. The conclusion, consequently, is that in order to arrive at a predicting equation for forecasting the demand for capital goods, some of the important underlying variables and factors to observe, in addition to the above, are: (*a*) the operating rate, or the ratio of production to capacity in the chief-user industries; (*b*) the profits of the user industries; and (*c*) labor wage rates such as average hourly earnings which, when combined with other relevant measures stated above, yield a *pressure index* (see Chapter 1) which serves as an indication of management's desire to incur defensive investment in cost-saving capital equipment.

Particular Demand

The factors that seem to be most important in determining the overall demand for capital goods are not necessarily the same as those which determine the demand for particular kinds of capital goods. One of the chief reasons for this is that many capital goods differ widely between their physical and economic life expectancies, and since their purchases are motivated by cost-saving factors, it is the economic life of the good that is of primary importance from a sales forecasting standpoint. Thus, certain types of capital goods, such as industrial abrasives, have both a short physical and economic life expectancy. Certain other types of capital goods have long physical life expectancies, but obsolescence causes a shortening of their economic lives, as in the case of style changes and their effect on automobile dies, the introduction of jets in place of conventional airliners, and the replacement of steam locomotives by diesels. Finally, there are still other types of capital equipment such as certain basic installations, for example, telephone systems, which with suitable modifications to meet long-run shifts in demand, can be made to last for many years.

It follows from this that most capital goods can also be grouped into fairly homogeneous demand categories, although not perhaps in the same way as consumer goods. A classification is needed which is logical, consistent, and practical. The arrangement selected here is based upon a four-way grouping:

1. The demand for *total capital goods*. This has already been discussed, utilizing the type of approach described above.

2. The demand for a *class of capital goods*. This approach involves the establishment of a relationship between the class of capital goods concerned and the demand for total capital goods. It is illustrated below in a study of the capital goods component of total electrical machinery.

3. The demand for a *type of capital good*. Emphasis here is placed on requirements that occur in specific markets. An illustration is the demand for machine tools, a study of which is presented later in this chapter.

4. The demand for a *specific capital good*. The approach employed in this case is to relate demand to the next higher group of capital goods which utilize the particular product. Thus, a study of the demand for oil-well drilling bits, based upon requirements for new oil wells, is illustrated later in the chapter.

It is to the last three categories, and the applications of each, that we now turn our attention. Each group presents different problems and hence must be subjected to a different type of analysis. As in the previous chapters, the techniques employed are graphic rather than mathematical so that the essential relationships can be more readily visualized.

DEMAND FOR ELECTRICAL EQUIPMENT CAPITAL GOODS

What techniques may be employed to analyze the demand for a class of capital goods? Are the techniques basically the same for all capital goods? The answers to these and many related questions are given in this and the following two sections, in which several demand studies for capital goods are explained and illustrated. We may begin with electrical equipment as representing a class of capital goods, and then proceed to narrower groupings in order to illustrate the principles and practices involved for different kinds of products. As we shall see, there is much to be learned from such comparative studies, from an economic as well as statistical standpoint.

Raw Data

One of the difficulties in attempting to forecast the demand for particular capital goods is to obtain a meaningful measure of the physical output of the product. Since the statistical series that would be most desirable is not always in existence, it is often necessary to construct it from available data and facts. Thus, in the present study, it would not have been meaningful to analyze the number of electrical measuring devices, instruments, and electronic control devices produced each year, because the enormous range of sizes and uses of such products would result in an extremely heterogeneous series which is of little or no practical value. Since no satisfactory series could be found it was necessary to construct a series for electrical equipment capital goods production.

How was this series constructed? The Federal Reserve Board has, since 1947, published an index of electrical equipment production. (Prior to 1947, the Board reported production of total machinery, both electrical and nonelectrical.) This index was utilized, along with the Board's separate indexes of radio and television production, statistical data from the 1947 *Census of Manufactures*, and the later *Survey of Manufactures*, to compile

TABLE 8–1

FACTORS DETERMINING DEMAND FOR ELECTRICAL EQUIPMENT CAPITAL GOODS

Year	Index of Electrical Machinery Capital Goods 1947–49 = 100 E	Total Capital Goods Production 1947–49 = 100 C	Year	Index of Electrical Machinery Capital Goods 1947–49 = 100 E	Total Capital Goods Production 1947–49 = 100 C
1927	30	43.6	1942	145	192.2
1928	38	47.1	1943	206	278.1
1929	45	55.2	1944	214	277.2
1930	34	41.5	1945	167	198.9
1931	22	26.8	1946	85	97.0
1932	14	15.4	1947	102	102.7
1933	17	19.5	1948	103	106.1
1934	22	27.1	1949	95	91.2
1935	27	31.3	1950	101	104.7
1936	30	40.8	1951	124	133.9
1937	37	47.4	1952	156	156.0
1938	25	28.1	1953	175	172.4
1939	33	39.3	1954	154	152.9
1940	42	56.8	1955	166	164.0
1941	80	101.8	1956	188	179.4

Source: Calculated from Federal Reserve Board data.

an index of the capital goods produced by the electrical equipment industry. Briefly, the procedure consisted of constructing an index for the period
1927 to 1946, and then splicing it with the Federal Reserve Board's index
which has been available since 1947. The result, along with an index of
total capital goods production covering the same years, is shown in Table
8–1, and graphically in Figure 8–1. The index, "electrical equipment capital goods production," thus becomes the dependent variable in this study,

FIGURE 8–1

CAPITAL GOODS COMPONENT OF ELECTRICAL EQUIPMENT DATA

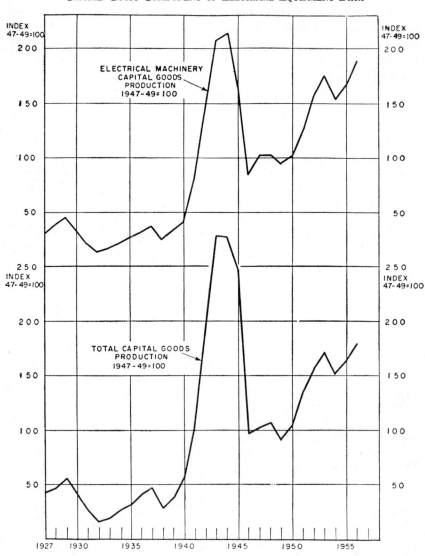

and consists of the output of such products as: (1) electrical industrial apparatus, communication equipment, and radar; (2) insulated wire and cable, and batteries; and (3) X-ray machines, therapeutic devices, and similar products.

Analysis

The analysis of demand for electrical equipment capital goods can now be accomplished in three basic steps: (1) compare production of these goods with total capital goods production, (2) remove the effects of total capital goods production, and (3) study the residual time series. Let us see how this is accomplished.

The object of the study is to relate electrical equipment production to total capital goods production. Since the two series are already closely related—indeed, one is actually a segment of the other—it may be assumed a priori that a one-to-one relationship exists. That is, on the average, a 1 per cent change in total capital goods production tends to be associated with a 1 per cent change in electrical equipment capital goods production, other things remaining equal, so that the elasticity may be said to be unity.

In order to put the series on comparable scales so that the graphic method of fitting yields the maximum likelihood solution, it is first necessary to divide each series by its standard deviation, s or σ, either symbol being widely used. As explained earlier, this procedure eliminates the influence of the units in which the data are quoted, so that the slope of the regression line expresses the true relation between the variables.[2]

Table 8–2 presents the steps involved in the analysis. In Figure 8–2, the electrical equipment series, E, expressed in terms of its standard deviation, s_E, is plotted against the total capital goods production series, C, also in terms of its standard deviation, s_C, resulting in the regression line as shown. The drift of the points away from the regression line during the postwar period reflects the growing importance of electronic equipment for both civilian and military uses.

The effects of total capital goods production on electrical equipment capital goods production must now be removed. This is accomplished by subtracting from the yearly value of the electrical series the corresponding point on the regression line. This point is computed from the relationship

$$y_c = .95x$$

where x refers to total capital goods production expressed in terms of its standard deviation.

The residual series is next plotted as a time series in Figure 8–3. The chart reveals a fairly tight relationship for the prewar period, with the average deviation well inside the $\frac{1}{2}$ standard deviation limit. The relationship was improved, however, by putting in a trend at .01 standard devia-

[2] See, for example, pp. 74–75 for a further explanation, and Chapters 5 and 6 for illustrative applications to several studies.

TABLE 8-2

ANALYSIS OF DEMAND FOR ELECTRICAL EQUIPMENT CAPITAL GOODS

(s = Standard Deviation)

Year	(1)* Index of Electrical Machinery Capital Goods (1947–49=100) E	(2)* Index of Total Capital Goods Production (1947–49=100) C	(3)† Electrical Capital Goods Index $s_E = \frac{(1)}{s_{(1)}}$	(4)† Total Capital Goods Index $s_C = \frac{(2)}{s_{(2)}}$	(5)† Electrical Machinery Excluding Capital Goods Production $y_c = .95x$ where $x = (4)$	(6)† (3) Adjusted for (5) $(5)-(4)$	(7)† Net Growth Trend	(8)† Demand for Electrical Machinery Capital Goods $(7)+(5)$	(9) Index of Demand for Electrical Machinery Capital Goods (1947–49=100) $(8) \times s_{(1)}$	(10) Ratio of Production to Demand $(1)/(9)$
1927	30	43.6	.475	.593	.563	−.088	.01	.573	36	.833
1928	38	47.1	.602	.641	.609	−.007	.01	.619	39	.874
1929	45	55.2	.713	.751	.713	.000	.01	.723	46	.978
1930	34	41.5	.538	.565	.537	+.001	.01	.547	35	.971
1931	22	26.8	.348	.365	.347	+.001	.01	.357	23	.957
1932	14	15.4	.222	.210	.200	+.022	.01	.210	13	1.074
1933	17	19.5	.279	.265	.252	+.017	.01	.262	17	1.00
1934	22	27.1	.348	.369	.351	−.003	.01	.361	23	.957
1935	27	31.3	.428	.426	.405	+.013	.01	.415	26	1.038
1936	30	40.8	.475	.555	.527	−.052	.01	.537	34	.882
1937	37	47.4	.586	.645	.613	−.027	.01	.623	39	.949
1938	25	28.1	.396	.382	.363	−.033	.01	.373	24	1.042
1939	33	39.3	.523	.535	.508	+.015	.01	.518	33	1.00
1940	42	56.8	.665	.773	.734	−.069	.01	.744	47	.893
1941	80	101.8	1.267	1.385	1.316	−.049	.01	1.326	84	.952
1942	145	192.2	2.297	2.616	2.485	−.188	.01	2.495	158	.918
1943	206	278.1	3.263	3.795	3.596	−.333	.044	3.640	230	.896
1944	214	277.2	3.389	3.772	3.583	−.194	.087	3.670	232	.918
1945	167	198.9	2.645	2.707	2.572	+.073	.131	2.703	171	.977
1946	85	97.0	1.346	1.320	1.254	+.002	.175	1.429	90	.833
1947	102	102.7	1.615	1.398	1.328	+.287	.218	1.546	98	1.040
1948	103	106.1	1.631	1.444	1.372	+.259	.262	1.634	103	1.000
1949	95	91.2	1.505	1.241	1.179	+.326	.306	1.485	94	1.011
1950	101	104.7	1.600	1.425	1.354	+.246	.349	1.703	108	.935
1951	124	133.9	1.964	1.822	1.731	+.233	.393	2.124	134	.925
1952	156	156.0	2.471	2.123	2.017	+.454	.437	2.454	155	1.006
1953	175	172.4	2.772	2.346	2.229	+.543	.480	2.709	171	1.023
1954	154	152.9	2.439	2.081	1.977	+.462	.524	2.501	158	.975
1955	166	164.0	2.629	2.232	2.120	+.509	.567	2.687	170	.976
1956	188	179.4	2.978	2.441	2.319	+.659	.611	2.930	185	1.016

*Cols. 1, 2 from Table 8-1.

†Cols. 3-8: In standard deviations.

FIGURE 8–2

ELECTRICAL EQUIPMENT CAPITAL GOODS INDEX (IN STANDARD DEVIATIONS) VERSUS
TOTAL CAPITAL GOODS PRODUCTION (IN STANDARD DEVIATIONS)

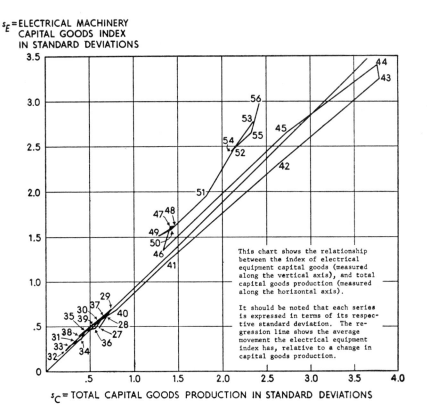

This chart shows the relationship
between the index of electrical
equipment capital goods (measured
along the vertical axis), and total
capital goods production (measured
along the horizontal axis).

It should be noted that each series
is expressed in terms of its respective standard deviation. The regression line shows the average
movement the electrical equipment
index has, relative to a change in
capital goods production.

tions for the 1927–41 period. As for the postwar period, there has been a
decided uptrend of the electrical index relative to the total capital goods
index. As the trend line shows, electrical equipment production has risen
by about .04 standard deviation more than that indicated by the change in
total capital goods production.

Conclusion

The separate relationships may now be combined and translated back
into the original index numbers. When this is done, the final predicting
formula, estimated graphically (see pp. 67–68), is:

$$E = .95 \frac{C}{s_C} + f(t) s_E$$

FIGURE 8-3

CAPITAL GOODS INDEX IN STANDARD DEVIATIONS EXCLUDING TOTAL CAPITAL GOODS
PRODUCTION VERSUS TIME

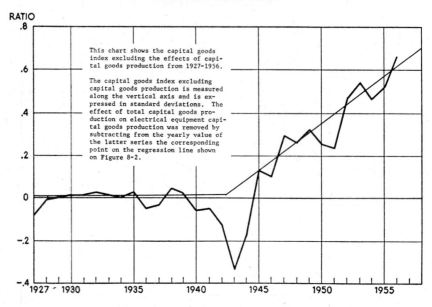

where

E = Electrical equipment capital goods production.

C = Total capital goods production.

s_C = Standard deviation of total capital goods production.

$f(t)$ = .0100 for the period 1926–41. Since 1942, $f(t)$ = .0436t + .0100, where t = the date year minus 1942.

s_E = Standard deviation of electrical equipment capital goods production.

A final test of the analysis is made in Figure 8–4, in which the actual series of electrical equipment capital goods production is plotted as a percentage of the calculated values for the analysis period. In most of the years (excluding the war years) the deviations are within a 5 per cent range. During the 1950–52 period output was retarded, but this deficiency probably reflected the expansion in armament output at that time. Since then the output has moved more or less in line with the indicated requirement levels.

Is this analysis of the demand for electrical equipment capital goods of any value to a particular firm engaged in the production of specific products in this field? The answer is yes. Unit sales data could be compared directly with the original series, or dollar sales may be compared with the production indexes multiplied by an appropriate price index. The analysis of the specific sales series would then proceed in exactly the same

FIGURE 8–4

Demand for Electrical Equipment Capital Goods, Unexplained Variation

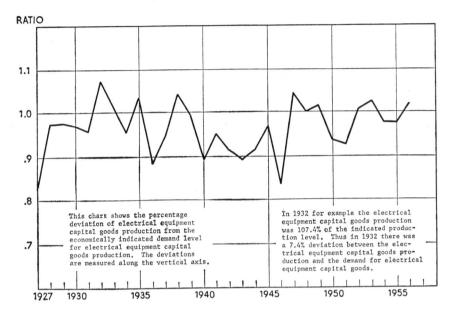

This chart shows the percentage deviation of electrical equipment capital goods production from the economically indicated demand level for electrical equipment capital goods production. The deviations are measured along the vertical axis.

In 1932 for example the electrical equipment capital goods production was 107.4% of the indicated production level. Thus in 1932 there was a 7.4% deviation between the electrical equipment capital goods production and the demand for electrical equipment capital goods.

way as the present analysis, although it might be necessary to include a trend or perhaps some other factor to account for any systematic deviations that may occur.

DEMAND FOR MACHINE TOOLS

Several indexes of criteria for forecasting machine tool new orders have been developed over the years. Prior to 1949, the procedure employed was to relate machine tool new orders to the total level of industrial activity as measured by the Federal Reserve Board (FRB) index, the change in production levels, industrial capacity, and changes in wage rates. After 1949, it was found that better results were obtained by placing increasing reliance on an index of metal and metal products production. This index, which is a special classification of the FRB index of industrial production, includes the principal customers of the machine tool industry— the automobile, iron and steel, nonferrous metals, machinery, and transportation equipment industries. The user industries and their operating rates must thus be recognized in a study of the demand for machine tools, just as in a study of the demand for any other capital good. The way in which these and related factors were incorporated in a recent study of the demand for machine tools is noted in the following paragraphs.

TABLE 8-3

FACTORS DETERMINING DEMAND FOR MACHINE TOOLS

	(1)	(2)	(3)	(4)	(5)	(6)	(7)	(8)	(9)
	Volume of New Orders	Metal and Metal Products Production	Metal and Metal Products Production 3 Months Later	Average Hourly Earnings in Manufacturing	Per Cent Change in Average Hourly Earnings	Federal Reserve Index of Industrial Production	Productive Capacity	Ratio of Production to Capacity	Metal-Working Machinery and Equipment Prices
	$ Millions, 1947–49 Prices	1947–49 = 100		Dollars per Hour	Ratio	1947–49 = 100	1947–49 Production Level = 100	Ratio	1947–49 = 100
Year	D_t	P_t	$P_{t+\frac{1}{4}}$	H_t	$\dfrac{H_t}{\frac{1}{2}(H_{t-1}+H_{t-2})}$	I	C	I/C	P
1921	14.9	18	22	.51	1.00	31	50	62	76.5
1922	44.1	32	35	.48	.90	39	49	80	67.0
1923	105.3	43	42	.52	1.05	47	51	92	71.2
1924	73.0	39	40	.55	1.09	44	53	83	69.2
1925	125.1	42	44	.55	1.02	45	54	83	67.2
1926	133.0	48	47	.55	1.00	51	57	89	65.1
1927	111.6	45	46	.55	1.01	51	59	86	62.7
1928	200.4	50	52	.56	1.02	53	61	87	63.2
1929	230.8	58	54	.566	1.02	59	64	92	65.5
1930	94.7	43	39	.552	.98	49	67	73	60.0
1931	53.6	27	24	.515	.92	40	68	59	55.0
1932	27.9	16	18	.446	.84	31	66	47	52.3
1933	37.7	22	24	.442	.92	37	64	58	52.0
1934	71.4	28	30	.532	1.20	40	63	63	56.6
1935	127.2	36	39	.550	1.13	47	62	76	56.3
1936	210.7	48	50	.556	1.03	56	64	88	56.7
1937	213.4	55	52	.624	1.13	61	68	90	62.3
1938	87.5	42	43	.627	1.06	48	70	69	62.3
1939	238.2	46	50	.633	1.01	58	71	82	61.5

Year								
1940	577.4	62	70	.661	1.05	67	76	88	62.4
1941	1310.6	93	104	.729	1.13	87	86	101	64.7
1942	2664.6	138	146	.853	1.23	106	104	102	67.6
1943	454.6	171	174	.961	1.22	127	123	103	67.6
1944	846.2	181	109	1.019	1.12	125	135	93	67.6
1945	661.1	133	122	1.023	1.03	107	140	76	68.2
1946	330.1	87	90	1.086	1.06	90	110	82	75.3
1947	219.6	101	102	1.237	1.17	100	110	91	93.6
1948	224.8	104	102	1.350	1.16	104	118	88	100.8
1949	168.4	95	100	1.401	1.08	97	129	75	105.6
1950	545.0	115	119	1.465	1.07	112	138	81	112.0
1951	1194.8	130	133	1.59	1.11	120	150	80	125.8
1952	757.4	140	145	1.67	1.10	124	159	78	128.4
1953	607.4	159	158	1.77	1.08	134	167	80	131.1
1954	376.9	141	144	1.81	1.05	125	172	73	133.1
1955	618.7	160	163	1.88	1.05	139	171	81	142.5
1956	568.1	165	167	1.98	1.07	143	172	83	156.4

Source: National Machine Tool Builders Association; *Federal Reserve Bulletin*; Bureau of Labor Statistics.

TABLE 8–4
ANALYSIS OF DEMAND FOR MACHINE TOOLS

Year	(1) Volume of New Orders	(2) Metal and Metal Products Production 3 Months Lead	(3) Per Cent Change in Average Hourly Earnings	(4) Metal and Metal Products Index Adjusted for Hourly Earnings	(5) Adjustment for Metal and Metal Products Production and Hourly Earnings	(6) New Order Equivalent of Metal and Metal Products Production and Hourly Earnings
	$ Millions, 1947–49 Prices	1947–49 = 100	Ratio	Index		$ Millions, 1947–49 Prices
	D_1	$= P_{t+\frac{1}{4}} = P_t'$	$\dfrac{H_t}{\frac12(H_{t-1}+H_{t-2})} = H_t'$	$(P_t')(H_t')$	y_c	$\dfrac{\dfrac{D_1}{H_t}}{\frac12(H_{t-1}+H_{t-2})} = D_1'$
	From Table 8–3			(2)×(3)	$y_c = 2.72x - 17.6$ where $x = (4)$	(1)/(3)
1921	14.9	22	1.00	22.0	42.2	.353
1922	44.1	35	.90	31.5	68.1	.648
1923	105.3	42	1.05	44.0	102.1	1.031
1924	73.0	40	1.09	43.6	101.0	.723
1925	125.1	44	1.02	45.0	104.8	1.194
1926	133.0	47	1.00	47.1	110.5	1.204
1927	111.6	46	1.01	46.2	108.1	1.032
1928	200.4	52	1.02	53.2	127.1	1.577
1929	230.8	54	1.02	55.0	132.0	1.748
1930	94.7	39	.98	38.2	86.3	1.097
1931	53.6	24	.92	22.1	42.5	1.261
1932	27.9	18	.84	15.0	23.2	1.203
1933	37.7	24	.92	22.1	42.5	.887
1934	71.4	30	1.20	35.9	80.0	.893
1935	127.2	39	1.13	44.0	102.1	1.246
1936	210.7	50	1.03	51.4	122.2	1.724
1937	213.4	52	1.13	58.7	142.1	1.512
1938	87.5	43	1.06	45.7	106.7	.820
1939	238.2	50	1.01	50.6	120.0	1.985
1940	577.4	70	1.05	73.4	182.0	3.173
1941	1310.6	104	1.13	117.2	301.2	4.357
1942	2664.6	146	1.23	179.1	469.6	5.674
1943	454.6	174	1.22	211.4	557.4	.816
1944	846.2	169	1.12	189.8	498.7	1.697
1945	661.1	122	1.03	126.0	325.1	2.034
1946	330.1	90	1.06	95.4	241.9	1.365
1947	219.6	102	1.17	119.5	307.4	.714
1948	224.8	102	1.16	118.6	305.0	.737
1949	168.4	100	1.08	108.3	277.0	.608
1950	545.0	119	1.07	127.0	327.8	1.663
1951	1194.8	133	1.11	147.6	383.9	3.112
1952	757.4	145	1.10	158.8	414.3	1.828
1953	607.4	158	1.08	170.5	446.2	1.361
1954	376.9	144	1.05	151.2	393.7	.957
1955	618.7	163	1.05	171.2	448.1	1.381
1956	568.1	167	1.07	178.7	468.5	1.213

TABLE 8-4 *(Continued)*

	(7)	(8)	(9) Volume of New Orders Adjusted for Metal and Metal Products Production, Hourly Earnings and Ratio of Production to Capacity	(10)	(11)	(12)	(13)
	Ratio of Production to Capacity	Adjustment of Ratio of Production to Capacity		Net Growth Trend	Demand for Volume of New Orders	Metal-Working Machinery and Equipment Prices	Demand for Volume of New Orders
	Ratio	Ratio	Ratio	Ratio	$ Millions, 1947–49 Prices	1947–49 =100	Millions $
	I/C	$f(I/C)$	$[D_1'/f(I/C)] = \left[\dfrac{D_1/H_t}{\frac{1}{2}(H_{t-1}+H_{t-2})}{f(I/C)}\right]$	$f(t)$	$\dfrac{y_c}{\times}$ $f(I/C)$ $\times$ $f(t)$	P	D
Year	From Table 8-3	Regression Estimates from Fig. 8-7	(6)/(8)	Trend Estimate from Fig. 8-8	(5)×(8) ×(10)	From Table 8-3	(11)×(12)
1921	62	.95	.372				
1922	80	1.28	.506				
1923	92	1.70	.606	.58	100.6	71.2	71.6
1924	83	1.36	.532	.65	89.3	69.2	61.8
1925	83	1.36	.878	.72	102.6	67.2	68.9
1926	89	1.56	.772	.79	136.2	65.1	88.7
1927	86	1.45	.712	.86	134.8	62.7	84.5
1928	87	1.48	1.065	.93	174.9	63.2	110.5
1929	92	1.70	1.028	1.00	224.4	65.5	147.0
1930	73	1.11	.988	1.00	95.8	60.0	57.5
1931	59	.92	1.371	1.00	39.1	55.0	21.5
1932	47	.87	1.383	1.00	20.2	52.3	10.6
1933	58	.91	.975	1.00	38.7	52.0	20.1
1934	63	.95	.940	1.00	76.0	56.6	43.0
1935	76	1.18	1.056	1.00	120.5	56.3	67.8
1936	88	1.52	1.134	1.00	185.7	56.7	105.3
1937	90	1.60	.945	1.00	227.4	62.3	141.7
1938	69	1.03	.796	1.00	109.9	62.3	68.5
1939	82	1.34	1.481	1.00	160.8	61.5	98.9
1940	88	1.52	2.088	1.00	276.6	62.4	172.6
1941	101	2.42	1.798	1.00	728.9	64.7	471.6
1942	102	2.45	2.316	1.00	1150.5	67.6	777.7
1943	103	2.48	.329	1.00	1382.4	67.6	934.5
1944	93	1.75	.970	1.00	872.7	67.6	589.9
1945	76	1.17	1.738	1.00	380.4	68.2	259.4
1946	82	1.34	1.019	1.00	324.1	75.3	244.0
1947	91	1.65	.433	1.00	507.2	93.6	474.7
1948	88	1.52	.485	1.00	463.6	100.8	467.3
1949	75	1.15	.529	1.00	318.6	105.6	336.4
1950	81	1.31	1.269	1.00	429.4	112.0	480.9
1951	80	1.27	2.450	1.00	487.6	121.1	590.5
1952	78	1.22	1.498	1.00	505.4	128.5	649.4
1953	80	1.27	1.072	1.00	566.7	131.1	742.9
1954	73	1.20	.798	1.00	472.4	133.1	628.8
1955	81	1.31	1.054	1.00	587.0	142.6	837.1
1956	83	1.36	.892	1.00	637.2	156.4	996.6

Raw Data

Of the economic variables affecting the demand for machine tools, three are of particular importance: (1) production of metal and metal products; (2) the rate of change of hourly earnings; and (3) the rate of total industrial production relative to total capacity.

How are these variables utilized in the construction of a model of the demand for machine tools? The first, metal and metal products, can be utilized in a lead-lag manner because new orders for machine tools are of necessity placed on the basis of future production plans, and these orders have been found to precede the output of metals and metal products by about three months, as shown by the two upper panels of Figure 8–5. The second variable, rate of change of hourly earnings, has cost effects which are ultimately absorbed and reflected, in about two years, by the total industrial production index. Hence, the percentage change in average hourly earnings from the average level of the preceding two years is a labor cost variable that may be employed. Finally, the third variable, rate of operations, consists of the ratio of industrial production to industrial capacity. The former is measured by the FRB index; the latter is an index compiled for this particular study and expressed in terms of the production index. It is constructed in three steps: (1) total industrial capacity is estimated on the basis of actual production in high-output years; (2) the change in capacity between these benchmark years is then analyzed in terms of data on manufacturers' expenditures for capital equipment (adjusted for price changes) and a calculated average retirement rate; and (3) capacity levels in the interbench-mark years, as well as in the current period, are then estimated in the same manner. It has been found that this derived measure of the operating rate in total industry is a rather sensitive measure of changes in the demand for machine tools, particularly when operations exceed a level of about 85 per cent.

Analysis

Table 8–3 and Figure 8–5 reveal the important variables in the machine tool study for the period 1921–56, while Table 8–4 contains the highlights of the analysis. Let us examine this table and the corresponding charts briefly.

Figure 8–6 shows the relationship between (1) domestic machine tool new orders, adjusted for changes in prices, and (2) production of metals and metal products (with a three-month lead) adjusted for changes in hourly earnings. Since changes in hourly earnings are associated with changes in the demand for machine tools, the combined variable is simply the product of the volume of new orders for machine tools and the change in hourly earnings. The regression line, therefore, represents the average aggregate effect of changes in this combined variable on changes in the volume of new orders for machine tools. Deviations of actual orders from

FIGURE 8–5

Machine Tools Data

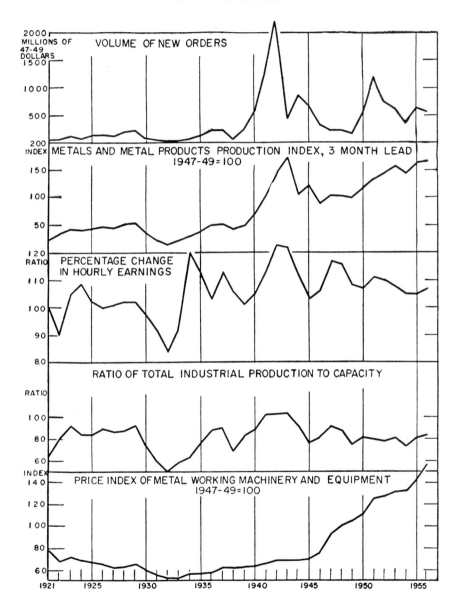

this regression line represent the effects of other economic variables and errors in the data. If we denote the combined variable as x_1, the formula for the regression line may be estimated (see pp. 67–68) as:

$$y_c = 2.72x_1 - 17.6$$

Since the slope is the coefficient of x_1, it means that for every change of one unit in the adjusted index of metals and metal products production, the demand for machine tools changes in the same direction by $2.72 million (expressed in constant prices).

Changes in the ratio of production to capacity, referred to here as the *operating rate*, also affect new orders for machine tools. In Figure 8–7, the volume of new orders adjusted for metals output and for changes in hourly earnings is plotted against the operating rate. The dependent variable was adjusted by dividing the new-orders figure for each year by the corresponding point on the regression line. As shown by the curved regression line, the adjusted volume of new orders turns up sharply as production approaches 100 per cent of (rated) capacity. The relatively flat nature of the regression line toward the left side of the chart indicates a small elasticity of demand for machine tools when production rates are low, while the curved end toward the right reveals an elasticity well above unity when the operating rate reaches about 85 per cent.

FIGURE 8–6

VOLUME OF DOMESTIC MACHINE TOOL NEW ORDERS VERSUS PRODUCTION OF
METALS AND METAL PRODUCTS (3 Month Lead) ADJUSTED FOR THE
CHANGE IN AVERAGE HOURLY EARNINGS

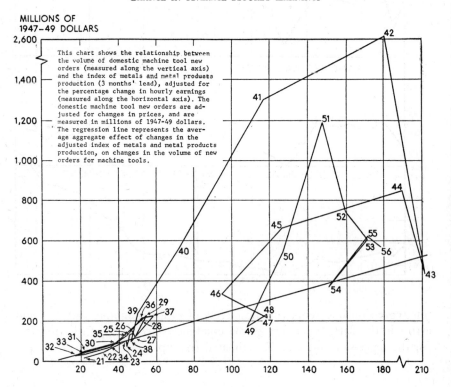

MILLIONS OF
1947–49 DOLLARS

This chart shows the relationship between the volume of domestic machine tool new orders (measured along the vertical axis) and the index of metals and metal products production (3 months' lead), adjusted for the percentage change in hourly earnings (measured along the horizontal axis). The domestic machine tool new orders are adjusted for changes in prices, and are measured in millions of 1947–49 dollars. The regression line represents the average aggregate effect of changes in the adjusted index of metals and metal products production, on changes in the volume of new orders for machine tools.

FIGURE 8-7

VOLUME OF DOMESTIC MACHINE TOOL NEW ORDERS ADJUSTED FOR METALS
AND METAL PRODUCTS PRODUCTION AND PER CENT CHANGE IN
HOURLY EARNINGS VERSUS PER CENT OF CAPACITY UTILIZED

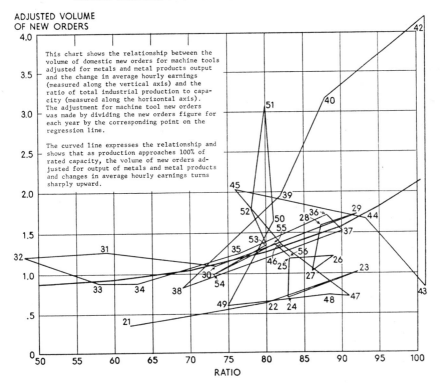

The curved regression line is thus drawn on the basis of economic judgment, for by statistical criteria alone it would be impossible to tell from the pattern of the scatter whether the line should be curved or straight. In drawing this regression line, the years 1939–41 and 1950–52 were ignored because they were years of unusual demand for machine tools due to military needs. It may also be noted that there are actually two regression lines, the major one already discussed, and a minor one for the 1920's, which is of about the same relationship as the major one, but at a lower level. A shift in levels has thus occurred, which was taken into account by a net growth trend, as shown in the next chart.

Conclusion

After the effect of all of these factors are removed, there is still some residual variation, indicating that other factors may be incorporated in the analysis to explain the remaining variations. This residual variation is plotted

FIGURE 8–8

VOLUME OF DOMESTIC MACHINE TOOL NEW ORDERS ADJUSTED FOR METALS
AND METAL PRODUCTS PRODUCTION AND PER CENT CHANGE IN
HOURLY EARNINGS AND PER CENT OF CAPACITY UTILIZED

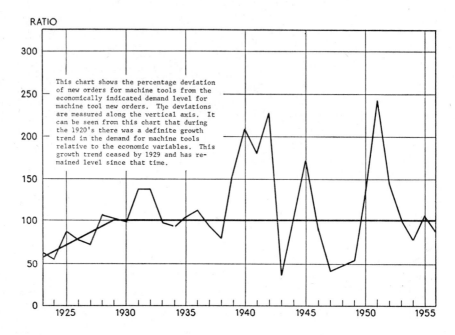

against "time" in Figure 8–8. As can be seen from the chart, there was a definite growth trend in the demand for machine tools during the 1920's relative to the economic variables used. This was due to the newly emerging mass production industries which, by the 1930's, had grown large enough to warrant the building of their own machine tool shops. The result was a partial loss of a segment of the domestic market for the tool builders, and hence a cessation of the net growth in machine tool demand.

The remaining significant deviations can be explained by: (1) the two wars and the preparation periods for them, during which times there were abnormally high demands for machined metals and hence for machine tools; and (2) the low sales level during 1947–49, due largely to government sale of surplus machine tools to nonmilitary users, thereby cutting into the demand for new machine tools.

When the equations of the separate regression lines are combined, they produce the final predicting equation

$$D = \left(2.72P_{t+\frac{1}{4}} \frac{H_t}{\frac{1}{2}(H_{t-1} + H_{t-2})} - 17.6\right) f(I/C) f(t) P$$

where

D = Demand for machine tools, measured by new orders.

P_{t+1} = Production of metals and metal products with a three-month lead.

H_t = Average hourly earnings in the year t.

$f(I/C)$ = Effect of changes in the rate of operations on the demand for machine tools.

$f(t)$ = Net growth or time trend, whose value is 1.00 after the year 1930.

P = BLS index of prices of metal working machinery.

FIGURE 8–9

MACHINE TOOL NEW ORDERS: DEMAND VALUES OF NEW ORDERS
AND ACTUAL VALUE OF NEW ORDERS 1923–1956

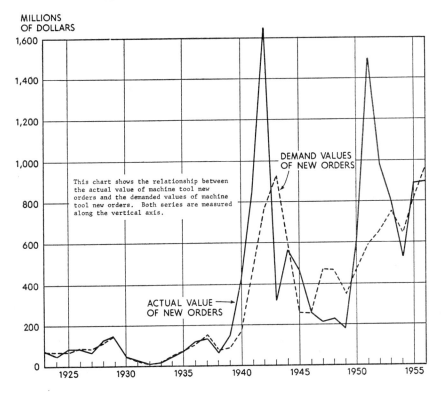

Since a formula is never as readable as a chart, Figure 8–9 presents a comparison of the actual and calculated values. The dashed line, of course, is the graphic counterpart of the formula. With the exception of the unusual demand years noted above, the fit appears to be a good one for the period covered.

DEMAND FOR OIL-WELL DRILLING BITS—FOOTAGE DRILLED

Having explained and illustrated the procedures used in forecasting the demand for both a class of capital goods and for a type of capital good, we may concentrate now on the problems involved in dealing with a specific capital good. The product in question is drilling bits, specifically those used in the drilling of oil wells. But since these drilling bits are demanded according to requirements for new oil wells, and the latter, in turn, may be measured by the total amount of oil-well footage drilled each year, the dependent variable used for the study will be footage drilled. The method for translating the results back into the demand for drilling bits will then be explained in the concluding portions of this section.

Raw Data

Despite the romantic connotations that have been attached to the search for oil—connotations in the form of wildcat dreams, hopes, and windfall profits—it appears that the amount of drilling done each year is a function of economic rather than emotional factors. Is it possible, therefore, to predict with reasonable accuracy the amount of drilling that will be done? The answer is yes, provided the determining variables can be identified, measured, and correctly incorporated in the predicting equation. Let us see how this may be done.

Profit, or rather the expectation of profit, is the predominant motivating factor in the search for oil. Future profit, of course, is the difference between future income, determined by the future output of the well and price of crude oil, and expenses, which include the cost of such factors as land, labor, equipment, and money, that is, interest on borrowed funds to finance exploration. Footage drilled, therefore, may be assumed to vary directly with expected income and inversely with costs. The problem, then, is to obtain satisfactory measures of these variables so that they may eventually be incorporated in a meaningful equation. Since the measures that are best theoretically are usually impossible to obtain, substitute or proxy variables must be employed as the closest approximations.

To estimate income, we need a measure of its components—output and price. As a measure of output, the series selected was the index of crude petroleum production published by the American Petroleum Institute; as a measure of prices, the BLS index of crude petroleum prices was chosen. Income, of course, is the product of output and price, but since output per well is regulated, or, if not regulated, can be fairly well predicted once the well is proven, income is generally determined by price.

Concerning costs, the most important parts of total cost are the prices of oil field machinery, pipes, and so forth, which are represented here by the BLS index of oil field machinery prices. The total cost, of course, also varies significantly with the amount of footage drilled. As for interest, variations in rates have had little measurable effect upon total footage drilled. One reason is that price changes have often incorporated the influence of interest rates. A net residual trend, therefore, is included in the analysis to account both for systematic variations resulting from changes in the interest rate, and for deviations of the proxy variables from the true measures of underlying economic change.

The above variables constitute the chief factors determining the demand for footage drilled, and are shown in Table 8–5 and Figure 8–10. When the variables are properly combined or related as explained in the following paragraphs, it is found that total footage drilled varies directly with total petroleum output and crude oil prices, and indirectly with the index of oil field machinery prices.

Analysis

Since petroleum prices are the chief factor determining income, and oil machinery prices are the chief factor affecting costs, it follows that the ratio of the two would serve as a useful pressure index of profitability, and hence a good combined measure or independent variable affecting the amount of footage drilled. In Figure 8–11, therefore, footage drilled is plotted against this price ratio, the data being obtained from Table 8–5, or from the accompanying analysis table, Table 8–6. The price ratio, of course, does not show why footage drilled increased over time, but rather how it behaved over the business cycle. The regression line (explained further in the following paragraph) shows that on the average a 1 per cent change in the price ratio is associated with a 1 per cent change in footage drilled, other things remaining the same. The footage-drilled series is next adjusted for the effects of the price ratio by dividing the former series by the latter.

The adjusted footage-drilled series is then plotted against the index of total domestic production in Figure 8–12. There is an implicit assumption here that as cyclical demand for petroleum products expands, the flow per well is increased. This leads to greater profit per well and hence induces drilling for new wells. Two definite relationships emerge, one for prewar and one for postwar, with a considerable shift between the two. The more recent or postwar relationship is such that, on the average, a 1 per cent change in petroleum production is associated with about a 1.9 per cent change in footage drilled, other things remaining equal. This relative elasticity indicates that the greater the output of petroleum, the greater the demand for new wells as measured by footage drilled adjusted for the price ratio. The shift in the relationship between the prewar and postwar period explains the somewhat unusual regression line drawn previously in Figure 8–11. This single line representing the period as a whole is actually an average of two separate regression lines that might have been drawn through the prewar and postwar data, respectively.

In the light of the relationship just established, the footage-drilled figures are adjusted for the effects of varying petroleum production by di-

TABLE 8–5

FACTORS DETERMINING DEMAND FOR FOOTAGE DRILLED

Year	(1) Footage Drilled, Thousands of Feet F_1	(2) Crude Petroleum Price Index ———(1947–49	(3) Oil Field Machinery Price Index =100)———	(4) Price Ratio P/M	(5) Total Domestic Petroleum Production (000's of Barrels)	(6) Index of Production, 1947–49 = 100 I
1925.......	76,595	71	65.3	108.7	791,907	38.6
1926.......	82,447	80	63.2	126.6	805,291	39.2
1927.......	72,267	55	60.9	90.3	942,348	45.9
1928.......	74,295	50	61.3	81.6	946,609	46.1
1929.......	88,053	54	63.6	84.9	1,062,649	51.8
1930.......	68,762	50	58.2	85.9	953,331	46.5
1931.......	37,892	27	53.4	50.6	896,524	43.7
1932.......	47,682	37	50.7	73.0	822,471	40.1
1933.......	39,568	28	50.5	55.4	940,834	45.8
1934.......	56,141	42	55.0	55.0	946,324	46.1
1935.......	68,745	41	54.6	75.1	1,037,800	50.6
1936.......	80,997	46	55.0	83.6	1,144,959	55.8
1937.......	105,099	50	60.5	82.6	1,331,127	64.9
1938.......	90,585	48	60.5	79.3	1,267,466	61.8
1939.......	85,523	43	59.7	72.0	1,319,110	64.3
1940.......	96,183	43	60.6	71.0	1,412,081	68.8
1941.......	99,348	48	62.9	76.3	1,486,518	72.4
1942.......	67,903	50	65.6	76.2	1,472,364	71.7
1943.......	61,992	51	65.6	77.7	1,595,729	77.8
1944.......	84,378	51	65.6	77.7	1,780,350	86.8
1945.......	92,982	51	66.2	78.5	1,828,539	89.1
1946.......	101,125	60	73.0	82.2	1,851,748	90.2
1947.......	112,816	81.6	92.9	87.8	1,989,850	97.0
1948.......	136,709	109.9	100.8	109.0	2,167,264	105.6
1949.......	138,617	108.5	106.4	102.0	1,999,215	97.4
Avg. 47–49.	129,381			99.6	2,052,110	
1950.......	159,762	108.4	108.7	99.7	2,155,693	105.0
1951.......	176,757	109.0	119.9	90.9	2,452,676	119.5
1952.......	188,378	109.0	120.1	90.8	2,513,733	122.5
1953.......	198,433	117.0	125.1	93.5	2,596,166	126.5
1954.......	209,502	120.3	129.5	92.9	2,567,628	125.1
1955.......	228,530	120.5	134.8	89.4	2,766,325	134.8
1956.......	235,221	121.1	143.4	84.5	2,905,588	141.6

Source: *World Oil;* Bureau of Labor Statistics; American Petroleum Institute.

viding footage drilled adjusted for prices by the index of petroleum production raised to the 1.9th power. The resulting series is footage drilled
adjusted for prices and production, and is plotted against time in Figure
8–13. There was apparently a smoothly declining trend from 1925 to 1944,
and thereafter a stable relationship between footage drilled and the factors
determining it. What explanation can be given for this? The answer probably is that the declining trend reflects the need for drilling to greater depths
to obtain a strike. As the depth increased, the cost per well increased beyond
that measured by the index of machinery prices. It would be possible to test
the validity of this assumption by introducing data on the average depth of
new wells, and using these along with interest rate data to eliminate the
time trend and some of the remaining deviations. This, however, is unnecessary; the relationship in its present form is quite adequate for practical forecasting. By being on the alert for major changes in depth in the future, the
analyst can use the residual time trend without any danger.

In Figure 8–14, the percentage deviations of footage drilled from the
calculated values are plotted. Note that in only three years of the entire
analysis period did the actual data deviate by more than 10 per cent from
the calculated, and since 1949 only one year, 1953, showed more than a
5 per cent deviation.

Conclusion

Combining the variables, the predicting equation derived in this study
is

$$F = .02296I^{1.9} (P/M)T$$

where

> F = Footage drilled.
> I = Index of domestic petroleum production.
> P/M = Ratio of petroleum prices to oil field machinery prices.
> T = Net trend (= 1.00 from 1944–56).

How might this long-term analysis of the demand for footage drilled
be applied to a short-term analysis, that is, less than a year? First, an analysis
of seasonal variations is made by the standard ratio-to-trend method. Drilling, it is found, tends to be a little below average in the first half of the
year, and a little above it in the second half. The third quarter is usually
the high for the year, although the deviations from average in each quarter
are not large. This is the only further adjustment necessary.

Useful forecasts can now be made on a quarterly basis by forecasting
the independent variables, crude oil prices, machinery prices, and petroleum
output by quarters and inserting the forecasts in the formula. The results
are the quarterly forecasts on an annual level. If these totals are divided by
4 and the quotient multiplied by the seasonal factor, the quarterly forecast
on a quarterly level is obtained. This forecast can then be used to make fore-

TABLE 8-6

ANALYSIS OF DEMAND FOR FOOTAGE DRILLED

Year	(1) Footage Drilled (000's of Ft.) F_1	(2) Price Ratio P/M	(3) Footage Drilled Adjusted for Price Data (Ratio) $\frac{F_1}{P/M}$	(4) Domestic Petroleum Production (Millions of Bbls.)	(5) Index of Domestic Petroleum Production (1947–49 =100) I	(6) Adjustment for Domestic Petroleum Production (Millions of Ft.) $.02296\,I^{1.9}$	(7) Footage Drilled Adjusted for Price Ratio and Domestic Petroleum Production (Ratio) $\frac{F_1/P/M}{.02296\,I^{1.9}}$ (3)/(6)	(8) Trend of (7) (Ratio) T	(9) Demand for Footage Drilled (000's of Ft.) F (2)×(6)×(8)	(10) Ratio of Footage Drilled to Demand (Ratio) F_1/F (1)/(9)
			From Table 8–5							
1925	76,595	108.7	70.5	791,907	38.6	23.7	2.97	2.71	69,810	1.097
1926	82,477	126.6	65.1	805,291	39.2	24.5	2.66	2.67	82,823	.996
1927	72,267	90.3	80.0	942,348	45.9	32.9	2.43	2.63	78,137	.925
1928	74,295	81.6	91.0	946,609	46.1	33.3	2.73	2.58	70,099	1.060
1929	88,053	84.9	103.7	1,062,649	51.8	41.5	2.49	2.54	89,484	.984
1930	68,762	85.9	80.0	953,331	46.5	33.8	2.37	2.50	72,575	.947
1931	37,892	50.6	74.9	896,524	43.7	30.1	2.49	2.43	37,009	1.024
1932	47,682	73.0	65.3	822,471	40.1	25.5	2.56	2.37	44,129	1.081
1933	39,568	55.4	71.4	940,834	45.8	32.9	2.17	2.30	41,929	.944
1934	56,141	76.4	73.5	946,329	45.1	33.3	2.21	2.24	56,986	.985
1935	67,845	75.1	90.3	1,037,800	50.6	39.7	2.21	2.17	64,688	1.049
1936	80,997	83.6	96.9	1,144,959	55.8	47.8	2.03	2.07	82,717	.979
1937	105,099	82.6	127.2	1,321,127	64.9	63.7	1.99	1.98	104,188	1.009
1938	90,585	79.3	114.2	1,267,466	61.8	58.0	1.96	1.88	86,461	1.048
1939	85,523	72.0	118.8	1,319,110	64.3	62.6	1.89	1.74	78,442	1.091

1940	96,183	71.0	135.5	1,412,081	68.8	91.8	1.47	1.59	103,636	.928
1941	99,348	76.3	130.2	1,486,518	72.4	78.4	1.66	1.45	86,739	1.145
1942	67,903	76.2	89.1	1,472,364	71.7	77.0	1.16	1.30	76,271	.890
1943	61,992	77.7	79.8	1,595,729	77.8	89.9	.887	1.16	84,026	.738
1944	84,378	77.7	108.6	1,780,350	86.8	110.7	.981	1.01	86,870	.971
1945	92,982	78.5	118.4	1,828,539	89.1	118.6	.998	1.00	93,100	.999
1946	101,125	82.2	123.0	1,851,748	90.2	119.1	1.032	1.00	97,900	1.033
1947	112,816	87.8	128.5	1,989,850	97.0	136.7	.940	1.00	120,020	.940
1948	136,709	109.0	125.4	2,167,264	105.6	160.6	.780	1.00	173,050	.790
1949	138,617	102.0	135.9	1,999,215	97.4	137.8	.986	1.00	140,560	.986
Avg. 47–49	129,381	99.6		205,211						
1950	159,762	99.7	160.2	2,155,693	105.0	159.0	1.007	1.00	158,520	1.008
1951	176,757	90.9	194.5	2,452,676	119.5	203.3	.956	1.00	184,800	.956
1952	188,378	90.8	207.5	2,513,733	122.6	213.0	.974	1.00	193,400	.974
1953	198,432	93.5	212.2	2,596,166	126.5	226.5	.936	1.00	211,780	.937
1954	209,502	92.9	225.5	2,567,628	125.1	221.7	1.017	1.00	205,960	1.017
1955	228,530	89.4	255.6	2,766,325	134.8	225.5	1.000	1.00	228,420	1.000
1956	235,221	84.5	278.4	2,905,588	141.6	280.6	.992	1.00	237,110	.992

FIGURE 8–10

FOOTAGE DRILLED DATA

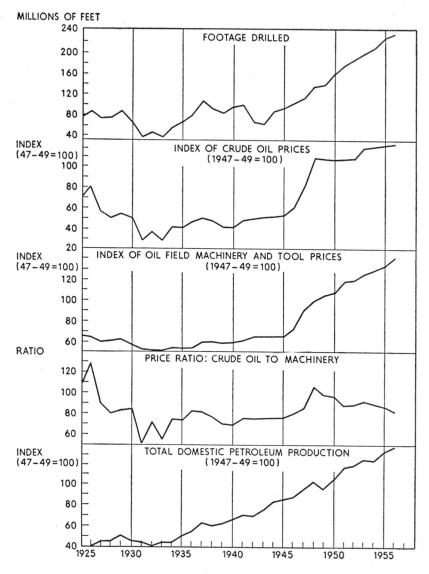

casts of specific capital goods related to footage drilled, such as bits, drilling mud, and pipe. The first two of these are products which are consumed upon use, while the last is a capital good which will remain in use for the life of the well.

FIGURE 8–11

FOOTAGE DRILLED VERSUS PRICE RATIO

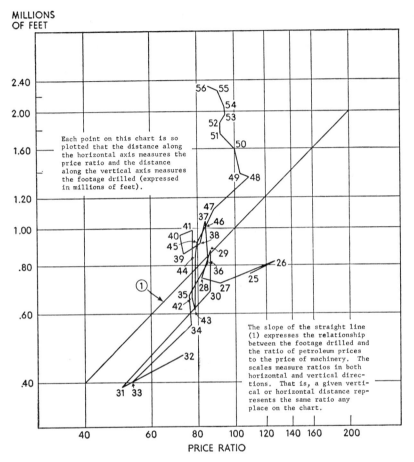

Each point on this chart is so plotted that the distance along the horizontal axis measures the price ratio and the distance along the vertical axis measures the footage drilled (expressed in millions of feet).

The slope of the straight line (1) expresses the relationship between the footage drilled and the ratio of petroleum prices to the price of machinery. The scales measure ratios in both horizontal and vertical directions. That is, a given vertical or horizontal distance represents the same ratio any place on the chart.

A considerable amount of subsidiary information is immediately obtainable from a good forecast of footage drilled. Since the average depth per well has been found to vary slowly from year to year, this study can be used as an analysis of the number of wells drilled. Such information would be of value to producers of oil well machinery, although the problem is admittedly complicated by the fact that a drilling rig is moved from a well and used for another as soon as the well is completed. In fact, the number of wells drilled each year is somewhere in the vicinity of 50,000, while the number of drilling rigs used for the purpose is only a few thousand. Nevertheless, some useful relationships could be derived that would serve as a guide for forecasting, if desired.

FIGURE 8–12

FOOTAGE DRILLED ADJUSTED FOR PRICE RATIO VERSUS INDEX
OF DOMESTIC PETROLEUM PRODUCTION
1947–1949 = 100

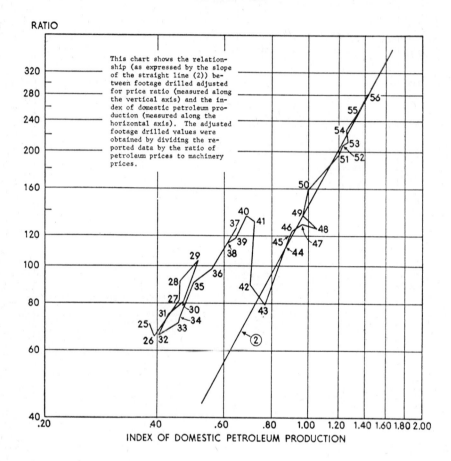

Sellers of drilling mud, pipe, and drilling bits would probably find that their sales varied directly with footage drilled. With respect to drilling bits, however, there are three complicating factors: (1) about 10 per cent of the wells drilled each year are by cable rigs, which do not use drilling bits; (2) increases in efficiency have reduced the number of bits needed per foot; and (3) the number of bits required is greatly affected by the type of soil or rock that must be drilled. It should, therefore, be possible to relate total bits sold to total footage drilled and arrive at an equation which, when adjusted by some sort of trend to take into account the other factors, would explain the movements in total bits sold.

FIGURE 8–13

FOOTAGE DRILLED ADJUSTED FOR PRICE RATIO AND PETROLEUM PRODUCTION

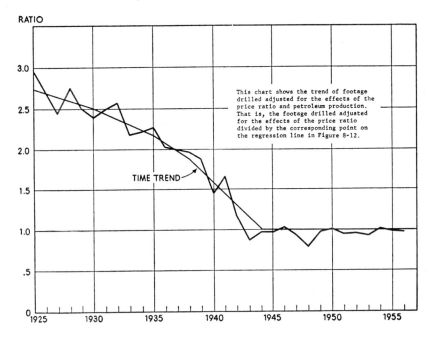

This chart shows the trend of footage drilled adjusted for the effects of the price ratio and petroleum production. That is, the footage drilled adjusted for the effects of the price ratio divided by the corresponding point on the regression line in Figure 8-12.

TIME TREND

FIGURE 8–14

DEMAND FOR FOOTAGE DRILLED UNEXPLAINED VARIATION

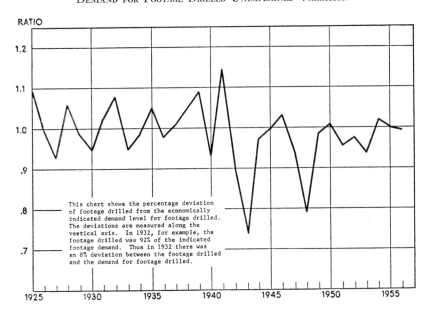

This chart shows the percentage deviation of footage drilled from the economically indicated demand level for footage drilled. The deviations are measured along the vertical axis. In 1932, for example, the footage drilled was 92% of the indicated footage demand. Thus in 1932 there was an 8% deviation between the footage drilled and the demand for footage drilled.

QUESTIONS

1. How does the definition of capital goods as given in the text compare with more traditional definitions? Explain or account for the difference, if any, from a forecasting standpoint.

2. In discussing the demand for capital goods, why is a distinction made between "aggregate demand" and "particular demand?"

3. On the basis of the equation of aggregate demand for capital goods, and the discussion of that equation, develop a generalized "basic equation" as was done in the previous chapters for consumers' goods.

4. State at least three different ways in which particular capital goods may have to be classified in order to analyze the demand factors affecting them.

5. In general, what types of variables would you look for in attempting to analyze the demand for particular types of capital goods? Explain.

Chapter 9

FORECASTING SALES OF
CONSTRUCTION MATERIALS

Economists have long been interested in construction activity as an indicator of the economy's health and as a basis for explaining business fluctuations. The latter have been particularly emphasized in much of the literature of business cycles, primarily because investment expenditures and construction activity are so closely related and, in turn, exercise such profound effects on income, employment, and other major economic variables.

Much of the research done in forecasting construction has been confined either to construction activity as a whole or to some large segment of it such as building construction. This leaves much to be desired from a businessman's as well as economist's standpoint, since there are many narrower categories that need to be forecast, which, when taken together, comprise the construction industry. The techniques that may be used to arrive at such predictions, and the principles underlying these techniques, are the subject matter of this chapter. As in the previous chapters, it is appropriate to begin with an explanation of the underlying demand determinants and then apply the principles that are derived to actual case studies.

DEMAND DETERMINANTS

What is the construction industry? Actually it is a composite of various economic entities, which, for prediction purposes, may be conveniently classified into two categories, private and public. The economic behavior of each entity is to some extent (with qualifications discussed below) independent of the others. Thus, in the area of private construction, residential building evidences many of the same demand characteristics as consumers' durable goods and often changes in a pattern that differs substantially from industrial and utility construction. These last two have economic characteristics of capital goods. In public construction, building streets and sewers may exhibit economic patterns significantly different from those of dam and river-and-harbor projects. It is necessary, therefore, to divide the two categories of construction, private and public, into further homogeneous subdivisions in order to arrive at a sound basis of measurement and prediction.

What types of subdivisions are suggested? A breakdown that has yielded meaningful results has been: (1) *private construction*, composed of (*a*) residential, (*b*) industrial, (*c*) railroad and other utility, (*d*) commercial, (*e*) institutional, and (*f*) farm; and (2) *public construction*, consisting of (*a*) streets, sewers, and water systems, (*b*) highways, (*c*) schools, (*d*) administrative buildings, (*e*) military, and (*f*) all others, including public industrial, utility, commercial, and residential. The demand factors that are significant with respect to these subdivisions will be discussed in later paragraphs. First, however, some comments on the general aspects of demand will prove useful.

General Considerations

As implied above, certain relationships tend to exist between particular subdivisions of public and private construction. Thus, the development of residential communities gives rise to a need for new streets, sewer and water systems, schools, and administrative buildings such as fire stations and city halls. Other types of public construction, such as river and harbor improvement, highway construction, and the like, are not directly related to residential building but are scheduled instead according to regional needs and the available supply of labor and materials. It is the latter that is of particular concern to us in this chapter.

As with capital goods demand, forecasts of construction materials lend themselves to an *end-use* type of approach. For certain materials such as steel and Portland cement, both of which are used in varying proportions in almost all types of construction, a chief problem is to relate their sales to construction activity. A rough measure of the latter that is usually employed is an index of construction contracts awarded. More precise results can be obtained, however, by developing a new index of contracts awarded, with construction contracts weighted for each of the twelve groups outlined above by the amount of the material (e.g., cement or steel) used in each group. Examples of such indexes will be presented in later sections with applications to actual studies.

Other types of construction materials, such as plumbing goods and valves and fittings on the one hand, and lumber and plywood on the other, have more specific end-use markets and may be handled accordingly. Thus, plumbing goods sales are primarily affected by residential and commercial construction and slightly less by private institutional and public school construction. In contrast, sales of valves and fittings are much more dependent on industrial than residential construction. Lumber's primary market is residential construction, with secondary uses by railroads (for ties) and electric utilities (for poles), and with varying consumption rates by practically all other areas of construction. Douglas fir plywood, on the other hand, finds almost half of its market in residential construction and maintenance, and the balance primarily in commercial and highway construction, and in industry for cabinets, partitions, tables, signs, and packaging of heavy goods. Both lumber and plywood have different growth patterns relative to the activity of their end uses. Lumber, it appears, is gradually losing position while plywood is rapidly gaining.

On the basis of the above discussion, it would seem that the sale of construction materials ought to exhibit a fairly smooth relationship with a total or weighted index of construction awards. In reality this has not occurred because (1) construction maintenance expenditures have been large and are still growing, and (2) construction material contractors and dealers frequently buy for inventory well in advance of their needs, usually for speculative or protective purposes. Two demands, a maintenance demand and an inventory demand, are thus created, which tend to distort actual manufacturers' sales of construction materials as compared to contracts awarded.

How can this distorted relationship be corrected? The approach used here is to add to contracts awarded a measure of maintenance demand and a measure of inventory demand, since these are the two variables that must be allowed for. Maintenance expenditures correlate well with gross national product and certain of its components; inventory demand, since it results from speculative and protective motives, is generally a function of changes in wages per hour, monetary and fiscal policies, unusual government demand, and similar factors that may be inflationary or deflationary. The analysis, therefore, can be conducted along the same lines as in earlier chapters, by isolating and measuring relevant variables in order to determine their weights or significance in the total relationship.

Private Construction

Against this general background of demand factors and their influence on construction as a whole, what can be said about the forces determining the level of construction activity in the particular subdivisions of private and public construction that were outlined earlier? We may begin with the six groups comprising the private sector and point out the essential demand determinants for each, and then proceed to a similar discussion of the public sector. This will provide a sounder basis for comprehending the empirical studies that constitute the remainder of the chapter.

Residential Construction. The most important factors tending to influence the amount of new housing that the public will be able to buy are: (1) the number of purchasing units such as families or households (households being preferred since they include single individuals living separately and more than one family living together); (2) the number of vacancies or, equivalently, the percentage of occupancy; (3) construction costs relative to rental value or, almost equivalently, construction costs relative to disposable income; (4) taxes and carrying charges; and (5) the long-term interest rate. Actual construction of houses may differ from demand for short-run periods, but these factors have been found to produce a good fit under normal conditions. And even under certain abnormal conditions such as occurred for several years after World War II when demand greatly exceeded supply, a model utilizing these variables along with estimates of labor and materials supplies served to forecast the end of the period of excess demand and the return to normal activity.

Industrial Construction. Building activity in industry is usually undertaken in order to reduce costs and expand capacity. The economic behavior pattern of industrial construction, therefore, may be expected to be similar to that of capital goods. This means that new industrial construction contracts depend for the most part upon the following factors: (1) the production of, or new orders for, manufactured goods and industrial raw materials; (2) the trend in manufacturing production costs; and (3) the operating rate, or the ratio of industrial production to industrial capacity. Operating rate, was stressed as an important variable in the discussions in the previous chapter dealing with capital goods, and the method of estimating it was explained. As a further guide in making the estimation, it may be noted that such industries as steel and paper regularly release their operating rates to the press, while several trade associations in other major industries collect the information for their members and release it on request.

A significant factor to keep in mind when attempting to forecast industrial construction has been the sharply declining trend in the demand for industrial space relative to industrial production. That is, the demand for industrial space per unit of industrial production has been declining significantly, or in a somewhat similar vein, production per square foot of plant has been rising significantly. Statistically, this tendency can be accounted for by including a time trend in the analysis; economically, it can be explained by technological factors such as the utilization of better equipment and production methods. These new production methods have influenced the physical nature of industrial buildings as well, by bringing about a shift from the older multistory type of factory building to the newer and more efficient unilevel kind.

Railroads and Utility Construction. The building of railroad and other transit facilities has exhibited a pattern similar to that of industrial construction but with a considerably sharper downward trend. In contrast, electric light and power, and gas and oil pipeline construction have risen relative to industrial construction, while telephone and telegraph construction has sometimes risen and sometimes fallen. How can this information be utilized for a forecast of utility construction? The best approach appears to be that of discovering the theoretical forces which have been primarily responsible for past trends in utility construction relative to industrial construction, and then projecting these trends in the light of the theory and the statistical relationships.

Commercial Construction. The average of residential and industrial construction rates determines the rate of commercial construction, with a time lag introduced. That is, commercial building typically stems from residential and industrial building erected a short time previously, because the former must often be serviced by stores and the latter by offices and warehouses. Two sets of forces, one depressing, the other stimulating, have been at work in affecting the demand for commercial construction: (1) The demand-depressing conditions are reflected primarily in a declining utilization of floor space and warehouse facilities per unit of goods distributed, and have been due mainly to technological advancements in marketing as evidenced by improved materials-handling equipment and prepackaging techniques. (2) The demand-stimulating factors for commercial construction, on the other hand, are the result of increasing incomes and leisure time as seen by the growth in recreational and resort facilities, libraries, and similar "luxury" attributes of an expanding economy.

Farm Construction. This segment represents only 5 per cent of total private construction, but nevertheless provides an important market for lumber and other building materials. The demand for farm construction depends upon (1) the number of farm families, (2) their incomes, and (3) their need for houses, implement sheds, barns, garages, and the like. Basic changes in the character of agriculture have been taking place for many years, particularly in the direction of increased mechanization, and hence consolidation, of farms. These and other factors have led to a demand for more modern homes, barns, and sheds for businessmen-farmers.

Private Institutional Construction. The construction of hospitals, colleges, and buildings for a variety of educational and charitable activities, comprise what is largely the category of private institutional construction. This variable fluctuates according to (1) changes in the character and age of the population, (2) general economic conditions of the previous year, and (3) tax laws as they effect personal income, because disposable income in any year is fairly well related to the number and size of new endowments and, in turn, to the following year's building. With respect to private hospitals, the increasing cost of their operation and their difficulties of financing pose a problem as to their future growth. It is possible, therefore, that they will be replaced by subsidized or public hospitals in the years to come.

Public Construction

Most of the important categories of public construction have been discussed, either explicitly or implicitly, in the paragraphs above. Thus, the construction of streets and sewer-and-water systems, as already pointed out, must keep pace with changes in population growth; and public hospitals and institutions, it appears, will share an increasing proportion of the construction of such facilities in view of the rising costs of the services they render. The important categories remaining that warrant separate attention are schools and highways, and these may be discussed briefly as follows.

Schools and Highways. (1) The most significant factors affecting the over-all demand for educational facilities are the proportion of the population of school age and the level of disposable income. Construction of educational facilities amounted to about 50 per cent of total public construction in the 1920's, about 25 per cent during the 1930's, and has since been over 50 per cent. With the rising proportion of school-age children, the demand for all types of school buildings from elementary through college is rapidly increasing, and their financing is certain to become a growing economic problem for many communities in the near future. (2) The demand for new highway construction depends almost entirely on the number of vehicle miles of travel. This, in turn, is a function of real disposable income and the availability of leisure time, both of which exhibit significant growth trends. Assuming that the superhighway or turnpike will be the ultimate form of highway travel for at least the next decade, a practical upper limit to automobile speeds (of about 75 miles per hour) has been reached, and hence a higher volume of highway construction per vehicle mile will be necessary as the number of vehicle miles continues to grow.

Conclusion

The complex nature of the markets for construction materials makes the forecasting of their sales extremely difficult. Nevertheless, progress can be made in the right direction by approaching the problem from the standpoint of end-use analysis. This was the approach employed in the previous chapter in forecasting the sales of particular kinds of capital goods, and it will be seen shortly to be equally important, if not more important, in predicting the demand for construction materials.

Briefly, the procedure followed is to relate the demand for the material to some measure or measures of activity in the end-use markets or to some proxy measure such as an index of total business activity. Three measures of business activity often used for this purpose are (1) total industrial production or a relevant segment of it, (2) activity in the consuming or end-use industries, or (3) a segment of gross national product. An index of construction contracts awarded, of course, would be a measure closely related to the sale of construction materials, but such an index would not necessarily measure the demand for construction materials for maintenance.

Unfortunately, data on construction contracts awarded are still sketchy. Series that have become available for the United States as a whole only in the last few years fluctuate considerably more than construction activity itself. Hence, in the case studies that follow, data.on construction put in place rather than contracts awarded have been used, even though the former series lags behind the latter. Nevertheless, the gain in using the more comprehensive series more than offsets the loss incurred by not using the early turning series.

The series employed in the following studies is a joint estimate of the Departments of Commerce and Labor and is reported in terms of value in

1947–49 prices. By adjusting the series for changes in dollar value due to changes in prices, the result obtained is physical volume of construction put in place. As a measure of the remaining source of demand, which we call "maintenance demand," proxy variables such as industrial production and real disposable income (i.e., disposable income corrected for changes in the cost of living) are employed because more reliable series do not exist. Sometimes the proxy variables used enter directly into the correlations, but generally in an explicit manner as an explanation of some end-use index.

DEMAND FOR PLYWOOD

The increasing demand for plywood in almost every field of construction has resulted in a mushrooming rate of production during the past three decades. In the mid-twenties production of plywood was in the vicinity of 150 million square feet per year; by the mid-fifties it was 5 billion square feet per year, an increase of over 3,000 per cent in 30 years. What are the reasons for this remarkable expansion of output? One factor of considerable importance is cost, for although plywood prices are relatively higher than lumber prices, the savings in labor costs of putting the plywood in place more than offset the price differences. Another factor is the technical superiority of plywood, which, for physical reasons, makes it preferable to lumber in particular construction uses. Let us see, therefore, the procedure that may be used in arriving at a forecasting model for this product.

Analysis

The sale of plywood depends on (1) activity in the end-use markets, and (2) the development of new uses for the product. As a measure of activity in end-use markets, an end-use index was constructed in the following way.

First, the various markets for plywood were defined and measured, based on published reports of the trade association and various government agencies. Seven consuming markets for plywood were found to be of importance, of which five were directly related to some sector of construction and the remaining two were measures of maintenance and total production, respectively. The names of the seven markets and their symbols are given in columns 2 through 8 of Table 9–1. Second, the respective markets as shown in the table were weighted by the proportion of plywood consumed by each in the early fifties, and then combined in an additive manner to form the final end-use index, E:

$$E = .333R + .044I + .028C + .107N + .016F + .265B + .207P$$

Thus, in the base period 1951–52 from which the weights for plywood consumption were selected, residential construction, R, utilized 33.3 per cent of plywood production; industrial construction, I, utilized 4.4 per cent and so on. The sum of the weights, of course, is 100 per cent.

TABLE 9-1

Demand for Plywood

(Dollar Amounts in Millions of 1947–49 Dollars)

Year	(1) Production (Millions of Sq. Ft.)	(2) Residential Construction, Total R	(3) Industrial Construction, Total I	(4) Commercial Construction, Total C	(5) Nonresidential Building Total N	(6) Farm Total F	(7) Building Maintenance B	(8) F.R.B. Industrial Production Index (1947–49 = 100) P	(9) Calculated Demand (Millions of Sq. Ft.) D
1924	125	$10,455	$ 960	$1,506	$2,053	$607	$2,892	44	131
1925	153	11,514	1,067	1,950	2,554	623	3,102	49	148
1926	173	11,570	1,511	2,269	2,775	596	3,273	51	155
1927	206	10,818	1,484	2,365	2,790	714	3,526	51	225
1928	276	9,958	1,710	2,306	2,788	676	3,733	53	291
1929	358	7,250	2,081	2,263	2,747	622	3,892	59	330
1930	305	4,261	1,307	1,811	2,906	409	3,611	49	294
1931	235	3,486	617	1,040	2,734	238	3,128	40	265
1932	200	1,658	220	598	1,879	105	2,726	31	201
1933	390	1,237	516	376	1,015	139	2,505	37	324
1934	384	1,515	512	455	1,239	166	2,772	40	383
1935	480	2,528	400	561	1,218	314	3,275	47	490
1936	700	3,899	648	740	2,313	394	3,710	56	680
1937	725	4,224	1,042	866	1,753	480	3,720	61	723
1938	650	4,219	526	633	2,092	407	3,511	48	691
1939	950	5,615	614	649	2,726	508	3,804	58	898

Year									
1940	1,200	6,308	1,255	764	1,523	573	4,002	67	927
1941	1,620	7,216	3,900	840	1,330	666	4,116	87	1,136
1942	1,782	3,935	6,216	286	740	490	3,487	106	1,007
1943	1,430	2,695	3,184	58	344	473	3,260	127	901
1944	1,440	1,572	2,382	96	393	425	3,325	125	844
1945	1,200	1,928	2,210	337	616	377	3,900	107	891
1946	1,395	6,590	2,278	1,597	1,105	1,097	6,193	90	1,425
1947	1,630	8,230	1,919	921	1,179	1,459	7,212	100	1,635
1948	1,871	9,780	1,524	1,208	1,983	1,485	7,373	104	1,864
1949	1,897	9,834	1,127	990	2,997	1,479	7,443	97	1,931
1950	2,551	13,340	1,216	1,224	3,363	1,583	7,135	112	2,530
1951	2,866	11,313	2,611	1,233	3,700	1,616	7,159	120	2,786
1952	3,072	11,322	3,293	986	3,397	1,643	7,318	124	3,098
1953	3,670	11,824	3,241	1,497	3,448	1,484	7,205	134	3,538
1954	3,822	13,058	2,943	1,778	4,081	1,420	7,547	125	4,043
1955	4,934	15,291	2,534	2,526	4,243	1,350	8,100	139	4,881
1956	5,172	13,838	2,642	2,730	4,231	1,266	8,500	143	5,173

Source: Douglas Fir Plywood Association; Department of Commerce; *Construction Review; Federal Reserve Bulletin.*

FIGURE 9–1

PLYWOOD DEMAND—RAW DATA

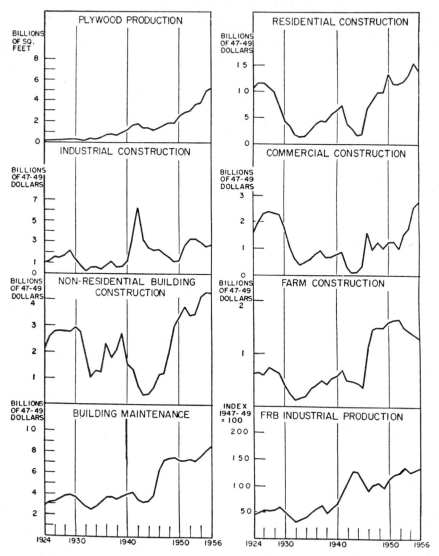

After plotting the separate variables as in Figure 9–1, the problem is to relate plywood production to the weighted end-use index. But first, both series are placed on comparable scales, as explained in previous chapters, by dividing them by their respective standard deviations. In this way the regression coefficient is influenced only by the relation between the variables and not by the units in which the variables are quoted. The resulting regression line after the variables are plotted against each other is shown in

FIGURE 9-2

PLYWOOD PRODUCTION EXPRESSED IN STANDARD DEVIATIONS VERSUS END-USE INDEX
EXPRESSED IN STANDARD DEVIATIONS

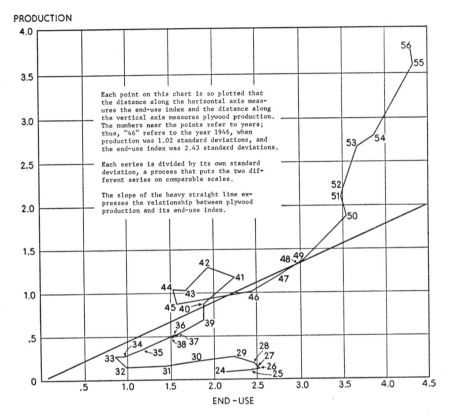

Figure 9-2. The drift of the points away from the regression line since 1949 is a reflection of the substantial growth pattern mentioned earlier, and is due to the discovery of new uses for plywood, as well as extensive advertising and promotional efforts.

If the ratio of actual production to the regression line is calculated and the ratio is plotted against time, the effect on plywood demand of factors other than the end-use index is obtained. This is shown graphically in Figure 9-3. The heavy line, of course, is a time trend representing factors other than the end-use index. Three distinct growth phases are noticeable: (1) The first, between 1924 and 1932, is virtually a typical logistic growth cycle, starting slowly, then accelerating, and then slowing down by 1932. Between 1932 and 1933, plywood production nearly doubled despite a slight decline in the end-use index, probably because of the introduction of plywood sheathing, the growing use of the concrete form panel, and, most important, speculative inventory buying in anticipation of higher

FIGURE 9–3

PLYWOOD DEMAND NET GROWTH TREND

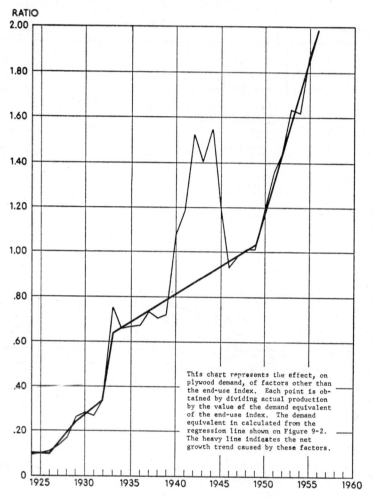

This chart represents the effect, on plywood demand, of factors other than the end-use index. Each point is obtained by dividing actual production by the value of the demand equivalent of the end-use index. The demand equivalent in calculated from the regression line shown on Figure 9-2. The heavy line indicates the net growth trend caused by these factors.

prices under the NRA. (2) The second growth phase occurred in the period 1933–49. Changes in plywood demand due to factors other than end use remained below the growth trend during most of the prewar period, owing to the generally depressed conditions of the time. During the war, production of plywood greatly exceeded civilian demand, but this "excess" was absorbed by military requirements (for example, barracks construction), which are not measured in the end-use index. (3) Since 1949, the industry has been in a third phase of expansion, reflecting both the savings in labor cost from the use of plywood and the development of new as well as existing uses of the product. Thus from 1949 to 1956, plywood production increased 173 per cent while the end-use index rose only 41 per cent. The difference, 132 per cent, is a measure of the nonend-use factors contributing to the growing demand for plywood.

Conclusion

The two independent variables, the end-use index and the net growth or time trend, may now be combined to produce an equation of the demand, D, for plywood:

$$D = .4486 \frac{E}{sE} f(t) \, {}^{s}P$$

where

$E =$ End-use index.
${}^{s}E =$ Standard deviation of the end-use index.
${}^{s}P =$ Standard deviation of plywood production.
$f(t) =$ Net growth or time trend.

A comparison of the calculated and actual values is shown in Figure 9–4, while the percentage deviations of the actual from the calculated values is presented in Figure 9–5. Annual forecasts of the demand for plywood can be made, therefore, by first forecasting construction activity and then the net growth trend. The former can be developed from principles presented in Chapter 3; the latter requires continuous study of the industry, for growth is inherently an *ex post* rather than *ex ante* concept and can be established only after the growth has taken place. Until growth is realized, its future can at best be only estimated by projecting historical data.

FIGURE 9–4

PLYWOOD DEMAND—ACTUAL PRODUCTION AND CALCULATED DEMAND

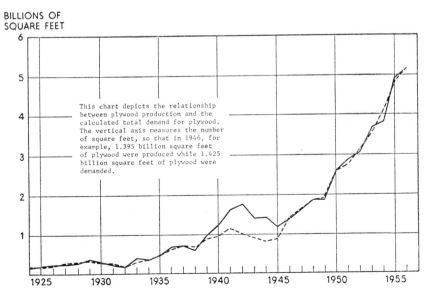

BILLIONS OF
SQUARE FEET

This chart depicts the relationship between plywood production and the calculated total demand for plywood. The vertical axis measures the number of square feet, so that in 1946, for example, 1.395 billion square feet of plywood were produced while 1.425 billion square feet of plywood were demanded.

FIGURE 9–5

PLYWOOD DEMAND—UNEXPLAINED VARIATION

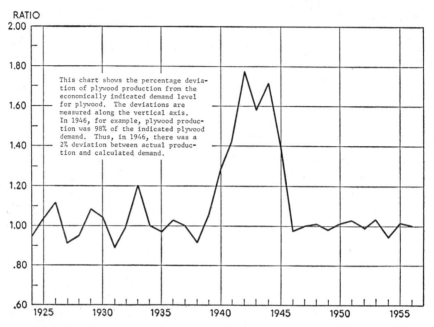

This chart shows the percentage deviation of plywood production from the
economically indicated demand level
for plywood. The deviations are
measured along the vertical axis.
In 1946, for example, plywood production was 98% of the indicated plywood
demand. Thus, in 1946, there was a
2% deviation between actual production and calculated demand.

Forecasts of less than a year must take account of seasonal variations. Satisfactory results can be achieved by taking the seasonal variation as the average deviation of the monthly or quarterly data from its twelve-month moving average. When this is done, the analysis indicates a peak for plywood production during the first quarter, a low during the third quarter, and a moderately stable variation in between. Forecasts of seasonally adjusted demand or sales on a quarterly basis can be calculated by substituting quarterly forecasts of construction activity and net growth trend into the formula. The results multiplied by the seasonal factors yield forecasts of actual sales.

DEMAND FOR PORTLAND CEMENT

Portland cement has important uses throughout the construction industry. It is a major raw material in the construction of highways, dams, military installations, airports, and other public projects, as well as being of considerable significance in many areas of private construction. Thus Portland cement is a relatively small part of the total raw materials used in residential construction, but the volume of residential construction is large enough to create a sizeable demand for Portland cement.

Analysis

An analysis of the demand for Portland cement reveals that the sale of the product depends primarily on two factors: (1) the level of construction activity and (2) the competitive position of cement relative to structural steel, masonry, and other substitutes. As in the previous study of plywood, the problem with cement is to compare its output with a weighted index of activity in the major markets. Each market is weighted according to its relative importance to total consumption in the 1947–49 period. The result is an end-use index which serves as a measure of the first variable mentioned above. The second variable, which is the competitive position of cement relative to substitutes, can then be handled as in the plywood study by an ordinary time trend.

In the previous section of this chapter, the construction industry was divided into about a dozen separate markets, each one reasonably homogeneous in that it embraced a type of construction activity which responded fairly consistently with the economic forces at work. For the present study a regrouping of construction markets into three broad categories was found to be more suitable because of the product involved. The three market categories employed were: producers' plant, p, including private, public, and utility construction; highway construction, h; and all other construction, a. Each of these markets was then weighted according to its relative contribution to total consumption, based on published reports of the Department of Commerce on cement use by major sectors of the construction industry for the years 1947–49. According to the Commerce Department's estimates, the allocation of total cement produced during that period was: $p = 19.5$ per cent; $h = 16.5$ per cent; and $a = 64$ per cent.

To construct an end-use index, that is, a measure of activity in end-use markets, two steps were involved: (1) A separate series for p, for h, and for a, was calculated from Commerce Department data on expenditures for construction put in place. The three series, adjusted for price changes, are shown in Table 9–2, and graphically, along with Portland cement shipments, in Figure 9–6. (2) Each of the three series was then indexed on a 1947–49 = 100 base, weighted according to its particular percentage contribution as stated above, and all three were then combined to form a total market index. In other words, the formula for constructing the end-use index, E, was

$$E = .195P + .165H + .640A$$

where P, H, and A are indexes of producers' plant, highway, and "all other" construction, respectively, and the coefficients are the weights according to the percentage of total cement allocated to p, h, and a in 1947–49.

The series "Portland cement shipments" was chosen as a measure of demand, D. Both series, D and E, were then divided by their respective standard deviations in order to place the data on comparable scales. D,

TABLE 9–2

DEMAND FOR PORTLAND CEMENT
(Dollar Amounts in Millions of 1947–49 Dollars)

	(1)	(2)	(3)	(4)	(5)	(6)
Year	Shipments Millions of Barrels	Producers' Plant Construction	Highway Construction	All Other Construction	Total	Calculated Demand Millions of Barrels
		P	H	A		D
1920	96.0	$3,956	$ 674	$ 7,813	$12,443	84.5
1921	95.1	3.428	1,058	9,421	13,907	96.0
1922	116.6	3,889	1,192	13,834	18,915	122.2
1923	135.9	4,613	983	15,048	20,644	131.2
1924	145.8	4,747	1,257	16,987	22,991	147.8
1925	156.7	5,251	1,448	18,907	25,606	163.8
1926	161.8	6,223	1,486	19,316	27,025	170.8
1927	170.9	6,388	1,726	19,199	27,313	174.0
1928	175.5	6,411	1,947	18,411	26,769	172.1
1929	169.4	7,031	1,978	15,736	24,745	160.6
1930	158.7	5,860	2,548	12,643	21,051	145.9
1931	126.5	3,462	2,542	11,101	17,105	120.9
1932	80.6	1,794	2,259	7,565	11,618	86.4
1933	64.1	1,432	1,567	6,137	9,136	65.3
1934	75.9	1,584	1,636	7,277	10,497	71.7
1935	75.2	1,665	1,448	9,243	12,356	78.1
1936	112.8	2,366	2,151	12,682	17,199	109.4
1937	113.8	3,151	2,064	12,125	17,340	110.7
1938	106.3	2,210	2,492	12,301	17,003	110.7
1939	122.7	2,426	2,478	14,963	19,867	122.8
1940	130.4	3,030	2,409	15,329	20,768	126.0
1941	167.6	3,792	1,739	20,332	25,863	147.2
1942	185.3	2,065	931	23,404	26,400	142.7
1943	127.6	1,139	516	14,433	16,088	88.3
1944	94.3	1,506	461	9,520	11,487	66.5
1945	106.4	2,507	526	9,548	12,581	74.9
1946	169.6	5,461	1,074	16,135	22,670	140.8
1947	187.5	5,234	1,532	19,530	26,296	168.3
1948	204.3	5,512	1,672	22,416	29,600	192.6
1949	206.1	5,095	2,128	23,750	30,973	209.2
1950	226.0	5,229	2,367	27,532	35,128	235.4
1951	241.2	6,079	2,349	27,063	35,491	238.6
1952	251.1	6,089	2,489	27,863	36,441	245.7
1953	260.9	6,666	2,851	28,147	37,664	257.8
1954	274.1	6,634	3,689	29,827	40,150	282.8
1955	296.3	7,729	3,812	32,261	43,802	306.5
1956	311.6	8,450	3,920	31,063	43,433	306.5

Source: Same as Table 9–1.

FIGURE 9–6

Portland Cement Demand—Raw Data

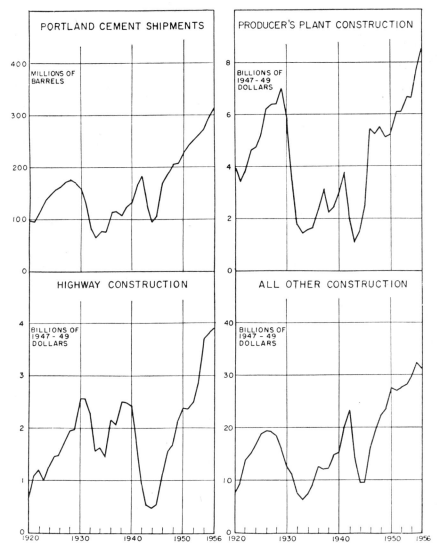

expressed in standard deviations, was next plotted against *E*, also expressed
in standard deviations, as in Figure 9–7. The relationship obtained was an
upward-sloping regression line at a 45-degree angle to the base, indicating
a *D-E* relationship of unit elasticity, that is, a 1 per cent change in the end-
use index is accompanied by a 1 per cent change in the shipments of Portland cement.

The remaining steps in the analysis involved the determination of the

FIGURE 9–7

PORTLAND CEMENT DEMAND—PORTLAND CEMENT SHIPMENTS EXPRESSED IN
STANDARD DEVIATIONS VERSUS END-USE INDEX EXPRESSED
IN STANDARD DEVIATIONS

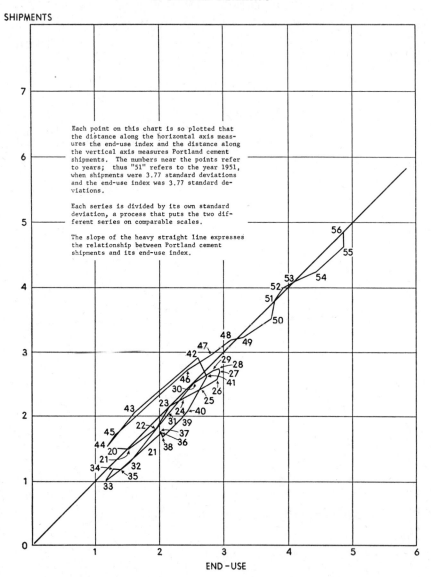

SHIPMENTS

Each point on this chart is so plotted that
the distance along the horizontal axis measures the end-use index and the distance along
the vertical axis measures Portland cement
shipments. The numbers near the points refer
to years; thus "51" refers to the year 1951,
when shipments were 3.77 standard deviations
and the end-use index was 3.77 standard deviations.

Each series is divided by its own standard
deviation, a process that puts the two different series on comparable scales.

The slope of the heavy straight line expresses
the relationship between Portland cement
shipments and its end-use index.

END–USE

effects of factors other than construction activity. This was done by calculating the ratio of actual shipments to shipments that would be expected
on the basis of the regression estimates of Figure 9–7. The resulting ratio,
representing the "unexplained variations" between shipments and end-use

demand, was then plotted as a time series, that is, against time, to determine the trend of the nonend-use factors. The outcome of this step appears in Figure 9–8. The heavy trend line indicates three distinct phases of long-run change: (1) the period prior to 1940 during which time Portland cement suffered a decline in competitive position owing to lower comparative costs

FIGURE 9–8

PORTLAND CEMENT DEMAND—NET GROWTH TREND

This chart represents the effect of factors other than the end-use index on Portland cement demand. Each point is obtained by dividing actual shipments by the value of the demand equivalent of the end-use index, which is calculated from the regression line shown on Figure 9-7. The heavy line indicates the net growth trend caused by these factors.

of substitutes; (2) the war and postwar period in which the previous downward trend was sharply reversed, owing to large military needs, shortages of competing materials such as steel, and many technological advances resulting in new and improved types of concrete; and (3) the period since 1948 in which shipments owing to nonend-use factors appear to have been fairly stabilized.

Conclusion

The combination of the two independent variables, the end-use index and the time trend, produces the demand equation for Portland cement. The equation is

$$D = \frac{E}{{}^sE} f(t) \; {}^sS$$

where

$D =$ Demand for Portland cement, measured by shipments.
$E =$ End-use index.
${}^sE =$ Standard deviation of the end-use index.
${}^sS =$ Standard deviation of Portland cement shipments.
$f(t) =$ Net growth or time trend.

FIGURE 9–9

PORTLAND CEMENT DEMAND—ACTUAL SHIPMENTS AND CALCULATED DEMAND

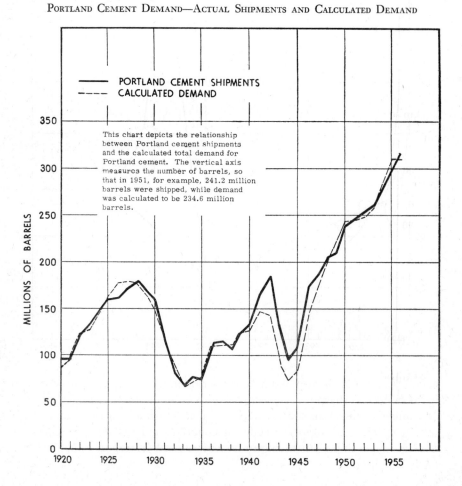

FIGURE 9-10

PORTLAND CEMENT DEMAND—UNEXPLAINED VARIATION

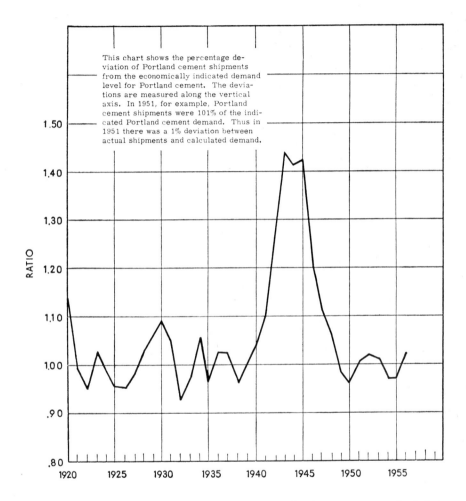

This chart shows the percentage deviation of Portland cement shipments from the economically indicated demand level for Portland cement. The deviations are measured along the vertical axis. In 1951, for example, Portland cement shipments were 101% of the indicated Portland cement demand. Thus in 1951 there was a 1% deviation between actual shipments and calculated demand.

The graphic result is shown in Figure 9–9, while the percentage deviation of the actual from the calculated values appears in Figure 9–10.

Forecasts of demand for Portland cement can be made, on an annual basis, by forecasting construction activity in the end-use markets and by projecting the net growth factor—and on a quarterly or monthly basis by including the normal seasonal variations. With respect to the latter, quarterly shipments of Portland cement exhibit a wide variation from the average annual level. They rise to a peak of about 20 per cent above average during the second and third quarter when outdoor construction is at a high, decline somewhat in the fourth quarter, and reach a trough in the first quarter of 30 per cent below the annual average when outdoor construction is virtually at a standstill because of cold weather in many parts of the country.

Finally, to complete the forecast, the probable change in inventory demand must be estimated. This is often quite difficult, but there are certain variables that can be observed as a guide in making such predictions. They include the relation between contract awards and monetary changes, labor demands and their possible effect on cement prices, and changes in productive capacity. In other words, a close contact with production and market conditions in the industry is necessary if correct forecasts are to be made.

DEMAND FOR IRON AND STEEL PRODUCTS

The construction industry utilizes iron and steel products of various kinds such as fabricated structural steel, galvanized steel sheets, steel line pipe, rails, concrete reinforcing bars, pressure pipe, soil pipe, conduit pipe, nails, steel piling, and so forth. In measuring the demand for iron and steel products, it is obviously not feasible to deal with each of these products separately. A practical method of attack, therefore, is to group the products into one category by the use of an index number.

The Department of Commerce has available an index of major iron and steel products shipped to the construction industry. This index is on a 1947–49 base, and consists of data collected on the above as well as other items, based on information obtained from trade associations such as the American Institute of Steel Construction, the American Iron and Steel Institute, and the National Electrical Manufacturers' Association, and governmental agencies such as the Bureau of the Census. Current figures on production are published monthly and annual figures are available back to 1947. This is the measure of output, therefore, that is employed in the following analysis of demand for iron and steel products.

Analysis

Although information as to the relative amounts of steel consumed by the various segments of the construction industry is unavailable, some preliminary research revealed that most of the items included in the output index mentioned above were of negligible importance in the construction of residential buildings, but of major importance in the construction of highways and industrial, commercial, and most nonresidential buildings. Therefore, as a measure of demand in the end-use markets, the series employed is the value of expenditures for new construction put in place less residential. The expenditure series is available from the Department of Commerce and is adjusted for changes in prices to yield an index of end-use activity on a 1947–49 base. The relevant data for the study are presented in Table 9–3.

After a comparison of the two variables, output and end use, as shown

TABLE 9–3

DEMAND FOR IRON AND STEEL PRODUCTS

(Dollar Amounts in Millions of 1947–49 Dollars)

Year	(1) Production (Index 1947–49 =100) P	(2) Total New Construction	(3) Residential	(4) Total Nonresidential	(5) Calculated Demand D
1947........	97	$19,084	$ 8,230	$10,854	94
1948........	102	22,227	9,780	12,447	102
1949........	101	23,530	9,834	13,696	107
1950........	120	27,993	13,340	14,653	109
1951........	123	28,332	11,313	17,019	120
1952........	113	29,123	11,322	17,801	118
1953........	128	30,459	11,824	18,635	123
1954........	120	32,603	13,058	19,545	128
1955........	133	35,702	15,291	20,411	131
1956........	141	34,933	13,838	21,095	133

Source: Same as for Table 9–1.

in Figure 9–11, the next step is to plot the two indexes against each other in the form of a scatter diagram. As in several previous studies, each variable is divided by its standard deviation and thereby expressed in standard deviation units, thus making the two variables more comparable. The resulting regression line expressing the relationship between output and end use is shown in Figure 9–12.

Factors other than end use are at work in influencing the construction industry's demand for iron and steel products. These other factors include (1) the availability of the product, (2) the degree to which other products may be substituted, and (3) the relative costs of iron and steel products as compared to the costs of substitutes. The net effect of all of these factors can be accounted for by dividing actual output for each year by the corresponding value of end-use demand as determined from the regression line in Figure 9–12. The resulting ratios express the percentage of actual to calculated requirements, and when plotted as a time series as in Figure 9–13, they exhibit a trend line which shows the average effect of factors other than end use in influencing steel output.

Conclusion

The net growth trend of iron and steel products used by the construction industry indicates a gradual loss of competitive position from 1947 to 1952. This was the period of intense steel shortage. Since 1952 the trend of factors other than end-use activity undertook a change in the direction of what appears to be somewhat greater stability.

FIGURE 9–11

STEEL DEMAND—STEEL PRODUCTION OUTPUT INDEX

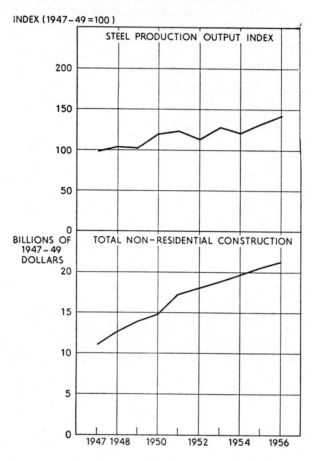

The demand equation for iron and steel, as measured by construction activity and the net trend of all other factors, may be expressed by the formula

$$D = 1.548 \frac{E}{{}^{s}E} f(t) \, {}^{s}P$$

where

$D = $ Demand.
$E = $ End-use index.
${}^{s}E = $ Standard deviation of the end use index.
${}^{s}P = $ Standard deviation of the production or output index.
$f(t) = $ Net growth trend.

FIGURE 9–12

STEEL DEMAND—STEEL OUTPUT INDEX EXPRESSED IN STANDARD DEVIATIONS
VERSUS END-USE INDEX EXPRESSED IN STANDARD DEVIATIONS

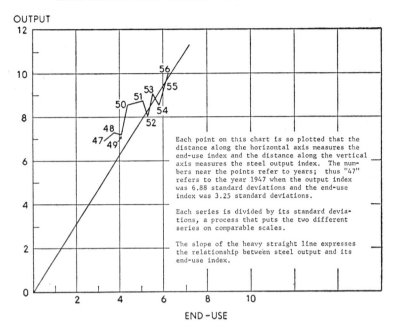

Each point on this chart is so plotted that the distance along the horizontal axis measures the end-use index and the distance along the vertical axis measures the steel output index. The numbers near the points refer to years; thus "47" refers to the year 1947 when the output index was 6.88 standard deviations and the end-use index was 3.25 standard deviations.

Each series is divided by its standard deviations, a process that puts the two different series on comparable scales.

The slope of the heavy straight line expresses the relationship between steel output and its end-use index.

FIGURE 9–13

STEEL DEMAND—NET GROWTH TREND

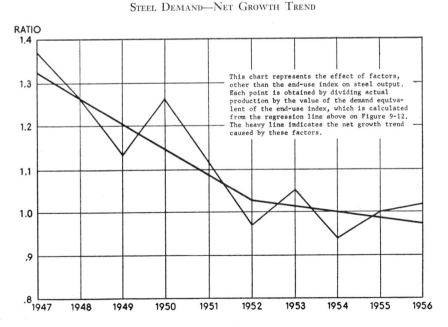

This chart represents the effect of factors, other than the end-use index on steel output. Each point is obtained by dividing actual production by the value of the demand equivalent of the end-use index, which is calculated from the regression line above on Figure 9-12. The heavy line indicates the net growth trend caused by these factors.

The relationship between actual steel output and the calculated demand is shown graphically in Figure 9–14, while the unexplained variation, measured by the percentage deviation of actual output about the calculated demand level, is presented in Figure 9–15.

FIGURE 9–14

<small>STEEL DEMAND—ACTUAL OUTPUT AND CALCULATED DEMAND</small>

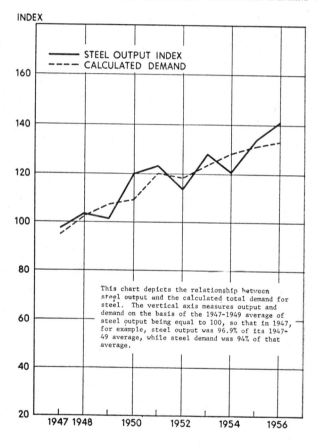

This chart depicts the relationship between steel output and the calculated total demand for steel. The vertical axis measures output and demand on the basis of the 1947-1949 average of steel output being equal to 100, so that in 1947, for example, steel output was 96.9% of its 1947-49 average, while steel demand was 94% of that average.

DEMAND FOR PLUMBING FIXTURES

A final illustration of the application of econometric techniques to the forecasting of construction materials can be seen in the following model of the demand for plumbing fixtures. As in all the previous studies, this too employed the same basic principles. Some modifications in techniques were used, however, in order to adapt the particular problem to the required type of analysis. Hence it should be instructive to outline the procedure em-

FIGURE 9–15

STEEL DEMAND—UNEXPLAINED VARIATION

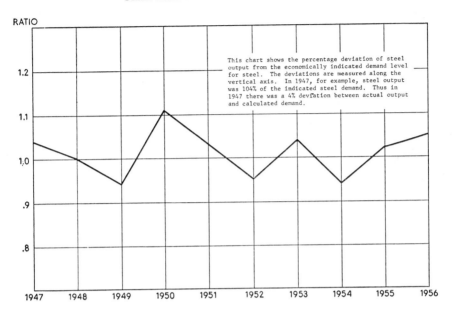

This chart shows the percentage deviation of steel output from the economically indicated demand level for steel. The deviations are measured along the vertical axis. In 1947, for example, steel output was 104% of the indicated steel demand. Thus in 1947 there was a 4% deviation between actual output and calculated demand.

ployed in order to provide a basis for comparing the various models that have been constructed in this chapter.

Analysis

A composite index of plumbing fixtures, representing the production of such items as bathtubs, kitchen sinks, commodes, flush tanks, lavatories, and other miscellaneous fixtures, is published quarterly and annually by the Department of Commerce. Physical production is multiplied by the average price for the year 1947, and the total value of all goods (in terms of constant 1947 dollars and therefore excluding changes in price) is indexed with the 1947–49 average equal to 100. This index, therefore, is the measure of output used in the present study.

How is a measure of end use obtained? Virtually all types of construction activity, with the exception of highway and public utility construction, makes significant use of plumbing fixtures of various kinds. Although definitive data on the consumption of plumbing fixtures by the various segments of the construction industry is unavailable, some preliminary research indicated that roughly 50 per cent of all plumbing fixtures are installed in residential buildings and the remaining 50 per cent, therefore, is allocated to the nonresidential sector. An index of end-use activity can thus be calculated in three steps: (1) an index of residential construc-

TABLE 9–4

DEMAND FOR PLUMBING FIXTURES

Year	(1) Production Index (1947–49 = 100) P	(2) Total	(3) Residential R	(4) Total Nonresidential	(5) Highway and Public Utility	(6) Nonresidential Less Highway and Public Utility NR	(7) Calculated Demand D
			Construction Activity 1947–49, $ Millions				
1945	35	12,581	1,928	10,653	1,698	8,955	24
1946	66	22,670	6,590	16,080	2,805	13,275	83
1947	94	26,296	8,230	18,066	4,028	14,038	93
1948	112	29,600	9,780	19,820	4,638	15,182	105
1949	93	30,973	9,834	21,139	5,279	15,860	98
1950	125	35,128	13,340	21,788	5,368	16,420	125
1951	120	35,491	11,313	24,178	5,405	18,773	109
1952	95	36,441	11,322	25,119	5,683	19,436	103
1953	101	37,664	11,824	25,840	6,213	19,627	98
1954	111	40,150	13,058	27,092	6,855	20,237	111
1955	140	43,802	15,291	28,511	7,069	21,442	138
1956	123	43,433	13,838	29,595	7,336	22,259	126

Source: Same as for Table 9–1.

tion activity is computed; (2) expenditures for all nonresidential construction except highway and public utilities are indexed; and (3) the two indexes are then added together to form a single index. Utilizing the data in Table 9–4, the formula for this calculation is

$$E = .5R + .5NR$$

where

E = End-use index.

R = Index of residential construction expenditures.

NR = Index of nonresidential construction expenditures, less highway and public utility expenditures.

As in several previous studies, each series is then divided by its own standard deviation, and the series are plotted against one another as a scatter diagram. The result appears in Figure 9–17, the regression line indicating the relationship between the production of plumbing fixtures (on the vertical axis) and its calculated end-use market (on the horizontal axis). The formula for this regression line can be read directly from the chart as

$$D = -2.5 + 2\frac{E}{{}^{s}E}$$

where D = demand for plumbing fixtures, E = end-use index, and ${}^{s}E$ = standard deviation of the end-use index.

FIGURE 9–16

PLUMBING FIXTURES DEMAND—RAW DATA

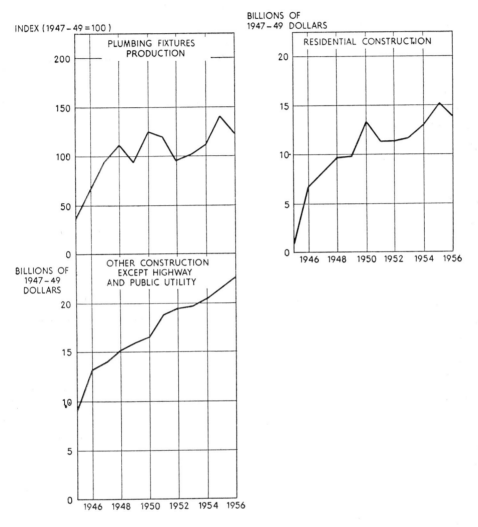

The drift of the points away from the regression line in Figure 9–17 indicates that factors other than end use have been exerting an influence on the demand for plumbing fixtures. In order to discover the influence of these nonend-use factors, the absolute deviations of the scatter from the regression line (percentage deviations could also have been used) are measured, and these differences are then plotted as a time series in Figure 9–18. Two trend lines can then be drawn: the first, from 1945–53, represents a decline of almost 4/10 of a standard deviation of production per year; the second, from 1953 on, is somewhat shallower and declines at about 1/10 of

FIGURE 9–17

PLUMBING FIXTURES DEMAND—PLUMBING FIXTURES PRODUCTION EXPRESSED
IN STANDARD DEVIATIONS VERSUS END-USE INDEX EXPRESSED
IN STANDARD DEVIATIONS

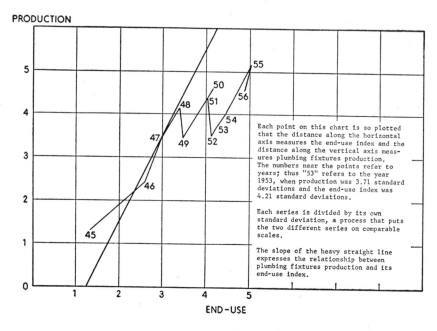

a standard deviation per year. Since homes are being built with more bathrooms and hence more plumbing fixtures, why should the trend of production be declining relative to demand originating in the end-use market? Apparently, some explanation is necessary.

The answer to the question lies in the interpretation of expenditures for construction. These expenditures are reported in constant 1947–49 dollars and hence, since they are adjusted for changes in prices, are more of a reflection of increases in physical volume than of increases in dollar value. Increases in physical volume, in turn, can result from: (1) increases in the number of units (homes) built, or (2) increases in the average size of the unit, either because of more rooms per unit or because of larger rooms. It is well known, of course, that high birth rates since World War II and high incomes have combined to cause an increase in both the number and the average size of dwelling units, the latter resulting from both a greater number of rooms per unit and larger rooms, in order to accommodate larger families. This is why the end-use index of activity in the plumbing goods market has expanded more rapidly than actual production (or consumption) of plumbing goods.

FIGURE 9–18

PLUMBING FIXTURES DEMAND—NET GROWTH TREND

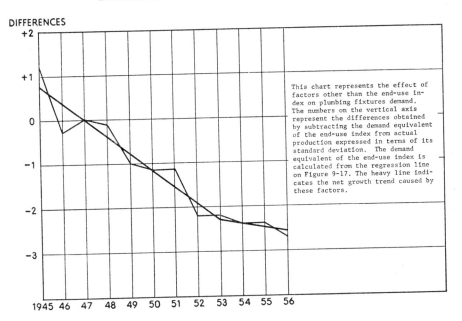

This chart represents the effect of factors other than the end-use index on plumbing fixtures demand. The numbers on the vertical axis represent the differences obtained by subtracting the demand equivalent of the end-use index from actual production expressed in terms of its standard deviation. The demand equivalent of the end-use index is calculated from the regression line on Figure 9–17. The heavy line indicates the net growth trend caused by these factors.

Conclusion

The trend toward larger homes has been leveling off in recent years. This, combined with the tendency for construction expenditures to reflect the increase in the number of units built more readily than the physical size of the units built, has produced a more stable net trend of plumbing fixtures production relative to the demand indicated by the end-use index.

A more complete formula expressing the demand for plumbing fixtures, therefore, is

$$D = -2.5 + 2\frac{E}{{}^sE} + f(t)\ {}^sP$$

in which

  D = Demand for plumbing fixtures.
  E = End-use index.
  ${}^sE$ = Standard deviation of the end-use index.
  $f(t)$ = Net growth trend.
  ${}^sP$ = Standard deviation of the production or output index.

The graphic form of the equation is shown by the dashed line in Figure 9–19, and the percentage deviations between the actual and calculated values are presented in Figure 9–20.

FIGURE 9–19

PLUMBING FIXTURES DEMAND—ACTUAL PRODUCTION AND CALCULATED DEMAND

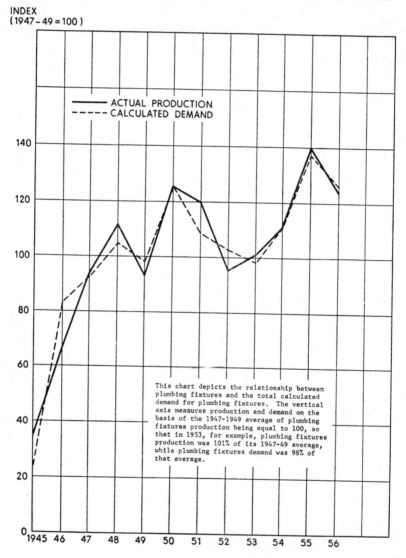

INDEX
(1947–49 = 100)

—— ACTUAL PRODUCTION
----- CALCULATED DEMAND

This chart depicts the relationship between plumbing fixtures and the total calculated demand for plumbing fixtures. The vertical axis measures production and demand on the basis of the 1947-1949 average of plumbing fixtures production being equal to 100, so that in 1953, for example, plumbing fixtures production was 101% of its 1947-49 average, while plumbing fixtures demand was 98% of that average.

SUMMARY

In forecasting the sale of construction materials, the first step is to classify the diverse construction industry into categories that are conven- ient for prediction purposes. A grouping into two categories, private and public, has been found useful for this purpose. These groups may then be further divided into narrower subgroups such as residential, industrial, rail-

FIGURE 9–20

PLUMBING FIXTURES—UNEXPLAINED VARIATION

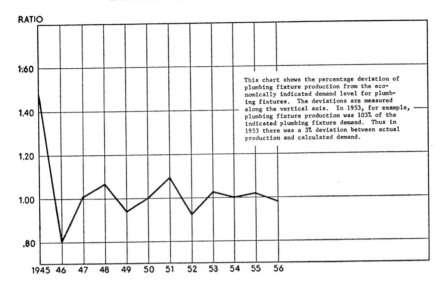

This chart shows the percentage deviation of plumbing fixture production from the economically indicated demand level for plumbing fixtures. The deviations are measured along the vertical axis. In 1953, for example, plumbing fixture production was 103% of the indicated plumbing fixture demand. Thus in 1953 there was a 3% deviation between actual production and calculated demand.

road, utilities, commercial, institutional, and farm construction, all in the category of private construction, and highways, street and water systems, schools, administrative buildings military, and "all others," all in the category of public construction. Particular demand factors exist which are significant to each of these subgroups, and the division of the construction industry into homogeneous classes such as these makes it possible to obtain more reliable measures of the actual demand forces that are at work.

After establishing a basis for classification, the actual techniques of measurement are fairly similar, with moderate variations employed in accordance with the particular product group in question, the availability of data, and the time period covered, that is, annual analyses, seasonal analyses, and so forth. Basically, the procedure is as follows. First, a series which can be satisfactorily forecast and which measures the changes in activity in each major end-use market is constructed. Second, each series is weighted according to its importance as a market for the specific product involved. Third, the separate weighted series are combined into a single end-use index, which then becomes the main independent variable in the analysis. And fourth, sales of the product are then correlated with this end-use series to obtain a measure of relationship. "Time" may also be incorporated as a second independent variable, thereby producing a net growth trend which explains most of the variations that remain after employing the end-use index. These techniques, as well as those developed in previous chapters, can thus be readily applied to an analysis and forecast of virtually any type of product.

QUESTIONS

1. Describe the nature of the classification employed in this chapter for forecasting sales of construction materials.
2. Outline briefly the basic steps involved in developing a model for forecasting sales of construction materials.
3. Can the end-use approach be employed in the forecasting of capital goods demand? Discuss.

INSTRUCTORS: Models in this and the previous chapter can serve as a strong basis for student projects. (See the Note to Instructors at the beginning of the book for specific suggestions.)

PART III

Forecasting the Total Economy

The previous chapters have illustrated the various ways in which econometrics can be employed as a forecasting tool by individual firms. Against this background, we turn now to a dicussion of some further theory and applications of econometrics, with emphasis on its role both as a sophisticated branch of economic analysis and as a powerful tool for total business and economic prediction.

The approach taken in the following two chapters is to discuss, first, a few of the more important economic and statistical aspects of econometric model building, and second, to describe and evaluate two widely known econometric models of the total economy. Some of the relatively simple concepts derived in previous chapters will be developed further, by introducing more realistic and complicated factors. In general, the discussion will be on a somewhat higher plane than any of the other chapters in the book, because aggregate or "macroeconometrics," which deals with models of the total economy (as distinguished from "microeconometrics" or models of individual sectors), involves uniquely complex economic and statistical problems which do not lend themselves to elementary exposition. Nevertheless, every effort will be made to present a treatment which is fairly comprehensible to the typical business or economics student who possesses only a modest background in statistics and economic theory.

Chapter 10

PRINCIPLES OF AGGREGATE ECONOMETRIC MODEL CONSTRUCTION

ECONOMIC PROBLEMS OF AGGREGATE MODELS

All economic forecasting rests, in the final analysis, on forecasts of how the main segments of the economy—national income and production, consumption and investment, and so on—will behave. These aggregate estimates are not always, indeed not usually, made explicit, but they always lie in the background of any forecast, no matter how specialized. To forecast the sales of a particular department store, for example, the forecaster might use the future trend of department store sales in general, together with an estimate of trends in local income generation. Both these variables depend in turn—in their different ways—on retail sales and state income. And these again will probably move in line with even larger magnitudes, such as national consumption and national income respectively. He would be a rash man who would forecast growing sales for a particular store without paying serious attention to the expected movements in national aggregates. It would certainly be possible for a particular store, or district, or even state, to experience rising sales and income at a time of countrywide recession, but it would be unlikely; and even in the favorable case, the fall in the national levels would reduce the local rate of expansion.

The matters dealt with in this and the next chapter are therefore central to the forecaster's problem. Even though the industry specialist may lack the time or resources to prepare his own estimates of global magnitudes, he should be aware of the nature and reliability of those outside forecasts that he does use. This leads to a crucial requirement for any set of predictions of aggregate variables, the nature of which is best seen by a simple example. Let us suppose that, on the basis of past trends in the variable, the forecaster estimates that gross national product (GNP) will rise from $500 billion this year to $520 billion next year, and that, again on its own past trends, consumption (C) is expected by the forecaster to increase from $300 billion to $310 billion. But suppose that there in fact exists a simple, stable relationship between C and GNP, given by the equation

$$C = -50 + 0.7\,GNP \tag{1}$$

Then if the forecaster's estimate of *GNP* is correct, his estimate of consumption expenditures will be too low by $4 billion, since the true estimate given by (1) shows $314 billion—an error of almost 30 per cent on the true value of the change in consumption ($4 billion in $14 billion). Alternatively, if the estimator's figure of consumption is correct, then the estimate of *GNP* is too high, by about $5.7 billion—an error of almost 40 per cent on the true value of the increase.

Of course this is a *very* simple example. Consumption depends on several other variables besides *GNP*—past levels of consumption, taxes, liquid assets, and stocks of consumer durables, to name only a few—and even the more sophisticated versions do not hold exactly; there is always a small unexplained residual to the most carefully thought out and fitted equation. But few would deny that *GNP* is a major influence on consumption, and that movements in the two variables are to some extent interrelated. This means that our forecasts of the various aggregate variables must be *consistent* with each other, that they must form an *integrated* set of predicted values, reflecting the underlying system of relationships between the variables concerned. Our hypothesis is that such an underlying *structure*, as it is usually called, exists and is sufficiently *uniform* through time to permit predictions to be based on our estimated approximations to it with a fair degree of accuracy.

It must be emphasized that this assumption is basic to all econometric studies, not just to complete models. Although grounded in economic theory, each application of the hypothesis must be justified in any particular situation. By careful selection among the various specifications suggested by economic theory, according to their explanatory power, one may be able to build a theoretical model of the actual structure that has considerable uniformity through time. For example, one may start out with the simple specification that consumption (C) is linearly related to disposable national income (Y_D), and estimate the two coefficients involved—slope and intercept. Suppose that this has been done using annual data from 1921 to 1955 (29 observations, excluding the war years 1941–46). Then the model may be tested for uniformity by seeing how well, given the actual Y_D in each of the years 1956–60, it "predicts" C in those years. If the results are close, then we have a uniform structure and *a fortiori* a forecasting equation in which we can place some reliance.

But if the results are not close, then two alternatives present themselves: (*a*) either C really does fluctuate rather wildly, so that it admits no uniform explanatory structure, or much more likely, (*b*) one or more important additional explanatory variables, suggested by theoretical considerations, have been omitted—for example, liquid assets in the hands of consumers or consumer loan interest rates. One may then add these to form a specification which is considerably more uniform, in the sense of the test described above. Eventually this iterative procedure of experimenting with different structures will usually produce uniformity in this sense, though there are cases where alternative (*a*) seems the only reasonable one; such cases usually turn out in practice to apply to variables the range of fluctuation of which is quite small.

A uniform structure may be said to have been achieved when the residuals from the test (that is, actual C minus estimated C, using the true values of Y_D) are both "small" and randomly distributed in sign. (There exist statistical tests for the randomness of such runs of signs; see the more advanced texts cited in the bibliography in the Appendix.) A great temptation for beginning students is to try to add variables to the specification until as much as possible of the residual variance in the original data (in this case of 1921–55) is "explained." But a moment's thought will lead one to realize that it is usually possible to find *some* time series, no matter how irrelevant to the problem at hand, the addition of which will improve the original fit; or, failing that, to cook up some compound variable, without much economic meaning, which will equally well turn the trick. The addition of a time-trend term is far too often an example of this. In a minority of cases, it is true that there is a genuine and otherwise inexplicable persistent trend; much more often, it is a trick by the forecaster (or estimator of the past structure) to improve the fit of the equation without too much trouble or attention to meaningful structure.

The addition of such correlation-maniac's variables may play havoc with good forecasting, since there is little reason to expect them to contribute to a uniform structure. One must be very careful to retain only those that have a clear economic meaning for the problem at hand. The choice among variables that this problem involves is therefore an example of the *art* of the econometrician. There are no definite rules about such selection, and wisdom in the choice of specifications comes only with experience and maturity in the handling of econometric models. Perhaps the surest safeguard against the crass empiricism implicit in such doubtful procedures as that discussed above—no different in essence from that of naïve forecasting techniques—is for the econometrician to possess a solid basis in rigorous economic theory and a wide practical knowledge of how the economic system concerned actually works.[1]

[1] An analogy may be helpful here in clarifying this crucial point. In baseball it is not always or even usually the case that the best batters attain the season's highest batting averages. Random forces intervene in any one season which sometimes drive relative mediocrities to the top. The test of a good performer is the ability to maintain consistently high averages from season to season. Similarly a particular equation may perform well with a given set of data, but unless it has true quality (that is, faithfully reflects the true uniform structure), it will not predict further data well. We use the terminology "uniform structure" and "uniformity" in preference to the more appropriate words "stable structure" and "stability," since these latter words have a different and well-established meaning in economic theory; for similar reasons we do not use the words "constant structure" or "constancy."

Multiple Equation Systems

So far we have been dealing with structures or models consisting only of single equations. Matters become considerably more complicated when moving on to multiequation models. Let us take as a simple example that already given in Chapter 1, the do-it-yourself model invented by *Business Week*. Changing their notation a little to match our uniform symbolism, we write in addition to C and GNP, Y = national income; I = investment; T = tax receipts; and G = government expenditures. All these variables refer to the current year, denoted by a subscript t; in addition the model employs P_{t-1} = last year's profits. Since there are five variables to predict (Y_t, GNP_t, T_t, I_t and C_t) we need a five-equation model. The model reads

$$C_t = aY_t + b \tag{2}$$
$$I_t = cP_{t-1} + d \tag{3}$$
$$T_t = eGNP_t \tag{4}$$
$$GNP_t \equiv C_t + I_t + G_t \tag{5}$$
$$Y_t \equiv GNP_t - T_t \tag{6}$$

We write $\equiv$ in the last two equations to denote that these are *identities*, reflecting definitions of the variables involved, to be contrasted with the *behavior* equations (2) and (3) which reflect the way in which people—consumers and investors respectively—are assumed to behave, and the *institutional* equation (4) which makes explicit our very simple assumptions about the institutional restraints, in the form of the tax system, under which the economic system as a whole operates. A more extended model would also include *technical* equations, such as production functions.

Now if we substitute for Y_t in (2) from (6) we get

$$C_t = a(GNP_t - T_t) + b \tag{2a}$$

and substituting further for GNP_t and T_t from (5) and (4) respectively, we obtain

$$C_t = a(C_t + I_t + G_t) - aeGNP_t + b \tag{2b}$$

and again substituting for GNP_t

$$C_t = a(1-e)(C_t + I_t + G_t) + b \tag{2c}$$

which may be written

$$C_t = \frac{a(1-e)}{1 - a(1-e)}(I_t + G_t) + \frac{b}{1 - a(1-e)} \tag{2d}$$

It is tempting to say that we have replaced the independent variable Y_t in (2) by the independent variables I_t and G_t in (2d). But in what sense can either Y_t or I_t be considered independent? There are equations explaining each of them [(3) and (6)] already contained in the model! They are therefore in no sense variables independent of the *system*, and it is misleading to use the word independent at all in this context. Thus, equation (2d) is still not in a suitable form for forecasting purposes since I_t cannot move freely but has to obey the behavior relation (3).[2] The only truly independent variable in (2d) is current government expenditure G_t, which may plausibly be taken to be dependent mainly on factors *outside* the normal economic system, such as defense policy, social policy, and so on. Such variables are called *exogenous*, in contrast to the *endogenous* or *jointly dependent* variables (in this case Y_t, C_t, I_t, T_t, GNP_t) determined within and by the system. It must be emphasized that these terms only have meaning in the context of a particular theoretical model. A variable such as "exports from the United States" may be considered exogenous to a relatively simple model for the U.S. economy, but would be endogenous to a model attempting to explain movements in the whole world economy.

Generally speaking, the model builder will try to reduce the number of exogenous variables in his model to as few as possible, and to try to make those as predictable as he can by choosing, for example, demographic variables in the short run. On the other hand, he must also recognize that some variables simply are not determined by the day-to-day workings of the economic system but do help to determine the performance of that system. For a large country such as the United States, the most important exogenous variables for a short-run economy-wide forecasting model are those relating to government, such as expenditure, tax rates, and the quantity of bank money. For small countries, such crucially important variables as import prices and export prices are substantially determined outside their borders, and must therefore be regarded as exogenous in any meaningful model of the relevant economy.

Equation (2d) may be taken further by combining it with (3) to produce

$$C_t = \frac{ca(1-e)}{1-a(1-e)}P_{t-1} + \frac{a(1-e)}{1-a(1-e)}G_t + \frac{da(1-e)+b}{1-a(1-e)} \qquad (2e)$$

or, writing the coefficients more simply,

$$= a_1 P_{t-1} + a_2 G_t + a_3 \qquad (2f)$$

We have now explained C_t in terms of two nonendogenous variables, namely G_t (already discussed), and last year's profits.[3] Therefore, provided that we have made good estimates of a_1, a_2 and a_3, and that we make reasonable guesses as to what government expenditure will be (and provided that our model has a good uniform structure), then (2f) will enable

[2] Notice that our earlier example pointed to the need for the forecaster to take into account that a behavioral relation may exist between any pair of variables in making his predictions. The present example extends this by showing that he must take into account the whole *system* of relations governing the variables in which he is interested.

[3] Observe that since each equation of the model is linear, the forecasting equation is also linear. Linear systems predominate in practice because of their ease in handling. However both of the models discussed at length in the next chapter contain significant nonlinearities, the second model particularly so. This makes it more realistic but also that much more difficult to solve.

us to predict, say, next year's consumption from this year's data. But it does not enable us to go any further into the future than that, unless we are prepared either (*a*) to make profits an exogenous variable, guessing at its likely future values, or (*b*) to enlarge the model in order to make profits an endogenous variable (dare one say to "endogenize" profits?). Clearly procedure (*b*) is theoretically and practically the better course; the volume of profits earned is obviously not independent of the level of prosperity. Therefore, we might hypothesize that current profits depend linearly upon current national income and *last* year's investment expenditure. The relevant equation would read

$$P_t = kY_t + 1I_{t-1} + m \tag{7}$$

Substituting this expression for P_{t-1} in (2) we find that

$$I_t = ckY_{t-1} + c1I_{t-2} + cm + d \tag{3a}$$

Notice that we now have an equation explaining a current endogenous variable partly as a function of its *own* past values. Putting this explanation of I_t into (2f) via (2d) we obtain

$$C_t = a_1 kY_{t-1} + a_1 1I_{t-2} + a_2 G_t + a_1 m + a_3 \tag{2g}$$

Prediction from Complete Models

Notice that (2g) enables us now to predict indefinitely far into the future, given only the estimated course of the exogenous variable G_t, and initial values for the *lagged endogenous* variables Y_{t-1} and I_{t-2}. We would require, for example, 1959 national income (one-year lag), 1958 investment (two-year lag), and current government expenditure (exogenous) in order to predict 1960 consumption. But we could go on to predict 1961 consumption, for we would know 1959 investment, and the rest of the system would give us a value for 1960 national income. Again we could obtain 1962 consumption, using 1961 income and the 1960 value of investment given by the model, and so on.

In order to see this clearly, it is necessary to transform our set of six equations (2)–(7) to a set of six equations each like (2g), that is, each with a current endogenous variable on the left-hand side and *only* exogenous and/or lagged endogenous variables on the right-hand side of each equation. (These two latter types of variable—exogenous and lagged endogenous—are usually known collectively as the *predetermined variables* of the model.) If we do this, and adopt a new simple and uniform notation for the coefficients in each equation, we will get the transformed set given by

$$
\begin{aligned}
C_t &= c_{21}Y_{t-1} & &+ c_{23}I_{t-2} + c_{24}G_t + c_{25} & (2R)\\
I_t &= c_{31}Y_{t-1} & &+ c_{33}I_{t-2} \qquad\;\; + c_{35} & (3R)\\
T_t &= c_{41}Y_{t-1} & &+ c_{43}I_{t-2} + c_{44}G_t + c_{45} & (4R)\\
GNP_t &= c_{51}Y_{t-1} & &+ c_{53}I_{t-2} + c_{54}G_t + c_{55} & (5R)\\
Y_t &= c_{61}Y_{t-1} & &+ c_{63}I_{t-2} + c_{64}G_t + c_{65} & (6R)\\
P_t &= c_{71}Y_{t-1} + c_{72}I_{t-1} &+ &c_{73}I_{t-2} + c_{74}G_t + c_{75} & (7R)
\end{aligned}
$$

This set is obtained by taking (2g) and (3a), and working back from them through the system (4)–(7), in each case substituting expressions involving only predetermined variables. The coefficients c_{ij} written here so simply are of course quite complicated combinations of the coefficients of the original structural equations. Thus c_{71} is in fact $\dfrac{ck^2(1-e)}{1-a(1-e)}$, and c_{45} consists of the following terms:

$$\frac{acm(1-e)+ad(1-e)+b+cm+d}{1-a(1-e)}$$

Such a set of equations showing the explicit dependence of each dependent (that is, current endogenous variable) on the predetermined variables, is known as the "reduced form" of the model. Strictly speaking, this use of terminology is incorrect and without qualification would cause some qualms on the part of the technical econometrician, who formulates his equations as random relationships (discussed in the next section). The term "reduced form" was in fact given originally only to the corresponding concept in these systems of "stochastic" equations, as they are called, but is perfectly applicable here, where we are temporarily abstracting from statistical problems.

An interesting question is whether, knowing the coefficients c_{ij}, we can always get back to the coefficients of the original structural set. This is called the *identification problem* and again was originally formulated and has more importance in a stochastic context. It happens that our particular model is "identified" so that we can get back to the original model; indeed it is *over* identified. But it is quite possible that none or only a few equations in a model could be identified, that is, could be solved for the original coefficients in terms of the coefficients of the reduced form. Fundamentally, the trouble springs from the fact that the same reduced form can originate from more than one basic structure, so that in passing back from the reduced form, one may end up not necessarily with the unique original structure, but with any one of a whole set of such structures. The classical example is simple supply and demand analysis, where the data consist of market purchases and prices. Do these price-quantity series describe a demand function or a supply function, or some definite mixture of both? The answer will depend on the way in which the supply and demand functions and market adjustment mechanisms are formulated (i.e. with lags or not), but in the simplest model the answer is simply no; supply and demand curves will be inextricably mingled together by the observational data.[4]

[4] The best introductory work on identification is by T. C. Koopmans in Chapter II of *Studies in Econometric Method*, cited in the bibliography. The standard texts of Klein, Tintner and Valavanis all deal with the problem, which was perhaps first clearly stated by E. J. Working in 1927, in an article now reprinted in George J. Stigler and Kenneth E. Boulding (eds.), *Readings in Price Theory* (Homewood, Ill.: Richard D. Irwin, Inc., 1951).

It is very clear from the reduced form that, given initial values of Y and I and the projected course of government spending, it is possible to forecast all seven variables once we know the coefficients c_{ij}. To find Y_{1960} we need Y_{1959} and I_{1958}, plus G_{1960}. This value of Y_{1960} may then be used, in conjunction with I_{1959} and G_{1961} to find C_{1961}, I_{1961}, T_{1961} and GNP_{1961}, and with the addition of I_{1960} [forecast from (3R) using Y_{1959}, and I_{1958}] to forecast P_{1961}. The way in which subsequent years are forecast is plain; the entire interdependent model generates, with the aid of the exogenous variable G_t, the whole course of seven of the most important aggregate variables in the economy.

Notice that the reduced-form equations do not have the fairly obvious behavioral implications of the original model. They are the forecasting equations derived by algebraic manipulation of the original model. For strictly prediction purposes, with an unchanged structure, the reduced form is all that the forecaster needs. The coefficients of the reduced form are not *structural* coefficients in our original sense; for example, it is not possible to find out directly from the reduced form the value of the marginal propensity to consume, to use a well-known Keynesian concept, nor to find the value of the accelerator, even if it occurs in the original model. The student has been told that it is possible to go back if the equation is identified, but this ignores the realistic case where the equations concerned are stochastic; in that event, the interpretation of the structural coefficients derived from going back is usually not nearly so clear.

For some purposes, then, all that one needs is the reduced form. Its use here has been to bring out clearly the explicit or implicit dependence of each current endogenous variable on the predetermined variables. But for many other purposes it is essential also to know the coefficients of the original model—the *structural parameters*. For example, a change in the basic tax schedules would alter the structural parameters in (4), and although it is certainly possible then to recompute all the coefficients of the reduced form equations, it would be simpler and more meaningful to work with the original model.

Conclusion

The purpose of this first section has been to make clear that the concept of a general model or system of equations is a very powerful tool, enabling us to deploy the insights gained by many years of vigorous economic theorizing from Walras and Marshall to Keynes and beyond. Our particular example of a model has been fairly simple, purely for expository purposes; such a simple model is unlikely to have a sufficiently uniform structure for forecasting purposes, and actual models used for serious forecasting or analysis of past structure are considerably more complex. In the next chapter we shall take two of the most important complete econometric models, those of Klein-Goldberger and of the Econometric Institute, and examine their salient characteristics. But first we must repair a serious omission that has been made so far. In trying to explain the main concepts clearly, we have deliberately concentrated on the economic aspects of model building; but there are some very important statistical problems in connection with model construction, problems which have called forth some brilliant original research into previously unexplored areas of statistical inference, and which are inherent in all of this kind of work. It is to these problems that we now turn.

THE STATISTICAL BASIS OF ECONOMETRIC MODELS

It would be quite beyond the scope of this book to go into the statistical problems of model building in any detail. All that we can reasonably do in the short space available is to indicate the nature of a few of the problems involved, especially those most relevant to forecasting, and to guide the student to further reading. A thorough grasp of these matters requires a certain sophistication in statistical theory and mathematics; accordingly, the classified bibliography in the Appendix at the end of the book includes some basic statistical and mathematical textbooks to assist those who wish to pursue statistical analysis to a higher level.

"Unexplained" Factors: The Residual u_t

So far our formal exposition has deliberately left to one side one of the most central problems in econometrics. We have been arguing almost entirely as though our relations held *exactly*, as though, for example, if we knew the structural parameters of the consumption equation (2), we could forecast consumption exactly. More importantly, we have implied that the past series on consumption and income have obeyed (2) exactly. This is of course silly, only to be justified as a necessary technique of analytical exposition. The only structural equations that are obeyed exactly are the identities, which simply reflect the definitions that we—or the Department of Commerce—have agreed to use. Even the identities do not necessarily hold when there are errors of measurement, as is common enough in economic time series. Thus there is usually a statistical discrepancy between the two estimates of *GNP* calculated from the income and the product sides respectively, but this is usually small and random in effect. In this exposition we shall neglect almost entirely the problem of errors in measurement and the further problem of serial correlation. A useful first reference on both of these very important problems is Tintner's book, mentioned in the Appendix.

None of the other structural equations—behavioral, institutional, and technical—can be expected to hold exactly. The actual observations that we make are generated by a very complicated world from which our theoretical model can only hope to isolate the principal causal factors. There are a great many influences on national consumption, for example, and our model, if it is to remain simple enough for operational usefulness, specifies only those which theoretical considerations, practical knowledge, and the model builder's intuition consider the most important. Thus we might suppose that C_t depends on Y_t, Y_{t-1}, and C_{t-1} in the following way:

$$C_t = b_1 Y_t + b_2 Y_{t-1} + b_3 C_{t-1} + b_4 \qquad (8)$$

But because these are only our guesses of the principal factors affecting C_t, there will remain always a part of the value of C_t which is not explained by movements in the variables on the right-hand side. Sometimes the linear combination of these given by (8) will overstate the value of C_t actually observed, and sometimes they will understate it.[5] Therefore if we are to make (8) hold exactly, we must insert a further variable u_t (u being mnemonic for "unexplained") which, as it were, will "take up the slack" in the equation. Then our *randomized* or *stochastic* equation will read:

$$C_t = b_1 Y_t + b_2 Y_{t-1} + b_3 C_{t-1} + b_4 + u_t \qquad (8a)$$

Notice that u_t does not need a coefficient, since by definition it assumes the values required of it; unlike the other variables in the equation, it cannot be directly observed, so that there is no point in imputing a coefficient to it. An alternative and in some ways more enlightening way of writing (8a) is

$$u_t = C_t - b_1 Y_t - b_2 Y_{t-1} - b_3 C_{t-1} - b_4 \qquad (8b)$$

which says that u_t is the *residual* between the observed series C_t and the linear combination of the three observed series represented by the right-hand side of (8).

The whole statistical basis of econometrics turns on the properties that this residual may reasonably be expected to have. If we have truly isolated the main influences on C_t, the remaining influences will be a mixture of all sorts of small effects, some pulling one way, some the other, and some fluctuating both ways in effect. The cumulated effect of all these minor variables will therefore tend to be chance or random in operation, and hence u_t will be a *random variable*, whose expected value is likely to be close to zero, and which is also likely—since it is the sum of a number of small, presumably independent effects—to have a normal distribution.[6]

[5] Often, of course, errors of observation will cause the true value of C_t to be under- or overstated; but this is also true of the other variables in the equation. Stochastic models designed explicitly to take into account errors in observation, as well as errors in specification, involve much more difficulty, and have been little developed. It is doubtful whether they would lead to a substantive gain in predictive power, though perhaps they would improve our structural knowledge considerably.

[6] See any good textbook on statistics or probability for the proof of this classic *central limit theorem*, which is basic to a large part of statistical theory. In econometric models we also require that the value of u_t be independent of the values assumed by u_{t-1}, u_{t-2}, etc., so that u_t be serially uncorrelated. One often effective device for getting over this problem is the use of first differences, discussed in Chapter 4. For completeness' sake we should add that we require that the variance of our residual u_t be constant over time, which means essentially that the multitude of small causes underlying the random term should remain more or less constant in composition from period to period.

Moreover, it is also probable, as it is desirable, that it will be uncorrelated, or statistically independent, of movements in the observable explanatory variables.

All these required properties of the "disturbance term," as it is some-times called, turn on the correctness of the specification. If the model builder has left out some important structural variables, then it is unlikely that u_t will be a "normal" random variable with an average value of zero. It is more likely to have a systematic bias in its operation, and perhaps also to be correlated with movements of the explanatory variables; the same will apply, *mutatis mutandis*, if some inessential variables have been in-cluded. Notice that the ideal is not to make each value of u_t as small as possible, but to ensure that it is a *chance variable*. Of course the smaller its average value the better, but not at the cost of systematic bias, for such bias will turn out very badly when forecasting. It is generally better that one's predictions should be as likely to be too low as too high, rather than that they should systematically be on one side or the other. This is especially clear when forecasting for more than one period ahead; in this case pre-dicted data are required in order to produce predictions for further time periods.

Estimation Problems for Systems of Stochastic Equations

The classical method of making statistical estimates of the parameters b_1, b_2, b_3 and b_4 is to take a least-squares regression of the dependent vari-able C_t on the independent variables Y_t, Y_{t-1} and C_{t-1}. Since our data usually consist of a fairly small sample of observations on the structural relationship at work, our estimates will not be the true values of the param-eters, but only approximations to these values. It would be desirable that the larger the sample of independent observations,[7] the more closely our estimates approximate the true values; it would also be nice if on average we could expect our estimates to be close to the true values, rather than to be-tray a systematic bias. It so happens that, provided our conditions on u_t are satisfied and provided our independent variables really are independent,[8] our least-squares estimates possess both these properties of *consistency* and

---

[7] The word independent is essential here. The use of quarterly, monthly, or weekly series provide much more data, enabling us to see the relationship at work more often, and thus gain more information. But a corresponding price has to be paid, not only of harder processing work, but also because the problems of serial correlation and—sometimes—errors in observation are often more pressing the shorter the observa-tional period.

[8] We require also that the independent variables be independent of each other, that is, that they not be strongly intercorrelated (see Chapter 4). If they are—the con-dition is termed "multicollinearity" by Ragnar Frisch—the estimates of the parameters tend to fluctuate wildly with the omission or addition of an independent variable, and lose much of their significance.

unbiasedness respectively, as well as a few others; indeed, under these conditions the two basically different methods of least-squares and of maximum likelihood estimation mentioned earlier actually coincide and produce exactly the same results.

A slight word of warning is in order here. To be formally correct, it is necessary for the validity of these conclusions, and therefore of the inferences that we draw concerning the reliability and significance of the estimates, that the model be hypothesized independently of the data to which it is fitted. Now neither economic theory nor the forecaster's intuition is usually sufficiently developed to permit such sublime self-confidence. Every good econometrician will experiment on the data with different models (different variables and/or functional forms), before he arrives at one which he feels has a sufficiently uniform structure—or until his research resources run out. In either case the resulting model is not independent of the data, so that statistical tests of significance have to some extent to be taken with a grain of salt. This is as much a commentary on the current state of statistical theory as it is on the procedure of the econometrician; methods need to be devised that can test such nonindependent estimates.

The reader must bear in mind that the words *consistency* and *unbiasedness* used in this section are technical statistical concepts, and bear no relation to the use of similar terms in an economic context earlier in the chapter. The word "good" is used below in quotation marks for the reason that estimates that are not "good" are not necessarily at all bad, merely inconsistent and/or biased—in the statistical sense. One other technical point: least-squares estimation usually gives biased results, but maximum likelihood usually does, too. Maximum likelihood possesses very desirable asymptotic properties (see below) such as consistency and efficiency, but bias does not depend on sample size.

It would be tempting to conclude from this discussion that, provided we have been clever enough to specify the model well, so that the residuals obey our assumptions reasonably enough, least-squares estimation will produce "good" estimates of our parameters. But here we must call to mind the economic discussion of the last section. There is no sense in which all the variables on the right-hand side of (8a) can be said to be independent, for Y_t should clearly, in any forecasting scheme, be just as much an endogenous variable as is C_t, although it is true that Y_{t-1} and C_{t-1} are predetermined. We have seen that the words "independent variables" must be replaced, in a complete model, by "predetermined variables." Only when all the right-hand sides of equations like (8a) contain only predetermined variables can we be sure—without further investigation into the model's anatomy—that least-squares (l.s.) estimation will produce estimates with the desirable properties. We can see immediately that l.s. estimation of each equation separately of the reduced form of the model will give consistent estimates of the parameters of the *reduced form*. But it does not necessarily follow that the estimates of the parameters of the structural equations, arrived at by solving back from the stochastic equations of the reduced form through to the stochastic equations of the model, will also necessarily be "good" estimates; only in a very special case—the just-identified case, unlikely in practice—will this be so.

The basic problem is that, in a complete model, the usual distinction in regression analysis between dependent and independent variables has to assume new forms. Earlier analysts of the demand for food, for example, worried about whether they should take the regression of the "dependent" variable, quantity demanded, on the "independent" variable, price, or *vice versa*. Which was the dependent and which the independent variable? It is important to realize that the two different choices produce quite different results for the forecaster. But we can now see that the economic requirement that the forecaster specify the complete model which generated his observations, leads him to recognize that as a result his statistical procedures may have to be modified.

Such modifications in our estimating procedures were worked out, principally by statisticians associated with the Cowles Commission at the University of Chicago (now the Cowles Foundation at Yale), during the late 1940's. The statistical techniques needed to take full account of this "simultaneous-equations" approach are formidable in the extreme and expensive in computation time; they have seldom been used in practice. A somewhat less complicated method, much easier computationally, was also devised at Chicago, which meets many, though not all, of the conceptual objections made above; this is known as the *limited-information method*. So forceful and cogent were the criticisms of the Cowles Commission, and so impressive and obscure the alternative apparatus that they provided, that economists began to develop a feeling that, as Karl Fox has put it, least-squares estimation of single structural equations in a complete model is "wrong," and simultaneous-equations methods of estimation "right."

It must be made quite clear that the question here is not whether general models should be constructed as interdependent systems—they should, as indicated by the most elementary economic theory. The question is whether in estimating the parameters of this interdependent structure, the statistician should alter his classical methods originally devised for estimating parameters of single-equation models, not necessarily economic models. Of course for many single sectors of the economy, single equations are a reasonably good approximation from the economic point of view, and they have been extensively used and discussed in Part II. Similarly, least-squares estimation is usually appropriate for each such equation. But they all logically require exogenous variables which are usually endogenous to a complete economy-wide model; hence, scientific sectoral forecasting, as we emphasized early in this chapter, requires an underlying complete model, which it is better to have made explicit.

Defenses of Least-Squares Regression

In recent years, however, there has been a resurgence of interest in the applicability of least-squares regression estimates in complete models. This attack of the counterreformation has come from three sides, which we shall discuss below, adding for good measure some more practical observations of our own.

First has been the empirical comparisons between l.s. estimates and limited information (l.i.) estimates, based on the same data. Using synthetic data constructed with the help of the so-called Monte Carlo technique of producing mock-ups of actual stochastic models,[9] Wagner tested the performance of l.s. and l.i. estimators in each of two sets of 100 samples of only 20 observations on each variable. The reason behind this procedure is that many of the theoretical advantages of l.i. estimates refer to *asymptotic* properties, that is, they tend to hold for samples with a very large number of observations. It does not necessarily follow, therefore, that these properties will also hold in small samples ("large" and "small" are relative terms here; perhaps 100 observations is a rough-and-ready dividing line). In fact, one of the l.i. properties did not hold in Wagner's samples, namely that of (asymptotic) *efficiency*. By this we mean that the l.i. estimates show a smaller sampling variability than any other such estimator, provided that the samples are large. In Wagner's set of samples, the sampling variability of the l.s. estimates was less than that of the l.i. method; but the l.s. estimates were more biased. On the one hand, then, l.s. estimates tended not to fluctuate so wildly as l.i. estimates, but on the other, this lessened fluctuation was not around the true value. Whether l.i. estimates are therefore "better" than l.s. estimates seems, in this example, a question of which criterion is more relevant to the question at hand.

A commonly accepted criterion of error (though by no means sacred) is to take the average squared value of the residuals. This can be expressed as an additive function of the squared bias and the sampling variance of the estimators; thus one can see that, on this test, l.s. may in fact be definitely better than l.i., depending on the size of bias to the size of variability. More complicated criteria of performance, for example, those suggested by statistical decision theory, often reduce in practice to the average squared error criterion, since this is the usual *loss function* of decision theory. There are theoretical reasons for this similarity of l.s. and l.i. estimates in small samples, which are mentioned in the papers by Fox and Christ cited at the end of the book.

In another piece of empirical testing, this time with real data, Karl Fox estimated the parameters of the Klein-Goldberger model by l.s. and compared them with Klein-Goldberger's original l.i. estimates. He found

---

[9] Monte Carlo methods are in wide use in the physical sciences, where they often afford easier routes to solving complex physical systems. The reference for Wagner's paper is given in the bibliography, as are all the other references.

strikingly little difference in estimates generated from the same data with the two different methods; and where there was some substantial discrepancy, as when the same coefficients estimated by the different methods had different signs, economic considerations indicated the superiority of the l.s. estimates.

The second approach—a detailed account of which lies beyond our object in this chapter—has been the invention of new estimating techniques which take some cognizance of the simultaneity of the model, but which are at the same time considerably simpler computationally than the Cowles Foundation methods. The principal figures in this development are Theil and Basmann, who independently developed strikingly similar approaches, the best name for which appears to be that of Theil, "two-stage least-squares"; for a good account, see Theil's recent book on forecasting.

The two-stage least-squares method consists essentially of the following: obtain the reduced form of the model and estimate it by l.s.; then from this reduced form, based on the known predetermined variables in the past, calculate the past values of the endogenous variables (the true values of these, of course, are already given by one's observations, but here we construct an artificial series). Then in any equation containing current endogenous variables on the right-hand side, as well as the left, use these estimated series of "observations" as the data for the right-hand side endogenous variables, and estimate the desired equation(s) by ordinary least-squares. Estimates obtained in this curious but relatively simple way possess many of the desirable large-sample statistical properties lacked by least-squares. Theil shows in fact that l.s., l.i., and "two-stage least-squares" all belong to a general class—the "K-class"—of estimating methods.

The third approach is methodologically much deeper and is associated mainly with Wold and, to a lesser extent, Strotz. This attacks the simultaneous-equation approach at its roots, denying the logical superiority which is claimed for it. The issues involved here are philosophical in nature, reflecting one's basic views about the organization of reality, and are reminiscent of the battle concerning the foundations of mathematics between the intuitionists and the believers in transfinite induction.

Wold maintains that most general systems are fundamentally *causal chains*, by which he means that we can almost always in principle isolate a causal sequence, however complicated, running from a causal variable, say x_1, which influences another, x_2, which in turn influences another, x_3 (probably in conjunction with x_1), and so on. Such a scheme can always be arranged in the following way. We adopt linear equations for convenience, but this is not necessary.

$$x_2 = a_{11} + a_{12}x_1$$
$$x_3 = a_{21} + a_{22}x_1 + a_{23}x_2$$
$$x_4 = a_{31} + a_{32}x_1 + a_{33}x_2 + a_{34}x_3$$
$$\cdots \cdots \cdots \cdots \cdots \cdots \cdots \cdots \cdots \cdots \cdots$$
$$x_n = a_{n-1,1} + a_{n-1,2}x_1 + a_{n-1,3}x_2 + \cdots \cdots \cdots + a_{n-1,n}x_{n-1}$$

(some of the coefficients can be zero, leaving "holes" in this triangular arrangement).

Such a system is *recursive*, that is, given only the value of one variable, x_1, one can solve in relatively easy successive stages for the rest. Each dependent variable can indeed be written solely as a function of x_1, probably of values of x_1 at different times, for in order to preserve simplicity we have ignored the fact that the scheme above is usually ordered in *time*. Hence the x_1 affecting x_3 may not be the same value of x_1 as that affecting x_2. To take a simple and unrealistic example, we might suppose that consumption of durable goods (x_2) at time t depends on the stock of durable goods (x_1) at time $(t-1)$; and that savings (x_3) at time t depends on the stock of durable goods at time t plus the consumption of durable goods at time t. One can then see that, using the first relationship, we can substitute for durable goods consumption at time t, and say that x_3 at time t depends on x_1 at time t and at time $(t-1)$. It is apparent that very complex causal time paths can be constructed, all of which reduce in the end to equations, however complicated, depending on x_1 alone; there might, for example, be a dozen or more terms involving x_1 at various times in the final solution of any endogenous variable. Such an equation, involving x_1 at different time periods, is called a *difference equation*.

We have written the recursive system in its exact form for simplicity. But, of course, for econometric work each equation of the system must have its random term u_t, preferably with the properties already discussed. Similarly, we have argued as though there were only one final (predetermined) variable such as x_1; in any actual model there will normally be several, and the "final" equations will accordingly contain terms involving some or all of these basic causal variables.

Conclusion. Linear recursive systems have two great virtues: (*a*) they are easy to solve, since the direction of causation always runs one way, and (*b*) least-squares estimation of the parameters of each equation, taken singly, produces estimates having many desirable statistical properties even though the equations are part of a complete model.[10] We do not have to bother with the reduced form. It is therefore clearly of great importance whether such systems can be regarded as good representations of reality. To discuss this at all adequately would lead us far too deep, but one very interesting and sophisticated interpretation of simultaneous-equations models is worth mentioning, even in as brief a treatment as this.

In this interpretation, "the world" is held to be basically recursive, to be accounted for by a causal chain model. But the time lags involved are held to be so short, relative to the data available, that this temporal chain aspect of the model has to be suppressed, and it emerges as a simultaneous-equations model. Thus, the reactions in the behavioral equations of the recursive model may run in terms of weeks, days, or even hours, whereas

---

[10] This result, due to Wold, is valid under very general conditions, the most important of which is that the residuals be uncorrelated with the explanatory variables.

the data may only be annual. In such an event, we are forced to construct a model which eliminates all these brief lags, and concentrate on the grosser elements of the system. For example, we may have, in the simultaneous-equations model, current (annual) consumption dependent on current (annual) income, even though we may have good reasons for believing that in fact there is a one-week or one-month lag in consumption after receipt of income. Such a fine structure cannot withstand the blunderbuss of our crude data collection system. Notice that models based on, say, quarterly data, even though they bring their own problems, as we have seen, may therefore have the additional advantage of enabling a more recursive system to be articulated, and therefore may give us greater confidence in least-squares estimation.

The State of the Debate

What are we to make of this argument over methods of estimation? So far it has borne all the marks of the dialectic: thesis by the Cowles Foundation—antithesis by the "conservatives"—and a synthesis in the work of Theil and his colleagues. It is in the latter direction that the most promising line of approach would appear to be found. The supposition that the world is necessarily a causal chain seems difficult to swallow, and, more importantly, almost inherently untestable. It seems more reasonable to suppose that some functional relationships do operate simultaneously. Yet one is reluctant to abandon the relative flexibility of least-squares type methods for too heavy a reliance on methods apparently theoretically more satisfactory; with the increased use of high-speed computers, however, it can be maintained that there is comparatively less advantage to the flexibility of least-squares methods.

There are some tricky unresolved problems here which would repay further investigation. For example, both the simultaneous-equations approach and Wold's methods very properly lay stress on the need to formulate the model in advance of the statistical estimation methods used (a corollary to this is the point, stressed by Valavanis, is that different types of forecasting situations may call for different estimation methods). Thus, when we take into account the structure of the whole model in estimating any particular equation, we are making an implicit assumption that our model is a reasonable reflection of reality. But what if this is not so? How adversely are the desirable statistical properties of our estimates affected, even though made by the most refined methods, when our model is not "right"? Little work has yet been done on this topic, which would not be relevant in a perfect world, where we could pursue the two goals, refining the model and refining the statistical methods, without thought of limitations on research resources.

In a world where choice is still a necessity, however, it is an open question as to which avenue to pursue most vigorously. In any actual situation the choice will probably depend on the investigator's temperament as much as on the objective needs of the study, which can never be known exactly. It is perhaps significant that those econometricians who have done most empirical work have—with the notable exception of Klein—tended to be conservative in their estimation methods, preferring to devote more time to improving the data available to them and to making better specifications; they have recently had the qualified but weighty support of Theil. The most ardent advocates of simultaneous-equations methods have tended not to pursue empirical work—again Klein is an exception, as is T. M. Brown. But of course these matters should be mainly a question of the distribution of the marginal amount of effort. It is just as perilous a procedure to concentrate on data improvement and to forget about problems of serial correlation, for example, as it is to devise delicate methods for a very crude explanatory equation. It is part of the flair of a good econometrician to know how to balance these requirements judiciously.

Linear and Nonlinear Models

All the methods developed so far apply to linear models. This is not so restrictive as it sounds, for it is possible, by introducing ratios, squares, logarithms of variables, and so forth, to make many nonlinear specifications linear in appearance. However, there are snags in this procedure. It will not usually do, for example, in a time series analysis to use current income and the square of current income, for these are highly intercorrelated. Similarly, one may in a particular equation use, say, the logarithm of new orders; this is all right if either (*a*) this is the only place in the model where new orders occurs, or (*b*) all the other equations containing the variable "new orders" have it also in logarithmic form. In either case we are dealing only with the variable "logarithm of new orders," which enters linearly into the model. If these conditions are not satisfied, however, then the system becomes nonlinear.

One interesting nonlinearity arises from the use of price and quantity indexes (see the section in the next chapter on the Klein-Goldberger model). In this case we have equations of the form, value = price × quantity, which is nonlinear in variables. By an ingenious trick, Tinbergen, in his famous study of the United States economy, linearized this multiplicative relation; but such a trick only holds adequately if the movements in the indexes are not too violent.

The problem of nonlinearity arises in the two main stages of statistical work, estimation of relationships and solution of the model (that is, feeding in values of exogenous variables and lagged endogenous variables in order to obtain predictions). For linear models, both these problems require considerable computation but are conceptually usually straightforward. For nonlinear models, the problems are much more severe. Since estimation methods for nonlinear simultaneous models are still only in their infancy, one is forced on to least squares for at least the nonlinear equations, or to more or less doubtful procedures of linearization. Solution of such nonlinear models can seldom be exact, and resort to iterative (trial-and-error) procedures is necessary.

All these complications mean, therefore, that the econometrician is usually very circumspect before allowing nonlinear relationships into his model. Provided that the expected range of variation of the variables is not very great, he is content to use his linear model, even though he thinks that the true structure is nonlinear. But sometimes, for example, at the crest of a boom, nonlinearity is of the essence of the problem, and loss of verisimilitude is too high a price to pay for computational convenience.

Computational Problems

Most complete aggregate econometric models call for formidable amounts of data processing—in the original preparation of series appropriate to the economic concepts of the model, in the estimation of the structural relationships, in the testing of hypotheses (serial correlation, significance of parameters, etc.), and in the preparation of predictions.

The advent of high-speed electronic computers has enormously widened the range of these models (in economics as in so many other sciences), and enabled far more complicated structures to be used. The Econometric Institute model, for example, discussed in the next chapter, already strains the memory capacity of the IBM 650, and will probably soon migrate to an IBM 704. Econometricians thus need a working familiarity with computer programming.

In some respects, one may regret the lessened dependence on more primitive methods of computing, such as automatic electric desk calculators, slide rules, or even graphic experimentation. These tools do necessitate a close confrontation of the student with the data, and although this introduces the danger of trying to fit the data well—to the detriment of good model building—it does mean that one gains greater insight into the nature of the processes which are actually at work. For experimental work, at least, the econometrician should retain the full battery of computational tools; the era of the megaton bomb has not completely done away with the necessity for infantry. It is greatly to be hoped that larger, more efficient and cheaper high-speed computers will become available, so that ever more realistic models may be constructed. But it is unlikely that the construction of a complete model adequate for forecasting purposes will ever be anything but an expensive business, requiring considerable research resources.

THE EVOLUTION OF MODEL BUILDING

In order to appreciate fully the nature of the achievements of model building to date, and the tasks that lie ahead, it is worthwhile to trace briefly the ways in which model building has developed. In doing so, we concentrate entirely on the evolution of general models and their problems; this is not an account of the history of econometrics as a whole, which would have to lay stress on the contributions of Irving Fisher, Charles Roos, Henry Schultz, and many others.

As so often happens with the history of ideas, it is difficult to say precisely how the concept of an aggregate econometric model took hold. Many streams of economic and statistical ideas contributed to it. The development of mathematical economics and of general equilibrium theorizing which took place in the last quarter of the nineteenth century, the growth of statistical theory at the hands of Karl Pearson and R. A. Fisher, and the continuing tradition of demand analysis among U.S. agricultural economists, all certainly played their part. Perhaps the most proximate cause was the remarkable work in mathematical economics and statistics during the early 1930's by Ragnar Frisch in Norway, especially his work on *confluence analysis*, in which he tackled the problem of intercorrelation of the explanatory variables with great generality. His work directly inspired Tinbergen, who in 1939 produced his massive and pioneering econometric study of the U.S. economy. On the theoretical side, Frisch deeply influenced Haavelmo, who in 1943 was the first econometrician to publish a clear account of the nature of the simultaneous-equations problem in statistical estimation.[11]

After Tinbergen's great breakthrough, the development of simple aggregate economic models set off by Keynes's *General Theory* in 1936, enormously simplified the theoretical background of aggregate econometric models, although it is sad to relate that Keynes in his review of Tinbergen's contribution showed as much misunderstanding of, as opposition to, the nature of the Dutch economist's achievement. After the war, the Keynesian tools showed up well in the early models by Klein and by Clark (see the bibliography for references), while the development of new statistical techniques proceeded apace. Von Neumann had during the war made practical contributions to the study of serial correlation in time series, and further testing devices were developed afterwards. A major influence was the enormous progress in data collection, especially in the field of national income accounting. Klein's 1950 study is an excellent blending of the two approaches—economic and statistical—but cannot be considered very useful as a forecasting model. Both Clark and Klein (the latter in association with A. S. Goldberger) continued to develop their models further; these revised versions are discussed in the next chapter.

Meanwhile, econometric models were being applied elsewhere. In Scandinavia and Holland, under the leadership of Frisch, Wold, and Tinbergen, considerable innovations were made, especially with the Dutch model, which was used for official forecasting. Similar models were constructed in Canada, largely under Klein's influence, and a model for Britain was devised during his stay there (1954 to 1958). However, all these developments (with the possible exception of those in Holland) have en-

---

[11] T. Haavelmo, "The Statistical Implications of a System of Simultaneous Equations," *Econometrica*, Vol. XI (1943), pp. 1–12.

countered considerable resistance from administrators and others (including a large number of economists) who have been skeptical about the usefulness of such work. The performance of the latest Klein and Clark models would seem to indicate that such skepticism is misplaced. There are many problems still remaining in their specification, estimation, and solution, but these are steadily being overcome. Meanwhile, they represent an enormous improvement over any other method of preparing rational and consistent predictions for the whole economy. It is therefore regrettable that, at a time when research money is so freely available in so many sciences, so little is available for further experimentation in econometric model building.

Perhaps a word should also be said concerning the progress of inter-industry models of the economy. These, which have attained their importance through the pioneering and persistence of W. Leontief of Harvard, are also in a sense aggregate econometric models, since they take an economy-wide view, certainly involve difficult measurements, and can be used for prediction. However, they are more closely tied to a particular theoretical structure than is the type of model discussed in this chapter and, being based on cross-section data, are less probabilistically oriented; in consequence, they are of less use for *general* economic forecasting. However, the two approaches can usefully supplement each other, especially as the aggregate models are broken down into several sectors. A recent study which is to some extent a blend of the two types of analysis is K. J. Arrow and M. Hoffenberg, *A Time Series Analysis of Inter-Industry Demands* (North Holland, 1959).

QUESTIONS

See end of next chapter.

Chapter 11

APPLICATIONS OF
AGGREGATE ECONOMETRIC
MODELS

In the last section of Chapter 10, we briefly reviewed the development of aggregate econometric models, and in the bibliography at the end of the book, we give a fairly complete list of such models as have been constructed for the U.S. economy. It is something of a paradox that, while in several other countries complete models are undergoing continued development, in the United States only a few can be said to be significantly active. Of these the best known by far is the Klein-Goldberger model, originally published in 1955, and on which sporadic work has since been done. But it would be wrong to say that it is currently receiving that degree of continued revision necessary for the maintenance of a good forecasting tool. A second model, developed by Colin Clark, first individually and then at the Econometric Institute, has for various reasons not been available in published form. It has received continuous development by a sizable research team for the past seven years, and is now probably the most ambitious American attempt to design a model suitable for forecasting. Two others—those of Klein and Suits respectively—are in active preparation but have not yet (Spring, 1961) been published; the new Klein model is based on quarterly data.

In this chapter we shall discuss each of the first two models in turn, not in any spirit of competition between them, but because each exemplifies certain problems of model building, some of which are common to both and some of which are peculiar to the particular model. It is not part of our task to attempt a complete description of each model, since to do so would require far too much space; good short descriptions and analyses of the Klein-Goldberger model can be found in the review articles by Christ and by Fox already cited. Rather, we shall select certain problems posed by each model—predominantly economic rather than statistical problems—and discuss these fairly adequately. But the reader must bear in mind that these are only some of the more salient features of the models and that very much more remains than can be touched on here.

One important distinction between the two models should be borne in mind throughout. The Klein-Goldberger model (abbreviated hereafter to KGM) evolved from Klein's original model developed at the Cowles

Foundation, and its authors have always had mainly academic requirements in mind. There has, it is true, been a good deal of effort devoted by the authors to making it a good forecasting tool, but mainly for use by government and the general public; many of its features reflect this. The Econometric Institute model (EIM) however, although developed from the original academically oriented model by Clark published in 1949, has grown out of all recognition from that prototype, and in directions influenced by the requirements for short-term business forecasting, especially for industrial use. These two quite different emphases are important to the understanding of the different features of each model; one must always remember that they are not trying to do exactly the same things.

THE KLEIN-GOLDBERGER MODEL

The KGM uses mainly the categories of national income accounting and is estimated by using annual data from 1929 to 1941, and 1946 to 1952—twenty observations in all (an earlier version, reported in the same monograph, only utilized data to 1950). Our comments will stem from each of these three aspects of the model.

General Features

First, it is highly aggregative. There are twenty endogenous variables, so there must of necessity be twenty equations. Of these, five are identities, and the remaining fifteen estimated or stochastic equations (there are in addition five tax variables, with five equations explaining them, which enable forecasts to be made of tax yields even though only the exogenous tax rates are forecast). There are stochastic equations for consumption, gross private investment, corporate savings, corporate income, depreciation, private wage bill, private gross national product, wage rates, imports, private agricultural income, agricultural prices, household liquid assets, business liquid assets, short-term interest rates, and long-term interest rates. The five identities enable forecasts to be made of the following five variables as well: price index of GNP, nonwage nonfarm income, stock of capital goods, corporate surplus, and national income. There are twenty exogenous variables of which the most important are government expenditures in various sectors, the number of hours worked, exports, tax rates, some demographic variables, and "time" (to account for some otherwise unexplained trends).

Of the fifteen stochastic equations, four (those relating corporate profits to nonwage nonfarm income, agricultural prices to the GNP price index, long-term interest rates to short-term, and short-term interest rates to excess reserves), are essentially empirical in character (i.e., were not hypothesized prior to examining the data but were devised to fit the data), and hence are not, in the KGM terminology, "structural." Essentially this appears to mean that our confidence in their expected continuation into the future is less than that in their more "structural" cousins.

This may seem a complicated model, and it is; but it is still too small to admit of anything but a highly compressed account of the interaction of the various sectors of the economy. Four of the fitted equations refer to the money market, two to agriculture, two to the corporate sector, and two to wages and the wage bill. Only one equation refers to consumption, which is therefore left in aggregate form, rather than subdivided into durables, nondurables, and services. More important, gross private investment is left as one variable, and its very important components—producers' durables, business construction, residential construction, and inventory change—are not distinguished. Klein and Goldberger admit that this is a major defect of their model, since different factors affect the different categories of invest-ment. For example, they found no place for the long-term interest rate as an explanatory variable for investment, thus reaching conclusions similar to those of many other empirical studies of gross investment. Yet they con-cede that it is more than likely that long-term interest rates are relevant to residential construction. Similarly, by lumping inventory change in with investment, they are to some extent precluded from a detailed study of inventory cycles, which are the predominant form of fluctuation in eco-nomic activity in the United States since World War II.[1]

The precise degree of "aggregation" that an aggregate econometric model should have for good prediction is a very difficult problem. On the one hand, by being highly aggregative, one runs the risk of ignoring uni-form relationships that hold for the component items, and therefore of missing chances to establish a uniform structure. On the other hand, it not infrequently happens that relationships which do not hold well for each of a large number of finely divided sectors, tend to be much more uniform when these sectors are combined together in one; this would be especially true if there are strong substitution or complementarity relationships be-tween the sectors. Again, a fairly disaggregated model yields much greater information than a smaller model, but this has to be balanced against the greater complexity involved, which not only implies greater computation but also often confuses the essential nature of the processes at work, proc-esses which are more clearly seen in a less complex model. In any case there can be no clear-cut answer to the question. Different forecasting needs, as we have seen, call for different types of models, and the degree of aggrega-tion is just one way in which model-types can differ.

The second important point to notice about the KGM is that it is based mainly on the national income categories of the Department of Com-merce. Since the Department constantly revises its data, this means that the model has continually to be re-estimated. Just after the KGM was com-

[1] In his recent book, Goldberger attributes most of the failure of the KGM to call turning points correctly over the period 1929–52 to the faulty specification of this investment equation. This valuable book uses the method of reduced forms on a linearized version of the KGM in order to investigate its anatomy and physiology; but it is not primarily concerned with the KGM as a forecasting tool.

pleted, extensive revisions of the basic data were announced in mid-1954! Such heartbreaks are of the essence of applied econometrics, but they at least provide the opportunity for constant improvement of the model. Another implication of working with Department of Commerce income data is that one has to begin one's observations when they begin (1929) and this means that the number of annual observations available is quite small. A model working in terms of the index of industrial production, for example, would not have this problem (but would have the data revision problem). For many other reasons, however, a model of this latter type would probably not be so meaningful as one concerned with income and product data.

Problems of Deflation for Price Changes

A major problem arising with all models using data on value flows is that of deflation for changing prices. A complete treatment of this lies outside our scope (see Christ's review article for a more extensive account), but the nature of the problem can be indicated. It is forced on us by two contradictory requirements of our models. First, the identities which hold between the various value flows of a model (for example, private consumption plus gross private investment plus net foreign balance plus government expenditure equals gross national product) all hold between *current money values* of the variables concerned. They are accounting identities, and accountants' balance sheets must work in current dollars, not deflated dollars. On the other hand, it would not make sense to suppose that many of the structural relationships of the model hold in money terms. Such relationships as production functions, which attempt to express the total quantity of output as a function of the quantities of factors of production (usually labor and capital investments) available, are essentially "real" equations, and to use monetary values uncorrected for changes in the prices of output, labor, and capital goods would lead to error.

It is of little use to deflate all variables by the same price index, since this simply multiplies the whole model by a constant factor, and leaves the essence of the problem unchanged, for the problem arises from differing movements in relative prices of the various sectors concerned. If we deflate each sector by its own price index, we then have the problem of accounting for the movements of each index, thus adding considerably to the size of the model. But at least this will enable us to work our equations in real terms, and then get back *via* our endogenous price indexes (and further definitional equations of the nonlinear form, price $\times$ quantity $\equiv$ value) to making forecasts of current dollar values. There are, however, some difficult problems associated here with the deflation of series which do not represent actual quantities of goods and services, such as income flows; Christ points out how this affects the KGM income equation.

These problems of working with real and money values in the model have sometimes not been faced as squarely as they should in some of the econometric models listed in the bibliography, although Tinbergen's original model was very careful on this point; but there are clear signs of improvement in this direction in the future.

The Use of Annual Data

The third main aspect to the KGM is that it is a model based on annual data. This has two important effects, of which the first and most obvious is that it only allows us to forecast by yearly intervals, since all the lags involved have to be in multiples of one year. The use of data closer together—for example, quarterly data—would enable the structure of these lags to be more finely articulated and, of course, permit forecasts every quarter, which is of major importance for business use. The use of quarterly data has many problems of its own, however. First, since many of the quarterly estimates are based on interpolations of annual data—interpolations which are often rather mechanical in nature—there is the risk that successive estimates in the series are not independent, so that serial correlation becomes a problem. Of perhaps greater importance is the seasonal adjustment that has to be made in each series, if we are to correct for the systematic influences of each annual cycle due to the seasons. There have been ambitious attempts to account for seasonal movements by introducing appropriate factors in the stochastic equations themselves, but it seems simpler to accept the official adjustments made to the data where available and to make adjustments of one's own where these are not available. This means that in a quarterly model the forecasts are made of seasonally adjusted data, not the actual measurements that are made each quarter. Notice that this is not a problem peculiar to aggregate models; it affects all forecasting based on time series, and is perhaps particularly serious for such methods as the diffusion index approach described in Chapter 1.

A second effect of using annual data is that it shortens considerably the number of observations available, so that the parameter estimates lack the reliability that long series of observations can give them. On the other hand, as discussed above, unless the quarterly (or monthly) data are truly independent observations, the increased number that their use brings is purely specious; and the use of some methods of seasonal adjustment does have the effect of smoothing the data too much for good estimation.

An interesting problem arising from this shortness of time series was particularly important in the KGM and affects all such models not using ordinary least-squares estimation. It will be recalled that all the other methods described involved taking the regression of each endogenous variable on its reduced form equation, that is, on each of the predetermined variables. Now, in the KGM there are more predetermined variables than there are observations, so that such a procedure is impossible; there are not enough observations to estimate all the parameters. Even if the number of predetermined variables is only close to the number of observations available, one is still in trouble, because there are very few degrees of freedom available to make statistical fitting reliable. One way around this—adopted in the KGM—is to include only those predetermined variables that seem the most important; but then the strict logic of the simultaneous-equations methods has been abandoned, and it is difficult to know how to assess the meaning of the estimates obtained. It is not really enough just to "capture the spirit of simultaneity," as Klein and Goldberger claim (page 47). A more refined trick recently developed by the Dutch econometricians, Klock and Mennes, is to take what are known as the "principal components" of all the predetermined variables, and use those as explanatory variables in the reduced form. This seems to work very well, and opens up promising avenues for future exploration, since there is a well-developed literature, both in statistics and psychology, on these principal components.

Types of Forecasting

Forecasting, or prediction (to use the more academically acceptable word), is often regarded as the critical test of any economic theory, particularly of any econometric model. This is largely as it should be. There are many interesting questions about the nature of past structures on which econometrics can throw a great deal of light, but almost always the question at the back of our minds, even in these historical studies, is: How does this fit the facts now, or in what definite way has the structure changed? And these questions are asked basically because we want to predict the future course of events.

In order to eliminate ambiguity, it is necessary to distinguish three different situations in which we make estimates of future behavior and, for the purposes of this chapter, to give them separate names. The first, called here simply "free forecasting," is forecasting pure and simple. At any given time t, we know nothing about the future development of any of the variables, endogenous or exogenous, and we are required to estimate the future course of all of them. In order to do this, we have to guess at the future course of the exogenous variables, and from these and the model, estimate the future course of the endogenous variables. Thus this is a test of the forecaster as well as of his model, for it requires him to predict both exogenous and endogenous variables.

The second situation, which we call "conditional forecasting," is simply a test of the model, and is in no sense a projection into the future. Suppose that in 1960 we have a model which was estimated with data up to 1958, and that we have all the data for 1959. Then a test of the model is to assume that the exogenous variables take their correct 1959 values, and to estimate the values of the endogenous variables for 1959 thus generated by the model. These are then compared with the actual values we already possess.

A third situation, called here "alternate forecasting," has for its purpose neither a statement of what will happen, nor of what would have happened if the world had been like the model, but a prediction of the outcome of different lines of policy. Thus the government may ask the model builder: What will be the effect on output, income, interest rates, and employment if personal income taxes are reduced by 10 per cent? Or by 5 per cent? Or by 15 per cent? These alternative projected values are fed into the model as different sets of values of the exogenous variables, and the resulting outcomes calculated. All of these predictions may have turned out wrong in the actual outcome, but this kind of use of the model may nevertheless be the best way of judging the total effects of differing lines of policy (for such purposes it is perhaps not so important that the model be extremely good at short-run forecasting). This use of econometric models is very common in Holland and Scandinavia and is certainly one of the objects of the KGM; in the nature of the case, however, little testing of the efficiency of a model in this regard is possible unless the policy maker has control over all the exogenous variables, which is very unlikely.

Forecasting with the Klein-Goldberger Model

Both conditional forecasting and free forecasting were used in the KGM, the former for the early model fitted on data to 1950, the latter on both models. The conditional forecasts for 1951 and 1952 turned out quite well, with the most serious errors occurring in investment (as our discussion above would lead us to expect), and prices. Investment was understated in both cases and the extent of the price rise overstated. Apart from the bad specification of its equation, the Korean War may have had much to do with the underestimate of investment, while apparently the excessive rise in prices forecast was due to insufficient account being taken of increases in productivity. Although the supply side of the model was a considerable improvement over the original Klein model published in 1950, much more remains to be done here, especially for a period like the last few years, when the economy has been running fairly close to full employment but showing a small and fairly persistent rise in prices.

In his latest work, Goldberger shows that the KGM is really made up of two sectors, the "real," which accounts for the GNP and its components; and the "monetary," which deals with prices, interest rates, and wages. He considers that the real sector of the model is quite a good representation of reality, apart from the investment equation, but that the monetary sector is not, and that the apparent dichotomy between the two sectors is due to a failure of model building rather than a feature of reality. This is an opinion that we share, though it is only fair to point out that the theoretical and the empirical elucidation of the relationships between these two sectors are two of the most difficult tasks in economics.

In preparing their free forecasts, Klein and Goldberger each time tried several varying sets of assumptions about future government tax and expenditure policy and, therefore, each time produced several alternate forecasts. In each case, they guessed at the tax rates the government would have in force during the coming period, and by means of the five tax equations incorporated in the model, predicted the corresponding current dollar tax yields. Such alternate forecasts, as we have noted, would be of considerable use for government, especially as their computations indicated that the impact effect of government spending is apparently smaller than many economists have believed. The short-run multiplier, according to their calculations, was substantially less than 2 during this period; Goldberger's estimate in his recent book is around 1.4. These low estimates stem essentially from the important role of lagged variables, but because the data used are annual, the lags specified may be too long, and these "impact multiplier" estimates may accordingly be a little low.

Since they were mainly concerned with free forecasting, Klein and Goldberger were in each case forced to select one of their varying assumptions as the most likely to occur (they point very sensibly to the great need for careful guessing of the exogenous variables, especially those relating to government policy). Forecasting for 1953 with their early model, they anticipated a general rise in activity over the year, a forecast at variance with much expert opinion of the time and one which turned out to be correct. But observe that with their annual model they were not able to anticipate the downturn which actually occurred in the second half of the year. So, although their forecasts of *levels* were quite good, they were quite unable, by the nature of their model, to predict the *movements* in the economy during the year. For the main purposes of their investigations, this was perhaps not a great drawback; but for short-run business forecasting, it is a serious handicap. In order to spot a turning point more than six months ahead, they would have had to forecast for two full years, with the corresponding greater uncertainty about exogenous variables two years hence.

The revised model, estimated on data through 1952, was used to forecast 1954, and here again the performance was for the most part quite good. The worst estimates of the forecast prepared in December, 1953, were the gross overstatement of the degree of rise in both prices and wage rates and an underestimate of the amount of unemployment. Both of these failures point again to a weakness in the supply side of the model, as well as reflecting the incorrect assumptions about the exogenous variables (these made government expenditure fall by $1.2 billion when in reality it fell by $6.5 billion).

From a methodological point of view, there are several interesting aspects to the way in which forecasts from the KGM were prepared. In working out the final equations for forecasting, they obtained a pair of simultaneous nonlinear equations in national income and the GNP price deflator. These could not be solved exactly, so a guess was made of the pair of values of the two variables that would satisfy the two equations, and a trial-and-error technique was used to find answers which were correct to within the required degree of approximation. From these two values, the appropriate levels of the other variables in the system could then be calculated.

The Use of Recent Data

In estimating a model, one normally uses all the data that are available at the time; but it is costly to re-estimate the model as each set of additional data becomes available. Thus one might work hard on a model and estimate it for data through 1959; in early 1961 one may wish to prepare forecasts for the whole of that year. Then what should one do with the 1960 data? Ideally the whole model should be re-estimated, but this is a lengthy and costly business, both in the estimation of the equations and in the necessarily altered computer programs required for the solution.

The fresh data from 1960 must be allowed to influence the model somehow, however, for otherwise, valuable information on the structural uniformity of the model is being thrown away. Suppose, for example, that the last three years of the sample period (1957 to 1959) had shown that consumption was consistently overestimated by its equation (or equations); this run of three negative residuals (actual figures minus estimated) could have occurred by chance, but is more likely to indicate that the consumption equation(s) is (are) incorrectly specified. If the 1960 information again shows that consumption has been overestimated, then the evidence on bias in the equation becomes almost conclusive, while an underestimation would lend support to the hypothesis that the run was due to chance. In the former case, either the equation must be re-estimated or, if the implications of this are too expensive, it must be adjusted in some way to correct temporarily for the bias in the equation, pending re-estimation at some time in the future.

Klein and Goldberger computed all the residuals in their equations over the previous five years, and examined their time patterns for persistent bias. If there had been runs of four or five years of sizable residuals, each of the same sign, and if there was independent evidence (for example, from consumer intentions surveys and so on) to confirm the existence of such bias, they used the latest residual to adjust the constant term in the appropriate equation, in order to make the corrected residual zero. Thus, suppose the consumption equation had overestimated for the last few years, and that there was either some outside evidence to indicate where their equation was wrong, or some similar evidence to show that overestimation would be likely in the future; then if the last residual was, say, $3.5 billion, they reduced the constant term in the equation by that amount; and correspondingly for underestimation. They would then use the corrected equation in preparing forecasts.

Such a procedure can obviously have its dangers and is equally obviously far removed from the mechanical unthinking use of formulas that many nonmathematicians associate with mathematical methods of prediction. But the skillful econometrician uses such devices to take account of all the extraneous information at his command. The use of a complete econometric model greatly economizes on the number of separate judgments that the forecaster has to make and contributes greatly to the consistency of his predictions; but in no sense does it obviate the need for flair and good judgment. *The good econometrician must be first and foremost a good economist.*

Long-Run Properties of the Klein-Goldberger Model

Although in this book we are mainly interested in models that will prove efficient at short-run forecasting, it is of interest to see how well our models acquit themselves over the longer run. Failure in this regard would not invalidate a model's claim to be a good short-run forecasting tool, but success would contribute substantially to our belief that it is a good representation of the economic system.

Klein and Goldberger did not test their model in this way, but such a test was performed subsequently in an article by Dr. and Mrs. I. Adelman. Using a slightly revised version of the KGM, and making extrapolations of the exogenous variables far into the future, they showed that the model very rapidly lost any trace of fluctuation and gave simple growth trends of each of its variables over the long-run. Thus, if one takes the view that fluctuations are inherent in an economic system characterized by free enterprise, the KGM is not a good representation of its workings.

On the other hand, one may believe that the oscillations often observed in aggregate time series are not generated by the economic process itself, but are the response of that system to various erratic shocks which beset it through time, as a pendulum will oscillate regularly even when struck in a random fashion. Acting on this hypothesis, the Adelmans submitted the KGM to a random series of such additions to and subtractions from the various equations, with quite remarkable results. It gave cycles of the length and amplitude that are commonly observed and conformed very well with the usual pattern of lead-lag relationships through the business cycle.

These results are very interesting, but not, of course, conclusive evidence that the business cycle is the response of an essentially linear system to random shocks. A model which as it were generates its own "shocks" may be a much better representation of reality than the KGM. But the Adelmans' results certainly provide solid evidence on the other side. The long-run performance of the KGM is therefore difficult to evaluate. It may be excellent or mediocre, depending on one's views of the way in which growth under capitalism proceeds. If cycles are inherent in that process, the KGM is a poor map of the economic world; if they are not, and are the result instead of the system's response to "the slings and arrows of outrageous fortune," then the KGM is quite remarkably good as a general representation, though not necessarily as a short-run forecasting tool.

THE ECONOMETRIC INSTITUTE MODEL

As we noted in the introduction to this chapter, the Econometric Institute model (EIM) has evolved by an almost continuous sequence of changes from the original model published by Colin Clark in 1949. Until 1958, the model's development was privately financed, but at that time it became part of the Econometric Institute's operations. The superior research resources of the Institute enabled progress on the model to be accelerated. Of particular help was the Institute's extensive collection of unpublished data and the detailed set of sector equations developed by the late Charles Roos and his colleagues.

The model has always been mainly an instrument for short-run business forecasting, and this aim has to some extent governed its directions of change. Because of advances in economic theory, statistical and computational techniques, and the availability of data, the EIM is in a constant state of flux, improvements being made continuously. Therefore, the model we shall discuss is not that which is currently being used, since that itself would be somewhat out-of-date as a description of the Institute's forecasting model by the time this book is published. The model presented here is that which was in use during the latter half of 1958 and early 1959, and is in broad outline similar to that used currently. The present tense will be used throughout in discussing this earlier model, but this must not mislead the reader into believing that it is now operational.

Many of the problems of model building and prediction from these models are common to each and have already been discussed in the last chapter and this. Such topics as the use of tax equations, the degree of aggregation, deflation for price changes, serial correlation, and estimation methods are just as relevant to the EIM as they were to the KGM and other models; but they have already been dealt with (however briefly), and will not be discussed again here. Our treatment of the EIM can accordingly be relatively brief, and we shall concentrate on the nature of the economic structure of the model.

General Features

The EIM consists of 79 equations, which accordingly explain 79 endogenous variables. Of these, 49 are identities, 3 are tax equations (in the sense used in discussing the KGM), and the remaining 27 are behavioral or technical equations. There are 15 exogenous variables, of which 6 (labor force, productivity trend, time, depreciation factors for consumer durables, construction, and total capital stock) are assumed to be "automatic" trend variables in character. The remaining 9 require judgment as to their future behavior, and here the research experience of the Econometric Institute's entire staff is utilized. These variables are the raw material price index, farm and rentier income, government transfer payments, net foreign investment, net exports of durable goods, government purchases of goods and services (estimated category by category), Aaa bond yields, business liquid assets, and consumer liquid assets.

The list of endogenous variables is so long that it cannot be given here, but it includes all the usual components of gross national product, broken down in considerable detail. Thus gross private investment is subdivided into residential construction, nonresidental construction, producers' durable equipment, and inventory change; consumption is divided into automobile consumption, other durables, nondurables, and services. Unlike with the KGM, the agricultural sector is not separately distinguished, partly because the Institute's clients are predominantly in commerce and industry, but mainly because it operates a sector model for farm products. (See Chapter 5 for some agricultural models.)

This exemplifies a feature of the Institute's approach to forecasting. It uses the complete aggregate model to forecast the main categories of the economy, concentrating especially on manufacturing, and uses sector models to forecast individual industry behavior, using as some of the explanatory variables the forecast aggregate variables from the main model. The use of these "satellite" models (see Part II) is a good compromise between the conflicting demands for the simplicity in aggregate models and for the comprehensiveness in coverage that integrated forecasting requires. Karl Fox has pointed to the need for these satellites, and although the KGM began to develop such ideas, it did not carry them very far. These models provide a much more rational frame of reference for consistent specialist forecasting than hitherto, one in which specialized knowledge of the behavior of particular sectors can be combined with a comprehensive view of the economy. The satellite models need not necessarily be dependent only on the results predicted by the sector equations; specialist knowledge of the sector comes in when judging the likely future uniformity of the structure that has been built, for example, by analysis of residuals. As always, the function of mathematical and statistical techniques is to reduce the area in which judgments are needed, so that the wisdom and experience of the forecaster can be concentrated on the crucial issues.

The Manufacturing Sector

Even this aggregate model, however, goes into great detail concerning one sector—manufacturing. Just over half of the equations in the EIM are concerned with this sector alone. There are two main reasons for this. The first is simply that forecasts of such things as new orders, sales, production, inventories, and unfilled orders in the various manufacturing categories (capital goods, other durable, and nondurable), all of which the EIM provides, are extremely useful in business planning, probably more useful than the usual GNP categories in providing direct guides for careful business decisions.

The second reason is more technical, and concerns the handling of inventory change. All the downturns since World War II have been predominantly inventory recessions, and there is every likelihood that this phenomenon will continue. This means that if we are to forecast efficiently, we must pay great attention to the way in which these inventory recessions are generated. This cannot be done at all well with a model that does not separate inventory change from total private investment, as in the KGM. Since most of the endogenous variability in inventory change comes from manufacturing and commercial inventories[2] it is to these sectors that we must turn. On examination, the behavior of the various categories of manufacturing—capital goods, other durables, and nondurables—turned out to be very different, requiring different explanatory structures.

A main feature of this manufacturing sector is the essential role played by new orders in motivating production and inventory change. This means that great care has to be taken to find cogent explanations of these new orders in the various categories. In the "other durable" sector, the rate of change of sales, and the inventory/sales ratio are used as explanatory variables and give good results, while in the capital goods sector, lagged corporate profits, lagged gross profit margins, and the utilization of capacity are important. By relating movements in these various new orders series to past movements of the system, the model acquires a definite dynamic pattern. It is one of the main findings of the model that increases in government expenditure only affect the economy slowly, in this confirming the findings of the KGM on short-run multipliers. On the other hand, it appears that sudden cessations of government spending, especially when coupled with high interest rates, are enough to push the economy on to a downward path.

The contributions of the various parts of the manufacturing sector are aggregated to form total change in manufacturers' inventories, and from this, total change in all nonfarm inventories is found by means of what Klein and Goldberger would term "empirical" rather than "structural" stochastic equations. In a sense the whole of this considerable edifice of forty-one equations for the manufacturing sector (twenty-seven identities and fourteen behavioral equations)[3] is needed only to get at two variables—producers' durable equipment and inventory change—which are components of GNP. But looking at it in this way obscures the fact that most of the other variables are of interest for their own sake and, even

[2] One difficulty with the analysis of inventory change is that it is a notoriously hard quantity to measure, due mainly to the problems of revaluation of existing inventories when prices change. This means that preliminary estimates by the Department of Commerce are frequently extensively revised, as are already established estimates. In such unavoidable circumstances it is difficult to know how well one is forecasting this strategic variable.

[3] The large number of identities in this sector is due to the numerous accounting relationships which must hold between the variables involved, for example, Sales = Production *less* Addition to Inventories, and Change in Unfilled Orders = New Orders *less* Sales, for each of the various categories.

more important, that it is only by going carefully into the structure of this sector that the dynamics of inventory fluctuations are laid bare.

The Logical Structure of the Model

The EIM is a quarterly model, by which we mean that all its behavioral equations are estimated on the basis of quarterly data (it utilizes all the postwar data, which give around fifty observations on each variable), that its lags are based on intervals of one quarter, and that its predictions are made by quarters. The model is usually used to predict six quarters ahead.

As we have seen, the use of quarterly data brings great advantages, in providing more data for good estimation and in making it possible to spot turning points accurately. It also brings its own problems, especially those of seasonal adjustment and serial correlation, to which careful attention must be paid. Of great importance for the EIM is that, by permitting lags to be specified with considerable accuracy, the model can become much more *recursive* (defined earlier, in Chapter 10) than if it had been only an annual model.

In fact, the EIM is almost recursive,[4] a fact which makes it far easier to solve than a more simultaneous model and which gives us more confidence in the validity of the least-squares estimation method used. With such almost complete recursion it is very unlikely that the use of more complex methods of estimation would prove worthwhile, especially as some of the equations are nonlinear.

The methods used to predict with the model are made much simpler because of the simply ordered way in which the equations can be set out. Estimates of the various exogenous variables are prepared (for some purposes alternative hypotheses are presented, as with the KGM), and their first quarter's estimates fed into the equations. Two guesses as to GNP in the next quarter are then made, one just higher than is at all possible, one just lower. Then, since the rest of the model is recursive, with the direction of causation running one way all the time, it is possible to take, say, the high value of GNP and from this, plus the exogenous variables and the lagged endogenous variables, to forecast man-hours worked. From this latter variable and utilization of capacity plus the appropriate exogenous variables, one can attain an estimate of wage rates which, combined with man-hours, gives the total wage bill.

The ratio of gross profits to labor income can then be estimated as a function of GNP and capacity utilization, and this gives gross profits.

---

[4] A note for technicians: by this we mean that the "matrix" of coefficients of the current endogenous variables of the model is specified to be very nearly triangular, save for one row. Complete recursiveness is equivalent to triangularity of the matrix of a linear system. We put "matrix" in quotes here since the EIM is not linear, and therefore the concept of a matrix does not strictly apply. But the qualitative picture should be clear, especially since most of the equations are linear in the variables.

From there one can go on to corporate profits, disposable income, consumption, and so on right through the system, since the equations can be set out in such a way that the dependent variable in, say, the forty-seventh equation depends only on exogenous and lagged endogenous variables and on at most a few of the endogenous variables that have already been estimated in the first forty-six equations.

At the end of all this one will have two sets of estimates of each endogenous variable, and by adding together the appropriate set of variables (consumption, gross private investment, net foreign investment, and government purchases of goods and services), one can get two new estimates of gross national product. These two new values can then be used as the basis for an iterative procedure that will converge to approximate solutions for all the variables of the whole system for the first quarter. We say approximate, since the system is nonlinear, and its true solution is therefore nonlinear; but our trial-and-error procedure attempts only a linear approximation. Since the range of the values concerned is quite small, however, and the system is not too nonlinear, this approximation is quite close (a small segment of a relatively flat arc looks very much like a straight line).

This procedure, therefore, gives estimates of the endogenous variables for the first quarter of the forecast period. The same procedure is repeated for the second and subsequent quarters, using the estimated values of the exogenous variables and the forecast values for earlier quarters of the appropriate endogenous variables, in those equations where lagged endogenous variables are used. Thus, if one equation has, say, consumption lagged by two quarters as an explanatory variable, the forecast from that equation for the third quarter of the forecast period will use as a predetermined variable the forecast value of consumption for the first quarter. The forecasts therefore tend to become rather less reliable, the further the model is projected into the future, a feature which the model shares with all forecasting methods. For this reason the model is restricted to forecasting six quarters ahead, which is sufficient for most short-run business planning and at the same time well within the margin of reliability.

Forecasting with the Econometric Institute Model

The EIM and its predecessors have given good service as forecasting tools, and have usually managed to predict some months ahead the turning points of the postwar recessions. The model has not been submitted to a long-run test, or a conditional forecast, but it was used to estimate the course of the economy during 1957 and 1958, using true values of the exogenous variables. This was not a conditional forecast, since the model had been estimated on data covering most of the forecast period (through the second quarter of 1958); on the other hand, neither was it a test simply of how well the model mirrors the past behavior of the economy, since the forecast and not the actual values of the lagged endogenous variables were used in going from quarter to quarter of the forecast period.

This mixed test produced excellent results. It predicted the downturn in the middle of 1957 with great accuracy, and the beginning of the recovery in early 1958. Throughout its existence, the EIM has paid as much attention to the accuracy of its forecasts of *movements* in the economy as to its forecasts of levels. It is therefore of considerable importance that the model accurately captures the timing of such elusive phenomena as inventory recessions.

CONCLUSION

We have already noted that the EIM is being continually improved. One recent move has been to analyze more deeply the monetary sector of the economy, which is mainly exogenous in the version described here. Further attention to the equations for consumer durables is also indicated by the wealth of recently published detailed econometric studies in this field, though no revisions may turn out to be required. The recent radical changes in the Federal Reserve Board's indices of industrial production also necessitate a revision of the manufacturing sector equations, which utilize this data indirectly.

Such constant changes and attention to detail are of the essence of a serious, continuing, econometric program. At no time can one say that this is the best that can be done; there is always room for improvement. But the promising performance of such models as the KGM and the EIM in forecasting the economy with considerable accuracy (even though the research resources available have not been great by comparison with many programs in, say, the physical sciences) inspire workers in the field with the belief that even greater success is around the corner. As our theoretical knowledge and empirical experience grow and as the quantity of resources available for such work increases, the prospect of really close accuracy in short-run forecasting will come within our grasp.

QUESTIONS

1. "The ultimate objective of an econometric model is to obtain a good fit." Discuss this statement in the light of this and the previous chapter.

2. Review this and the previous chapter, and make a list of the various technical terms, both economic and statistical, that you encounter. Write brief definitions of these terms in your own words and explain carefully their meaning and significance within the general scheme of econometrics.

3. Using the terms collected in answering the above question, write an essay on the nature, scope, and content of econometrics with emphasis on its usefulness in forecasting.

CLASSIFIED

Appendix

BIBLIOGRAPHY

BOOKS

The student who wishes to pursue his work in aggregate econometric models further, should embark on the following course of reading, which will lead him by graduated steps to the heart of modern econometrics. Along the way he (or she) may feel the need to supplement his mathematical and his statistical knowledge, so that appropriate textbooks in that area are also included.

A second list of monographs and articles refers to particular topics that we have touched upon, in both theoretical and applied fields. Articles bearing on econometric models appear occasionally in almost all the usual learned journals of economics, and regularly so in *Econometrica, Journal of the American Statistical Association, Journal of Farm Economics,* and *International Economic Review.* The series of monographs issued by the Cowles Foundation is concerned almost wholly with mathematical economics and econometrics, while the series *Contributions to Economic Analysis,* edited by Tinbergen and others, and published by the North Holland Publishing Company, has a very strong econometric bias, though uneven in quality. The remarkable series of books on statistics published by Wiley is also of interest for econometricians.

BEACH, E. F. *Economic Models; an Exposition.* Wiley, 1957.

A useful first introduction to the subject, which also develops a few of the easier mathematical and statistical tools required.

TINBERGEN, J. *Econometrics.* McGraw-Hill, 1951.

An elementary book, but very useful for its author's concern for both theoretical tools and empirical relevance.

There is rather a jump in sophistication to the level of:

VALAVANIS, S. *Econometrics.* McGraw-Hill, 1959.

This is a brilliant, rather partisan, account of the logic of the maximum likelihood, simultaneous-equations approach. Although in places it is somewhat wilfully elliptical and not easy to follow for the relative beginner, it is always stimulating to learn from an original mind.

KLEIN, L. *A Textbook of Econometrics*. Row, Peterson, 1953.

This is a very different kind of textbook from that of Valavanis. Solid and, within its self-imposed limits, thorough, it should be the serious worker's *vade mecum*, as befits a work from the leading American academic econometrician. It is, however, rather heavily slanted in favor of Cowles Foundation methods of estimation.

A useful supplement to this is:

TINTNER, G. *Econometrics*. Wiley, 1952.

This deals with a large number of topics omitted by Klein, especially those concerned with time-series analysis. It contains a wealth of techniques, examples, and references.

THEIL, H. *Economic Forecasts and Policy*. North Holland, 1958.

This is the most ambitious application of the techniques of mathematical economics and econometrics to the problems of forecasting yet published. In many cases the procedures described are impractical with our present knowledge of the data, but there is little doubt that it is in these directions that scientific forecasting will gradually move. Of most relevance for this chapter is the description of Theil's "K-class estimators," which include l.s., l.i. and two-stage least-squares as special cases.

In the course of reading these textbooks, the student will be constantly referred to three classic monographs on modern econometrics. These are:

HAAVELMO, T. "The Probability Approach in Econometrics," *Econometrica*, Vol. XII, July, 1944 (Supplement).

This is a very careful exposition of the nature of the problems of inference in complete equation systems.

KOOPMANS, T. C. (ed.). *Statistical Inference in Dynamic Economic Models*. Cowles Commission Monograph No. 10. Wiley, 1950.

The basic source of most of the statistical methods devised to cope with the simultaneous-equations problem. Unfortunately, much of it suffers from an excessively precious notation and needless search for overgeneralization.

HOOD, W. C., and KOOPMANS, T. C. (eds.). *Studies in Econometric Method*. Cowles Commission Monograph No. 14. Wiley, 1953.

This is a considerably simpler exposition of the main methods contained in Monograph No. 10, plus reprints of some excellent earlier articles by Girshick, Haavelmo, and Koopmans, and further developments in the Cowles Commission methods by other authors.

This concludes the list of econometrics books per se, though it must be stressed that we have had in mind only the development of complete *aggregate* models and have not attempted a reading list suitable for the whole very wide range of modern econometrics.

Assuming that the student is primarily an economist, he will probably get his best first training in mathematical economics from such books as:

ALLEN, R. G. D. *Mathematical Analysis for Economists.* St. Martin's Press, 1938.

—————. *Mathematical Economics.* St. Martin's Press, 1956.

BRENNAN, JR., M. J. *Preface to Econometrics.* Southwestern, 1960.

BUSHAW, D. W., and CLOWER, R. W. *Introduction to Mathematical Economics.* Irwin, 1957.

HENDERSON, J. M., and QUANDT, R. E. *Microeconomic Theory: A Mathematical Approach.* McGraw-Hill, 1958.

LEWIS, J. P. *An Introduction to Mathematics for Students of Economics.* St. Martin's Press, 1954.

MEIR, R. C., and ARCHER, S. H. *An Introduction to Mathematics for Business Analysis.* McGraw-Hill, 1960.

TINTNER, G. *Mathematics and Statistics for Economists.* Rinehart, 1953.

As he goes through these he will probably feel the need for supplementary work on specifically mathematical textbooks, of which many excellent examples exist. A sophisticated calculus text is:

COURANT, R. *Differential and Integral Calculus* (2 Vols.). Interscience, 1953. However, many other calculus texts on various levels are available.

Good survey books on modern elementary mathematics are:

ALLENDOERFER, C. B., and OAKLEY, C. O. *Principles of Mathematics.* McGraw-Hill, 1955.

—————. *Fundamentals of Freshman Mathematics.* McGraw-Hill, 1959.

KEMENY, J. G., SNELL, J. L., and THOMPSON, G. L. *Introduction to Finite Mathematics.* Prentice-Hall, 1958.

Of especial usefulness in advanced economic theory and econometrics:

BELLMAN, R. E. *Introduction to Matrix Analysis.* McGraw-Hill, 1960.

There are now several good textbooks on statistics available, ranging from the first four below, which require no knowledge by the reader other than high school mathematics and adult intelligence, to the more specialized books beyond:

WALLIS, W. A., and ROBERTS, H. V. *Statistics: A New Approach.* Free Press, 1956.

SCHLAIFER, R. *Probability and Statistics for Business Decisions.* McGraw-Hill, 1959.

DIXON, W., and MASSEY, F. *Introduction to Statistical Analysis.* 2d ed. McGraw-Hill, 1957.

CHERNOFF, H., and MOSES, L. E. *Elementary Decision Theory.* Wiley, 1959.

There are many good books on mathematical statistics proper, of which the following are a good sample:

MOOD, A. M. *Introduction to the Theory of Statistics.* McGraw-Hill, 1950.

FRASER, D. A. S. *Statistics: An Introduction.* Wiley, 1958.

CRAMER, H. *Mathematical Methods of Statistics.* Princeton, 1946.

Sooner or later a solid groundwork in probability will also be required, and this is provided in the following books:

FELLER, W. *Introduction to Probability Theory and Its Applications*, Vol. I. 2d ed. Wiley, 1957.

PARZEN, E. *Modern Probability Theory and Its Applications.* Wiley, 1960.

There are very many recent works on programming for digital electronic computers, of which the following are representative:

LIVESLEY, R. K. *An Introduction to Automatic Digital Computers.* Cambridge Press, 1957.

JEENEL, J. *Programming for Digital Computers.* McGraw-Hill, 1959.

But the rapid technical developments in this field will no doubt necessitate a constant stream of new works.

MONOGRAPHS AND ARTICLES

These fall into two groups, those concerned with theoretical problems of aggregate econometric models and those with empirical problems. The latter can be read with profit at an early stage in one's econometric career. The paper of the former type quoted here almost all require rather specialized knowledge.

Theoretical Problems of Model-Building

The various pieces of empirical information concerning the relative merits of l.s. and l.i. estimation methods are given in:

WAGNER, H. "A Monte Carlo Study of Estimates of Simultaneous Linear Structural Equations," *Econometrica*, Vol. XXVI (1958), pp. 117–33.

FOX, K. A. "Econometric Models of the U.S. Economy," *Journal of Political Economy*, Vol. LXIV (1956), pp. 128–42 (reprinted in K. A. Fox, *Econometric Analysis for Public Policy*, Iowa State Press, 1958, the rest of which may be read with profit).

CHRIST, C. F. "Aggregate Econometric Models," *American Economic Review*, Vol. XLVI (1956), pp. 385–408.

Both of these are review articles on the Klein-Goldberger model, and belong in the next section as much as here.

The alternative methods of estimation that have been put forward are discussed in Theil's book already cited, and in:

BASMANN, R. L. "A Generalized Classical Method of Linear Estimation of Coefficients in a Structural Equation," *Econometrica*, Vol. XXV (1957), pp. 77–83.

NAGAR, A. L. "The Bias and Moment Matrix of the General K-class Estimators of the Parameters in Simultaneous Equations," *Econometrica*, Vol. XXVII (1959), pp. 575–95.

KLOEK, T., and MENNES, L. B. M. "Simultaneous Equations Estimation Based on Principal Components of Predetermined Variables," *Econometrica*, Vol. XXVIII (1960), pp. 45–61.

The best discussion of causal-chains *versus* simultaneous equations is to be found in:

WOLD, H., and STROTZ, R. H. "A Triptych on Causal Systems," *Econometrica*, Vol. XXVIII (1960), pp. 417–63.

This consists of three articles and the last paper, by Wold, contains an extensive bibliography of the debate.

Empirical Applications of Model-Building for Short-Run Forecasting

U.S.A.

TINBERGEN, J. *Statistical Testing of Business-Cycle Theories*, Vol. I, "A Method and Its Applications to Investment Activity"; Vol. II, "Business Cycles in the United States of America, 1919–1932." League of Nations, Geneva, 1939.

CLARK, COLIN. "A System of Equations Explaining the U.S. Trade Cycle, 1921–1941," *Econometrica*, Vol. XVII (1949), pp. 93–124.

KLEIN, L. R. *Economic Fluctuations in the United States 1921–1941*. Cowles Commission Monograph No. 11. Wiley, 1950.

CHRIST, C. F. "A Test of an Econometric Model of the United States 1921–1947," *Conference on Business Cycles*, pp. 35–107. Universities-National Bureau Committee, 1951.

KLEIN, L. R., and BARGER, H. "A Quarterly Model for the U.S. Economy," *Journal of the American Statistical Association*, Vol. XLIX (1954), pp. 413–37.

KLEIN, L. R., and GOLDBERGER, A. S. *An Econometric Model of the United States 1929–1952*. North Holland, 1955.

LIU, T. C. "A Simple Forecasting Model for the U.S. Economy," *International Monetary Fund Staff Papers*, Vol. IV (1955), pp. 434–66.

ADELMAN, I., and ADELMAN, F. L. "The Dynamic Properties of the Klein-Goldberger Model," *Econometrica*, Vol. XXVII (1959), 596–625.

GOLDBERGER, A. S. *Impact Multipliers and Dynamic Properties of the Klein-Goldberger Model*, North Holland, 1959.

U.K.

KLEIN, L. R., BALL, R. J., and HAZLEWOOD, A. "Econometric Forecasts for 1959," *Bulletin of the Oxford University Institute of Statistics*, Vol. XXI (1959), pp. 3–16.

KLEIN, L. R., and BALL, R. J. "Some Econometrics of the Determination of Absolute Prices and Wages," *Economic Journal*, Vol. LXIX (1959), pp. 465–82.

CANADA

Brown, T. M. "Some Recent Econometric Developments," *Canadian Journal of Economics and Political Science*, Vol. XXV (1959), pp. 23–33.

(This is concerned also with general methodological developments.)

INDIA

Narasimhan, N. V. A. *A Short-Term Planning Model for India*. North Holland, 1956.

HOLLAND AND SCANDINAVIA

Theil, H. *Economic Forecasts and Policy*, Part III.

In addition, econometric studies of other countries appear from time to time, some of them available only in mimeographed form—for example, the memoranda of the Oslo Institute of Economics in Norway.

INDEX

INDEX

Names of authors appearing in the classified bibliography, pp. 398–403, are not included in this index.

R

Random variable, 370
Randomized equation, 370
Randomness, meaning of, 42
Raw materials
    examples of, 206
    price determinants, 141 ff.
Recursive, 376
Reduced form, 367
Reference cycle, 10–11
Refrigerator sales, model of, 252–79
Regression
    concept of, 43–45
    estimate, refrigerator model, 263 ff.
    partial, meaning of, 51
Relationships, additive vs. multiplicative, 66 ff.
Replacement; *see also* specific models
    demand, consumers' durables, 241–42
    sales, automobile model, 248
Residual method, 8, 9
Residual u_t, 369 ff.
Residuals, unexplained, reasons for, 60
Retail sales, automobile model, 248–49
Roos, C. F., 7, 244, 294

S

Sales force polling, 17
Sales, sources of data, 28
Sample surveys, as a forecasting method, 14 ff.
Scale, adjustment for, 74–75
Schultz, H., 244
Schweiger, I., 17
Scrappage, as replacement demand, consumers' durables, 242
Seasonal, defined, 6
Semimanufactured goods, price determinants, 141 ff.
Serial correlation, 9, 70
Short-term money rates, model of, 191–95
Siegelman, L., 40
Simple correlation, meaning of, 44
Simultaneous-equation models, 364–66
Single equations vs. systems of equations, 68, 364 ff.
Slope-intercept formula, 52
Slutsky-Yule effect, 9
Snyder, R. M., 25
Sources of data
    commonly used indexes, 34
    general, 23–25
    special, 25–28
Specific metals, price determinants, 171 ff.
Specifying the model, 371 ff.
Spencer, M., 40
Spot market prices, nature of, 30–31
Sprowls, R. C., 10

Stable structure, in models, 363
Standard deviation, adjusting for scale, 74–75
Statistical Abstract of the United States, 24
Statistical inference, meaning of, 42
Steel, iron and, prices, 171–72
Stigler, G. J., 367
Stochastic equations, 367, 370 ff.
Stock market model, 195–203
Strotz, R. H., 375 ff.
Structural uniformity, in models, 362–63
Style factor, women's outerwear model, 236–37
Substitute or price factor, beer model, 228–29
Substitute or proxy variable, 72
Successive approximation, method of, 58
Suits, Daniel, 252
Supernumerary income, nature of, 33
Supply-demand factors affecting prices, 94 f.
Survey of Current Business, 24–25
Survey Research Center, 16
Survival coefficients, table of, 256
Survival functions, refrigerators, 253–54

T

Taxable bond yields, model of, 184–86
Technical equations, 364
Technological factors affecting prices, 96, 98
Television sales, model of, 279–90
The Econometric Institute, Inc., computation of discretionary income, 207
The Econometric Institute Model, 392–97
    forecasting, 396–97
    general features, 392–93
    logical structure, 395–96
    manufacturing sector, 393–95
Thomsen, F. L., 59
Time lags and time trend, 71–72
Time series analysis, 5
Time trend, as "catchall" variable, 59–61, 71–72, 363
Time-use characteristics, consumers' durable goods, 240
Tinbergen, J., 380
Tintner, 40, 367
Treasury (new) bill rate, model of, 195–96
Trend, defined, 6
Trend projection, as forecasting method, 7
Two-point formula, 52
    on arithmetic scales, 67
    on logarithmic scales, 68
    on semilogarithmic scales, 68
Two-stage least squares, 375

This book has been set on the Linotype in 10 and 9 point Janson, leaded 2 points. Chapter numbers and titles are in 18 point Spartan Medium. The size of the type page is 27 x 47 picas.